Second Language Interaction
in Diverse Educational Contexts

Language Learning & Language Teaching (LL&LT)

The LL&LT monograph series publishes monographs, edited volumes and text books on applied and methodological issues in the field of language pedagogy. The focus of the series is on subjects such as classroom discourse and interaction; language diversity in educational settings; bilingual education; language testing and language assessment; teaching methods and teaching performance; learning trajectories in second language acquisition; and written language learning in educational settings.

For an overview of all books published in this series, please see
http://benjamins.com/catalog/lllt

Editors

Nina Spada
Ontario Institute for Studies in Education
University of Toronto

Nelleke Van Deusen-Scholl
Center for Language Study
Yale University

Volume 34

Second Language Interaction in Diverse Educational Contexts
Edited by Kim McDonough and Alison Mackey

Second Language Interaction in Diverse Educational Contexts

Edited by

Kim McDonough
Concordia University

Alison Mackey
Georgetown University

John Benjamins Publishing Company

Amsterdam / Philadelphia

The paper used in this publication meets the minimum requirements of the American National Standard for Information Sciences – Permanence of Paper for Printed Library Materials, ANSI z39.48-1984.

Library of Congress Cataloging-in-Publication Data

Second language interaction in diverse educational contexts / Edited by Kim McDonough and Alison Mackey.
p.   cm. (Language Learning & Language Teaching, ISSN 1569-9471 ; v. 34)
Includes bibliographical references and index.
1. Second language acquisition--Study and teaching. 2. Language and languages--Study and teaching. 3. Multicultural education. I. McDonough, Kim, editor of compilation. II. Mackey, Alison, editor of compilation.
P118.2.S4354   2013
418.0071--dc23   2012044698
ISBN 978 90 272 1309 9   (Hb ; alk. paper)
ISBN 978 90 272 1310 5   (Pb ; alk. paper)
ISBN 978 90 272 7234 8   (Eb)

John Benjamins Publishing Co. · P.O. Box 36224 · 1020 ME Amsterdam · The Netherlands
John Benjamins North America · P.O. Box 27519 · Philadelphia PA 19118-0519 · USA

Table of contents

List of contributors

Rebekha Abbuhl
California State University Long Beach
1250 Bellflower Blvd
Long Beach, CA
USA
rabbuhl@csulb.edu

Steffi Ammons
Georgetown University
German Department
Intercultural Center 468
Washington, DC 20057
USA
sa585@hoyamail.georgetown.edu

Júlia Barón
University of Barcelona
Dept Filologia Anglesa i Alemanya
Centre Ciutat, Plaça Universitat, Edifici
Històric, Altell Pl. 2a
Gran Via Corts Catalanes, 585
08007 Barcelona
Spain
juliabaron@ub.edu

María Basterrechea
University of the Basque Country (UPV/EHU)
Escuela Universitaria Politécnica
de Donostia-San Sebastián
Dpto. de Filología Inglesa y Alemana
Europa Plaza 1
20018 Donostia-San Sebastián
Spain
maria.basterrechea@ehu.es

Rob Batstone
University of Auckland
Department of Applied Language
Studies and Linguistics
Private Bag 92019
Auckland
New Zealand
r.batstone@auckland.ac.nz

Sigrun Biesenbach-Lucas
Georgetown University
Center for Language, Education,
& Development
Bunn Intercultural Center 481
Washington, DC 20057
USA
sea2skye@aol.com

Joseph Collentine
Northern Arizona University
Modern Languages, Box 6004
Flagstaff, AZ 86001
USA
joseph.collentine@nau.edu

Karina Collentine
Northern Arizona University
Modern Languages, Box 6004
Flagstaff, AZ 86001
USA
karina.collentine@nau.edu

Natalia Dolgova Jacobsen
Georgetown University
Department of Linguistics
Poulton Hall, Suite 229
1421 37th St NW
Washington, DC 20057
USA
ndj5@georgetown.edu

Lyn Fogle
Mississippi State University
Department of English
Drawer E
Mississippi State, MS 39762
USA
ewf30@msstate.edu

Akiko Fujii
University of the Sacred Heart, Tokyo
4-3-1 Hiroo
Shibuya, Tokyo 150-8938
Japan
afujii@u-sacred-heart.ac.jp

María del Pilar García Mayo
University of the Basque Country (UPV/EHU)
Paseo de la Universidad 5
Dpto. de Filología Inglesa y Alemana
Facultad de Letras
01006 Vitoria-Gasteiz
Spain
mariapilar.garciamayo@ehu.es

Roger Gilabert
University of Barcelona
Dept Filologia Anglesa i Alemanya
Centre Ciutat, Plaça Universitat,
Edifici Històric, Altell Pl. 2a
Gran Via Corts Catalanes, 585
08007 Barcelona
SPAIN
rogergilabert@ub.edu

Phillip Hamrick
Georgetown University
Department of Linguistics
Poulton Hall, Suite 229
1421 37th St NW
Washington, DC 20057
USA
ph239@hoyamail.georgetown.edu

Trude Heift
Simon Fraser University
Department of Linguistics
Burnaby, BC V5A1S6
Canada
heift@sfu.ca

Teresa Hernández González
Concordia University
Department of Education
1455 de Maisonneuve Blvd. West
Montreal, QC H3G 1M8
Canada
teresa@education.concordia.ca

Talia Isaacs
University of Bristol
Graduate School of Education
35 Berkeley Square, Clifton
Bristol, BS8 1JA
United Kingdom
talia.isaacs@bristol.ac.uk

YouJin Kim
Georgia State University
Department of Applied Linguistics
and ESL
34 Peachtree Street, Suite #1200
Atlanta, GA 30302-4009
USA
ykim39@gsu.edu

Katie Kim
Georgetown University
Department of Linguistics
Poulton Hall, Suite 229
1421 37th St NW
Washington, DC 20057
USA
katie.j.kim12@gmail.com

Julie Lake
Georgetown University
Department of Linguistics
Poulton Hall, Suite 229
1421 37th St NW
Washington, DC 20057
USA
jbl34@georgetown.edu

Alison Mackey
Georgetown University
Department of Linguistics
Poulton Hall, Suite 229
1421 37th St NW
Washington, DC 20057
USA
mackeya@georgetown.edu

Kim McDonough
Concordia University
Department of Education
1455 de Maisonneuve Blvd. West
Montreal, QC H3G 1M8
Canada
kim.mcdonough@concordia.ca

Jenefer Philp
Lancaster University
Department of Linguistics and English
Language
County South
Lancaster LA1 4YL
United Kingdom
j.philp@lancaster.ac.uk

Patrick Rebuschat
School of Linguistics and English
Language
Bangor University
College Road
Bangor, Gwynedd LL57 2DG
United Kingdom
p.rebuschat@bangor.ac.uk

Claire Renaud
Arizona State University
Department of English
PO Box 870302
Tempe, AZ 85287-0302
USA
claire.renaud@asu.edu

Shannon Sauro
Faculty of Education and Society
Malmö University
205 06 Malmö
Sweden
Shannon.Sauro@mah.se

Corinne Seals
Georgetown University
Department of Linguistics
Poulton Hall, Suite 229
1421 37th St NW
Washington, DC 20057
USA
cas257@hoyamail.georgetown.edu

Ellen Johnson Serafini
Georgetown University
Department of Spanish and Portuguese
Box 571039
Intercultural Center 403
Washington, DC 20057
USA
esj23@hoyamail.georgetown.edu

Bryan Smith
Arizona State University
Department of English
PO Box 870302
Tempe, AZ 85287-0302
USA
bryansmith@asu.edu

Kerstin Sondermann
Georgetown University
Department of Linguistics
Poulton Hall, Suite 229
1421 37th St NW
Washington, DC 20057
USA
ks394@georgetown.edu

Kaitlyn Tagarelli
Georgetown University
Department of Linguistics
Poulton Hall, Suite 229
1421 37th St NW
Washington, DC 20057
USA
tagarelk@gmail.com

Mari Takada
Dokkyo University
Department of German
Faculty of Foreign Languages
1-1 Gakuen-cho, Soka-shi
Saitama 340-0042
Japan
tmari@dokkyo.ac.jp

Paul D. Toth
Temple University
Department of Spanish
and Portuguese
Anderson Hall 441
1114 West Berks Street
Philadelphia, PA 19122-6090
USA
ptoth@temple.edu

Elvis Wagner
Temple University
Curriculum, Instruction and Technology
in Education Department
459 Ritter Hall
1301 Cecil B. Moore Ave
Philadelphia, PA 19122-6092
USA
elvis@temple.edu

Atsuko Watanabe
International Christian University
College of Liberal Arts
3-10-2 Osawa, Mitaka, Tokyo
181-8585
Japan
atsuko@icu.ac.jp

Heather Weger
Georgetown University
Center for Language, Education,
& Development
Bunn Intercultural Center 481
Washington, DC 20057
USA
hdw2@georgetown.edu

Paula Winke
Michigan State University
Second Language Studies, Linguistics
and Languages
A-745 Wells Hall
East Lansing, MI 48824
USA
winke@msu.edu

Nicole Ziegler
Georgetown University
Department of Linguistics
Poulton Hall, Suite 229
1421 37th St NW
Washington, DC 20057
USA
nz45@georgetown.edu

Preface

Interaction in diverse educational contexts, a volume in the Language Learning and Language Teaching series from John Benjamins, brings together empirical research studies that explore interaction in a wide range of educational settings. In this volume, we include work that takes a cognitive, brain-based approach to studying interaction, as well as work that takes a social, contextual perspective on interaction. We define interaction quite broadly, with a primary focus on oral interaction as is typical in the field, but also inclusively because in some authentic educational contexts, face-to-face interaction is not a viable option for teachers, so we include work that involves interaction between learners and technology (for example, software and clicker-based response systems). Also, although most of the chapters we include here analyze the linguistic or discourse features of interaction between learners and their interlocutors, in some educational settings, interaction can serve other purposes, such as to inform placement and testing decisions. Therefore, we include studies where the goal is evaluating the use of interaction for making such judgments. We include interaction as it is traditionally studied, where interactional features are examined to see if they are associated with developmental challenges and outcomes, but we also include factors that impact learners' production as they interact in different contexts. The studies here investigate interactions with different interlocutors (i.e., learner-learner, learner-teacher), in a variety of environments (i.e., classrooms, interactive testing environments, conversation groups) and through different modalities (i.e., oral and written, face-to-face and technology-mediated). We include studies that explore L2 learners' orientation to, use of and acquisition of language forms (morpho-syntax, lexicon, and pragmatics) during collaborative activities, the nature of the interactions they have with peers and teachers, and the opportunities for learning that occur during face-to-face and computer mediated interactions.

Throughout this volume the common thread is interaction research that is situated in educational settings. By this, we mean existing instructional contexts, as opposed to settings that have been established exclusively for research purposes. Choosing to work in authentic contexts like these inevitably has implications for the level and type of experimental control that is possible, as practitioners naturally and appropriately prioritize instructional goals and learner needs over the needs of researchers. Each chapter reflects the following two principles:

1. The research study was carried out in an authentic educational setting (classroom, computer laboratory, conversation group)
2. The study either (a) reports the findings of research in which the materials and activities are representative of this instructional context and its stakeholders, or (b) describes the learning potential and/or outcomes of naturally occurring interactions which are being engaged in for the purposes of second language learning, testing, or use.

In our editorial role, our overarching goal for the volume was for each of the chapters to contribute something new or different to the field of interaction work. By this, we mean that at least one aspect of the research (context, design, coding, analysis) included something not typically seen in the interaction field. We did this because we wanted to provide a picture of the rich and diverse range of educational settings that offer potential for interaction researchers, both currently, and in the hope of sparking potential new directions for future research in the field to develop. For example, interaction in conversation group settings would seem to be an obvious avenue for researchers, with its naturally occurring features, potential for in-depth qualitatively driven insights into the patterns we typically manipulate experimentally, and its authentic, intrinsically motivated setting. Yet, to our knowledge, the studies we include here are the only ones of this kind in the interaction field to date.

This volume is divided it into the following thematic sections: (i) interaction in L2 classrooms; (ii) interaction involving technology; and (iii) interaction in other educational settings. Part I focuses on interaction in L2 classroom settings, beginning with YouJin Kim's study, *Promoting attention to form through task repetition in a Korean EFL context*, which investigates the modulation of Korean EFL learners' attention to linguistic form during collaborative tasks when task variables, specifically task repetition and procedural repetition, are manipulated. Using language related episodes (LREs) as a measure of the learners' attention to form during peer interaction, Kim offers a unique view into issues that directly impact pedagogical interventions in the classroom. In Chapter 2, *Language-related episodes during collaborative tasks: A comparison of CLIL and EFL learners*, María Basterrechea and María del Pilar García Mayo assess whether collaborative tasks differentially impact attention to form depending on the learning environment, comparing a content-and-language-integrated-learning (CLIL) classroom and an English-as-a-foreign-language (EFL) classroom. Using a dictogloss task to index collaborative work, Basterrechea and García Mayo explore whether learners attend to the present tense marker –s. In Chapter 3, Roger Gilabert and Júlia Barón's study, *The impact of increasing task complexity on L2 pragmatic moves*, explores the intersection of task complexity, interaction and interlanguage pragmatics. Gilabert and Barón measure the impact of cognitive task demands on the use of Catalan/Spanish bilingual L2 learners' English pragmatic performance, operationalized through the number and variety of resulting pragmatic moves. In Chapter 4, *Tasks and traditional practice activities in a foreign language classroom context*, Mackey et al. compare the effectiveness of traditional and communicative tasks at facilitating question development in a Japanese university EFL setting. In Chapter 5, *Building explicit L2 Spanish knowledge through guided induction in small group and whole class interaction*, Elvis Wagner and Paul Toth explore the interrelation between analytic talk and classroom context (small group or teacher-fronted interaction) in a consciousness-raising task that uses inductive reasoning with L2 learners of Spanish. In the final chapter in this section, *Classroom interaction and learning opportunities across time and space*, Rob Batstone and Jenefer Philp investigate the wide-ranging interactions that occur in L2 classrooms, ranging from teacher-fronted activities to pair and small group work. Batstone and Philp analyze data from advanced L2 English learners in an English for Academic Purposes (EAP) classroom to document how learners' interactions occur in both public and private spaces.

The studies in Part II explore interactions involving technology. The first three chapters report studies involving computer-mediated interaction, in which learners used computers as a medium for interaction. This section begins with Shannon Sauro's Chapter 7, *The cyber language exchange: Cross-national computer-mediated interaction*, in which text-chat interaction between L2 English learners in Sweden and preservice English teachers in the United States was analyzed. Sauro investigates whether telecollaboration (i.e., the text-chat interaction) provided L2 learners with opportunities for corrective feedback and therefore enhanced their attention to form. In Chapter 8, *Using eye tracking as a measure of foreign language learners' noticing of recasts during computer-mediated writing conferences*, Bryan Smith and Claire Renaud use eye-tracking in an effort to untangle noticing and learning in a computer-mediated setting. Smith and Renaud explore the link between second language recasts, noticing, and learning during computer-mediated communication between L2 learners of Spanish and German and their instructors. In Chapter 9, *A corpus approach to studying structural convergence in task-based Spanish L2 interactions*, Joseph Collentine and Karina Collentine use corpus-linguistic tools to investigate how Spanish L2 learners converge in their use of specific grammatical forms while carrying out SCMC tasks in a virtual 3-D environment. The last two chapters in this section take a different perspective on interaction, focusing on interactions between learners and technology. In Chapter 10, *Preemptive feedback in CALL*, Trude Heift investigated whether two types of preemptive feedback were differentially effective in a CALL environment for beginner and intermediate L2 learners of German. And in the last chapter in this section, Chapter 11, *Learner perceptions of clickers as a source of feedback in the classroom*, Ellen Johnson Serafini investigates how Spanish L2 learners perceive their use of learner response systems (or *clickers*) as a source of feedback and whether their perceptions vary based on the nature of the feedback provided by the clickers.

Part III explores interaction in other educational settings, beginning with Chapter 12, *International engineering graduate students' interactional patterns during a paired speaking test: Interlocutors' perspectives*, in which Talia Isaacs investigates the types of speaker relationships that unfold when L2 English speakers are paired up for an oral assessment task.

Also situated in a testing context, Paula Winke in Chapter 13, *The effectiveness of interactive group orals for placement testing*, takes an assessment-oriented approach to the study of interaction by examining the reliability and validity of using task-based, peer group orals for placement testing. The last two chapters describe the types of interactions that occur in conversation group settings. In Chapter 14, Ziegler et al., explore how German L2 learners develop their conversational style over the course of several conversation group meetings. Finally, in the last chapter, *Language production opportunities during whole-group interaction in conversation group settings*, Kim McDonough & Teresa Hernández González analyze the language production opportunities that preservice teachers create during whole-group interaction when they facilitate conversation groups as part of the practical training requirements of their teacher education program.

Acknowledgements

First, we would like to thank the editors of the *Language Learning & Language Teaching* series at John Benjamins, Nina Spada and Nelleke Van Deusen-Scholl, for their helpful suggestions throughout the process of writing the proposal, preparing the chapters, and editing the final volume. We are also grateful to Kees Vaes at John Benjamins for his consistent support for the book. We would like to thank Paula Kielstra for her assistance with the page proof corrections. Most of all, we would also like to thank all contributors to this volume for participating in this project and for their patience with our requests for just one more revision.

Part I

Interactions in L2 classrooms

Chapter 1

Promoting attention to form through task repetition in a Korean EFL context

YouJin Kim
Georgia State University

This chapter compares the impact of task repetition and procedural repetition on Korean EFL learners' ($n = 48$) attention to linguistic form during collaborative tasks. Two EFL classes were randomly assigned to carry out three collaborative tasks with either task repetition or procedural repetition. The learners' and the teacher's perceptions about task performance were elicited through questionnaires and a semi-structured interview with the teacher. The learners' task interaction was analyzed in terms of language-related episodes (LREs), and the questionnaire and interview responses were analyzed qualitatively. Results indicated that repeating the same task procedure was useful for encouraging LREs, especially when different content was provided each time. Implications for research and teaching are discussed.

Introduction

Over the past few decades, task-based language teaching (TBLT) has attracted the attention of second language acquisition (SLA) researchers, curriculum developers, and language teachers (Bygate, Skehan, & Swain 2001; Ellis 2003; Robinson 2011; Samuda & Bygate 2008; Van den Branden 2006; Van den Branden, Bygate, & Norris 2009). A number of SLA studies have used oral interactive tasks to provide linguistic input as well as to elicit second language (L2) learners' oral production. One topic that has generated a great deal of interest is how the design of tasks and task implementation factors differentially mediate interactional features during task performance. Most studies tend to analyze task performance during learner-learner interaction (Adams 2007; Kim & McDonough 2011; Leeser 2004; Gilabert & Barón, this volume; Basterrechea & García Mayo, this volume) and as a result, less is known about the role of teachers during learners' task-based interaction.

Despite growing empirical evidence documenting the significance of task design factors, important pedagogical questions regarding how tasks should be sequenced and implemented in task-based syllabi have not been widely investigated (Robinson 2009). For instance, one important pedagogical issue in need of empirical investigation is whether or not repeating different characteristics of tasks in the foreign language (FL) classroom enhances the benefits of task-based interaction. This chapter reports on a study that investigates the relationship between task repetition, learners' attention to linguistic forms, as well as learners' and teacher's perceptions about task-based interaction. Following Samuda and Bygate's (2008) call for more task-based research in ecological contexts, the current study was carried out in English as a foreign language (EFL) classes in Korea and focuses on two types of classroom interactions: learner-learner and teacher-learner.

Learner-learner interaction during task-based instruction

Conversational interaction is believed to facilitate the process of second language (L2) learning by exposing learners to meaningful input, providing them with feedback on their linguistic performance and allowing them to produce and modify their output (Gass 2003; Gass & Mackey 2007; Long 1996; Swain 1995). When learners experience a breakdown in communication, they might receive feedback on their erroneous production, may modify their output, or, when interacting with another learner, may even engage in metatalk. These features of interaction are hypothesized to help learners notice gaps between their current knowledge and the target language. To date, a substantial amount of research has examined these claims, and it is generally accepted that features of L2 oral interaction facilitate language learning (Gass & Mackey 2007; Mackey 2007a, 2007b). Given that pair and group work is widely implemented in language classroom contexts, a large number of studies have explored how to promote learner-learner interaction, and more recently a growing number of studies has investigated whether learners can serve as, and even be trained as, feedback providers (e.g., Adams 2007; Kim & McDonough 2008, 2011; McDonough 2004; Nuevo 2006; Sato & Lyster 2012). Overall, these studies have demonstrated that learners are able to attend to language form during task performance, discuss language issues explicitly, and more importantly, they can be providers of feedback.

The degree to which learners pay attention to form during learner-learner interaction has been shown to vary considerably depending on factors related to both (1) learners' individual differences such as age, gender, proficiency, pair dynamics, and level of engagement, and (2) task design and task implementation, such as planning time, task complexity, and task familiarity (e.g., Kim 2009; Kim & McDonough 2008, 2011; Gilabert & Barón, this volume; Leeser 2004; Mackey, Kanganas, & Oliver 2007; McDonough 2004; Neuvo 2006; Philp, Oliver, & Mackey 2006; Révész 2011; Watanabe & Swain 2007). In terms of learner factors, previous research suggests that collaborative pair dynamics, high levels of engagement, and interaction with a dyadic partner of a higher proficiency level facilitates interaction. However, the findings related to task design factors have not been conclusive, suggesting that some interactional features (e.g., comprehension check, recasts, language related episodes) are differentially affected by certain task variables more than others (Kim 2009; Nuevo 2006; Révész 2011). Task repetition is one such example, and one that has not been widely explored (Samuda & Bygate 2008).

Task repetition and task-based language teaching

According to Samuda and Bygate (2008), task repetition provides multiple opportunities for learners to rephrase or try out new aspects of language in the same or in a similar context/task, and as such it may help to draw learners' attention to form during task performance. From a theoretical point of view, repeating a task is key for interlanguage restructuring because it provides the opportunity for learners to first focus on expressing meaning, and then when repeating the task, they have more attentional capacity to focus on form (Ellis 2003).

To date, a majority of task repetition studies have been based on psycholinguistic work (e.g., Levelt's speech production model). Bygate (1996, 2001) argued that L2 learners have to figure out the relationship between the conceptual content of their messages and the formulation possibilities under time pressure. When carrying out oral tasks, learners are primarily concerned with content generation. However, once learners are familiar with the message content, they can allocate more of their attention from content to the selection and monitoring of appropriate language, which can facilitate the quality of oral production (Bygate 1999). By repeating tasks, learners are expected to keep their previous oral production phases (i.e., conceptualization, formulation and articulation) in their memory store and reuse them on the second occasion (Bygate 2001). From a skill acquisition theory perspective, DeKeyser (1998:49) refers to repeated "behaviour" (i.e., performing a communicative task) when describing why task repetition is an important task design element to consider in FL classrooms:

> repeated behaviors … allow the restructuring of declarative knowledge in ways that make it easier to proceduralize and allow the combination of co-occurring elements into larger chunks that reduce the working memory load.

Previous task repetition studies have tested the benefits of task repetition mainly by exploring the extent to which task repetition impacts accuracy, complexity, and fluency of L2 oral production during task performance. For instance, Bygate (2001) found that memories of a previous task experience positively affected oral performance in the areas of fluency and complexity especially. In a recent study, Ahmedian and Tavakoli (2010) also found a positive relationship between task repetition and task planning on all three areas of EFL learners' oral production (accuracy, complexity, and fluency).

While the studies mentioned above were conducted in monologic contexts, task repetition has also been examined in a conversational interaction setting. For instance, Plough and Gass (1993) compared a task familiar group and a task unfamiliar group's use of discourse (e.g., overlaps, interruptions) and interactional features (e.g., confirmation checks, clarification requests). They operationalized task familiarity as learners' familiarity with task procedures through task repetition. Results showed that the task unfamiliar group produced more interruptions, whereas the task-familiar group used more interactional features. One of the few classroom-based task repetition studies is Lynch and Maclean

(2000) which investigated task repetition effects with advanced learners in an English for Specific Purposes course. Learners participated in a "poster carousel" which first involved making a poster based on a research article and then they visited each other's posters to ask questions. Lynch and Maclean (2000) operationalized task repetition as "recycling" or "retrial", where the communication goal was the same, but the content varied depending on the partners' questions about the posters. The findings indicated that immediate repetition of tasks had positive effects on both accuracy and fluency.

Mackey, Kanagas, and Oliver (2007) compared the differential effects of procedural and content repetition. Procedural familiarity was operationalized as the learners' prior experience of procedural aspects of a task, whereas content familiarity was operationalized as previous content knowledge. A total of 40 young ESL learners completed four tasks in pairs. The results revealed that more negotiation of meaning was found when the learners were not familiar with the procedure and content of the task. However, procedural familiarity provided more opportunities for feedback. Because their focus was task familiarity as opposed to task repetition, the findings were not discussed in terms of whether and in what ways the amount or type of focus on form during task performance changed through repetition.

Overall, previous studies investigating the relationship between task repetition and L2 oral performance have generally found that the quality of L2 learners' oral output was positively influenced by task repetition. However, the majority of previous studies were conducted using similar task types (e.g., story retelling) in monologic speaking contexts. Furthermore, the role of different characteristics of task repetition (e.g., repeating the same content or procedure) has not been systematically researched. To date, only two studies have addressed these concerns by examining the role of different characteristics of task repetition in relation to learners' linguistic development during learner-learner interaction.

Gass, Mackey, Fernandez, Alvarez-Torres and Fernández-García (1999) investigated the role of content repetition on language development in terms of overall proficiency, morphosyntax ("ser" and "estar" in Spanish), and lexical sophistication. They hypothesized that repeating tasks with the same content while following the same procedure would allow learners to allocate more attentional resources to linguistic forms. A total of 108 Spanish L2 learners were assigned to either a same content group, a different content group, or a control group. The same content group watched the same Mr. Bean episode three times, followed by a fourth Mr. Bean video which had a different content. In contrast, the different content group watched four different Mr. Bean episodes. The control group watched the first and the fourth videos only. Learners were asked to retell the story after each viewing. The findings suggested that the same content group showed higher overall proficiency gains and more lexical sophistication. In terms of learners' accurate use of "estar," the different content group showed higher gains in accuracy.

In order to investigate how different task repetition features influence the benefits of task-based interaction, Patanasorn (2010) examined the effects of procedural, content, and task repetition on the accuracy of simple past tense use, following a pretest-posttest-delayed posttest design. Ninety-two Thai EFL learners were randomly assigned to the three repetition conditions: procedural repetition, content repetition, and task repetition. Each group carried out three collaborative tasks targeting the simple past tense. Procedural repetition was operationalized as carrying out tasks which had the same procedure but different content. The content repetition group was operationalized as engaging in tasks that had the same content but different procedures. Task repetition was operationalized as carrying out tasks with the same procedures and content three times. The oral production test used was a story retell task based on a silent film. Results indicated that the procedural repetition group's accuracy of the simple past developed the most compared to the other two groups, which did not show improvement in the use of the past tense.

In sum, task repetition is one task implementation variable found to affect L2 learners' language production and development, as it allows them to place increased attention on making more fluent, accurate, and complex form-meaning connections (Ahmadian & Tavakoli 2010; Bygate 2001; Patanasorn 2010). However, it is unclear whether it is repeating the same task content or the same task procedure that makes the difference. In addition, previous research has focused on oral performance and/or posttest results without reporting on learners' interaction patterns over time. Language instruction often involves task repetition, thus it is an important factor to consider when implementing collaborative tasks in language classroom. Yet, little is known about how repeating tasks would affect interactional features between learners, in addition to their subsequent language use. For instance, Patanasorn (2010) was the first study to examine the effects that different task repetition variables have on linguistic development over time when collaborative tasks are used with adult learners in EFL contexts. However, this study focused on the outcome of each repetition condition, and did not address what happened during task-based interaction. Because pair and group work is relevant for task-based instruction in classroom contexts, it is also necessary to explore various factors affecting potential interaction-driven language learning during task performance.

One other area that has been under-researched is the role of the teacher during task-based interaction (Samuda 2001). To my knowledge, there is no reported research focusing on teachers and how they implement or perceive the value of task repetition in class. In order to better understand the occurrence of learning opportunities in natural classroom settings, both learner-learner and teacher-learner interaction need to be investigated in task-based interaction studies. Furthermore, the learners' and the teacher's perceptions towards task performance and task repetition require investigation so that their perspectives can be considered in teaching and research contexts.

This chapter describes a study that explored the effects of different task repetition characteristics on junior high school EFL learners' attention to linguistic forms during task-based interaction. Specifically, the role of procedural repetition (i.e., repeating the same task type with different content) versus task repetition (i.e., repeating the same task content and task procedure) was investigated. The current study operationalized attention to form as the learners' production of Language Related Episodes (LREs) during task-based learner-learner interaction. Additionally, the learners' and the teacher's perceptions about the usefulness of task repetition were examined.

The study was guided by the following research questions:

1. Do task repetition and procedural repetition affect learners' attention to linguistic forms differently during task performance?
2. How do task repetition and procedural repetition influence learners' perceptions of their task performance?
3. What opinions does the teacher have about the different characteristics of task repetition?

Method

Design of the study

The current study employed a between-groups design to investigate the impact of task repetition and procedural repetition on learner-generated focus on linguistics forms (both with the teacher and between learners), as well as their perceptions towards task performance in English. Following Patanasorn (2010), task repetition was operationalized as carrying out tasks that had the same procedures and same content during three consecutive lessons (see Table 1). Procedural repetition was operationalized as providing three information gap tasks during three consecutive lessons that followed the same procedure, but with different content each time.

Table 1. Operationalization of different task repetition conditions

	Procedure	Content
Procedural repetition	Same procedure (+)	Different content (−)
Task repetition	Same procedure (+)	Same content (+)

The study was carried out with two intact groups at a junior high school in Korea. One class was randomly assigned to the task repetition group, while the other class was assigned to the procedural repetition group. Both quantitative and qualitative data were used to answer the three research questions.

Participants

EFL learners

The participants in this study were 48 female Korean middle school students who were enrolled in two classes of a required English course at a private, all-girls school in South Korea. Originally a total of 58 students were enrolled in both classes. However, 10 students were excluded from the data set because they either did not complete all tasks or their recordings were not comprehensible. The participants ranged in age from 12 to 14 years old, with a mean age of 13.47 years ($SD = .54$). All participants had taken at least four years of required English classes in elementary school. Their average previous English instruction time was 6.25 years ($SD = 1.75$). Their regular curricula included four hours of a mandatory English course per week; three hours was spent with their regular (Korean L1) English teacher and one hour was with a native English speaking teacher. The textbook used in the course with the Korean English teacher was organized by different themes, and each unit presented different functional expressions, target grammatical features, and vocabulary. With the native English speaker teacher, the students often practiced speaking and listening skills and played English games. Most students reported taking extra English lessons in their free time, with a mean of 5 hours per week ($SD = 3.43$). They reported that on average, two instructional hours were spent practicing oral communication skills in English per week.

At the school where the study was conducted, learners are grouped together based on having a similar level of English language proficiency. This policy is known as ability grouping for English instruction (see Kim 2012). Students are divided into three levels (low, mid, high) based on their mid-term and final exam results. The learners that took part in the current study belonged to the high group classes (i.e., students who are above the 30th percentile).

Teacher

The teacher participant, Miran (Pseudonym), was the Korean English teacher. Miran was a 42 year-old female who had 20 years of teaching experience at the same school where the study took place. She had obtained an MA degree in English education in South Korea and lived in Australia for one year when she attended an Intensive English program.

Materials

Tasks

Three communicative tasks were created in an effort to appeal to students' interests and develop their ability to talk about previous events in English: (1) hosting an American friend; (2) describing school events/activities; and (3) talking about candidates for mayor. Because learners were in an EFL context, their real-world need for using English was rather limited. Therefore, tasks were designed based on their school events (e.g., athletic meetings, birthday party, school festival) as well as on current social issues at the time of data collection (e.g., mayoral election). The task repetition group repeated the first task (i.e., hosting an American friend) three times, while the procedural repetition group carried out all three tasks one time each.

All three tasks were information-exchange tasks (each learner in the pair held information that had to be shared), and followed the same procedure. Learners were provided with the same amount of visual input (e.g., number of pictures, words provided along with each picture) across all three tasks. The common outcome across tasks was to exchange necessary information and prepare a report form to present to the entire class based on the information exchanged between learners. Table 2 below describes the procedure of each task.

Table 2. Task descriptions

	Hosting an American friend	Describing school events	Discussing candidates for mayor
Step 1	Both learners looked at pictures about what they did with an American friend in Korea.	Both learners looked at pictures about their school events.	Both learners looked at pictures about two candidates' life histories.
Step 2	Each learner had different events on different days.	Each learner had different events.	Each learner had different information.
Step 3	Both learners created an information report form presenting what their American friend did while visiting Korea.	Both learners created an information report form presenting on the events each school had in the Spring term.	Both learners created an information report form presenting complete information about the candidates' background.

Learner questionnaire

The student questionnaire consisted of 16 Likert-scale items. Seven questions targeted language anxiety (e.g., I am afraid of speaking in front of my classmates) and six questions were related to learner-learner interaction during tasks. Additionally, one question asked to what extent learners enjoyed the task ("likeability") (i.e., I enjoyed carrying out the tasks.), and one question addressed the helpfulness of task performance to improve their English ("helpfulness") (i.e., I believe that the tasks were helpful to improve my English). Finally, the last question asked about the extent to which learners liked the topic(s) of the tasks ("topic interests") (e.g., I found the topic(s) during the three tasks interesting.). In the current study, each group's responses to the three questions focusing on likeability, helpfulness, and topic interests are discussed. Each item presented the student with six options: strongly agree, agree, somewhat agree, somewhat disagree, disagree, strongly disagree.

Interview questions

After completing the three tasks, the researcher carried out a semi-structured interview with the Korean English teacher. During the interview, two issues were addressed: (1) How do you feel about using collaborative tasks in your class? and (2) What characteristics of task repetition seemed beneficial for promoting learning opportunities?

Procedure

The tasks were administered during three regularly-scheduled classes over a one-week period. Each task was carried out during a 45-minute class period, which consisted of short pretask activities (planning time), the main task, and posttask activities. Given that previous interaction studies have highlighted the potential benefits of guided task planning (e.g., Foster & Skehan 1996; Mochizuki & Ortega 2008; Kim & McDonough 2011), learners were provided with task models (2 minutes each) during their planning time in the pre-task phase. During this phase, the researcher and the teacher demonstrated the task in order to promote collaborative task performance and reinforce focus on form techniques. Learners were then given 25–30 minutes to complete the main task. As described in the previous section, the task repetition group repeated the same task ("Hosting an American friend") three times, whereas the procedural repetition group carried out three different tasks (thus following the same procedure but differing in content only). In real classroom contexts it would be rare for the learners to repeat the same task three times without any changes. For that reason the learners in the task repetition group were asked to work with different partners each time. This way they received different input on the same topic from each partner. In order to provide the same condition in terms of interlocutor, the procedure repetition group also changed their partners for each task.

While carrying out each task, learners were required to complete the report forms while exchanging information for the class presentation. During the posttask activity, the teacher asked learners to present to the class what they had put on their task worksheet. On the fourth day of the study, learners were given about 20 minutes to complete the background and perception questionnaire, and afterwards, a semi-structured informal interview was carried out with the teacher.

Data coding

All task-based interaction data were recorded and transcribed by the researcher and a research assistant. The transcribed data were analyzed for learners' attention to linguistic forms, or LREs, which were further broken down into two categories: grammatical versus lexical. Next, LRE resolution was coded for whether the LRE was resolved, unresolved, or incorrectly resolved. Lastly, all LREs were coded according to having taken place between two learners or a learner and the teacher.

LREs

LREs, are defined as "any part of a dialogue where the students talk about the language they are producing, question their language use, or correct themselves or others" (Swain & Lapkin 1998: 326). Grammatical LREs included students' discussion about grammatical features of English. A total of eight issues were addressed during grammatical LREs: (1) tense (e.g., past tense), (2) word form (e.g., gerund -ing forms), (3) sentence structure (e.g., passives), (4) plurality (e.g., singular vs. plural), (5) article use, (6) prepositions, (7) question formation (e.g., inversion), and (8) pronoun (e.g., his vs. hers). A grammatical LRE in which two learners discussed sentence structure (i.e., passive construction) is illustrated in (1). Learner 2 explicitly pointed out Learner 1's incorrect use of active voice and suggested the use of passive voice.

(1) 1   Learner 1: She elected as city councilor.
     2   Learner 2: She was elected 아냐? (Shouldn't we say "she was elected"?)
     3   수동태잖아 (It is a passive voice)
     4   Learner 1: She was elected as city councilor. She was very sincere and honest.

In terms of lexical LREs, the students in the current study focused on a total of four issues: (1) meaning (i.e., From English to Korean), (2) English translation (From Korean to English), (3) pronunciation, and (4) spelling. In the lexical LRE shown in (2), Learner 1 did not know how to say "watered" in English (i.e., English translation), and Learner 2 provided an appropriate word in English (Line 2):

(2) 1   Learner 1: no but I 물주다 ("water"). 식물에 물주다 뭐라 그러지?
         (How do you say "muljuda" in English?)
     2   Learner 2: watered.
     3   Learner 1: I watered some flowers.

In terms of resolution of LREs, correctly resolved, unresolved, and incorrectly resolved LREs were coded following previous studies (e.g., Kim & McDonough 2008; Leeser 2004; Swain & Lapkin 1998). For the correctly resolved LREs, the study considered both learner-learner and teacher-learner interaction, and it compared the extent to which the teacher or learners contributed to correctly resolving LREs. Thus two sub-categories were identified: correctly resolved LREs by the teacher and correctly resolved LREs by learners. LREs that were correctly resolved by the learners were illustrated in (1) and (2), and an LRE that was correctly resolved by the teacher is provided in (3).

(3) 1   Learner: He 노력하다가 try, 노력했다가 뭐예요?
         (The present form is "try" then what is the past form of "try"?)
     2   Teacher: He tried
     3   Learner: Ah… He tried to collect money.

Reliability and analysis

An independent rater coded a subset of the data (20%). The Pearson's *r* for interrater reliability was .94 for the classification of LREs, and .92 for the resolution of LREs. Any disagreements were resolved through discussion. Individual Mann-Whitney tests, non-parametric independent samples *t*-tests, were used to compare the number of LREs generated by each group. For the questionnaire data, independent samples *t*-tests were run. Alpha was set at .05 for all statistical tests. Finally, the interview data were analyzed qualitatively.

Results

The first research question investigated how task repetition and procedural repetition affected junior high school EFL learners' attention to linguistic forms during task performance. To answer this question, LRE types (i.e., lexical, grammatical) and resolution of LREs were analyzed. Table 3 displays the descriptive statistics by group for lexical and grammatical LREs that occurred during the treatment tasks.

Table 3. Types of LREs by group and task

| Group | Lexical LREs | | | | Grammatical LREs | | | |
| | Task repetition | | Procedural repetition | | Task repetition | | Procedural repetition | |
	M	*SD*	*M*	*SD*	*M*	*SD*	*M*	*SD*
Task								
Friend	10.96	3.88	11.92	5.74	7.87	3.24	10.36	4.73
School	6.78	3.01	12.96	4.54	7.17	2.92	14.16	7.23
Mayor	5.35	2.95	18.40	4.69	11.48	4.13	12.00	5.10
Total	23.09	6.53	43.28	8.06	26.52	6.28	36.52	11.39

In terms of the total number LREs (both lexical and grammatical LREs), the procedural repetition group produced more ($M = 79.80$) LREs than the task repetition group ($M = 49.61$). The procedural repetition group produced a mean of 43.28 lexical LREs and 36.52 grammatical LREs, whereas the task repetition group had a mean of 23.09 lexical LREs and 26.52 grammatical LREs. The total number of lexical and grammatical LREs across all three tasks was compared using Mann-Whitney tests (non-parametric independent samples t-tests). The results indicated that the procedural repetition group produced significantly more lexical LREs ($Z = 5.80$, $p = .00$) and grammatical LREs ($Z = 3.50$, $p = .00$) than the task repetition group.

To explore what learners focused on during the LREs, a more detailed analysis of the focus of each LRE was conducted. The majority of the lexical LREs occurred when the learners could not come up with an English equivalent (i.e., English translation) or when they did not understand the meaning of words in the task input (i.e., meaning). Among the four foci of lexical LREs (i.e., meaning, English translation, spelling, pronunciation), both pronunciation and spelling for each task had mean scores below 1, therefore Figure 1 only illustrates the occurrence of LREs focusing on meaning and English translation.

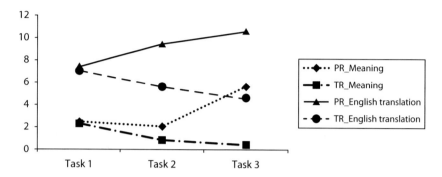

Figure 1. The occurrence of LREs focusing on meaning and English translation

(Note: PR = Procedural repetition, TR = Task repetition)

This figure shows that the number of LREs targeting meaning and English translation increased over time by the procedural repetition group, whereas the opposite pattern was found with the task repetition group.

Figure 2 illustrates the occurrence of grammatical LREs focusing on the two most widely addressed grammatical structures: verb tense (e.g., simple past) and word forms (e.g., using base forms after modal verbs).

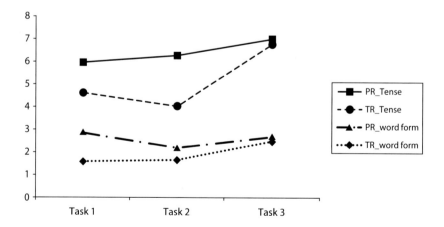

Figure 2. Grammatical LREs focusing on tense and word forms

As shown in Figure 2, all learners tended to produce more grammatical LREs focusing on tense and word forms during task 3 than task 1.

Next, resolution of LREs was also considered, looking at correctly resolved LREs, incorrectly resolved LREs, and unresolved LREs. In addition, correctly resolved LREs were further divided into learner-resolved and teacher-resolved.

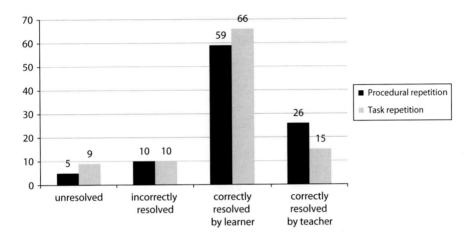

Figure 3. Resolution of LREs (%)

A visual inspection of Figure 3 reveals that the procedural repetition group resolved about 85% of LREs (learner + teacher corrected) with the remainder incorrectly resolved (10%) or unresolved (5%). The task repetition group resolved about 81% of their LREs, leaving 9% unresolved and 10% incorrectly resolved. When considering who contributed to correctly resolved LREs, 59% of the LREs were resolved correctly by learners and 26 % of the LREs were by the teacher in the procedural repetition group. On the other hand, for the task repetition group, 66% of the LREs were resolved correctly by learners and 15 % of the LREs were by the teacher. The results also show that the majority of LREs resolved by the teacher targeted English translation when learners asked questions such as "How do you say X in English?"

The second research question compared learners' attitudes towards task performance between the procedural repetition and the task repetition groups. Their responses on three questions were presented in Figure 4: Likeability, Helpfulness, and Topic interest. Each item has a minimum of 1 (strongly disagree) and a maximum of 6 (strongly agree) (see the materials section for each statement).

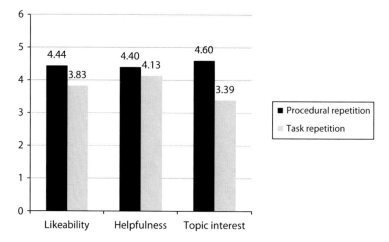

Figure 4. Learner perceptions towards task performance

As shown in Figure 4, overall, the procedural repetition group had more positive perceptions towards task performance than the task repetition group in regards to all three perception variables explored: how much they liked carrying out the tasks, how helpful the tasks were to improve their English skills, and how interesting the task topics were. The results of the independent t-test with an adjusted alpha ($\alpha = 0.017$) showed that there was no significant difference between the procedural repetition group and the task repetition group in terms of likeability, $t(1, 46) = 1.78$, $p = .08$ and helpfulness, $t(1, 46) = .97$, $p = .34$. However, the procedural repetition group found the topics of tasks significantly more interesting than the task repetition $t(1, 46) = 4.21$, $p = .00$.

The third research question focused on the teacher's perceptions towards the role of task performance, particularly in reference to different characteristics of task repetition in promoting English learning. This research question was addressed using qualitative data from the interview. For example, overall, Miran found the tasks useful for helping learners use English in class in meaningful contexts, as demonstrated below:

> The tasks were designed to encourage learners to talk about what they are familiar with. Thus students seemed to have a lot of ideas to discuss when carrying out the tasks. I was happy to see that students had opportunities to speak in English with their partners.

However, Miran also shared her concerns related to a lack of linguistic resources available to the learners:

> Although students saw task modelling before carrying out the task, it seems like it would have been more helpful for students if useful expressions or vocabulary items had been provided beforehand. Students would not feel that they learned something unless new vocabulary items or grammatical features were introduced.

With regards to the different characteristics of task repetition (e.g., task repetition versus procedural repetition), Miran mentioned that she was able to see some benefits of repeating the same task three times; for instance, students seemed to build confidence in carrying out the task in English. Also, because they had become familiar with the tasks, no detailed instruction was required, saving some valuable class time. More time could be dedicated to learner-learner interaction, for example. On the other hand, Miran shared that some students tended to lose motivation easily, especially when they had to repeat the same task for the third time. Thus, in regards to task repetition, Miran said the following:

> My students are young learners who easily become tired of doing the same thing. Thus although repeating the same tasks seem to have many benefits such as building fluency, I heard some students saying "again?" when the same content was introduced. Because of this reason, providing different contents but requiring the same procedure seems to keep students' interest high. Because they are not used to carry out tasks like these, keeping the same procedure is a good decision. However, again, I think it is important to provide some sample sentences and vocabulary words that they can use during tasks.

To summarize, the results of research question 1 demonstrated that the procedural repetition group produced significantly more LREs than the task repetition group. With regards to the occurrence of LREs over time, although the total number of both lexical and grammatical LREs decreased for the task repetition group, the amount of grammatical LREs increased over time. In terms of the resolution of LREs, both groups showed a similar pattern, with the majority of LREs being resolved correctly. However, the procedural group showed more reliance on the teacher's input to successfully resolve these LREs, particularly when they did not know how to express their ideas in English. To answer the second research question, the results suggest that both procedural and task repetition groups agreed that their task performance experience was somewhat helpful to improve their English skills. However, the task repetition group did not find the topic of the tasks as interesting as the procedural group, which could be because they received the same content three times. Finally, while the teacher highlighted the benefits of task repetition for both learners and for lesson implementation, it was also mentioned that young learners can easily lose interest when there is not enough new content between activities. Thus, the teacher also referenced the need to provide learners with more task-relevant input in the pre-task phase, irrespective of the task repetition type to be carried out.

Discussion

In the task repetition literature, one underexplored topic is how different characteristics of task repetition impact learners' attention to linguistic forms during task performance over time. Another underexplored topic is more pedagogically based and it is teachers' and learners' perceptions towards task repetition. This study has attempted to fill these gaps. It partially replicated Patanasorn (2010) and also provided an analysis of how learners addressed linguistic issues and to what extent teacher-learner interaction was initiated during pair work.

The findings of the current study were in line with previous task familiarity studies. For instance, Mackey, Kanganas and Oliver (2007) found that young learners working through unfamiliar tasks in terms of content and procedure produced more interactional feedback on non-target like utterances to each other. A similar pattern was found in the current study, particularly with lexical LREs; the procedure repetition group produced more lexical LREs than the task repetition group who became more familiar with the topic (i.e., hosting an American friend) over time.

When examining the number of lexical LREs over time, the task repetition group had fewer lexical LREs each time they repeated the same content, whereas the procedural repetition group produced an increasing number of lexical LREs over time. Two main foci of lexical LREs, meaning and English translation, followed the same pattern. This result showed that young learners in the current study were in need of more linguistic resources, particularly vocabulary items, to complete tasks with new content. During the interview, Miran suggested that providing learners with useful vocabulary items or expressions before starting the task seems necessary to help learners carry out the task successfully. Her comments were in line with teachers' comments in Carless (2007) which focused on the importance of providing more help with basic English grammar before adopting a task-based approach. However, findings on the occurrence of LREs supported previous learner-learner interaction studies (e.g., Adams 2007; Basterrechea & García Mayo, this volume; Kim & McDonough 2008; Leeser 2004) in that learners were able to seek out assistance either from their peers or the teacher during task performance. From a pedagogical point of view, the extent to which pre-generated vocabulary/expression lists would help learners to complete the tasks more successfully, compared to learner-generated focus on form during the task, needs further investigation.

In terms of grammatical LREs, although no clear pattern was found, learners in both groups produced more grammatical LREs during Task 3 than Task 1. Overall, the total amount of LREs during each task produced by the task repetition group was constant because fewer lexical LREs and more grammatical LREs were produced over time. For the procedural repetition group, the amount of LREs increased each time. This finding highlights the importance of familiarity with the task procedure and suggests that repeating tasks with the same procedure may help learners to try to elaborate their ideas by using new expressions because of the extra attention available to focus on linguistic forms (both lexical and grammatical) during task performance. However, repeating both procedure *and* content was not as effective as keeping the same procedure with various topics. This result may be because learners' task engagement is also influenced by affective factors such as motivation and willingness to communicate (Dörnyei & Kormos 2000). The learner perception data, particularly focusing on their likeability of tasks and interest in topics during tasks, indicated that this may be the case with the learners in the present study. An area of further research would be to replicate this study in other contexts and with different age groups.

An interesting finding from this study is that learners who repeated the same task three times and had the same content were able to resolve LREs between each other more than the procedural repetition group. Mackey, Kanganas and Oliver (2007) also found that learners who were familiar with the procedure had more opportunities to use feedback, and there was more incorporation of feedback by learners engaged in familiar tasks in terms of content and procedure. An example of how two learners from the task repetition group resolved LREs during task 3 is shown in (4). The two learners in this example correctly resolved lexical LREs (lines 3 and 5) as well as a grammatical LRE (line 7).

(4) 1   Learner 1: I I visit, I visited relatives with Laura. We helped my relatives and and
     2   I planted flower, flowers. Dig 가 뭐야? (what does "dig" mean?)
     3   Learner 2: dig 가 땅을 파다. (providing Korean translation)
     4   Learner 1: We digged a hole and we planted 다양한이 뭐야? (How do you say "dayanghan" in English?)
     5   Learner 2: Various
     6   Learner 1: various vegetables. We we felt very very hot. And there and we eat we eat we eat lunch, lunch.
     7   Learner 2: and we ate a lunch 지. ([you should say] "and we ate a lunch".)

On the other hand, the procedural group asked for more input from the teacher in order to resolve LREs. Example (5) shows two learners in the procedural group as they requested the teacher's help when they could not resolve the LRE themselves (line 5). Because the procedural repetition group was required to produce a new variety of lexical items and grammatical features each time, the linguistic demands for each task may have been higher than the task repetition group, which caused the learners to look for additional assistance.

(5) 1   Learner 1: On March 11, we had volunteer work. I had a volunteer.
     2   Learner 2: We volunteered at a park. We go out and we volunteered at a park. We we 줍다가 뭐지? (How do you say "jupda" in English?
     3   Learner 1: pick
     4   Learner 2: Pick up garbage?
     5   Learner 1: 선생님 줍다가 영어로 뭐예요? (Teacher, how do you say "jupda" in English?)
     6   Teacher: 주웠다? (juetda?) picked up
     7   Learner 2: we picked up garbage and we plants planted flowers.

Lynch and Maclean (2000) found that learners benefited from the opportunity to recycle communicative content as they repeated the same tasks. In terms of accuracy development, Patanasorn (2010) found that procedural repetition was more beneficial for promoting accurate production of the simple past than other types of task repetition. The current study provides additional evidence for the role of task repetition, both repetition of the procedure, and repetition of the procedure and content. However, the benefits were different depending on the type of task repetition. The junior high school learners in the current study were not familiar with carrying out collaborative tasks in class, and the different aspects of repetition seemed to be useful for encouraging learners to pay attention to language codes, particularly with the procedural repetition group. While repeating the same procedure with different topics, learners' attentional resources could have been directed to using different lexical and grammatical structures. In particular, verb tense, one of the main grammatical LRE targets was addressed increasingly with different verbs over time in the procedural repetition group. In comparison, repeating the same task with the same content did not encourage learners to attend to the use of different verbs as much.

To my knowledge, most previous classroom-based learner-learner interaction studies have not addressed the occurrence of teacher-learner interaction, which is a natural interaction pattern in any language classroom. The current study found that learners in the procedural repetition group tended to utilize more teacher input during task performance. Because the majority of LREs resolved by the teacher focused on finding an English translation, it seems clear that the teacher serves as an important linguistic resource in task-based language teaching. This finding also underscores the importance of examining task-based instruction in classroom contexts. Samuda (2001: 137) claimed that teachers "lead from behind" to support learning processes during pair and small group work. The current study confirms the teacher's positive role in task-based learner-learner interaction, showing how the teacher can provide additional support which helps to guide learners' attention towards form-meaning relationships.

With regards to the learners' and the teacher's perceptions towards task performance and task repetition, both students and the teacher found the tasks helpful for developing their English skills. However, the teacher expressed her concern about repeating both content and procedure, claiming that learners might lose interest over time with this kind of task repetition. Her concerns were somewhat reflected on the learner questionnaire results illustrating that although both groups found the task sequences they performed helpful, the task repetition group did not show strong interest in the topic of the tasks. Future research studies could investigate whether task repetition promotes developmental outcomes even through it is associated with decreased interest in the topics.

Important pedagogical implications for EFL task-based instructional contexts can be drawn from results of the current study. Researchers have expressed concerns regarding the implementation of task-based instruction in EFL contexts (e.g., Carless 2007; Swan

2005) in part because the amount of EFL learners' English instruction, as well as language input, is often limited. However, previous task-based interaction studies have supported the benefits of learner-learner interaction in various foreign language contexts (e.g., Kim & McDonough 2008, 2011; Leeser 2004; McDonough 2004; McDonough & Sunitham 2009). Findings of the current study suggest positive outcomes for the use of task-based learner-learner interaction in EFL middle school contexts, along with a potential optimal way to implement task-based instruction. Ensuring learners' familiarity with task procedures while providing them with new content seems to be a useful way to implement communicative tasks in a foreign language classroom context in Korea.

The current study also provided evidence regarding how the patterns of learners' attention to linguistic forms changed as they repeated tasks. However, these results should be considered with caution. For instance, the findings suggests that as the learners repeated the same task three times, the number of lexical LREs decreased constantly; grammatical LREs did not seem to be strongly affected by task repetition until the third time that they performed the task. Thus, when deciding on repetition conditions, teachers need to take target aspects of linguistic forms and the goals of the task into consideration as well as considering whether task repetition can lead to boredom.

Limitations of the current study must also be noted. First, the study was carried out at an all-girls junior high school in South Korea. Thus the results cannot be generalized to different educational contexts, and future research will need to examine different populations of learners across contexts. The study was also carried out with only one task type, information-exchange, and future studies using a variety of task types are necessary, particularly studies that explore different task design factors such as task complexity. Additionally, the current study did not take individual differences into consideration (e.g., anxiety, task motivation). For instance, learners with higher language anxiety might benefit from repeating tasks more than learners with lower language anxiety. From a pedagogical point of view, these issues are critical for language practitioners. Furthermore, the current study investigated only two repetition conditions: repeating the same content and procedure vs. repeating the same procedure with different content. In order to understand the role of different aspects of repetition in task-based instruction more in depth, other conditions such as "no repetition" and "content repetition with different procedures" need to be included. Future studies could also examine task repetition and repeated phrases or chunks of language from a sociocultural perspective, looking at phrases repeated during task repetition as a socio-cognitive tool (e.g., DiCamilla & Anton 1997). Finally, the current study addressed only one teacher's contribution to learner-learner interaction. More systematic research is warranted investigating how teachers can promote students' understanding of form-meaning relationships. This kind of research would be beneficial for teacher development in TBLT.

Conclusion

The purpose of this study was to investigate (1) the effects of task repetition and proce-dural repetition on the quantity and quality of learners' LREs, and (2) the learners' and the teacher's perceptions about task repetition. The results showed that different aspects of repetition in task-based instruction affect the amount of learners' attention to differ-ent types of linguistic forms. Given the increased demands of implementing instruc-tional tasks in foreign and second language contexts, clearly a great deal more research is required to explore beyond individual task design factors, and also to address the bigger picture such as how to sequence tasks when designing task-based syllabi or larger curri-cula (e.g., McDonough & Chaikitmongkol 2007). The results suggest that teachers should consider different aspects of repetition as one of the factors important in the design and sequencing of tasks in task-based instruction.

References

Adams, R. (2007). Do second language learners benefit from interacting with each other? In A. Mackey (Ed.), *Conversational interaction in second language acquisition* (pp. 29–51). Oxford: Oxford University Press.

Ahmadian, M. J., & Tavakoli, M. (2010). The effects of simultaneous use of careful online planning and task repetition on accuracy, complexity, and fluency in EFL learners' oral production. *Language Teaching Research, 15,* 35–59.

Bygate, M. (1996). Effects of task repetition: Appraising the developing language of learners. In J. Willis & D. Willis (Eds.), *Challenge and change in language teaching* (pp. 136–146). Oxford: Heinemann.

Bygate, M. (1999). Task as the context for the framing, re-framing and unframing of language. *System, 27,* 33–48.

Bygate, M. (2001). Effects of task repetition on the structure and control of language. In M. Bygate, P. Skehan, & M. Swain (Eds.), *Task-based learning: Language teaching, learning, and assessment* (pp. 23–48). London: Longman.

Bygate, M., Skehan, P., & Swain, M. (2001). *Researching pedagogic tasks: Second language learning, teaching and testing.* Harlow: Longman.

Carless, D. (2007). The suitability of task-based approaches for secondary schools: Perspectives from Hong Kong. *System, 35,* 595–608.

DeKeyser, R. M. (1998). Beyond focus on form: Cognitive perspectives on learning and practicing second language grammar. In C. Doughty & J. Williams (Eds.), *Focus on form in classroom second language acquisition* (pp. 42–63). New York, NY: Cambridge University Press.

DiCamilla, F. J., & Anton, M. (1997). Repetition in the collaborative discourse of L2 learners: A Vygotskian perspective. *The Canadian Modern Language Review, 53,* 609–633.

Dörnyei, Z., & Kormos, J. (2000). The role of individual and social variables in oral task performance. *Language Teaching Research, 4,* 275–300.

Ellis, R. (2003). *Task-based language learning and teaching.* Oxford: Oxford University Press.

Foster, P., & Skehan, P. (1996). The influence of planning and task type on second language performance. *Studies in Second Language Acquisition, 18,* 299–323.

Gass, S. M. (2003). Input, interaction. In C. Doughty & M. Long (Eds.), *Handbook of second language acquisition* (pp. 224–255). Oxford: Blackwell.

Gass, S. M., & Mackey, A. (2007). Input, interaction and output in SLA. In J. Williams & B. VanPatten (Eds.), *Theories in second language acquisition* (pp. 175–199). Mahwah, NJ: Lawrence Erlbaum Associates.

Gass, S. M., Mackey, A., Fernandez, M., & Alvarez-Torres, M. (1999). The effects of task repetition on linguistic output. *Language Learning, 49*, 549–580.

Kim, Y. (2009). The effects of task complexity on learner-learner interaction. *System, 37*, 254–268.

Kim, Y. (2012). Implementing ability grouping in EFL: Perceptions of teachers and students. *Language Teaching Research, 16*, 289–315.

Kim, Y., & McDonough, K. (2008). The effect of interlocutor proficiency on the collaborative dialogue between Korean as a second language learners. *Language Teaching Research, 12*, 211–234.

Kim, Y., & McDonough, K. (2011). Using pretask modeling to encourage collaborative learning opportunities. *Language Teaching Research, 15*, 1–17.

Leeser, M. J. (2004). Learner proficiency and focus on form during collaborative dialogue. *Language Teaching Research, 8*, 55–81.

Long, M. (1996). The role of the linguistic environment in second language acquisition. In W. C. Ritchie & T. K. Bhatia (Eds.), *Handbook of Research on Language Acquisition* (pp. 413–468). New York, NY: Academic Press.

Lynch, T., & Maclean, J. (2000). Exploring the benefits of task repetition and recycling for classroom language learning. *Language Teaching Research, 4*, 221–250.

Mackey, A. (2007a). Interaction as practice. In R. DeKeyser (Ed.), *Practice in second language* (pp. 85–110). Cambridge: Cambridge University Press.

Mackey, A. (2007b). Introduction: The role of conversational interaction in second language acquisition. In A. Mackey (Ed.), *Conversational interaction in second language acquisition* (pp. 1–26). Oxford: Oxford University Press.

Mackey, A., Kanganas, A. P., & Oliver, R. (2007). Task familiarity and interactional feedback in child ESL classrooms. *TESOL Quarterly, 41*, 285–312.

McDonough, K. (2004). Learner-learner interaction during pair and small group activities in a Thai EFL context. *System, 32*, 207–224.

McDonough, K., & Chaikitmongkol, W. (2007). Teachers' and learners' reactions to a task-based EFL course in Thailand. *TESOL Quarterly, 40*, 107–132.

McDonough, K., & Sunitham, W. (2009). Collaborative dialogue between Thai EFL learners during self-access computer activities. *TESOL Quarterly, 43*, 231–254.

Mochizuki, N., & Ortega, L. (2008). Balancing communication and grammar in beginning-level foreign language classrooms: A study of guided planning and relativization. *Language Teaching Research, 12*, 11–37.

Nuevo, A. (2006). *Task complexity and interaction: L2 learning opportunities and development.* Unpublished doctoral dissertation, Georgetown University.

Patanasorn, C. (2010). *Effects of procedural content and task repetition on accuracy and fluency in an EFL contexts.* Unpublished doctoral dissertation, Northern Arizona University.

Philp, J., Oliver, R., & Mackey, A. (2006). The impact of planning time on children's task-based interactions. *System, 34*, 547–565.

Plough, L., & Gass, S. (1993). Interlocutor and task familiarity: Effects on interaction structure. In G. Crookes & S. Gass (Eds.), *Task and language learning: Integrating theory and practice* (pp. 35–56). Clevedon: Multilingual Matters.

Révész, A. (2011). Task complexity, focus on L2 constructions, and individual differences: A classroom-based study. *Modern Language Journal, 95*, 162–181.

Robinson, P. (2009). Syllabus design. In M. H. Long & C. Doughty (Eds.), *Handbook of second language teaching* (pp. 294–310). Oxford: Blackwell.

Robinson, P. (2011). Task-based language learning: A review of issues. *Language Learning, 61* (Supplement 1), 1–36.

Samuda, V. (2001). Guiding relationships between from and meaning during task performance: The role of the teacher. In M. Bygate, P. Skehan, & M. Swain (Eds.), *Task-based learning: Language teaching, learning, and assessment* (pp. 119–140). London: Longman.

Samuda, V., & Bygate, M. (2008). *Tasks in second language learning.* New York, NY: PalgraveMacmillan.

Sato, M., & Lyster, R. (2012). Corrective feedback and peer interaction for accuracy and fluency development: Monitoring, practice, and proceduralization. *Studies in Second Language Acquisition, 34,* 591–626.

Swain, M. (1995). Three functions of output in second language learning. In G. Cook & B. Seidlhofer (Eds.), *Principle and practice in applied linguistics: Studies in honor of H. G. Widdowson* (pp. 125–144). Oxford: Oxford University Press.

Swain, M., & Lapkin, S. (1998). Interaction and second language learning: Two adolescent French immersion students working together. *The Modern Language Journal, 82,* 320–337.

Swan, M. (2005). Legislation hypothesis: The case of task-based instruction. *Applied Linguistics, 26,* 376–401.

Van den Branden, K. (Ed.). (2006). *Task-based language education: From theory to practice.* Cambridge: Cambridge University Press.

Van den Branden, K., Bygate, M., & Norris, J. (Eds.) (2009). *Task-based language teaching: A reader.* Amsterdam: John Benjamins.

Watanabe, Y., & Swain, M. (2007). Effects of proficiency differences and patterns of pair interaction on second language learning: Collaborative dialogue between adult ESL learners. *Language Teaching Research, 11,* 121–142.

Author note

I would like to thank the editors, Kim McDonough and Alison Mackey for their support and helpful suggestions throughout the project. Special thanks also go to Nicole Tracy-Ventura, Melissa Baralt, and Heidi Vellenga for their insightful comments at different stages of the project. I am grateful to all the learners and the teacher who participated in the study.

Chapter 2

Language-related episodes during collaborative tasks
A comparison of CLIL and EFL learners

María Basterrechea and María del Pilar García Mayo
University of the Basque Country (UPV/EHU)

Recent research in different educational settings has provided support for the use of collaborative tasks in which learners consciously reflect on their own language (i.e., produce language-related episodes or LREs). However, little is known about whether learners in content-and-language-integrated-learning (CLIL) programs pay attention to formal aspects of language and whether that has an impact on their written production. This study investigates the effect of collaborative work on production of the present tense marker –s by eighty-one English-as-a-foreign-language (EFL) and CLIL adolescent learners during a dictogloss task. Results showed that CLIL learners produced more LREs than EFL learners and that there was a positive correlation between the number of LREs involving the target form and the learners' written text reconstructions.

Introduction

Interaction hypothesis (Long 1996) research has provided support for the facilitative role of interaction in the process of second language learning (Gass & Mackey 2007; Keck, Iberri-Shea, Tracy-Ventura, & Wa-Mbaleka 2006; Mackey & Goo 2007). Many empirical studies both in classroom and laboratory settings have investigated how negotiated interaction provides learners with comprehensible input, feedback and opportunities to produce modified output (García Mayo & Alcón Soler in press; García Mayo & Pica 2000; Mackey 2007; Mackey, Oliver, & Leeman 2003). Research has also provided support for the use of collaborative tasks, particularly form-focused activities which require learners to produce output. Through interaction, learners' attention may become focused on those parts of their interlanguage that deviate from the target language or on forms that are not yet in their interlanguage repertoire (Swain & Lapkin 2001). During collaborative tasks, learners may consciously reflect on their own language use and produce what has been referred to as language-related episodes (LREs), which were originally defined by Swain

(1998: 70) as "[…] any part of the dialogue in which students talk about the language they are producing, question their language use, or other- or self-correct."

Recent research has examined the amount and nature of LREs produced by learners in different settings (Adams & Ross-Feldman 2008; Alegría de la Colina & García Mayo 2007; Fortune 2005; García Mayo 2002a, 2002b; Leeser 2004; Williams 2001). However, little is known about a new learning context: Content-and-language-integrated-learning (CLIL) programs (Mehisto, Frigols, & Marsh 2008), which are becoming prevalent in Europe (Dalton-Puffer 2011; Ruiz de Zarobe & Jiménez Catalán 2009). Although some studies have investigated general discourse features in this setting (Dalton-Puffer 2007; Dalton-Puffer & Smit 2007), little is known about whether its special characteristics (more exposure to the target language and interactive methodology) have an effect on learners' attention to form.

Attention to form and LREs

A considerable body of research over the last 20 years has claimed that explicit attention to form facilitates second language (L2) learning (Norris & Ortega 2000; Spada & Tomita 2010). Schmidt (1990) operationalized attention as noticing, and argued that it is a necessary condition for language learning (but see Truscott (1998) for a different view). There are several levels of noticing: learners may *notice the gap* (Schmidt & Frota 1986) when they realize that the form they produced is different from the target language form. Learners may also *notice the hole* (Swain 1995) when they realize that they are not able to say what they want to say accurately or appropriately in the target language.

Attention to form is influenced by a learner's internal syllabus, with linguistic forms discussed during learner-initiated episodes incorporated in subsequent utterances more often than the forms targeted in teacher-initiated episodes (Ellis, Basturkmen & Loewen 2001). Similarly, Hanaoka (2007) pointed out that teachers' pedagogical intentions may differ from the learners' attentional focus. Learner attention to specific forms while performing a task may be more effective and more likely to be retained than forms pre-planned by the teacher.

One way to determine if learners consciously reflect on their own language use and whether the information generated has a subsequent effect on their interlanguage development is by examining the LREs they generate during collaborative work. LREs include conversational turns in which learners may question the meaning of a word, the correctness of a word's spelling, the pronunciation of a word or a grammatical form. They may implicitly or explicitly correct their own or another's usage of a word, form or structure (Leeser 2004). LREs have been claimed to represent second language learning in progress (Gass & Mackey 2007) and have received considerable attention in interaction research.

Researchers have examined the impact of different variables on the occurrence of LREs. Several studies have considered the effect of learner proficiency in the target language (Abadikhah & Mosleh 2011; Kim 2009; Kim & McDonough 2008; Leeser 2004; Watanabe

& Swain 2007; Williams 1999, 2001). The general finding is that the occurrence of LREs increases as the learners' proficiency level increases and that lower proficiency learners tend to focus more on meaning whereas more advanced learners focus on formal aspects. Task types and specific task features also impact the occurrence of LREs (Abadikhah 2011; Adams & Ross-Feldman 2008; Alegría de la Colina & García Mayo 2007; Azkarai Garai & García Mayo 2012; García Mayo 2002a, 2002b; Gilabert & Barón, this volume; Ismail & Samad 2010; Kim 2009; Niu 2009). For example, written tasks seem to draw learners' attention to language form to a greater extent than oral tasks and text reconstruction tasks elicit more LREs than opinion-gap tasks. Some studies have considered the relationship between LREs and L2 development (Adams 2007; Kim 2008; LaPierre 1994; McDonough & Sunitham 2009; Swain & Lapkin 1998, 2001; Williams 2001) and have shown that, in general, the LREs produced during collaborative tasks have a positive impact on L2 acquisition. LREs have also been considered in different educational contexts such as immersion (Swain 1998; Swain & Lapkin 1998, 2001), content-based instruction (Leeser 2004), foreign language settings (EFL: Abadikhah 2011; Alcón Soler & García Mayo 2008; Alegría de la Colina & García Mayo 2007; Azkarai Garai & García Mayo 2012; Baleghizadeh & Arab 2011; Kim, this volume; Kim & McDonough 2011) and, more recently, self-access environments (McDonough & Sunithan 2009; Yilmaz 2011). Little research has been done so far on the impact of learner variables on the occurrence of LREs (see Azkarai Garai & García Mayo 2012 and Ross-Feldman 2007 for gender and LREs).

Several researchers have investigated how to draw learners' attention to linguistic form (i.e. produce LREs) in meaning-bearing, close-ended information exchanges. This research has established that dictogloss (Wajnryb 1990) is an effective collaborative writing task for drawing learners' attention to form (Alegría de la Colina & García Mayo 2007; Kowal & Swain 1997; Leeser 2008; Swain 1998; Swain & Lapkin 2000, 2001). In a dictogloss task, a short text is read twice at normal speed: the first time learners listen, and the second time they jot down words. Then, individually or collaboratively, learners reconstruct the text in writing as faithfully as possible. A particular linguistic form can be embedded in the text that is used in a dictogloss task (Thornbury 1997).

Dictogloss tasks that involve collaborative, as opposed to individual, text reconstruction may be particularly useful for integrating attention to form and communicative interaction in ways that encourage learners to co-construct new knowledge. For instance, in an ESL context, Storch (1999) found that pair collaboration had a positive effect on learners' grammatical accuracy. In a subsequent study, Storch (2005) compared the text reconstructions of learners who collaborated in pairs to those of learners who worked individually. The findings indicated that the collaborative learners produced shorter texts, but their texts had better task completion, grammatical accuracy, and complexity. In terms of accuracy, Storch (2007) later reported only small differences in the mean accuracy of learners working in pairs and those working individually during a text-editing task. Interestingly, however, the dyads' oral interaction contained a high proportion of LREs that were resolved collaboratively.

In an EFL context, Kuiken and Vedder (2005) compared the text reconstructions of learners who collaborated or worked individually, specifically their use of passive constructions. Their results showed that although the collaborative text reconstructions did not contain more passives than the individual reconstructions, the learners' oral interaction included attention to form. Also in an EFL context, Baleghizadeh (2009, 2010) found that learners working collaboratively obtained significantly better results than those working individually. More recently, in a Spanish-as-a-foreign-language setting, Fernández Dobao (2012) compared small groups, dyads and individuals as they performed the same writing task. Her findings point to a more frequent attention to language form by the small groups, with members producing more LREs and solving a higher percentage of LREs than learners working in pairs.

In sum, the prior research suggests that collaborative dictogloss tasks help learners scaffold their contributions and pool their resources, thus generating more learning opportunities through attention to form. The present study similarly compares collaborative and individual text reconstruction, but expands the existing research by investigating a new educational setting, specifically content and language integrated learning.

Content and language integrated learning (CLIL)

CLIL is an umbrella term adopted by the European Network of Administrators, Researchers and Practitioners, which encompasses the learning of a non-language subject through a foreign language where the subject and language have a joint role. Recently, Dalton-Puffer (2011: 183) has described CLIL as "[...] an educational approach where curricular content is taught through the medium of a foreign language, typically to students participating in some form of mainstream education at the primary, secondary, or tertiary level." At least two languages are used to teach various subjects in the curriculum, one of which is the language used in mainstream education (generally the official state language), and the other a target language (which may be a foreign language, a regional or minority language, or another official state language), independently of language lessons (Eurydice European Network 2006).

As Dalton-Puffer also pointed out (2011: 183), CLIL shares many characteristics with content-based instruction and immersion education. However, CLIL has the following typical features: (a) CLIL has to do with the use of a foreign language mainly encountered in a classroom context, (b) the dominant CLIL language is English and (c) CLIL teachers are normally non-native speakers of the target language who are content experts. CLIL is claimed to promote the interrelationship between learning content, cognitive processes and linguistic demands, in order to emphasize the communication of subject matter and the development of language and thinking skills strategies (Coyle 2007). Learners in CLIL classrooms are exposed to more hours of target language input per week, and the interactive teaching approach is believed to enhance learning opportunities. Preliminary studies in content-based classrooms have shown that teacher-dominated discussion is the prevalent mode of classroom discourse. Teachers rarely provide incidental attention to form in response to learners' non-target-like utterances but rather, they react to the value of the content of those utterances (Pica 2002). There is still a lot of work to do regarding how much and in what respect CLIL learners perform differently than their mainstream counterparts and, if that is so, why (Dalton-Puffer 2011: 186). Numerous schools adopted CLIL programmes in Spain in the first decade of the 21st century, both in the public and private sectors. Every autonomous community has implemented CLIL differently, due to the decentralized nature of the Spanish educational system (Ruiz de Zarobe & Jiménez Catalán 2009). In the Basque Autonomous Community (BAC), where the current research was carried out, schools in the public and private sectors have recently launched a multilingual program in secondary education, adopting a CLIL program consisting of five to seven hours of school subjects in English per week during Compulsory Education (ages 4–16). Prior comparative studies of CLIL and EFL learners' competence in the BAC have reported mixed results. When overall linguistic competence (Lasagabaster 2008) and pronominal use, lexical verbs, and subordination (Lázaro Ibarrola 2012; Lázaro Ibarrola & García Mayo 2012) were measured, CLIL groups outperformed non-CLIL groups on all tests. However, no advantages for CLIL were found for the use of copula and auxiliary *be* (i.e., suppletive inflection) versus the use of third person singular morpheme *–s* and past tense morpheme *–ed* (i.e., affixal inflection) (García Mayo & Villarreal Olaizola 2011). Clearly, more research is needed to identify differences between CLIL and EFL learners using both overall proficiency measures and more fine-grained analyses of specific linguistic forms.

Purpose of the study

Little research to date has explored how collaborative tasks affect CLIL learners' attention to formal aspects of the target language. This chapter is a first step toward comparing the collaborative interactions of CLIL learners with those of their EFL counterparts. Based on the theoretical background and the findings from prior research three research questions were formulated:

1. Do learners attend to form during collaborative dictogloss tasks, as evidenced by their LREs, and do those LREs involve the target form?
2. Is there a relationship between the quantity and quality of the learners' LREs and their accurate use of the target form in their text reconstructions?
3. Does collaborative text reconstruction lead to more accurate production of the target form than individual work in CLIL and EFL settings?

Method

Setting and participants

The present study was carried out in the BAC with 81 Basque-Spanish bilingual EFL learners (age range 15–16) who were in their first year of post-compulsory secondary education. They were learners from three different schools in the BAC, two from the private sector and one from the public sector. Out of this sample, 41 learners had attended classes in schools that implement a CLIL program, whereas the rest of the learners (40) had had English as a school subject in traditional EFL classrooms. All the learners were from a model in the Basque school system in which all the subjects are taught through Basque (i.e. total immersion), except for the English, French and Spanish language classes. The CLIL learners in the study had participated in a project with 5 to 7 weekly hours of school subjects in English in Secondary Compulsory Education (including English as a school subject plus a content subject, such as History, Technology or Computer Science), whereas EFL learners had English as a school subject only 3 hours per week. All learners had been exposed to English since preschool in a classroom setting. In the four-year span in high-school, CLIL learners were exposed to English for about 684 hours, whereas EFL learners were exposed for about 456 hours.

Target form

The target form was the 3rd singular present tense (–s) morpheme in English, which was selected for two main reasons. First, despite years of exposure and explicit instruction, both anecdotal and empirical evidence has shown that Spanish L1 speakers (Dulay & Burt 1973) and Basque-Spanish bilinguals (García Mayo, Lázaro Ibarrola, & Liceras 2005; García Mayo & Villarreal Olaizola 2011; Villarreal Olaizola & García Mayo 2009) have difficulty producing it accurately in written and spoken discourse. Although Basque and Spanish, the first languages of our learners, are richly inflected languages in comparison to modern English, these learners have difficulty with this morpheme. Second, researchers have claimed that forms amenable to form-focused tasks are those that "[…] are not important for successful communication, for example, third person singular –s in L2 English" (Williams & Evans 1998: 140).

Procedure and materials

In the pre-treatment session, the learners took the Quick Oxford Placement test (Syndicate, UCLE 2001) so that their English level could be assessed and similar proficiency level pairs could be established for those working collaboratively. This is important as some studies (Philp & Mackey 2010) have mentioned that uneven proficiency in dyads may negatively affect their interaction. The learners' score was equivalent to B1 – lower intermediate (an independent user according to the Common Framework of

Reference for Languages (Council of Europe 2001).[1] This means that these learners are able to understand the main points of clear standard input on familiar matters regularly encountered in work, school, and leisure. They can also produce a simple connected text on topics which are familiar or of personal interest, describe experiences and events, and briefly give reasons and explanations for opinions and plans. The learners also completed a questionnaire about their sociolinguistic background and self-ratings in English.

In the treatment session, the learners completed a dictogloss task, which consisted of a short passage dealing with a topic familiar to the learners: MySpace. The passage included information about the potential dangers associated with this type of website.[2] The targeted form was embedded in the text, which contained 13 instances of the third person singular morpheme (see Appendix). The learners were not informed about the target form, and were asked to refrain from turning pages back and forth in their task materials so that they would not know the type of activity they would be asked to complete after listening to the passage. Some of the words considered the most difficult in terms of spelling (*psychologist, socialization*) were provided in the task materials in order to lessen their memory load and to minimize the amount of time that learners might devote to spelling issues.

The dictogloss task began by having the learners listen to the MySpace passage, read by a near-native speaker of English, and without writing anything down. They then listened to the passage again and were instructed to take notes in English. Finally, using their notes, the learners reconstructed the passage either collaboratively (CLIL $n = 24$, EFL $n = 16$) or individually (CLIL $n = 17$, *EFL $n = 24$*). The interaction between the learners who reconstructed the text collaboratively was recorded and transcribed for subsequent analysis.

Scoring and analysis

The transcripts from the learners who worked collaboratively were coded for LREs, which were then classified in terms of their linguistic focus (lexical or grammatical) and their outcome (correctly/incorrectly resolved or unresolved) following previous research (Alegría de la Colina & García Mayo 2007; Leeser 2004; Williams 1999). Grammatical LREs were segments in the data where the learners dealt with aspects of morphology or

---

1. The Common European Framework for Languages provides a basis for the mutual recognition of language qualifications across Europe. It also defines 6 levels of proficiency (from C2 – proficient user – to A1 – basic user) which allow learners' progress to be measured at each stage of learning and on a life-long basis, as well as a common basis for curriculum and materials design (Council of Europe 2001). The global scale is provided in the Appendix to this volume.

2. The text was an adapted version of a piece of news titled "The MySpace Age" retrieved on 1 September 2009 from the BBC News Magazine webpage (http://news.bbc.co.uk/2/hi/uk_news/magazine/4782118.stm)

syntax, whereas lexical LREs dealt with word meanings, word choices, use of prepositions and spelling. Self- repair, defined as any instance when a learner modified his/her own utterance in the turn or in an adjacent turn without input from his/her interlocutor (Adams & Ross-Feldman 2008), was included.

The following examples from the data illustrate the two categories of LREs. An example of a correctly solved grammatical LRE is provided in (1), in which the two learners deliberated over the verb tense of the verb *appear*. Learner 1 suggested that the tense should be past, but learner 2 rejected the suggestion, which represents a correct resolution because the text had been in present tense.

(1) Learner 1: new bands
     Learner 2: that don't appear
     Learner 1: appeared
     Learner 2: huh?
     Learner 1: appeared
     Learner 2: no that don't appear

A correctly resolved lexical LRE about word choice is provided in (2). Learner 1 proposed the use of *to be in touch*, but learner 2 was not sure about its meaning, and asked about it. Learner 1 provided the correct meaning of the expression through the Spanish translation (*mantener contacto o conectar*).

(2) Learner 1: to be in touch eh to be in touch
     Learner 2: what is the meaning of it?
     Learner 1: *para mantener contacto o* (to be in contact or)
     Learner 2: *conectar* (to connect)
     Learner 1: *sí para* (yes to) meet people to be in touch with
     Learner 2: with other people
     Learner 1: *vale* (alright)

The text reconstructions were coded in terms of the learners' production of the third person singular present tense marker. First obligatory contexts involving the 13 verbs provided in the original passage were identified. Then a frequency count of supplied morphemes was taken and afterwards the mean average score of morphemes supplied by the learners was calculated by total contexts. Oversuppliance of the third person singular present tense marker in non-obligatory contexts was not considered. Verb forms that were different from those in the original text were also ignored. Various rounds of coding by the two researchers resulted in an agreement of 97%.

Results and discussion

Our first research question asked whether the learners would attend to form during collaborative text reconstruction. Table 1 shows the number and type of LREs produced by the 20 dyads. Their interaction contained a total of 142 LREs, of which grammatical LREs occurred slightly more often (n = 73; 51%) than lexical LREs (n = 69; 49%).

Table 1. LREs by linguistic focus

	N (%)	Mean	SD
Grammatical LREs	73 (51%)	3.65	3.03
Lexical LREs	69 (49%)	3.45	2.67
Total	142	7.10	5.13

Table 2 displays the amount, type and resolution of LREs produced by dyads in the two contexts: CLIL (n = 12) and EFL (n = 8). The percentage of LREs by context is provided in parenthesis to account for the unequal number of learners in each context. Specific types of grammatical LREs that rarely occurred, such as word order, relative pronoun, case or number agreement, have been grouped in the category *other*.

Table 2. Amount, type and resolution of LREs by context

	Correct		Incorrect		Unresolved		Total	
	CLIL	EFL	CLIL	EFL	CLIL	EFL	CLIL	EFL
Lexical LREs								
word meaning/choice	21	9	3	1	1	0	25 (62.5%)	10 (37.5%)
preposition	7	2	6	3	1	0	14 (65.1%)	5 (34.8%)
spelling	11	2	0	0	1	0	12 (77.4%)	2 (22.6%)
Total							51 (66.7%)	17 (33.4%)
Grammatical LREs								
3rd singular	20	9	4	1	0	0	24 (61.5%)	10 (38.4%)
Tense	3	4	2	1	3	1	8 (47%)	6 (53%)
Determiner	7	3	0	0	1	0	8 (64%)	3 (36%)
Other	6	5	2	0	1	0	9 (54.5%	5 (45.4%)
Total							49 (57.6%)	24 (42.4%)

Overall CLIL learners produced more LREs than EFL learners across all categories, with the exception of tense. In terms of the target structure, 61.5% of the LREs produced by the CLIL learners and 38.4% of the LREs from the EFL learners involved 3rd person singular, with high rates of correct resolution shown by learners in both contexts (20/24 for CLIL and 9/10 for EFL). The findings reported so far seem to suggest that both CLIL and EFL learners do indeed focus on form and, most importantly, they focus on the feature they seem to have more problems with: the English third person singular marker. In Swain's

(1998:73) words: "Learners talk about what they *need* to talk about; that is, those aspects of language about which they are not sure. And that, in turn, will depend on their own current internalized state of knowledge about language and its use."

In order to address our second research question, which asked whether there is a relationship between the quantity and quality of learners' LREs and their production of the 3rd person singular present tense in the reconstructed text, correlations among the following variables were carried out: (a) all grammatical LREs focused on the 3rd person singular, (b) correctly resolved grammatical LREs involving 3rd person singular forms, and (c) the number 3rd singular forms in obligatory contexts produced in the reconstructed texts. Results from a Pearson correlation show a positive relationship between all LREs involving 3rd person singular and the correct number of instances of present tense morphology used in the reconstructed text in obligatory contexts ($r = .604$). There was also a positive correlation between correctly resolved grammatical LREs focused on the 3rd person singular and the correct number of instances of present tense morphology in the reconstructed text in obligatory contexts ($r = .551$).

Positive correlations were also found among these variables both for the CLIL and for the EFL groups as follows: in the CLIL group, there was a positive correlation between all grammatical LREs involving 3rd person singular and the correct number of instances of present tense morphology in the reconstructed text in obligatory contexts ($r = .539$) and also between grammatical LREs focused on the 3rd person singular correctly solved and the correct number of instances in the reconstructed text in obligatory contexts, ($r = .493$). For the EFL group there was a positive correlation between all the LREs focused on the target feature and the correct number of instances of present tense morphology in the reconstructed text ($r = .749$) as well as between the grammatical LREs involving 3rd person singular correctly solved and the correct number of instances in the reconstructed text in obligatory contexts ($r = .706$).

These findings point to a positive relationship between the quantity and quality (i.e. grammatical) of the LREs focused on the 3rd person singular marker –*s* (all and correctly solved) and the correct use of this grammatical feature in the written task; in other words, the more grammatical LREs related to 3rd person singular and the more correctly solved LREs used in oral interaction, the more accurate the production of the morpheme in obligatory contexts in the reconstructed text for both CLIL and EFL groups. However, we cannot conclude that the more LREs are produced, the better the results, but rather that those who performed better in the final written reconstruction also produced more LREs focused on the target item. Thus, we can claim that there is a relationship between accuracy (i.e. the final reconstruction of the text) and conscious knowledge of language. Learners use this explicit knowledge of language to edit their reconstruction collaboratively and they do it in an effective way.

The following Example (3) displays a grammatical LRE focused on the third person singular present morpheme –*s*, in which learner 2 recasted the verb *meet* produced by learner 1. As seen in the example, learner 2 referred to the target form explicitly and resolved the LRE correctly. Learner 1 believed that *meet* should agree with *people* (from the main clause) instead of with the subject of the relative clause (*she*).

(3) Learner 1:   and interesting people, who meet in parties *por ejemplo* (for example)
     Learner 2:   who (*uttered while writing*)
     Learner 1:   meet in parties
     Learner 2:   she meets in parties
     Learner 1:   no who meet in parties
     Learner 2:   meets *no tiene que ser* (no it has to be) meets *porque es tercera persona* (because it's third person)

The text reconstruction from that dyad is provided in (4). The learners produced the correct form of the verb *to meet*, which takes the 3rd person singular marker –*s* because it agrees with *she* in the relative clause, and not with *people* in the main clause.

(4) [...] she has 224 friends: of school and interesting people she **meets** in parties and travels. [...]

Another LRE involving the 3rd singular form is illustrated in (5). Learner 2 produced the verbs *see* and *know* without the required –*s* ending, which Learner 1 recasted. Due to the length of the LRE, the turns have been marked with letters for the reader's convenience.

(5) a. Learner 1:   she .... knows .... but she .... only .... sees .... them (*uttered while writing*)
     b. Learner 2:   see them
     c. Learner 1:   *esto está mal no?* (this is wrong, isn't it?)
     d. Learner 2:   she only see them
     e. Learner 1:   no sees
     f. Learner 2:   she only see from school and the other ones are people she know
     g. Learner 1:   she knows
     h. Learner 2:   she know
     i. Learner 1:   *¡a ver!, tercera persona* (pay attention!, third person)
     j. Learner 2:   but and the other ones are people she know
     k. Learner 1:   she knows
     l. Learner 2:   but you have eh we have written here the third person she knows but she only sees
     m. Learner 1:   she only sees them once in a while
     n. Learner 2:   see them, *es* (it's) see *es sin la s* (it's without the –s) the first one are the people she know

As seen in the example, learner 2 wrongly believed that the verbs should agree with *people* (turns b, d, f, h, j, n). In turn i, learner 1 used metalinguistic terms to describe the target form, perhaps as a way to encourage her partner to change his mind. Learner 1 insisted that the third person singular marker should be used (turns c, e, g, i, k, m), but after many turns of disagreement, they eventually came up with the correct form of the verb *knows* but not of *sees*. Thus, learner 1 accepted the incorrect form of this verb, because she failed to convince learner 2 that *sees* agrees with *she* and not with *people*.

In their text reconstruction, learner 1, who was in charge of the writing, had written both verbs correctly before the LRE began (as shown in turn a), but she ended up crossing out only the *–s* marker in *sees*, but not in *knows*. This suggests that she may have crossed out the *–s* in *sees* (marked by X in (6) below) in response to the complaints of learner 2. The relevant excerpt of their text reconstruction is shown in (6), where the outcome of the LRE is reflected in the text reconstruction. They produced the correct form of the verb *knows*, but not of the verb *sees*.

> (6)   [...] she has 224 friends. She has two different groups of friends. The first ones are the people she **knows** from school and the other ones are the people she **knows** but she only **seeX** them once in a while. [...]

LREs are also a demonstration of the learners' involvement in the decision-making process. Example (5) is a good example of active involvement. Storch (2002: 120) claimed that in negotiated interaction learners "[...] negotiate not only about the topic but also about their relationship [...]". The previous interaction (5) and the corresponding text reconstruction (6) showed a pattern of dyadic interaction with high equality, in which both members of the dyad worked together in all parts of the task and both were willing to offer and engage with each other's ideas, leading to resolutions that seemed acceptable to both learners. This is shown in the attitude of learner 1 towards her companion's (wrong) contribution on subject-verb agreement in *she see. Both members played a dominant role, but also discussed and even accepted the alternative views provided by their partner.

Finally, we explored whether collaborative text reconstruction led to more accurate use of the target form than individual text reconstruction in the two educational contexts. We hypothesized that CLIL learners would benefit more from collaborative tasks, since this teaching methodology relies on collaborative work extensively (Ball and Lindsay 2010) with activities that enhance peer communication and increase communicative competence. The correct number of 3rd singular *–s* produced by the CLIL and EFL groups collaboratively in obligatory contexts (13) were summed. Figure 1 compares the mean text reconstruction scores for the CLIL and the EFL learners who worked collaboratively and individually.

As the figure shows, CLIL learners who collaborated had higher text reconstruction scores than the other learners. The scores were submitted to a two-way ANOVA analysis, which showed that there was a significant interaction between context (CLIL versus EFL) and text reconstruction (collaborative versus individual): $F(1,76) = 4.132$, $p = .046$. To explore the interaction, means comparisons with a Bonferroni adjustment were performed and revealed the following significant contrasts. In terms of collaborative text reconstruction, CLIL dyads outperformed EFL dyads ($p = .011$). In the CLIL context,

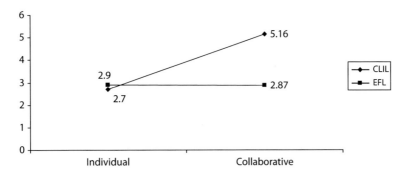

Figure 1. Mean scores for CLIL and EFL learners who collaborated and worked individually

dyads who collaborated outperformed learners who worked individually ($p = .007$). In other words, collaborative text reconstruction was more beneficial in the CLIL context than the EFL context.

Conclusion and future research

The present study investigated whether learners in two learning contexts, CLIL and EFL, would attend to formal aspects of language while engaged in a dictogloss task. Motivated by the fact that certain linguistic features (especially grammatical morphemes) consistently evade L2 learners' attention and lead to non-target like production, the target feature for the study was the 3rd person singular –s, a morpheme that has been shown to be persistently problematic for both Spanish and Basque-Spanish EFL learners. We were also interested in knowing whether collaborative work would yield more positive results for CLIL than for EFL learners, due to the different amount of exposure and the different teaching methodology in both settings.

The findings indicated that the 3rd person singular present tense marker is a problematic form for Basque-Spanish bilinguals. After many years of exposure and explicit instruction, these learners still overtly attend to this grammatical form, showing a need to discuss through collaboration, which may yield positive results. As reported above, both CLIL and EFL learners discussed the target form while collaborating, but CLIL learners produced more LREs than their EFL counterparts. The learners in the study were not aware of the fact that they were carrying out a form-focused task, with third person singular present morpheme –s as the focus under study. On the contrary, they were engaged in a meaning-focused, communicative task, where they reconstructed the information from a passage dealing with a topic of interest. During task completion, we identified numerous episodes in which the learners discussed 3rd singular forms which suggest that the dictogloss task was effective at promoting attention to form.

The results also show that attention to form during collaboration was associated with accurate use of 3rd singular forms in the text reconstruction. A statistically significant correlation was found between LREs (both all LREs involving 3rd person singular and those correctly solved) and accurate use of the target feature in the reconstructed texts for both CLIL and EFL. Based on the results, we can conclude that dictogloss tasks seem to promote attention to a specific grammatical form (–s), thus supporting one of the functions of output that Swain (1985, 1998) argued for.

In line with the previous comparative studies, the results indicate that collaborative text reconstruction yielded more positive results for CLIL than EFL learners. The greater exposure to the target language and the use of a task-based methodology provided in the CLIL context (Ball and Lindsay 2010) may enhance peer communication, promote the development of production strategies and engage learners in higher cognitive skills, thereby allowing them to benefit from collaborative tasks. The CLIL learners' advantages over their EFL peers might be attributed to CLIL methodology going beyond the language / content dichotomy and bringing together content (subject matter), communication (language), cognition (learning and thinking) and culture (social awareness and self and "otherness"), the 4Cs Framework (Coyle 2007). In fact, recent work by Moore (2011) has also reported that CLIL learners participate more frequently and more effectively in collaboration than EFL learners.

There are obvious shortcomings that should be acknowledged and addressed in future research. As the study was carried out in a particular instructional setting (CLIL and EFL courses in the BAC), the results might not be generalizable to other settings. The sample from each setting should be increased to confirm that CLIL learners benefited from collaborative dictogloss activities to a greater extent than EFL learners. Finally, the data in this paper come from just one task, dictogloss, and one grammatical marker, –s. Future research should explore the impact of task type on learners' attention to form (see chapters by Gilabert & Baron and Kim for examples), and investigate which morphosyntactic features are more amenable to form-focused tasks. The use of post-tests to assess the impact of LREs on learners' development in future studies would establish whether the benefits of collaboration persist over time. As suggested by Fortune (2005), another interesting line of research would be the analysis of the metalanguage used by both CLIL and EFL learners when engaged in LREs (see Wagner & Toth, this volume). Finally, future studies involving dyads should consider the impact of learners' roles and social factors on their collaboration. Recent work by Philp, Walter and Basturkmen (2010) has shown that personal and interpersonal factors affect learners' attention to form in task-based interaction.

References

Abadikhah, S. (2011). Investigating language-related episodes during mechanical and meaningful output activities. *International Journal of English Linguistics, 1*, 281–294.

Abadikhah, S., & Mosleh, Z. (2011). EFL learners' proficiency level and attention to linguistic features during collaborative output activities. *The Iranian EFL Journal, 7*, 179–198.

Adams, R. (2007). Do second language learners benefit from interacting with each other? In A. Mackey (Ed.), *Conversational interaction in second language acquisition* (pp. 29–52). Oxford: Oxford University Press.

Adams, R., & Ross-Feldman, L. (2008). Does writing influence learner attention to form? In D. Belcher & A. Hirvela (Eds.), *The oral/literate connection: Perspectives on L2 speaking/writing connections* (pp. 243–67). Ann Arbor, MI: University of Michigan Press.

Alcón Soler, E., & García Mayo, M. P. (2008). Incidental focus on form and learning outcomes with young foreign language classroom learners. In J. Philp, R. Oliver, & A. Mackey (Eds.), *Second language acquisition and the younger learner* (pp. 173–192). Amsterdam: John Benjamins.

Alegría de la Colina, A., & García Mayo, M. P. (2007). Attention to form across collaborative tasks by low-proficiency learners in an EFL setting. In M. P. García Mayo (Ed.), *Investigating tasks in formal language settings* (pp. 91–116). Clevedon: Multilingual Matters.

Azkarai Garai, A., & García Mayo, M. P. (2012). Does gender influence task performance in EFL. Interactive tasks and language related episodes. In E. Alcón Soler & M. P. Safont Jordá (Eds.), *Language learners' discourse across L2 instructional settings* (pp. 249–278). Amsterdam: Rodopi.

Baleghizadeh, S. (2009). Investigating the effectiveness of pair work on a conversational cloze task in EFL classes. *TESL Reporter, 42*, 1–12.

Baleghizadeh, S. (2010). The effect of pair work on a word-building task. *ELT Journal, 64*, 405–413.

Baleghizadeh, S., & Arab, F. (2011). The impact of pair work on promoting noticing among EFL learners. *The Southeast Asian Journal of English Language Studies, 17*, 18–31.

Ball P., & Lindsay, D. (2010). Teacher training for CLIL in the Basque Country: The case of the Ikastolas – in search of parameters. In D. Lasagabaster & Y. Ruiz de Zarobe (Eds.), *CLIL in Spain: Implementation, results and teacher training* (pp. 162–187). Newcastle upon Tyne: Cambridge Scholars.

Council of Europe. (2001). *Common European framework of reference for languages: Learning, teaching, assessment.* Cambridge: Cambridge University Press.

Coyle, D. (2007). Content and language integrated learning: Toward a connected research agenda for CLIL pedagogies. *The International Journal of Bilingual Education and Bilingualism, 10*, 543–562.

Dalton-Puffer, C. (2007). *Discourse in content-and-language-integrated learning (CLIL) classrooms.* Amsterdam: John Benjamins.

Dalton-Puffer, C. (2011). Content-and-language integrated learning: From practice to principles? *Annual Review of Applied Linguistics, 31*, 182–204.

Dalton-Puffer, C., & Smit, U. (Eds.), (2007). *Empirical perspectives on CLIL classroom discourse.* Frankfurt: Peter Lang.

Dulay, H. C., & Burt, M. K. (1973). Should we teach children syntax? *Language Learning, 23*, 245–258.

Ellis, R., Basturkmen, H., & Loewen, S. (2001). Preemptive focus on form in the ESL classroom. *TESOL Quarterly, 35*, 407–432.

Eurydice European Network. (2006). *Content and language integrated learning (CLIL) at school in Europe.* Available at http://eacea.ec.europa.eu/ressources/eurydice/pdf/0_integral/071EN.pdf (20 July, 2008).

Fernández Dobao, A. (2012). Collaborative writing tasks in the L2 classroom: Comparing group, pair and individual work. *Journal of Second Language Writing, 21*, 40–58.

Fortune, A. (2005). Learners' use of metalanguage in collaborative form-focused L2 output tasks. *Language Awareness, 14*, 21–38.

García Mayo, M. P. (2002a). The effectiveness of two form-focused tasks in advanced EFL pedagogy. *International Journal of Applied Linguistics, 12*, 156–175.

García Mayo, M. P. (2002b). Interaction in advanced EFL pedagogy: A comparison of form-focused activities. *International Journal of Educational Research, 37*, 323–341.

García Mayo, M. P., & Alcón Soler, E. (in press). Input, output. The interactionist framework. In J. Herschensohn & M. Young-Scholten (Eds.), *The handbook of second language acquisition*. Cambridge: Cambridge University Press.

García Mayo, M. P., & Pica, T. (2000). L2 learner interaction in a foreign language setting: Are learning needs addressed? *International Review of Applied Linguistics, 38*, 35–58.

García Mayo, M. P., & Villarreal Olaizola, I. (2011). The development of suppletive and affixal tense and agreement morphemes in the L3 English of Basque-Spanish bilinguals. *Second Language Research, 27*, 129–149.

García Mayo, M. P., Lázaro Ibarrola, A., & Liceras, J. M. (2005). Placeholders in the English interlanguage of Bilingual (Basque/Spanish) children. *Language Learning, 55*, 445–489.

Gass, S., & Mackey, A. (2007). Input, interaction and output in second language acquisition. In B. VanPatten & J. Williams (Eds.), *Theories in second language acquisition. An introduction* (pp. 175–199). Mahwah, NJ: Lawrence Erlbaum Associates.

Hanaoka, O. (2007). Output, noticing, and learning: An investigation into the role of spontaneous attention to form in a four-stage writing task. *Language Teaching Research, 11*, 459–479.

Ismail, L., & Samad, A. A. (2010). The effects of tasks on language-related episodes (LREs) during focus-on-form instruction. *Language Education in Asia, 1*, 87–98.

Keck, C. M., Iberri-Shea, G., Tracy-Ventura, N., & Wa-Mbaleka, S. (2006). Investigating the empirical link between task-based interaction and acquisition: A quantitative meta-analysis. In J. M. Norris & L. Ortega (Eds.), *Synthesizing research on language learning and teaching* (pp. 91–131). Amsterdam: John Benjamins.

Kim, Y. (2008). The contribution of collaborative and individual tasks to the acquisition of L2 vocabulary. *The Modern Language Journal, 92*, 114–130.

Kim, Y. (2009). The effects of task complexity on learner-learner interaction. *System, 37*, 254–268.

Kim, Y., & McDonough, K. (2008). The effect of interlocutor proficiency on the collaborative dialogue between Korean as a second language learners. *Language Teaching Research, 12*, 211–234.

Kim, Y., & McDonough, K. (2011). Using pre-task modelling to encourage collaborative learning opportunities. *Language Teaching Research, 15*, 183–199.

Kowal, M., & Swain, M. (1997). From semantic to syntactic processing. How can we promote it in the immersion classroom? In R. K. Johnson & M. Swain (Eds.), *Immersion education: International perspectives* (pp. 284–309). Cambridge: Cambridge University Press.

Kuiken, F., & Vedder, I. (2005). Noticing and the role of interaction in promoting language learning. In A. Housen & M. Pierrard (Eds.), *Investigations in instructed second language learning* (pp. 353–382). Berlin: Mouton de Gruyter.

LaPierre, D. (1994). Language output in a cooperative learning setting: Determining its effects on second language learning. MA thesis, University of Toronto.

Lasagabaster, D. (2008). Foreign language competence in content and language integrated courses. *The Open Applied Linguistics Journal, 1*, 31–42.

Lázaro Ibarrola, A. (2012). In what aspects are CLIL learners better than EFL learners? The case of morphosyntax. *IJES International Journal of English Studies, 12*, 79–96.

Lázaro Ibarrola, A., & García Mayo, M. P. (2012). L1 use and morphosyntactic development in the oral production of EFL learners in a CLIL context. *IRAL International Review of Applied Linguistics, 50*, 135–160.

Leeser, M. J. (2004). Learner proficiency and focus on form during collaborative dialogue. *Language Teaching Research, 8,* 55–81.

Leeser, M. J. (2008). Pushed output, noticing, and development of past tense morphology in content-based instruction. *Canadian Modern Language Review, 65,* 195–220.

Long, M. H. (1996). The role of the linguistic environment in second language acquisition. In W. C. Ritchie & T. K. Bhatia (Eds.), *Handbook of language acquisition: Vol. 2. Second language acquisition* (pp. 413–468). New York, NY: Academic Press.

Mackey, A. (ed.). (2007). *Conversational interaction in second language acquisition.* Oxford: Oxford University Press.

Mackey, A., & Goo, J. (2007). Interaction research in SLA: A meta-analysis and research synthesis. In A. Mackey (Ed.), *Conversational interaction in second language acquisition* (pp. 407–472). Oxford: Oxford University Press.

Mackey, A., Oliver, R., & Leeman, J. (2003). Interactional input and the incorporation of feedback: An exploration of NS-NNS and NNS-NNS adult and child dyads. *Language Learning, 53,* 35–66.

McDonough, K., & Sunitham, W. (2009). Collaborative dialogue between Thai EFL learners during self-access computer activities. *TESOL Quarterly, 43,* 231–254.

Mehisto, P., Frigols, M., & Marsh, D. (2008). *Uncovering CLIL: Content and language integrated learning in bilingual and multilingual education.* Oxford: MacMillan.

Moore, P. (2011). Collaborative interaction in turn-taking: A comparative study of European bilingual (CLIL) and mainstream (MS) foreign language learners in early secondary education. *International Journal of Bilingual Education and Bilingualism, 14,* 1–19.

Niu, R. (2009). Effect of task-inherent production modes on EFL learners' focus on form. *Language Awareness, 18,* 384–402.

Norris, J., & Ortega, L. (2000). Effectiveness of L2 instruction: A research synthesis and quantitative meta-analysis. *Language Learning, 50,* 417–428.

Philp, J., & Mackey, A. (2010). Interaction research: What can socially informed approaches offer to cognitivists (and vice versa)? In R. Batstone (Ed.), *Sociocognitive perspectives on language use and language learning* (pp. 210–228). Oxford: Oxford University Press.

Philp, J., Walter, S., & Basturkmen, H. (2010). Peer interaction in the foreign language classroom: What factors foster a focus on form? *Language Awareness, 19,* 261–279.

Pica, T. (2002). Subject matter content: How does it assist the interactional and linguistic needs of classroom language learners? *Modern Language Journal, 85,* 1–19.

Ross-Feldman, L. (2007). Interaction in the L2 classroom: Does gender influence learning opportunities? In A. Mackey (Ed.), *Conversational interaction in second language acquisition: A collection of empirical studies* (pp. 52–77). Oxford: Oxford University Press.

Ruiz de Zarobe, Y., & Jiménez Catalán, R. (2009). *Content and language integrated learning. Evidence from research in Europe.* Bristol: Multilingual Matters.

Schmidt, R. (1990). The role of consciousness in L2 learning. *Applied Linguistics, 11,* 129–158.

Schmidt, R., & Frota, S. (1986). Developing basic conversational ability in a second language. A case study of an adult learner of Portuguese. In R. Day (Ed.), *Talking to learn: Conversation in second language acquisition* (pp. 237–326). Rowley, MA: Newbury House.

Spada, N., & Tomita, Y. (2010). Interactions between type of instruction and type of language feature: A meta-analysis. *Language Learning, 60,* 1–46.

Storch, N. (1999). Are two heads better than one? Pair work and grammatical accuracy. *System, 27,* 363–374.

Storch, N. (2002). Patterns of interaction in ESL pairwork. *Language Learning, 52,* 119–158.

Storch, N. (2005). Collaborative writing: Product, process and students' reflections *Journal of Second Language Writing, 14,* 153–173.

Storch, N. (2007). Investigating the merits of pair work on a text editing task in ESL classes. *Language Teaching Research, 11,* 143–159.

Swain, M. (1985). Communicative competence: Some roles of comprehensible input and comprehensive output in its development. In S. Gass & C. Madden (Eds.), *Input in second language acquisition* (pp. 235–253). Rowley, MA: Newbury House.

Swain, M. (1995). Three functions of output in second language learning. In G. Gook & B. Seidlhofer (Eds.), *Principle and practice in applied linguistics* (pp. 125–144). Oxford: Oxford University Press.

Swain, M. (1998). Focus on form through conscious reflection. In C. Doughty & J. Williams (Eds.), *Focus on form in classroom second language acquisition* (pp. 64–81). Cambridge: Cambridge University Press.

Swain, M., & Lapkin, S. (1998). Interaction and second language learning: Two adolescent French immersion students working together. *The Modern Language Journal, 82,* 320–337.

Swain, M., & Lapkin, S. (2000). Task-based second language learning: The uses of the first language. *Language Teaching Research, 4,* 251–274.

Swain, M., & Lapkin, S. (2001). Focus on form through collaborative dialogue: Exploring task effects. In M. Bygate, P. Skehan, & M. Swain (Eds.), *Researching pedagogic tasks: Second language learning, teaching, and testing* (pp. 99–118). New York, NY: Longman.

Sydicate, U. C. L. E. (2001). *Quick Placement Test.* Oxford: Oxford University Press.

Thornbury, S. (1997). Reformulation and reconstruction: Tasks that promote "noticing". *ELT Journal, 51,* 326–335.

Truscott, J. (1998). Noticing in second language acquisition: A critical review. *Second Language Research, 14,* 103–135.

Villarreal Olaizola, I., & García Mayo, M. P. (2009). Tense and agreement morphology in the interlanguage of Basque-Spanish bilinguals: Content-based learning vs the learning of English as a school subject. In Y. Ruiz de Zarobe & R. Jiménez Catalán (Eds.), *Content and language integrated learning (CLIL): Evidence from research in Europe* (pp. 157–175). Bristol: Multilingual Matters.

Wajnryb, R. (1990). *Grammar dictation.* Oxford: Oxford University Press.

Watanabe, Y., & Swain, M. (2007). Effects of proficiency differences and patterns of pair interaction on second language learning: Collaborative dialogue between adult ESL learners. *Language Teaching Research, 11,* 1221–142.

Williams, J. (1999). Learner-generated attention to form. *Language Learning, 51,* 303–346.

Williams, J. (2001). The effectiveness of spontaneous attention to form. *System, 29,* 325–340.

Williams, J., & Evans, J. (1998). What kind of focus and on which forms? In C. Doughty & J. Williams (Eds.), *Focus on form in classroom second language acquisition* (pp. 139–155). Cambridge: Cambridge University Press.

Yilmaz, Y. (2011). Task effects on focus on form in synchronous computer-mediated communication. *The Modern Language Journal, 95,* 115–132.

Appendix

Dictogloss passage

MySpace is the most popular social website. People can create their own homepage, list their favourite music bands and films, and meet people with similar likes and dislikes.

Betty Smith is 25 years old and works in the music industry; she loves MySpace. She has 224 friends on it. Some are good friends from school, others are interesting people she meets in parties when she travels to New York. In her homepage you can also find a list of music bands she likes. She speaks with people on the website about new bands that appear on MySpace every day.

Peter Jones discovers new music bands on MySpace that do not appear on television or the radio. He says that he meets a lot of people on MySpace, too, but only a few are true friends.

Not everybody likes MySpace; Bill Davis, psychologist, believes that teenagers use this type of website to avoid real-life socialization, and to show others how many friends they have. But, as Mr. Davis says, real friends are always less than 10. Apart from that, showing your personal life to strangers can be dangerous.

Author note

The authors want to thank the editors for their invitation to contribute to this volume. Thanks also go to Michael J. Leeser (Florida State University) for assistance with statistical analyses and for his helpful suggestions, and to Tiffany Judy (University of Florida) for proofreading the manuscript. The research was supported by the following research grants: UFI11/06 from the University of the Basque Country (UPV/EHU); IT-311-10 from the Basque Government; and FF12009-10264 and CSD2007-00012 from the Spanish Ministry of Education.

Chapter 3

The impact of increasing task complexity on L2 pragmatic moves

Roger Gilabert and Júlia Barón
University of Barcelona

The study measures the impact of increasing cognitive task demands on the use of L2 learners' pragmatic moves. L2 Spanish/Catalan learners of English ($n = 36$) were grouped into pairs and performed two types of problem-solving tasks. Task complexity was independently measured by means of a learners' perceptions questionnaire, time on task, and time estimation. Interactions were analyzed for the use of requests and suggestions. Results showed an impact of task complexity on the number of moves for one of the tasks, indicating a clear task effect. No differences in terms of the variety of moves were found between the simple and complex versions of tasks. Results showed a clear task effect with some moves being exclusively associated with some tasks but not others.

Introduction

In classrooms around the world L2 learners are often faced with the need to resort to their pragmatic knowledge in order to get their peers to do things or to request permission from them. Often this is the consequence of engaging in task performance (e.g. through role-playing) in either pairs or groups. Both the design of the task as well as the fact that it happens in interaction are believed to affect the ways L2 learners use pragmatic moves on their way to accomplishing task goals. The aim of this paper is to bring together three areas within SLA that can help us understand how learners use their L2: task complexity, or the internal cognitive demands that language tasks impose on learners' processing and language use; interaction, or the way in which learners interact and collaborate with one another to achieve task goals in the L2 and how they use and learn the language as they do so; and interlanguage pragmatics, which is the area in second language acquisition which is concerned with how learners use, develop and learn pragmatics in their second or foreign language. It is still an issue how learners' use of pragmatic devices may be affected by the design of the tasks they are asked to perform, and so in this paper a classroom-based experiment is used to measure the impact of increasing the cognitive demands of interactive tasks on learners use of pragmatic moves.

Task complexity: Definition, scope, and the issue of its independent measurement

In the context of second language acquisition, task complexity has been defined as the attentional, memory, and reasoning demands that the structure of a language learning task imposes on learners' processing (Robinson 2001). As an area of research, task complexity is one of the possible dimensions of task design that can be manipulated in order to systematically study its effects on second language use and learning. In the last few years, and supported by the Cognition Hypothesis (Robinson 2001, 2003, 2005), task complexity has attracted considerable research attention. It has done so because it can be associated with crucial areas of second language acquisition such as needs analysis (Long 2005), which can be used to establish the characteristics of target tasks and their degree of complexity, information of paramount importance for the development of pedagogic tasks; task sequencing (Levkina & Gilabert 2011), which is concerned with how tasks can be best organized in a syllabus to maximize second language production and learning; task performance (Robinson 1995, 2001, 2007, 2011; Ishikawa 2001, 2007; Rahimpour 1997; Kuiken, Vedder, & Mos 2005; Gilabert 2005, 2007a, 2007b, 2007c; Gilabert et al. 2011; Michel, Kuiken, & Vedder 2007; Kuiken & Vedder 2007; Ong & Zhang 2010; Kormos 2011; Michel 2011), which has been interested in understanding how task complexity can affect L2 learners' fluency, lexical complexity, structural complexity, and accuracy; development, which has been mainly studied through the provision of recasts during both simple and complex performance in order to see how complexity may differentially affect learning (Baralt 2010; Révész 2009; Nuevo 2006; Nuevo, Adams, & Ross-Feldman 2011; Révész, Mackey, & Sachs 2011). Also, more recently, as will be shown in the next section, task complexity has been studied in relation to interactive tasks.

While much has been learned about the effects of manipulating the cognitive demands of tasks on L2 performance and learning, a crucial issue that task complexity studies still need to address in a systematic way is the independent measurement of cognitive task complexity. By drawing on Robinson's Triadic Componential Framework (2001b; Robinson & Gilabert 2007), most studies so far have set up different levels of cognitive task complexity by drawing on various interpretations and typically dichotomous (i.e. a simple task versus a complex task) operationalizations of cognitive variables such as the number of elements in a task (+/− elements), the reasoning demands (+/− reasoning) they impose on learners, or their degree of displaced past time reference (+/− here-and-now). Researchers conducting those studies have then looked at performance or learning results and explained them against their operationalizations of task complexity. This, critical voices suggest, is evidence of such studies falling into the trap of circularity and have stressed the need to independently measure task complexity rather than using the effects on performance and learning to refer back to and confirm differences in task complexity. Few studies so far have attempted to confirm whether learners' perception matched the intended operationalizations of task complexity. One way to measure students' perception of task complexity has been the use of affective variable questionnaires immediately after task performance. (Robinson 2001; Robinson 2007b; Gilabert 2007b;

Gilabert 2007c; Gilabert et al. 2009) by means of which learners are asked to rate on a Likert scale the levels of difficulty, stress, confidence, interest, and motivation in performing the tasks. Such questionnaires can provide information about whether L2 learners actually find a complex task significantly more difficult than a simple one. A second method, so far only employed by Baralt (2010) in the task complexity domain, has been the report by learners of their estimated time on task immediately after task performance. From the work on time estimation in cognitive psychology (Macar et al. 1994; Casini et al. 1997; Chastain et al. 1997) we have learned that typically during time performance we pay attention to both the performance of the task and the approximate time the task is taking us. Several experiments have shown that the higher the cognitive load, the less attention is devoted to keeping track of time. In this study, both independent measures of task complexity are used.

Task complexity in relation to interaction

Studies looking at task complexity have mainly been monologic in nature and it has not been until recently that task complexity has been studied in relation to interaction. Driven by the impetus of the Interaction Hypothesis (Long 1996), studies on interaction have focused on the effects that engaging in interaction may have for L2 learners' interlanguage development. In the 1980s and 1990s, many studies focused on the relationship of negotiation and comprehensible input, which in turn led researchers to focus on conversational episodes such as clarification requests, confirmation checks, and comprehension checks (see for example Pica et al. 1993). From the mid-1990s onwards, researchers interested in the effects of interaction on development enlarged the scope to include language-related episodes and recasts as potential contributors to learning. As for language-related episodes, many claimed that development is fostered by such episodes because learners engage in processes such as hypothesis testing, noticing, self-repair, and metalinguistic talk (Swain & Lapkin 1995, 1998, 2001; Swain 1995, 1998; Lyster & Ranta 1997; Lyster 1998; Alegría de la Colina & García-Mayo 2007), all of which are processes which are thought to be conductive to second language learning. The literature on recasts, on the other hand, has shown the most robust links existing between interaction and L2 development. Some examples are the association of interaction and past tense acquisition (Han 2002; McDonough 2007), interaction and the acquisition of verbal morphology (Ishida 2004; Iwashita 2003), and question development (Mackey & Philp 1998 – for a review of the principles of interaction see Gass & Mackey 2007; for an example of meta-analysis providing evidence of the positive effects of recasts on learning particularly in laboratory settings see Mackey & Goo 2007). Only recently some studies (Robinson 2001; Robinson 2007; Gilabert, Barón & Llanes 2009; Gilabert, Barón & Levkina 2011) have started to look at how increasing task demands may affect the occurrence of conversational moves such as clarification requests, confirmation checks, comprehension checks, LREs or recasts. No studies in this area, however, have looked at how task complexity may affect pragmatic use by L2 learners in spite of the natural association existing between pragmatics and interaction.

Interlanguage pragmatics

Within the wide field of pragmatics, it is Interlanguage Pragmatics (ILP) which brings together second language acquisition and pragmatics. ILP has aimed at analyzing how learners of a foreign language acquire and produce the pragmatics of the target language (Kasper 1996). More recently, there has been an increasing interest in also examining how L2 pragmatics develops over time (Achiba 2003). Most of the research within ILP has focused on speech acts with requests being the most researched speech act, probably because it is one of the most commonly used acts in everyday conversations and because when produced by NNSs inappropriate requests might be realized. One of the main aims of analyzing how learners use speech acts in the L2 is to see how they differ from the target norm. Regarding requests, many studies have looked at the level of directness of the requests produced by learners, especially if the target language is English. What has commonly been found is that learners with low proficiency tend to produce more direct requests, whereas more proficient learners tend to use more indirect requests together with mitigation (Ellis 1992; Trosborg 1995; Hill 1997; Rose 2000; Achiba 2003; Hassall 2003; Félix-Brasdefer 2007).

With a similar aim to those studies which have examined the use of requests, other studies have analyzed different speech acts (e.g. apologies, suggestions, rejections, complaints, compliments, giving advice, offers, among many others) to measure learners' pragmatic compentence (Scarcella 1979; Schmidt 1983; Schmidt & Frota 1986; Trosborg 1987, 1995; Takahashi & Dufon 1989; Bardovi-Harlig & Hartfort 1993; Rose 2000; Matsamuura 2003; Barron 2003; Martínez-Flor 2004; Koike & Pearson 2005; Martínez-Flor & Fukuya 2005; Pearson 2006; among others). Most of these studies, though, have focused on ESL contexts and stay-abroad experiences, in which typically changes regarding learners' pragmatic performance and competence can be noticed. The few studies which focus on EFL contexts tend to study the effects of pragmatic instruction, leading to the conclusion that teaching the L2 pragmatics, explicitly or implicitly, leads to positive effects on learners' acquisition of target language pragmatics (García 1989; Bouton 1996; Jeon & Kaya 2006; Bardovi-Harlig & Griffin 2005; Alcón 2008; Alcón & Martínez-Flor 2008).

Regarding task complexity, few studies in ILP have analyzed the possible effects of task complexity on learners' pragmatic performance. A single study by Taguchi (2007) can be found which studied the effects of task difficulty in the production of requests and refusals in different power relation situations. In this study task difficulty was operationalized as the social distance between the participants. The results of Taguchi's study showed that in the situations where there was a higher power relation, speech rate was generally slower and learners with low proficiency level needed more planning time.

Research questions

As far as we know, no studies so far have brought together our knowledge of task complexity, interaction, and interlanguage pragmatics. The goal of this chapter is therefore to analyze how increasing the cognitive demands of tasks during interaction may affect the use of pragmatic moves in the L2. The study is exploratory in nature and is concerned with pragmatic use rather than development. In order to achieve such a goal, two research questions are advanced:

1. What is the impact of increasing task complexity on the overall number and variety of pragmatic moves?
2. What is the impact of increasing task complexity on the number and variety of specific pragmatic moves?

While the Cognition Hypothesis (Robinson 2001, 2003, 2005) makes predictions for performance (i.e. enhanced complexity and accuracy at the expense of fluency on more complex tasks), and for enhanced interaction (i.e. more interactive moves will results from increases in task complexity), it does not make any predictions regarding pragmatic moves. Given the quantitative nature of our study, we cannot draw any directional hypotheses from the pragmatic literature which has shown that more difficult tasks cause the use of more indirect requests. We may speculate, however, that dealing with more cognitively complex tasks may result in a greater quantity and a wider variety of pragmatic moves because learners need to work out multiple issues. A greater quantity of moves can be expected because the more difficult nature of the solutions may force learners to consider several alternatives. A wider variety may be predicted because learners may be expected to avoid repetition of the same moves during their interactions.

Method

Participants

Thirty-six participants grouped in eighteen dyads volunteered to take part in the study. They were all Catalan/Spanish bilinguals taking English as a foreign language and their ages ranged between 19 and 21 years. They came from two intact groups; in one group participants were in their third year of an advertising degree at a private university in Barcelona, Spain; in the other group students were in their first year of their undergraduate degree in English Studies also in Barcelona. Based on the results of a task-based needs analysis in the advertising sector, students at the private university follow a task-based program to learn English through the performance of advertising-related tasks, such as ad campaign presentations, production meetings, or focus group meetings which they typically perform in pairs or small groups. In the English Studies degree at the public institution, learners follow a program which includes topic-based oral tasks in which they are asked to engage in discussions and problem-solving in small groups in relation to issues such as internet downloading, surveillance at the workplace, or the ethics of cloning. In both institutions, oral task-based performance in pairs is not only part of their programs but also of their final evaluation. Students were at B1 level (as reported by both institutions) in the Common European Reference for Languages (CEFR) global scale (provided in the Appendix to this volume), and so they were all expected to sustain a conversation with a reasonable level of fluency, providing straightforward descriptions in a linear sequence of points. At that level in those institutions students are presented with tasks at the B2 level, that is, tasks that require from them clear descriptions, the expression of viewpoints and the development of arguments. It is important to point out that the participants in this study were not receiving any explicit pragmatic instruction at the time of data collection. In sum, participants in both groups were therefore thought to be homogeneous in terms of proficiency, age, type of instruction, and social position.

Task complexity as an independent measure

As we saw in the introduction, the Cognition Hypothesis provides us with a general definition of the construct of task complexity. Robinson (2001:28) says that: "task complexity is the result of the attentional, memory, reasoning, and other information processing demands imposed by the structure of the task on the language learner." At a more specific level, we define complex reasoning as the coordinated use of multiple cognitive processes such as comparing, classifying, induction, deduction, error analysis, constructing support, abstracting or analyzing perspectives. The specific operationalization of task complexity is specified below for each of the tasks used in the experiment.

Task materials and operationalization of task complexity

Two tasks were used in this experiment since it was believed that beyond the effects of manipulating task complexity, task type has consistently shown to play a role in determining L2 performance (for some examples see Foster & Skehan 1996; Skehan & Foster 1997; Gilabert 2007; Gilabert et al. 2009). A problem-solving/decision-making task used in previous studies (Gilabert 2007; Gilabert et al. 2009) was chosen for the experiment (see Appendix A). In this first task, which we will refer to as the 'fire chief' task, learners are presented with a building where a fire has broken out. They are instructed to collaboratively decide which actions to take in order to save as many people as possible, to specify in what sequence, and to justify both the chosen actions and their sequence. In terms of the operationalization of task complexity, in the simple version of the task participants find different groups of people scattered around the building. The people involved have no particular roles and they present similar levels of risk. Additionally, because participants have enough resources (i.e. two fire trucks and one helicopter) they can choose what to do and in what order without the need to prioritize some actions over others. Events and characters are loosely connected (e.g. there is smoke as a consequence of the fire but it is being blown away by the wind) and so participants are expected to make decisions which are autonomous in nature.

The complex version, on the other hand, presents participants with people at different levels of risks (e.g. an injured person at the top of the building, a man trapped in the elevator, an elderly person) which, coupled with the fact that they have limited resources (i.e. only one fire truck), force them to prioritize some actions over others. In this complex version events and elements are more intricately connected (e.g. the smoke is coming into the building and the fire has started to burn the elevator shaft). The sources for this particular operationalization are needs analysis and the ergonomics literature. During needs analysis (Gilabert 2005), this task was selected as part of scenario planning during crisis management and experts helped us identify the elements that make the task more or less difficult (e.g. different risk levels, combinations of events and people involved). As for the ergonomics literature, we learned from Quesada et al. (2005:6), that complex problem-solving tasks are situations that are: "(1) dynamic, because early actions determine the environment in which subsequent decisions must be made and features of the task environment may change independently of the solver's actions; (2) time-dependent, because decisions must be made at the correct moment in relation to environmental demands; and (3) complex, in the sense that most variables are not related to each other in a one-to-one manner".

From a task complexity perspective, we expected the simple version to engage learners in few cognitive processes (e.g. comparing, deduction) as opposed to the complex version of the task (e.g. comparing, inducing, deducing, constructing support, error analysis, analyzing perspectives). From an information distribution perspective, the 'fire chief' task is a two-way, split information task in which learners share the same goal and which therefore renders it a convergent task.

As for the second task (see Appendix B), which we will refer to as the "party task", learners are presented with a role-play in which three flat mates want to hold a party. Both student A and student B are involved in the interaction and they have their own preferences, and at the same time they must also take into account the preferences of a third flat mate who is not present in the conversation. The requirements of the third flat mate are the same for the simple and complex version. In the simple version, the requirements of student A and student B complement the requirements of their flat mate (e.g. the flat mate wants only 5 people coming to the party, student A wants to bring 3 friends and student B wants to bring 2). In order to agree, learners need to apply one-step decisions involving few mental skills (e.g. comparing and deducing). In the complex version, conflict of interests was built into the task so as to have learners engage in multiple-step decisions (e.g. student A wants to bring 7 friends and student B wants to bring 4 while the third flat mate only wants 5 friends to come).

Apart from the problem-solving and decision-making literature we consulted to detect the factors affecting complex problem-solving and decision-making, during piloting of the party task we found out that conflicting interests forced learners to engage in more complex negotiation involving more reasoning and therefore the use and combination of more mental skills. From an information perspective, the party task is a two-way, shared information task in which participants have divergent goals in the complex version. The two tasks are both decision-making tasks since they force learners to generate and apply criteria to select from among seemingly equal alternatives, and they are also problem-solving in the sense that they ask the participants to overcome constraints that are in the way of reaching goals.

Beyond the theoretical operationalization of task complexity, three independent measures of task complexity were used in the study. The first one is affective perception by which learners are asked to fill out a 9-point Likert scale questionnaire at the end of each task performance (see Appendix C). Affective perception has been previously tested in several studies (Robinson 2001; Gilabert 2007b; Gilabert 2007c; Gilabert et al. 2009). The second measurement was time on task. While the two tasks include a similar number of elements and events and complexity only affects the relationships between those elements and events, it was expected that time on task could indirectly inform us of the cognitive load of each task, with the more complex tasks taking longer to perform. Thirdly, and as was seen before, time estimation (Macar et al. 1994; Casini et al. 1997; Chastain et al. 1997) has been used in cognitive psychology and at least one in task complexity studies (Baralt 2010) as an independent measurement of task cognitive load. For time estimation we calculated the distance between real and perceived time (regardless of whether participants under- or overestimated the time it took them to complete the task). It was believed that for confirmation of the differences in task complexity students should perceive the most complex task as significantly more difficult, take a significantly longer time in completing it, and be significantly less accurate at estimating the time they needed to complete the task.

Experimental design and procedure

Table 1 shows that the sequence of presentation followed a Latin Square design in order to minimize carry over effects.

Table 1. Latin Square design for the presentation of tasks during the experiment

	Task 1	Task 2	Task 3	Task 4
Sequence 1 $n=5$ dyads	Fire chief simple	Fire chief complex	Party simple	Party complex
Sequence 2 $n=4$ dyads	Fire chief complex	Fire chief simple	Party complex	Party simple
Sequence 3 $n=5$ dyads	Party simple	Party complex	Fire chief simple	Fire chief complex
Sequence 4 $n=4$ dyads	Party complex	Party simple	Fire chief complex	Fire chief simple

Data collection took place in a single one-and-a-half hour classroom setting. Students were organized in pairs and were assigned to one of the four sequences randomly. The same procedures were used in the two intact groups: instructions were given to the whole group, and then task 1 was delivered and performed, at the end of which students completed the affective variable and time estimation questionnaire. This operation was repeated for the three remaining tasks. There was minimal intervention of the teacher in each group except for the clarification of procedures. No task-related input or feedback was provided. All performances were audio recorded.

Coding and analysis of pragmatic moves

The CLAN version of Childes (McWhiney 1995) was used for the transcription of audio recordings. The pragmatic moves examined in the present study are mainly requests and suggestions. In order to measure the types of requests used by the learners, the classification by Ervin-Tripp (1976) and Blum-Kulka & Olshtain (1989) was followed. First of all, the data was analyzed by using all the request types proposed by the aforementioned studies. After analyzing all the data, it was found that not all the requests were used by the participants and, therefore, only the ones that were used at least once are reported in this study (see Appendix D). Other types of requests were found throughout the data, which matched Achiba's (2003) 'want statement'. This type of request was also included in our analysis but in a broader sense, including not only requests produced by means of the verb *want* but also all those requests which implied the speakers' willingness to get something (e.g I would like to eat paella).

Regarding suggestions, we followed Martínez-Flor (2004) categorization of suggestions. As with requests, first, all the types were used to analyze the data but we only report on the ones that appeared in the data at least once (see Appendix E). As with requests, other suggestions were found in the data, but they did not match any existing classification. Suggestions which were produced with the intention of expressing the speaker's future actions, similar to a decision, were also classified in this study as suggestions and called *decision*. Examples like *I will go and save the old man* were coded as *decision suggestions*, since they expressed what they were going to do with the aim of 'suggesting' a solution to the problem they were solving.

Given the exploratory nature of this study, statistical analysis of the outcome measures includes the ratio of moves and types in order to compensate for differences in text length, since the complex versions of tasks generated significantly longer texts which, as a consequence, contain a larger number of pragmatic moves. The ratio numbers can give us information about the specific effects of task complexity on pragmatic moves by compensating length of the learners' interactions by time, number of words, and number of turns. Hence, the results section will report on three types of figures: the number and types of pragmatic moves per minute, the number and types of pragmatic moves per 100 words, and the number and types of pragmatic moves per turn. The specific calculations are as follows:

a. the number of moves and types divided by the total amount of time and multiplied by 60
b. the number of moves and types divided by the total amount of words and multiplied by 100
c. the number of moves and types divided by the total amount of turns

Standard interrater reliability procedures were applied on 10% of the data for both transcription and coding with interrater reliability reaching 94%. All data were screened for normal distribution. Since most variables were not normally distributed, non-parametric tests were adopted. Descriptive statistics were used to obtain means and standard deviations. Wilcoxon signed ranked tests were used to analyze the potential differences between simple and complex versions of each tasks and between tasks. Alpha was set at 0.05.

Results

In this section we present results corresponding, first, to the independent measurement of task complexity and, second, to the two research questions. First descriptive statistics of overall number of moves and types are presented, followed by Wilcoxon paired samples comparisons of the simple and complex versions for each task. Following these, the same set of results are presented for the second question, and so the number of specific moves is presented followed by paired samples comparisons.

Independent measurement of task complexity

As can be seen from the results in Table 2, both the complex fire chief task and the complex party task were perceived as more difficult than their simple counterparts. Learners also took a significantly longer time to complete the complex version of tasks, which indirectly informs us of a potentially higher cognitive load of the task. They also were less accurate about time estimation after performing the complex versions of tasks. Time estimation showed a trend in the fire chief task and a significant difference in the party task. These three independent measures seem to suggest that the operationalization of task complexity worked for the two tasks and we can therefore state that we obtained two tasks at two different levels of cognitive complexity.

Table 2. Wilcoxon signed-rank test comparing simple and complex tasks

Simple vs complex	Affective perception	Time on task	Time estimation
Fire chief task	.015*	.000**	.083
Party task	.002**	.000**	.045*

Task complexity and total pragmatic moves

Table 3 below shows the descriptive statistics of the number of pragmatic moves per 60 seconds, per 100 words, and the number of moves per turn. The results of these three ratio measures show that, on average, participants produced a higher number of pragmatic moves when performing the complex version of the two tasks. Paired sample comparisons show the impact of task complexity on pragmatic moves to be significant when the ratio is obtained by means of time ($p = .008$) and by means of the ratio out of 100 words ($p = .035$). These two ratio measures do not show a significant effect of task complexity for the fire chief task. Finally, when divided by the number of turns, both tasks show a trend ($p = .076$ for the fire chief task; $p = .088$ for the party task) for the impact of task complexity on the number of pragmatic moves.

Table 3. Descriptive statistics for total number of pragmatic moves

	Task complexity	n	Fire chief task		Party task	
			M	SD	M	SD
Pragmatic moves x 60 seconds	Simple	18	2.42	1.35	3.38	1.47
	Complex	18	2.72	.87	4.93	2.72
Pragmatic moves x 100 words	Simple	18	1.83	1.02	2.51	1.03
	Complex	18	2.17	.68	3.03	.76
Pragmatic moves x turns	Simple	18	.36	.36	.27	.20
	Complex	18	.67	.66	.36	.21

As for the types of pragmatic moves, Table 4 shows that participant used a slightly wider variety of moves when producing the simple versions of tasks. This is the case when we consider the types of pragmatic moves per 60 seconds and the types of pragmatic moves per 100 words. The number of types per turn suggests that participants used a wider variety of types on the complex version of tasks. Pair wise comparisons, however, showed no significant effects between the simple and complex version for either task.

Table 4. Descriptive statistics for types of pragmatic moves

	Task complexity	n	Fire chief task		Party task	
			M	SD	M	SD
Types of pragmatic moves x 60 seconds	Simple	18	.97	.56	1.58	.65
	Complex	18	.82	.28	1.44	.62
Types of pragmatic moves x 100 words	Simple	18	.97	.56	1.58	.65
	Complex	18	.82	.28	1.44	.62
Types of pragmatic moves x turns	Simple	18	.14	.10	.11	.06
	Complex	18	.21	.27	.12	.10

Task complexity and specific pragmatic moves

As can be seen from the information in Table 5 and descriptive statistics provided in Appendix F, in all cases learners produced a higher number of specific pragmatic moves in the complex versions of tasks. If we consider moves related to probability/possibility (e.g. *we could ask your friends not to come*), we can see that differences between simple and complex are significant for the three ratio measures ($p = .009$ for possibility/probability moves every 60 seconds; $p < .009$ for moves every 100 words; and $p = .011$ for moves per turn) in the party task, which suggests both an effect of task and cognitive complexity on the pragmatic performance of learners. If we consider conditional moves (e.g. *I would go to the third floor first*), again more moves were used in the complex versions of tasks but none of the comparisons were significant. A similar pattern was found for *should* and *have to* (e.g. *we have to ask James*), since the complex versions showed a higher use of such moves without any significant differences existing between them. As for impersonal pragmatic moves, the complex versions of both tasks triggered the use of more imperatives but with no significant differences. In the case of decisions (e.g. *I will rescue the elderly man first*), no significant differences between simple and complex versions of tasks were found despite the fact that in all cases the complex tasks led learners to produce more pragmatic moves of this kind. Finally, want statements were only used in the party task and no significant differences were found between the simple and the complex versions of tasks.

Table 5. Wilcoxon signed-rank comparisons for simple and complex tasks by specific moves

Move type	Measure	Fire chief task	Party task
Possibility & probability	No. Pragmatic moves x 60 seconds	.831	.009**
	Pragmatic moves x 100 words	.868	.009**
	Pragmatic moves x turns	.124	.011*
Conditionals	Pragmatic moves x 60 seconds	.156	.754
	Pragmatic moves x 100 words	.140	.433
	Pragmatic moves x turns	.061	.433
Should & have to	Pragmatic moves x 60 seconds	.594	.203
	Pragmatic moves x 100 words	.826	.139
	Pragmatic moves x turns	.272	.139
Impersonal	Pragmatic moves x 60 seconds	.500	.213
	Pragmatic moves x 100 words	.500	.182
	Pragmatic moves x turns	.500	.110
Decision	Pragmatic moves x 60 seconds	.182	.285
	Pragmatic moves x 100 words	.203	.169
	Pragmatic moves x turns	.305	.074
Want statement	Pragmatic moves x 60 seconds	1.000	.327
	Pragmatic moves x 100 words	1.000	.679
	Pragmatic moves x turns	1.000	.420

*=p<.05; **=p<.01

Discussion

The aim of this exploratory study was to analyze the impact of increasing the cognitive demands of tasks on L2 pragmatic use during task-based interaction. Firstly, we made sure that our operationalization of task complexity was matched by learners' subjective perception and by indirect yet indicative data of increased cognitive load in the form of time on task and time estimation. Our data showed that learners perceived the most complex versions of tasks to be indeed more difficult, they took longer to complete them (and only higher reasoning demands can explain this), and were less accurate at estimating how long it had taken them to perform the task (see Table 2). We believe that by using those methods we avoided circularity and guaranteed that our operationalization of task complexity was confirmed by learners' perceptions.

Our first research question aimed at discovering how the number and types of requests and suggestions were affected by such increases in task complexity. As shown by descriptive statistics, overall learners used a larger number of pragmatic moves when tasks demands were higher and they used a similar variety of types with, as will be seen later, probably an overuse of certain types in association with certain tasks. Ratio measures (i.e. moves per minute, moves per 100 words, and moves per turn) showed either significant differences or a trend for the impact of task complexity on the pragmatic use of learners but only in the case of the party task, where almost all measures showed significant differences. But why would enhanced reasoning imposed by task design lead L2 speakers to use a larger number of moves? One explanation may be that higher task demands imposed a higher cognitive load at the level of conceptualization (Kormos 2006). Considering more complex, dynamic problems may have led participants to consider more reasons, more alternatives, and more possible solutions which, as a consequence, resulted in the use of more pragmatic moves. The higher reasoning skills (e.g. comparing, analyzing, deducing, inducing, error analysis, taking perspective) involved in negotiating the more complex problems imposed through task design may have pushed learners' interlanguage, and their pragmatic knowledge in particular, to meet those higher task demands. The excerpt in (1) from the complex version of the party task, where conflict of interests was built into the task, shows how both learners resort to suggestions in order to solve the conflict.

(1) *PAT: yeah but you said but you said a barbecue *what about* a paella? don't it sounds great?

    *MIQ: oh a paella I well it sounds great

    *PAT: mean you could be *we could do we could cook* two one with meat and one with

    *MIQ: I have I have *why can can't can we not* eh eh make an

    *PAT: oh yeah it's it's a good idea

    *MIQ: why do we have to chose between eh one thing and the other thing

    *PAT: true true but

    *MIQ: cause *we can do a barbecue* and *we can do a paella* as well

> *PAT: oh *a little bit of vegetables to all maybe*?
> *MIQ: yeah
> *PAT: but I
> *MIQ: so that eh James eh can be happily

The need to resort to pragmatic moves may not be so urgent when conflict of interest does not exist. The same pair performing the simple version of the party task is provided in (2).

(2) *PAT: what about the food?
     *MIQ: what about the food? eh you know I have em eh ha ha ha *I would really eh want to have* you know *a vari a variety of salads*
     *PAT: well that sounds great because
     *MIQ: but do you think
     *PAT: no
     *MIQ: yeah and James would be eh
     *PAT: happy too
     *MIQ: happy about it because you know he eh
     *PAT: he is still in the vegetarian
     *MIQ: in the vegetarian fix so it could be great what do you think?
     *PAT: perfect because I *want* to eat tofu and algae so

Associated with the first explanation, we believe more demanding tasks, which require more difficult solutions, may have geared learners towards the use of more pragmatic moves in order to mitigate their opinions and/or decisions. As suggested by Martínez-Flor (2004), suggestions may be used to include the listener in the decision-making process and they are less face threatening than other types of moves such as statements or imperatives. A second important question which can be drawn from our results is why task complexity pushed learners to use a wider variety of pragmatic moves in the L2. Why learners relied on a limited number of moves may be explained by the fact that there have only received minimal or no specific training in the use of pragmatic moves. Our results suggest that task complexity alone may not do the job of pushing learners into using a wider variety of moves, and that students may have stayed within a safe zone by resorting to the high frequency moves they feel comfortable with, hence task complexity only impacting on the number but not the variety of moves they used. It is an issue whether other kinds of manipulation of task design, beyond reasoning demands, can be applied to push learners into using a wider variety of pragmatic moves, or whether a wider variety of moves may be encouraged by the use of pedagogical interventions through focus on form techniques such as input flooding, input enhancement, or input elaboration prior to task performance. It is also an issue whether variety may be more affected by other factors, such as the learners' proficiency rather than by the cognitive complexity of the task.

As for research question 2, participants used certain types of suggestions and requests when tasks were made more demanding but not others, and they therefore confirm a clear task effect in the use of pragmatic moves as mediated by task complexity. As seen from the results (see Table 5), in the fire chief task conditionals were more often used in the most complex task than in its simple counterpart while want statements were not used at all. Regarding conditionals, we believe that the more complex nature of problems in the complex task, with its associated delicate solutions, may have prompted learners to take some distance from their statements and therefore mitigate them by means of conditionals (e.g. *I would first go to help the elderly man* instead of *I will go to help the elderly man*). As for want statements, it is reasonable to find more requests associated with the party task because of its nature (i.e. learners were specifically asked to ask for permission and to talk about their conditions/wants). Another striking result is the use of probability/possibility (e.g. *we could cook vegetarian paella*) in connection with the party task, which by far it is the most frequent kind of pragmatic move and much more so in the complex version of the task. An explanation may lay in the fact that since requests tend to be considered face-threatening acts suggestions may become a better alternative to get something done. Pragmatic moves such as *we could* or *we can,* which are very frequent in our data (to the point of being overused), may be used to suggest actions that include the interlocutor, leading to collaborative solutions, and which therefore avoid the face-threatening character of requests. In sum, it is obvious from the results obtained here that pragmatic moves may be task specific and that their use may be mediated by increases in task complexity, but a lot more research is needed to identify and/or design the types of tasks that will gear learners' attention towards the use of pragmatic moves.

Implications

One of the conclusions that can be drawn from the results of the experiment in this study is that manipulating task design, in this case by increasing the cognitive demands of tasks, may have the potential to affect L2 pragmatic use in positive ways. From a pedagogical point of view, the more complex versions of the tasks generated longer interactions and, as a consequence, the chances of using more pragmatic moves as well as many other interactive moves increased. From an SLA perspective, it seems that deliberately making tasks more complex may have drawn learners' attention to ways in which they could request things from the partners or make suggestions in order to find joint solutions to problems. Noticing (Schmitt 2001), L1-L2 comparisons (Doughty 2001) and hypothesis testing (Swain 1995) may have occurred as learners tried to negotiate complex solutions to complex problems. We have also seen that the type of task also determines the kind of moves that take place and so both design characteristics (e.g. task complexity) and the kind of tasks that learners are presented with need to be taken into account.

Limitations and questions for further research

Some obvious limitations of this study are the small number of participants which may render the results not generalizable to other populations. We also believe that a native speaker baseline would provide additional information about pragmatic use in the L1 in relation to task complexity, which is certainly worth exploring. Future directions of our research should include the study of mitigation (i.e. how students mitigate requests and suggestions by means of devices like 'maybe' or 'ok?') and the study of whole sequences, that is, how learners either accept or reject requests and suggestions. Other aspects that may be worth exploring are the role of proficiency and whether differences in proficiency within pairs/dyads affect the use of pragmatic moves. More studies like the one by Taguchi (2007) which looked at task difficulty from the point of view of social distances are also badly needed. Finally, a major concern should be how task design can be coupled with pragmatic instruction (e.g. recasts) in order to maximize learners' noticing, use, and practice of pragmatic moves on their way to becoming competent learners of an L2.

References

Achiba, M. (2003). *Learning to request in a second language: Child interlanguage pragmatics.* Clevedon: Multilingual Matters.

Alcón, E. (2008). Investigating pragmatic language learning in foreign language classrooms. *IRAL – International Review of Applied Linguistics in Language Teaching, 46,* 173–195.

Alcón, E., & Martínez-Flor, A. (Eds.). (2008). *Investigating pragmatics in foreign language learning, teaching and testing.* Clevedon: Multilingual Matters.

Alegría de la Colina, A., & García-Mayo, M. P. (2007). Attention to form across collaborative tasks by low proficiency learners in an EFL setting. In M. P. García-Mayo (Ed.), *Investigating tasks in formal language learning* (pp. 91–116). Clevedon: Multilingual Matters.

Baralt, M, (2010). *Task complexity, the Cognition Hypothesis and interaction in CMC and FTF environments.* Unpublished PhD dissertation, Georgetown University.

Bardovi-Harlig, K., & Hartford, B. (1993). Learning the rules of academic talk: A longitudinal study of pragmatic change. *Studies in Second Language Acquisition, 15,* 279–304.

Bardovi-Harlig, K., & Griffin, R. (2005). L2 pragmatic awareness: Evidence from the ESL classroom. *System, 33,* 401–415.

Barron, A. (2003). *Acquisition in interlanguage pragmatics: Learning how to do things with words in a study abroad context.* Amsterdam: John Benjamins.

Blum-Kulka, S., & Olshtain, E. (1989). Requests and apologies: A cross-cultural study of speech act realization patterns (CCSARP). *Applied Linguistics, 5,* 196–213.

Bouton, L. F. (1996). Pragmatics and language learning. In L. F. Bouton (Ed.), *Pragmatics and language learning, monograph series vol. 7* (pp. 1–20). Urbana-Champaign, IL: Division of English as an International Language, University of Illinois, Urbana-Champaign.

Casini, L., & Macar, F. (1997). Effects of attention manipulation on judgments of duration and of intensity in the visual modality. *Memory & Cognition, 25,* 812–818.

Chastain, G., & Ferraro, F. R. (1997). Duration ratings as an index of processing resources required for cognitive tasks. *The Journal of General Psychology, 124,* 49–76.

Doughty, C. (2001). Cognitive underpinnings of focus on form. In P. Robinson (Ed.), *Cognition and second language instruction* (pp. 206–257). Cambridge: Cambridge University Press.

Ellis, R. (1992). Learning to communicate in the classroom: A study of two language learners' requests. *Studies in Second Language Acquisition, 14,* 1–23.

Ervin-Tripp, S. (1976). Is Sybil there? The structure of some American English directives. *Language in Society, 5,* 25–66.

Félix-Brasdefer, J. C. (2007). Pragmatic development in the Spanish as a FL classroom: A cross-sectional study of learner requests. *Intercultural Pragmatics, 4,* 253–286.

Foster, P., & Skehan, P. (1996). The influence of planning and task type on second language performance. *Studies in Second Language Acquisition, 18*, 299–323.

García, C. (1989). Disagreeing in requesting by Americans and Venezuelans. *Linguistics and Education, 1*, 299–322.

Gass, S., & Mackey, A. (2007). Input, interaction and output: An overview. *AILA Review 19*, 3–17.

Gilabert, R. (2005). *Task complexity and L2 narrative oral production.* Unpublished PhD dissertation, University of Barcelona.

Gilabert, R. (2007a). Effects of manipulating task cognitive complexity on interactional modifications during L2 oral performance. Paper presented at the European Second Language Association (EUROSLA) 17 Conference, University of Newcastle, 11–14 September.

Gilabert, R. (2007b). The simultaneous manipulation of task complexity along planning and +/– Here-and-Now: Effects on L2 oral production. In M. P. García Mayo (Ed.), *Investigating tasks in formal language learning* (pp. 44–68). Clevedon: Multilingual Matters.

Gilabert, R. (2007c). Effects of manipulating task complexity on self-repairs during L2 oral production. *International Review of Applied Linguistics, 45*, 215–240.

Gilabert, R., Barón, J., & Llanes, M. A. (2009). Manipulating congnitive complexity across task types and its impact on learners' interaction during task performance. *International Review of Applied Linguistics, 47*, 367–395.

Gilabert, R., Barón, J., & Levkina, M. (2011). Manipulating task complexity across task types and modes. In P. Robinson (Ed.), *Second language task complexity. Researching the cognition hypothesis of language learning and performance* (pp. 105–138). Amsterdam: John Benjamins.

Han, Z. (2002). A study of the impact of recasts on tense consistency in L2 output. *TESOL Quarterly, 36*, 543–572.

Hassall, T. (2003). Requests by Australian learners of Indonesian. *Journal of Pragmatics, 35*, 1903–1928.

Hill, T. (1997). *The development of pragmatic competence in an EFL context.* Unpublished PhD dissertation, Temple University Japan.

Ishida, M. (2004). Effects of recasts on the acquisition of the aspectual form -te i-(ru) by learners of Japanese as a foreign language. *Language Learning, 54*, 311–394.

Ishikawa, T. (2007). The effects of increasing task complexity along the [+/– Here-and-Now] dimension on L2 narrative discourse. In M. P. García Mayo (Ed.), *Investigating tasks in formal language learning* (pp. 136–156). Clevedon: Multilingual Matters.

Iwashita, N. (2003). Negative feedback and positive evidence in task-based interaction: Differential effects on L2 development. *Studies in Second Language Acquisition, 25*, 1–36.

Jeon, E. H., & Kaya, T. (2006). Effects of L2 instruction on interlanguage pragmatic development: a meta-analysis. In J. M. Norris & L. Ortega (Eds.), *Synthesizing research on language learning and teaching* (pp. 165–211). Amsterdam: John Benjamins.

Kasper, G., & Schmidt, R. (1996). Developmental issues in interlanguage pragmatics. *Studies in Second Language Acquisition, 18,* 149–169.

Koike, D. A., & Pearson, L. (2005). The effect of instruction and feedback in the development of pragmatic competence. *System, 33*, 481–501.

Kormos, J. (2006). *Speech production and second language acquisition.* Mawah, NJ: Lawrence Erlbaum.

Kormos, J. (2011). Speech production and the Cognition Hypothesis. In P. Robinson (Ed.), *Second language task complexity. Researching the cognition hypothesis of language learning and performance* (pp. 39–60). Amsterdam: John Benjamins.

Kuiken, F., Mos, M., & Vedder, I. (2005). Cognitive task complexity and second language writing perfomance. In S. Foster-Cohen, M. P. García Mayo, & J. Cenoz (Eds.), *Eurosla Yearbook, Volume 5* (pp. 195–222). Amsterdam: John Benjamins.

Kuiken, F., & Vedder, I. (2007). Cognitive task complexity and linguistic performance in French L2 writing. In M. P. García-Mayo (Ed.), *Investigating tasks in formal language learning* (pp. 117–135). Clevedon: Multilingual Matters.

Levkina, M., & Gilabert, R. (2011). *Task sequencing in the L2 acquisition of spatial expressions.* Task-based Language Teaching Conference, Auckland, New Zealand.

Long, M. (1996). The role of the linguistic environment in second language acquisition. In W. Ritchie & T. Bhatia (Eds.), *Handbook of language acquisition. Vol. 2: Second language acquisition* (pp. 413–468). New York NY: Academic Press.

Long, M. (2005). *Second language needs analysis.* Cambridge: Cambridge University Press.

Lyster, R. (1998). Recasts, repetition, and ambiguity in L2 classroom discourse. *Studies in Second Language Acquisition, 20,* 51–81.

Lyster, R., & Ranta, L. (1997). Corrective feedback and learner uptake. *Studies in Second Language Acquisition, 19,* 37–66.

Macar, F., Grondin, S., & Casini, L. (1994). Controlled attention sharing influences time estimation. *Memory & Cognition, 22,* 673–686.

Mackey, A., & Goo, J. (2007). Interaction research in SLA: A meta-analysis and research synthesis. In A. Mackey (Ed.), *Conversational Interaction in Second Language Acquisition* (pp. 407–452). Oxford: Oxford University Press.

Mackey, A., & Philp, J. (1998). Conversational interaction and second language development: Recasts, responses, and red herrings? *The Modern Language Journal, 82,* 338–356.

MacWhinney, B. (1995). *The CHILDES project: Tools for analyzing talk* (2nd edn). Hillsdale, NJ: Lawrence Erlbaum Associates.

Martínez-Flor, A. (2004). The effect of instruction on the development of pragmatic competence in the English as a foreign language context: A study based on suggestions. Unpublished PhD dissertation. Universitat Jaume I.

Martínez-Flor, A., & Fukaya, Y. J. (2005). The effects of instruction on learners' production of appropriate and accurate suggestions. *System, 33,* 463–480.

Matsumura, S. (2003). Modelling the relationships among interlanguage pragmatic development, L2 proficiency, and exposure to L2. *Applied Linguistics, 24,* 465–491.

McDonough, K. (2007). Interactional feedback and the emergence of simple past activity verbs in L2 English. In A. Mackey (Ed.), *Conversational Interaction in Second Language Acquisition,* (pp. 323–338). Oxford: Oxford University Press.

Michel, M. (2011). Effects of task complexity and interaction on L2 performance. In P. Robinson (Ed.), *Second language task complexity. Researching the cognition hypothesis of language learning and performance* (pp. 141–174). Amsterdam: John Benjamins.

Michel, M., Kuiken, F., & Vedder, I. (2007). The influence of complexity in monologic versus dialogic tasks in Dutch L2. *International Review of Applied Linguistics, 45,* 241–259.

Nuevo, A. (2006). *Task complexity and interaction.* Unpublished PhD dissertation, Georgetown University.

Nuevo, A. M., Adams, R., & Ross-Feldman, L. (2011). Task complexity, modified output, and L2 development in learner–learner interaction. In P. Robinson (Ed.), *Second language task complexity. Researching the cognition hypothesis of language learning and performance* (pp. 175–202). Amsterdam: John Benjamins.

Ong, J., & Zhang, L. J. (2010). Effects of task complexity on the fluency and lexical complexity in EFL students' argumentative writing. *Journal of Second Language Writing, 19,* 219–233.

Pica, T., Kanagy, R., & Falodun, J. (1993). Choosing and using communication tasks for second language instruction. In G. Crookes & S. Gass (Eds.), *Tasks and language learning: Integrating theory and practice* (pp. 9–34). Clevedon: Multilingual Matters.

Pearson, L. (2006). Patterns of development in Spanish L2 pragmatic acquisition: an analysis of novice learners' production of directives. *The Modern Language Journal, 90,* 473–495.

Quesada, J., Kintsch, W. & Gomez, E. (2005). Complex problem-solving: A field in search of a definition? *Theoretical Issues in Ergonomics Science, 6,* 5–33.

Rahimpour, M. (1997). *Task condition, task complexity and variation in L2 discourse.* Unpublished PhD dissertation, University of Queensland.

Révész, A. (2009). Task complexity, focus on form, and second language development. *Studies in Second Language Acquisition, 31,* 437–470.

Révész, A., Sachs, R., & Mackey, A. (2011). Task complexity, uptake of recasts, and L2 development. In P. Robinson (Ed.), *Second language task complexity. Researching the cognition hypothesis of language learning and performance* (pp. 203–236). Amsterdam: John Benjamins.

Robinson, P. (1995). Task complexity and second language narrative discourse. *Language Learning, 45,* 99–140.

Robinson, P. (2001a). Task complexity, task difficulty, and task production: Exploring interactions in a componential framework. *Applied Linguistics, 22,* 27–57.

Robinson, P. (2001b). Task complexity, cognitive resources, and syllabus design: A triadic framework for examining task influences on SLA. In P. Robinson (Ed.), *Cognition and second language instruction,* (pp. 287–318). Cambridge: Cambridge University Press.

Robinson, P. (2003). The cognition hypothesis, task design, and adult task-based language learning. *Second Language Studies, 21*(2), 45–105.

Robinson, P. (2005). Cognitive complexity and task sequencing: Studies in a componential framework for second language task design. *International Review of Applied Linguistics, 55,* 1–32.

Robinson, P. (2007a). Criteria for classifying and sequencing pedagogic tasks. In M. P. García Mayo (Ed.), *Investigating tasks in formal language learning,* (pp. 7–26). Clevedon: Multilingual Matters.

Robinson, P. (2007b). Task complexity, theory of mind, and intentional reasoning: Effects on L2 speech production, interaction, uptake and perceptions of task difficulty. *International Review of Applied Linguistics, 45,* 193–213.

Robinson, P., & Gilabert, R. (2007). Task complexity, the cognition hypothesis and second language learning performance. *International Review of Applied Linguistics, 45,* 161–176.

Robinson, P. (2011). Second language task complexity, the Cognition Hypothesis, language learning, and performance. In P. Robinson (Ed.), *Second Language task complexity: Researching the cognition hypothesis of language learning and performance* (pp. 3–38). Amsterdam: John Benjamins.

Rose, K. R. (2000). An exploratory cross-sectional study of interlanguage pragmatic development. *Studies in Second Language Acquisition, 22,* 27–67.

Scarcela, R. (1979). On speaking politely in a second language. In C. A. Yorio, K. Perkins & J. Schachter (Eds.), *On TESOL '79: The learner in focus* (pp. 275–287). Washington DC: TESOL.

Schmidt, R. (1983). Interaction, acculturation and the acquisition of communicative competence. In N. Wolfson and E. Judd (Eds.). *Sociolinguistics and second language acquisition* (pp. 137–174). Rowley, MA: Newbury House.

Schmidt, R. (2001). Attention. In P. Robinson (Ed.), *Cognition and second language instruction* (pp. 3–32). Cambridge: Cambridge University Press.

Schmidt, R. (1983). Interaction, acculturation and the acquisition of communicative competence. In N. Wolfson and E. Judd (Eds.). *Sociolinguistics and second language acquisition* (pp. 137–174). Rowley, MA: Newbury House.

Schmidt, R., & Frota, S. N. (1986). Developing basic conversational ability in a second language: A case study of an adult learner of Portuguese. In R. Day (Ed.). *Talking to learn* (pp. 237–326). Rowley, MA: Newbury House.

Skehan, P., & Foster, P. (1997). Task type and task processing conditions as influences on foreign language performance. *Language Teaching Research, 1,* 185–211.

Swain, M. (1995). Three functions of output in second language learning. In G. Cook & B. Seidelhofer (Eds.), *Principles and practice in applied linguistics: Studies in honour of H. G. Widdowson* (pp. 125–144). Oxford: Oxford University Press.

Swain, M. (1998). Focus on form through conscious reflection. In C. Doughty & J. Williams (Eds.), *Focus on Form in Classroom SLA* (pp. 64–81). New York, NY: Cambridge University Press.

Swain, M., & Lapkin, S. (1995). Problems in output and the cognitive processes they generate: A step towards second language learning. *Applied Linguistics, 16*, 370–391.

Swain, M., & Lapkin, S. (1998). Interaction and second language learning: Two adolescent French immersion students working together. *The Modern Language Journal, 82*, 320–337.

Swain, M., & Lapkin, S. (2001). Focus on form though collaborative dialogue: Exploring task effects. In M. Bygate, P. Skehan & M. Swain (Eds.), *Researching pedagogic tasks: Second language learning, teaching and testing* (pp. 99–118). Harlow: Longman.

Taguchi, N. (2007). Task difficulty in oral speech act production. *Applied Linguistics, 28*, 113–135.

Takahashi, S., & Duffon, M. (1989). Cross-linguistic influence in indirectness: The case of directives performed by native Japanese speakers. Unpublished paper, Department of English as a Second Language. University of Hawai'i at Manoa. Honolulu.

Trosborg, A. (1987). Apology strategies in native/non-native speakers of English. *Journal of Pragmatics, 11*, 147–167.

Trosborg, A. (1995). *Interlanguage pragmatics: requests, complaints and apologies*. Berlin: Mouton de Gruyter.

Appendix A

Fire chief task

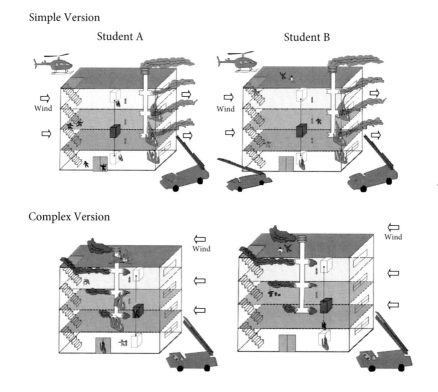

Simple Version

Student A   Student B

Complex Version

Appendix B

Party task

SIMPLE   COMPLEX

Role-play(1)

Imagine that you are room-mates and that you also live with
another friend, James. Student A wants to throw a party in the
house and he/she has to ask for permission to the other people
living in the flat. Student A has to ask for permission to Student B.
Student A has already asked James who will accept but with
some conditions.

James says...

– only 5 FRIENDS.
– only VEGETARIAN FOOD, NO MEAT.
– THURSDAY NIGHT.
– only MUSIC from the 80s and 90s.

STUDENT A's conditons are:

– invite 3 friends.
– to eat tofu and algi.
– to hold the party
  during the week.
– to have 'oldies'

STUDENT B's conditions are:

– to bring 2 friends.
– to have a variety of salads.
– to hold the party
  on Thursday or over the weekend.
– no preferences for music.

Role-play(2)

Imagine that you are room-mates and that you also live with
another friend, James. Student A wants to throw a party in the
house and he/she has to ask for permission to the other people
living in the flat. Student A has to ask for permission to Student B.
Student A has already asked James who will accept but with
some conditions.

James says...

– only 5 FRIENDS.
– only VEGETARIAN FOOD, NO MEAT.
– THURSDAY NIGHT.
– only MUSIC from the 80s and 90s.

STUDENT A's conditions are:

– to invite 7 friends.
– to have a barbecue for the party.
– to hold the party on Saturday
  night.
– to have live music at the party.

STUDENT B's conditions are:

– to bring 4 friends.
– to eat 'paella'.
– to hold the party
  on Friday night.
– to have a DJ, not live music.

Task adapted from the BAF project (Barcelona Age Factor, University of Barcelona)

Appendix C

Task performance questionnaire

Name: _____

Consider the tasks you have just performed.

How long did it take you to complete this task?
_____minutes

I thought this task   1 2 3 4 5 6 7 8 9   I thought this task
was **easy**   was **difficult**

I felt **frustrated**   1 2 3 4 5 6 7 8 9   I felt **relaxed**
doing this task   doing this task

I did **not** do this   1 2 3 4 5 6 7 8 9   I did this task **well**
task **well**

This task was   1 2 3 4 5 6 7 8 9   This task was
not interesting   **interesting**

I **don't want** to   1 2 3 4 5 6 7 8 9   I **want to do** more
do **more** tasks   tasks like this
like this

How long did it take you to complete this task?
_____minutes

Task 2

I thought this task   1 2 3 4 5 6 7 8 9   I thought this task
was **easy**   was **difficult**

I felt **frustrated**   1 2 3 4 5 6 7 8 9   I felt **relaxed**
doing this task   doing this task

I did **not** do this   1 2 3 4 5 6 7 8 9   I did this task **well**
task **well**

This task was   1 2 3 4 5 6 7 8 9   This task was
not interesting   **interesting**

I **don't want** to   1 2 3 4 5 6 7 8 9   I **want to do** more
do **more** tasks   tasks like this
like this

(Robinson 2001; Gilabert 2005)

Appendix D

Request types by source

Ervin-Tripp (1976)	Blum-Kulka & Olshtain (1989)
Need statement	Mood derivable
Imperatives	Explicit performative
Imbedded imperatives	Hedge performative
Permission directive	Locution derivable
Non-explicit question directives	Scope stating
Hints	Suggestory formulae
	Reference to preparatory conditions
	Hints/ Strong Hints

Appendix E

Suggestion types

Type	Strategy
Direct	Performative verb
	Noun of suggestion
	Imperative
	Negative Imperative
Conventionalized forms	Specific formulae
	Probability/Possibility
	Should/need
	Conditional
Indirect	Impersonal
	Hints

From Martínez-Flor (2004)

Appendix F

Descriptive statistics for specific moves

	Task complexity	Fire chief task		Party task	
Probability & possibility		M	SD	M	SD
Sum	Simple	3.39	3.76	2.11	1.41
	Complex	3.83	2.91	7.94	6.15
Moves x 60 seconds	Simple	.94	.96	.84	.78
	Complex	.95	.71	2.17	2.04
Moves x 100 words	Simple	.74	.79	.63	.55
	Complex	.74	.53	1.40	.84
Moves x turns	Simple	.10	.16	.07	.08
	Complex	.20	.24	.17	.11
Conditionals					
Sum	Simple	.89	.75	.67	.97
	Complex	2.06	2.12	1.61	2.70
Moves x 60 seconds	Simple	.29	.29	.23	.34
	Complex	.45	.46	.40	.79
Moves x 100 words	Simple	.74	.79	.16	.24
	Complex	.74	.53	.22	.33
Moves x turns	Simple	.04	.06	.01	.02
	Complex	.17	.34	.02	.03
Should + have to					
Sum	Simple	1.00	1.08	.72	1.96
	Complex	2.66	4.39	1.00	1.13
Moves x 60 seconds	Simple	.32	.36	.20	.60
	Complex	.58	.90	.24	.28
Moves x 100 words	Simple	.26	.31	.13	.40
	Complex	.44	.72	.16	.18
Moves x turns	Simple	.03	.04	.01	.05
	Complex	.11	.23	.01	.02
Impersonal					
Sum	Simple	.44	1.24	.28	.75
	Complex	.11	.32	1.06	1.16
Moves x 60 seconds	Simple	.20	.65	.13	.42
	Complex	.02	.07	.22	.25
Moves x 100 words	Simple	.13	.41	.10	.31
	Complex	.01	.05	.17	.19
Moves x turns	Simple	v.02	.09	.00	.02
	Complex	.00	.00	.01	.02

	Task complexity	Fire chief task		Party task	
Decision		M	SD	M	SD
Sum	Simple	1.50	3.66	.50	1.09
	Complex	2.11	3.04	.89	1.64
Moves x 60 seconds	Simple	.33	.60	.11	.26
	Complex	.49	.65	.21	.42
Moves x 100 words	Simple	.27	.49	.10	.25
	Complex	.41	.58	.14	.22
Moves x turns	Simple	.11	.35	.00	.02
	Complex	.14	.25	.01	.02
Want statements					
Sum	Simple	.00	.00	2.83	1.42
	Complex	.00	.00	4.61	2.52
Moves x 60 seconds	Simple	.00	.00	1.08	.77
	Complex	.00	.00	1.22	.79
Moves x 100 words	Simple	.00	.00	.82	.58
	Complex	.00	.00	.87	.55
Moves x turns	Simple	.00	.00	.10	.13
	Complex	.00	.00	.10	.07

Chapter 4

Tasks and traditional practice activities in a foreign language context

Alison Mackey[a], Akiko Fujii[b], Sigrun Biesenbach-Lucas[a],
Heather Weger[a], Natalia Dolgova Jacobsen[a], Lyn Fogle[c],
Julie Lake[a], Kerstin Sondermann[a], Kaitlyn Tagarelli[a], Mari Tsujita[d],
Atsuko Watanabe[e], Rebekha Abbuhl[f] and Katie Kim[a]

[a]Georgetown University / [b]University of the Sacred Heart, Tokyo / [c]Mississippi State University / [d]Dokkyo University / [e]International Christian University / [f]California State University at Long Beach

In this study, learners carried out tasks and traditional practice activities in an authentic instructional context: English as a Foreign Language (EFL) in Japan ($n = 37$). Learners' production on pre- and posttests was analyzed to investigate second language (L2) development with respect to the production of question forms. Quantitative results suggest that tasks and traditional practice activities were equally effective at promoting second language (L2) development. The results are discussed with respect to learners' beliefs and attitudes towards the type of L2 instruction they received and the role of context in L2 learning.

Introduction

Research that has emerged from the interactionist approach to second language acquisition (SLA) has found that learners benefit from interactions that maximize opportunities for learning in the form of modified input, corrective feedback, and modified output (Mackey & Goo 2007). Recent studies have found that tasks, in which learners interact to solve a problem or accomplish a goal, provide the ideal context for developmentally beneficial interactions. Bygate, Skehan, & Swain (2001) define a task as "an activity which requires learners to use language, with emphasis on meaning, to attain an objective" (p. 5), such as picture description, story retelling, and information gap activities.

Although tasks are considered to be effective teaching tools in English language classrooms (Ellis 2003; Long 1985), some researchers and practitioners have argued that they are not practical in certain educational contexts (e.g., Burrows 2008; Matsuura, Chiba, & Hilderbrandt 2001) or that teachers and learners are initially wary of such innovations (e.g., McDonough & Chaikitmongkol 2007) as they are of change in general. More research is needed to empirically examine the developmental outcomes of tasks in authentic classroom contexts. The current study was carried out in university classrooms in Japan in an EFL setting. Tasks designed by SLA researchers in partnership with language teachers were compared to more traditional practice activities.

Grammar teaching, corrective feedback, and tasks

Many second language (L2) teachers, researchers, and language learners agree that at least a minimal instructional focus on grammar is important for learners' development of language form. This instruction is usually followed by some sort of activity, including drills, tasks, or even a combination of both (Ellis, Basturkmen, & Loewen 2001). Tasks are believed to be especially beneficial for L2 development, as they require learners to "do" something with language, provide opportunities for both practice and negotiation of meaning, and create meaning-based contexts for linguistic forms (e.g., Bygate, Skehan, & Swain 2001; Ellis 2003, 2006; Long 2007). In addition, interaction that occurs during tasks helps draw learners' attention to areas of "mismatch" between their interlanguages and target languages. Tasks are also valued for the opportunities they create for implicit negative feedback on grammatical forms, something which is believed to be facilitative, if not necessary, for L2 development (Long 1996, 2007).

Empirical studies have provided evidence for an association between different types of tasks, corrective feedback, and L2 learning (e.g., Ellis, Tanaka, & Yamazaki 1994; Han 2002; Iwashita 2003; Loschky 1994; Mackey 1999; Mackey & Philp 1998; McDonough 2005; Silver 2000). Meta-analyses have also shown positive effects for task-based interaction on L2 development (Keck, Iberri-Shea, Tracy-Ventura, &Wa-Mbaleka 2006; Mackey & Goo 2007).

However, despite general enthusiasm in the field of SLA for various kinds of tasks, relatively little is known about their effectiveness as compared to the different types of "traditional" activities that are common in many EFL contexts, such as Japan. While there is great variety in what could be termed "traditional" activities, one common approach is the so-called "PPP" method which is tightly controlled by the teacher, beginning with a *presentation* (e.g., mini-lecture) of the target form(s). This is followed by *practice* of the target form(s), typically through the use of drills or other exercises, and then, finally, a more open stage where learners are given opportunities for *production* of the target form(s) in a dialogue, cued role play, or other activity. As Willis and Willis (1996) note, this approach has been valued for "encourag[ing] learners to produce language with a proper concern for form" (p. 44).

Although there has been much discussion on the relative merit of different approaches, few empirical studies have sought to directly compare the developmental effectiveness of tasks with more traditional activities. One recent exception is McDonough and Chaikitmongkol (2010). In this classroom-based study, the researchers compared information gap tasks implemented using a specific technique (collaborative syntactic priming) with the standard curriculum in a Thai EFL context to determine if there were differential effects on the target structure, *wh*-questions in English. Using a pretest, posttest, delayed posttest design, the researchers found that the class that completed the information gap tasks produced more *wh*-questions with auxiliary verbs than the class which did not do the task based activities.

Foreign language contexts

Another under-explored area concerns the effect of contextual factors (including second vs. foreign language contexts) on the effectiveness of classroom activities. As noted above, some researchers have questioned the effectiveness of tasks for developing linguistic knowledge in FL contexts (e.g., Burrows 2008; Carless 2004; Eguchi & Eguchi 2006; McDonough & Chaikitmongol 2007). Matters may be further complicated by the role of cultural background in influencing learners' receptivity to certain types of classroom activities. For example, Schultz (2001) examined student and teacher perceptions of grammar instruction and corrective feedback in two contexts, the U.S. and Colombia; she found that, in general, students and teachers from Colombia viewed traditional grammar teaching (with its emphasis on explicit grammar instruction and error correction) more favorably than their counterparts in the U.S. Also examining student preferences, Ockert (2005) found that EFL students in a small Japanese university preferred a particular order to instructional activities, with lecture and small-group activities followed by pair work. The challenges inherent to implementing task-based learning within a specifically Asian context are discussed in depth by Adams and Newton (2009). However, researchers have also reported positive effects for introducing tasks into the foreign language classroom (e.g. McDonough 2004; Tinker Sachs 2007; Weaver 2007) and favorable reactions to tasks in foreign language contexts such as Japan (e.g. Hood, Elwood, & Falout 2009).

Sheen's (2004) study is one of the few to investigate the EFL context and compare it with the ESL context. In her research, task-based learning with respect to the provision of interactional feedback was analyzed in four settings: (i) EFL in Korea, (ii) ESL in New Zealand, (iii) ESL in Canada, and (iv) French immersion in Canada. She reported that one type of corrective move, the recast, was the most common overall in all four contexts, but that it was more frequent in the Korean EFL and New Zealand ESL contexts as opposed to either Canadian context. In addition, modified output following recasts was more frequent in New Zealand and Korea than in the Canadian contexts. In other words, in Sheen's study the Korean EFL context had more recasts than ESL contexts. Lyster and Mori (2006) also looked at classroom interaction, comparing two immersion settings, French and Japanese, in terms of the provision of feedback and amount of learner uptake. The authors found that the recast was the most common form of feedback in both settings, but that French students produced more modified output after prompts and Japanese students produced more modified output after recasts. The results again suggest that context is an important variable in examining interactional tasks, and that FL contexts are particularly worth exploring. Taken together, these results suggest that context likely plays a role in the developmental effects of classroom activities. However, as Mackey and Goo (2007) note in their meta-analysis, more research into diverse learning environments is clearly necessary.

In sum, while there is empirical and theoretical support for the use of tasks in facilitating L2 learning, previous studies have indicated that more research is needed to determine the effect of contextual variables (such as setting, instructional context, and socio-cultural background) on the effectiveness of tasks. The current study aims to address this concern, exploring the effectiveness of tasks compared to more traditional grammar-focused practice activities in an authentic instructional foreign language context.

The research

This study investigated the effectiveness of activities that the teachers traditionally included as part of their lessons as well as the effectiveness of custom-made tasks with a more communicative orientation. The custom-made tasks were designed to provide both opportunities for targeted grammatical forms to occur, as well as opportunities for incidental corrective feedback after learner errors. The tasks were developed in researcher-teacher partnerships, to create pedagogically valid classroom tasks that were based on theory and research in SLA, while also being comparable and consistent with the teachers' usual activities to increase the ecological validity of the research. The study addressed the following research questions: Is there a relationship between activity type (tasks versus traditional practice activities) and L2 development in an EFL context?

Method

The study compares the effectiveness of tasks with traditional classroom activities in a Japanese university EFL setting. The procedure consisted of a pretest, treatment, posttest, and follow-up stimulated recall session. Two intact classrooms were studied: (i) one group of participants participated in a *task-based condition* and (ii) the other group participated in a *traditional activity condition*. The following sections describe the participants, instructional contexts, target structures, materials, and procedures used in the study.

Participants and instructional context

The EFL participants were 37 learners in an intensive English language program at a private university in Tokyo, Japan. There were 25 women and 13 men. All of the participants were native speakers of Japanese with an average of seven years of previous formal English instruction, representing a relatively homogenous group with regards to linguistic and cultural background. The age range was 18–20. The participants were enrolled in their first semester of university and represented a wide range of areas of study within the College of Liberal Arts. Entrance to the university was based on a competitive examination, which included a test of English. Placement into English classes was based on a university administered TOEFL test and an oral interview. The participants were drawn from two intact classes that met twice a week. Students were at the lower-intermediate level, which was characterized by an average TOEFL score of 450 (range = 340–493). The two instructors who are also co-authors of the current study were both female native speakers of Japanese who had near-native competence in English and extensive experience living and studying in English-speaking countries. One instructor was the coordinator of the academic speaking course with over 20 years of teaching experience at the university level in Japan, and the other instructor had seven years of experience in teaching Japanese and English as a foreign language at the university level.

The study was carried out in a course entitled "Academic Speaking," where the primary goal of the class was to develop learners' ability to communicate in an academic setting. Using a textbook titled *Communicating on Campus* (Hemmert & O'Connell 1998), the course covered topics such as making an appointment with a teacher, visiting a teacher's office, leading a class discussion, and making a short presentation to the class. The task-based materials developed for the study were also designed to simulate communicative needs in an academic or study abroad setting, such as taking notes, finding an apartment, or gathering information for a report. There was no explicit focus on grammar in the regular course syllabus. However, students were introduced to useful phrases and then given opportunities to practice these phrases in different activities. They were then expected to apply what they learned in their other English classes, in academic courses taught by English-speaking faculty, or in subsequent study abroad. All communication in class was conducted in English, as designated by the "English only" policy implemented and enforced throughout the English Language Program at the Japanese university where the study was conducted.

Target structures and measurement of development

Question forms were selected for the current study because they can be easily and reliably elicited through a variety of tasks and offer a reliable means for measuring linguistic development. A number of previous studies (e.g. Mackey 1999; Mackey & Oliver 2002; McDonough 2005; McDonough & Mackey 2006; Philp 2003; Silver 2000; Spada & Lightbown 1993) have demonstrated that L2 development can be effectively operationalized using the Pienemann and Johnston (1987) developmental sequence for question formation. In this sequence (see Table 1 below), a number of grammatical forms, including questions, develop in a set pattern. By targeting question forms for analysis, the results from the current study can be compared and discussed in relation to other studies that have also focused on these structures. More specifically, an analysis of question form development as a result of the two treatment conditions can contribute to what we know about the effectiveness of different tasks in classroom learning. In the current study, L2 development was operationalized as advancement in stage of question formation. For example, a learner assigned to Stage 3 in the pre-test developed if this learner was assigned to Stage 4 or higher in the post-test. Instructional materials targeted Stage 6 questions, the upper limit of the scale, so as to give all learners maximum opportunity to develop to the highest question stage.

Table 1. Examples of developmental question forms and stage ratings

Developmental stage	Examples
Stage 2 SVO? Canonical word order with question intonation	And you leave New York after? She doesn't remember?
Stage 3 Fronting Wh-/do/Q-word Direct questions with main verbs and some form of fronting	Do they remember the name of the city to immigrate? Is Mrs. Sato feel sad and scared to go abroad?
Stage 4 Pseudo-inversion: yes/no, copula Y/N In yes/no questions an auxiliary or modal is in sentence-initial position In Wh-questions the copula and the subject change position.	Were there any people who went to America with you? What was the name of the ship?
Stage 5 Do-/Aux-2nd Q-word à Aux/modal à subj. (main verb, etc.) Auxiliary verbs and modals are placed in second position to Wh-q's (& Q-words) and before subject (applies only in main clauses/ direct q's)	When did you immigrate to America? How many family members do they have? When will we have the next meeting?
Stage 6 Complex questions: Embedded questions with cancelled inversion Tag questions Negative questions	Would you tell me how long the test is? Do you know how we should prepare? Wasn't Hillview Apartment number 15, not 50? It's beautiful, isn't it?

Materials

The materials were designed to fit the purpose and focus of the ongoing English language instruction in the respective settings. As noted earlier, the materials were developed in partnership with the instructors for the classes studied and were pilot-tested with learners who did not participate in the current study but who were from a comparable population (enrolled in the same course taught by the same instructor in the previous semester). Developing pedagogically valid classroom tasks that were based on theory and research in SLA and were also comparable and commensurate with the teachers' usual activities was an important goal of the research design.

Pre- and post-tests

Three types of structure-focused monologic tasks (Find the Differences, Problem Solving, and Interview) were used for the pre-test and post-test. These tasks were designed to elicit the three target forms that are characteristic of Stage 6 of the Pienemann and Johnston

(1987) scale (see Table 2), tag questions, embedded questions and negative questions, and were developed specifically for the current study. Two of the three tasks (Find the Differences and Problem Solving) provided "task essential" (Loschky & Bley-Vroman 1993) contexts for advanced question forms (Stage 6), according to Pienemann and Johnston's (1987) 6-stage scale (see Table 1 above), in order to ensure that tests accurately measured learners' developmental stage. The third task, the interview task, provided a "task natural" context for all kinds of question forms. The post-test consisted of modified versions of the tasks used in the pre-test.

Tasks

In the task-based condition, learners were required to participate in role-play conversations with their partner. The tasks were designed to provide both opportunities for targeted grammatical forms to occur, as well as opportunities for incidental corrective feedback to be provided following errors. The scenarios for the role-plays took the form of comparing fictitious lecture notes, conducting interviews, or simulating academic discussions, all of which were accompanied by sufficient contextual prompts to elicit questions. In type and content they were very similar to the pretest material, but the focus was on structure-focused interaction rather than question formation. An example of one of the tasks used can be found in Appendix A.

Traditional classroom activities

The traditional classroom activities were created to fit into the "practice" stage of the classic Presentation-Practice-Production sequence (Willis 1996). Two types of elicited practice activities were designed: modeled elicitation and cued elicitation. Modeled elicitation was carried out in a teacher-fronted format, where learners immediately repeated the target structures (in this case, question forms modeled by their instructors). Cued elicitation was carried out in a teacher-fronted or a pair work settings. Learners were provided with oral cues and visual cues (via their handout), and expected to respond by producing the required target structure. An example of a handout used for the traditional practice activities is provided in Appendix B.

Table 2. Examples of prompts and expected responses for cued elicitation

Embedded questions	Negative questions
Prompt:	Prompt:
I want to know the location of the nearest supermarket.	*I am pretty sure that Mary lives in a dormitory.*
Learner response:	Learner response:
Do you know where the nearest supermarket is?	*Doesn't Mary live in a dormitory?*

Table 2 shows sample prompts that learners received in the lessons with traditional activities, along with expected learner responses. As shown in the examples, the prompts consisted of unrelated sentences and did not provide learners with an authentic communicative context for the target structures. Learners had opportunities to ask about instructions or unfamiliar vocabulary prior to practice of the targeted forms.

Questionnaire and stimulated recall

A questionnaire was distributed after the posttest and included questions to elicit learners' perceptions about the treatment materials and lessons as well as learners' awareness of the purpose of the study. The questionnaire was administered in Japanese, the native language of the participants, so that English language proficiency did not affect their responses. All participants' responses to the questionnaire were given anonymously, using a participant number. Finally, volunteers were solicited to participate in a stimulated recall interview (Gass & Mackey 2000). In this procedure, learners listened to excerpts from the audio recordings of the instructional lessons and reported what they had been thinking during the lessons.

Procedure

Overview

Because the study was conducted during regular class hours and as a part of the course curriculum, the task materials and the procedures were designed to fit as seamlessly as possible into the pedagogical framework of the classrooms.

Table 3. Procedure

	Traditional practice condition (N = 19)	Task-based condition (N = 18)
Day 1	Pretest (3 tasks)	Pretest (3 tasks)
Day 2	Teacher-led instruction (5 minutes)	Teacher-led instruction (5 minutes)
	Activity 1 (20 min.)	Task 1 (20 min.)
	Activity 2 (20 min.)	Task 2 (20 min.)
	Activity 3 (20 min.)	Task 3 (20 min.)
Day 3	Posttest (3 tasks)	Posttest (3 tasks)
Following week	Stimulated recall with volunteers	Stimulated recall with volunteers

First, on Day 1 (see Table 3), the students in both of the two intact classes carried out a set of three monologic tasks that served as a pretest. All students were given two minutes to complete each activity. The students were recorded individually using Olympus Voice-Trek digital voice recorders for a total of six minutes (for all three tasks). Then, on Day 2, one group of learners participated in a traditional practice activities condition (N = 19), and learners in the other intact classes (N = 18) participated in a task-based condition. Both conditions included three 20-minute practice activities or tasks that focused on the question forms targeted by the communicative tasks. Finally, on Day 3, learners carried out three monologic tasks, which served as a posttest. Like the pretest activities, learners were given two minutes each to complete each activity and were recorded individually for six minutes each. Immediately following the posttest activities, learners completed the questionnaire. During the week following the administration of posttests, stimulated recall sessions were conducted with volunteers from both classes.

Instructional conditions

As described above, three 20-minute practice activities or tasks were designed for each of the two instructional conditions. Each of the activities or tasks began with a five-minute teacher-fronted explanation of the grammar and appropriate use of question forms, including negative, embedded, and tag questions. The teacher-fronted explanation was then followed by either traditional practice activities (for the traditional practice condition) or tasks (for the task-based condition).

In the traditional activity condition, the teacher-fronted explanation was followed by teacher-led practice of the target structures, followed by learners' production of the structures in response to cues on their worksheets. As described above in the materials section, learners were given lists of sentences for all three tasks and instructed to form appropriate questions based on these. Learners took turns to transform the prompts into questions.

In the task-based condition, the teacher-fronted explanation was followed by role-play tasks, which were teacher-fronted for the first five minutes. During this time, the instructor engaged in interaction with the whole class and gave corrective feedback when necessary, after which the role-play continued in pairs.

To sum up, in both conditions the lesson began with teacher-fronted explanation, followed by teacher-led practice or task-based interaction, and then ended with pair work (again, practice or task-based interaction). Whereas the traditional activities provided learners with opportunities for practice (modeled elicitation and cued elicitation), the task-based activities consisted primarily of opportunities for production within the context of meaningful interaction with an interlocutor. Due to concerns by the language program about intrusiveness, and the concerns by the researchers to keep the context as close to an authentic classroom situation as possible, it was not possible to record each pair during the practice and task activities.

Stimulated recall interviews

Six volunteers (four from the group exposed to traditional classroom activities[1], and two from the group participating in communicative tasks) participated in stimulated recall interviews within a week of the posttest. As noted above, the stimulated recall involved having students listen to audio excerpts from the lessons and report on their thoughts at the time of the lesson. Then, the researcher asked more focused questions to elicit the learners' perceptions about the effectiveness of the instructional methods and materials used in the study. The elicitation took place in their L1, Japanese, except for two learners who requested to speak in English. The stimulated recall sessions were carried out with the second author.

Coding and analysis

All utterances from the pre- and post-tests were transcribed and coded for question stages (based on Pienemann & Johnston 1987). Question stages were assigned to each learner based on data from three different tasks on both the pre-test and the post-test. In order to assign an overall question stage to a learner, at least two different instances of a stage had to be present in at least two of the three tasks. Overall development was operationalized as movement to a higher stage in the post-test. Chi square tests for independence were performed to determine whether there was a relationship between activity type (traditional or communicative) and development, in both contexts.

Data were coded in two stages. First, a total of four raters each coded a subset of the question forms and assigned an overall question stage to the learners in their subsets, so that all question forms for each learner were coded. Next, 20% of the data coded by each rater was then coded by a second rater. Interrater reliability was calculated as simple percentage agreement. Agreement ranged from 84% to 91% and reached 100% after resolving disagreements. Then, one rater reviewed the entire data set to rule out instances of formulaic language use, which were defined as a repetition of the exact same question fragment more than two times over a short series of questions. Again, to establish interrater reliability, a second rater coded 20% of the entire data set for formulaic language use. Interrater reliability, calculated as simple percentage agreement, was 91% before and 100% after disagreements were resolved.

The distribution of stage assignments for the participants based on their pretests was as follows: 6 learners at Stage 3, 8 learners at Stage 4, and 5 learners at Stage 5 in the traditional practice condition, and 2 learners at Stage 3, 10 learners at Stage 4, and 6 learners at Stage 5 in the task-based condition.

Results and discussion

Task-based vs. traditional activities

The research question asked whether there was a relationship between activity type (traditional or task-based) and development (changes in learners' question stages before and after the instructional sessions) in this EFL context. Results indicated that in this context, 15 of 19 learners developed in the traditional activities group and 12 of 18 learners developed in the task-based activities group (see Table 4 below). The results of the Chi-square test for independence (with Yates continuity correction) indicated that there was no significant relationship between activity type and development, χ^2 (1, 37) = .221, p = .638.

Table 4. Task-based vs. traditional practice in an EFL context

	Traditional	Task-based
Developed	15	12
No development	4	6
Total	19	18

In sum, the results of the quantitative findings showed no differences in the effectiveness of the tasks and traditional practice activities, suggesting that previous researchers' claims about the value of tasks are not bound to a particular context or culture, and perhaps equally important, that there are benefits to both activity types, as well as a few limitations to be discussed below.

During the stimulated recall interviews, learners identified positive aspects of both tasks and traditional practice activities. Learners who engaged in the traditional practice activities appreciated in particular, the role of practice in alleviating anxiety and increasing confidence. For example, one learner stated, "I hadn't really used negative questions before this, and so I was unsure at first. I wanted to use this to ask this but I was pretty unsure. But after using it a number of times, I began to get it." Similarly, another learner mentioned that "I come, came to feel more comfortable through repeating … practice" and yet another learner in the task-based condition noted that "Yes [the practice was useful], because we repeated many times how to ask the question." Previous researchers have identified both general anxiety (a predisposition to be anxious) and language anxiety (feelings of apprehension associated specifically with learning a new language) as being obstacles to student learning (Elkhafaifi 2005; Horwitz 2001). For this reason, activities that serve to increase learners' confidence may facilitate the second language learning process. It may be the case that traditional practice activities, with their rote practice and memorization, are beneficial for at least some learners who experience language learning anxiety.

However, it also needs to be kept in mind that an activity that is stressful for one learner may be "comfortable" for another learner, and that language anxiety does not stem from classroom activities alone (Yan & Horwitz 2008). Obviously, it cannot be said unequivocally that traditional practice activities are less anxiety-inducing than communicative ones (see Horwitz 2010 for a recent overview of language anxiety). Put another way, as many other researchers and teachers have also concluded, our study supports the idea that there is probably no "one size fits all" approach to classroom activities.

Another benefit of the traditional practice activities was in helping learners practice structures they knew about but had never used. For example, one learner noted that "in high school, we mainly worked on reading comprehension of extended texts, and I had forgotten about these kinds of structures so I am glad we went over them again." Another learner commented that "in high school, … we did writing and reading and we studied complex grammar for university entrance examinations so there are a lot of expressions that I have seen before and I know them but I have never actually used them in speaking. So when we can focus on some expression in class, that is a good thing." For these students who had explicit grammatical knowledge about these structures, rote practice may have helped them transform "passive" knowledge into "active" knowledge (as one learner explained, "after repeating, the teacher often says to look up and say it, but when that happens its necessary to memorize it even for just a moment so I think maybe that is useful for learning it"). It may also build learners' sense of confidence to use a particular structure.

At the same time, learners also provided insight regarding the limits of traditional practice. One of the learners in the traditional practice condition commented, "But how should I use was not clear," indicating that the learner knew which structure to use but was unsure of *when* to use it. In contrast, the communicative condition provided learners with opportunities to make the connection between structure and context. One learner commented, "I realized in class that the conversation goes smoothly if I use these expressions, so … I think it will be convenient to use them in the future and I think there will be lots of situations when I can use them."

Taken together, these results imply that one activity type is not fundamentally more effective than another and that both have a role to play in helping learners make progress in the second language. As a number of researchers have noted, there is no magic bullet with respect to language teaching; teachers need to heed their own counsel about what works in their classrooms and with their learners. By open-mindedly considering a range of possibilities in the L2 classroom, "teachers [may] make more effective moment-by-moment decisions in harmony with how learners learn and …[challenge] teachers' sense of what is plausible and thereby keeping teaching vital" (Ellis 1997:78).

Limitations and conclusions

The current study provides evidence that in this small scale EFL context, learners benefited equally well from tasks and traditional practice activities, and held positive views of both. However, these results must be interpreted cautiously due to the limitations of the study. The sample size was small to begin with.

Other limitations concern the design and length of the study rather than the participants. While the type of treatments ensure a higher external validity because of their similarity to normal classroom activities, the necessity to fit the tests and practice sessions into regular classroom periods made it impossible to include a delayed post-test. For this reason, it was not possible to analyze long-term or delayed development, which has sometimes been documented in interaction research. Another limitation is due to the same reason: since treatments had to fit into a single class period, they necessarily had to be rather short. With three target structures, only a total of 15 to 20 minutes could be allocated to each one. After the teacher's explanations and brief group practice, this left only five minutes for pair activities. This may be too little time for learners to sufficiently practice a new form (or to become accustomed to the type of activity).

There were also differences in learners' pretest levels, which is inevitable in classroom rather than lab-based research. The traditional group had more lower level learners – making it a logical possibility that since more learners in the task group were already at higher stages they were better matched with the developmental opportunities provided by the tasks. There is also the issue that moving from Stage 5 to 6 may be more difficult because in tasks, Stage 6 questions are very difficult to constrain with obligatory production contexts. Future research would do well to try to match tasks and opportunities with developmental levels, to see if different results could be obtained.

Such future research, in addition to employing a larger sample size, measures of learners' developmental stages prior to treatment, and longer treatment sessions, should also undertake a careful analysis of transcripts of instructional sessions to investigate differences in quantity and quality of peer feedback and other opportunities for development. Since this study did not focus on the transcripts of the interactions during the instructional treatment, the quality of the interactions could not be compared between or within contexts. Future studies would also benefit from looking at individual learner differences (such as anxiety levels) and how they impact learners' development (and perceptions) in classes employing different types of activities.

Notes

One of the learners who volunteered for the interview was excluded from the pre/posttest analysis because part of her oral production data was lost due to technical difficulties.

References

Adams, R., & Newton, J. (2009). TBLT in Asia: Constraints and opportunities. *Asian Journal of English Language Teaching, 19*, 1–17.

Bygate, M., Skehan, P., & Swain, M. (Eds.). (2001). *Researching pedagogic tasks: Second language learning, teaching and testing.* Harlow: Pearson Education.

Burrows, C. (2008). Socio-cultural barriers facing TBL in Japan. *The Language Teacher, 32*, 15–19.

Carless, D. (2004). Issues in teachers' reinterpretation of a task-based innovation in primary schools. *TESOL Quarterly, 38*, 639–662.

Eguchi, M., & Eguchi, K. (2006). The limited effect of PBL on EFL learners: A case study of English magazine projects. *Asian EFL Journal, 8*, 207–225.

Elkhafaifi, H. (2005). Listening comprehension and anxiety in the Arabic language classroom. *The Modern Language Journal, 89*, 206–220.

Ellis, R. (1997). *SLA research and language teaching.* Oxford: Oxford University Press.

Ellis, R. (2003). *Task-based language teaching and learning.* Oxford: Oxford University Press.

Ellis, R., Basturkmen, H., & Loewen, S. (2001). Pre-emptive focus on form in the ESL classroom. *TESOL Quarterly, 35,* 407–432.

Ellis, R., Tanaka, Y., & Yamazaki, A. (1994). Classroom interaction, comprehension, and the acquisition of L2 word meanings. *Language Learning, 44,* 449–491.

Gass, S. M., & Mackey, A. (2000). *Stimulated recall methodology in second language research.* Mahwah, NJ: Lawrence Erlbaum Associates.

Han, Z.-H. (2002). A study of the impact of recasts on tense consistency in L2 output. *TESOL Quarterly, 36,* 543–72.

Hemmert, A., & O'Connell, G. (1998). *Communicating on campus.* Burlingame, CA: Alta Book Center.

Hood, M., Elwood, J., & Falout, J. (2009). Student attitudes toward task-based language teaching at Japanese colleges. *Asian Journal of English Language Teaching, 19, 19–47.*

Horwitz, B. (2001). *Communication apprehension: Origins and management.* San Diego CA: Singular.

Horwitz, E. K. (2010). Foreign and second language anxiety. *Language Teaching, 43,* 154–167.

Iwashita, N. (2003). Negative feedback and positive evidence in task-based interaction: Differential effects on L2 development. *Studies in Second Language Acquisition, 25,* 1–36.

Keck, C., Iberri-Shea, G., Tracy-Ventura, N., & Wa-Mbaleka, S. (2006). Investigating the empirical link between task-based interaction and acquisition: a quantitative meta-analysis. In J. M. Norris & L. Ortega (Eds.), *Synthesizing research on language learning and teaching.* Amsterdam: John Benjamins.

Long, M. H. (1985). A role for instruction in second language acquisition: Task-based language teaching. In K. Hyltenstam & M. Pienemann (Eds.), *Modeling and assessing second language development* (pp. 77–99). Clevedon: Multilingual Matters.

Long, M. H. (1996). The role of the linguistic environment in second languageacquisition. In W. C. Ritchie & T. K. Bhatia (Eds.), *Handbook of second language acquisition* (pp. 413–468). New York, NY: Academic Press.

Long, M. H. (2007). *Problems in SLA.* Mahwah, NJ: Lawrence Erlbaum Associates.

Loschky, L. (1994). Comprehensible input and second language acquisition: What is the relationship? *Studies in Second Language Acquisition, 16,* 303–323.

Loschky, L., & Bley-Vroman, R. (1993). Grammar and task-based methodology. In G. Crookes & S. M. Gass (Eds.), *Tasks and language learning: Integrating theory and practice* (pp. 123–167). Clevedon: Multilingual Matters.

Lyster, R., & Mori, H. (2006). Interaction feedback and instructional counterbalance. *Studies in Second Language Acquisition, 28,* 269–300.

Mackey, A. (1999). Input, interaction, and second language development: An empirical study of question formation in ESL. *Studies in Second Language Acquisition, 21,* 557–587.

Mackey, A., & Goo, J. (2007). Interaction research in SLA: A meta-analysis and research synthesis. In A. Mackey (Ed.), *Conversational interaction in second language acquisition: A collection of empirical studies* (pp. 407–452). Oxford: Oxford University Press.

Mackey, A., & Oliver, R. (2002). Interactional feedback and children's L2 development. *System, 30,* 459–477.

Mackey, A., & Philp, J. (1998). Conversational interaction and second languagedevelopment: Recasts, responses, and red herrings? *The Modern Language Journal, 82,* 338–356.

Matsuura, H., Chiba, R., & Hilderbrandt, P. (2001). Beliefs about learning and teaching communicative English in Japan. *JALT Journal, 23,* 69–89.

McDonough, K. (2004). Learner-learner interaction during pair and small group activities in a Thai EFL context. *System, 32,* 207–224.

McDonough, K. (2005). Identifying the impact of negative feedback and learners' responses on ESL question development. *Studies in Second Language Acquisition, 27,* 79–103.

McDonough, K., & Chaikitmongkol, W. (2007). Teachers' and learners' reactions to a task-based EFL course in Thailand. *TESOL Quarterly, 41,* 107–132.

McDonough, K., & Chaikitmongkol, W. (2010). Collaborative syntactic priming activities and EFL learners' production of *wh*-questions. *The Canadian Modern Language Review, 66,* 817–841.

McDonough, K., &Mackey, A. (2006). Responses to recasts: Repetitions, primed production, and linguistic development. *Language Learning, 56,* 693–720.

Ockert, D. (2005). Substantive scale verification: A likert scale analysis and critique of university student pedagogical activity preferences. *JALT Hokkaido Journal, 9,* 48–64.

Philp, J. (2003). Constraints on "noticing the gap". Nonnative speakers' noticing of recasts in NS-NNS interaction. *Studies in Second Language Acquisition, 25,* 99–126.

Pienemann, M., & Johnston, M. (1987). Factors influencing the development of language proficiency. In D. Nunan (Ed.), *Applying second language acquisition research* (pp. 45–141). Adelaide: National Curriculum Resource Centre, Adult Migrant Education Program.

Schultz, R. A. (2001). Cultural difference in student and teacher perceptions concerning the role of grammar instruction and corrective feedback: USA-Colombia. *The Modern Language Journal, 85,* 244–258.

Sheen, Y. (2004). Corrective feedback and learner uptake in communicative classrooms across instructional settings. *Language Teaching Research, 8,* 263–300.

Silver, R. E. (2000). Input, output and negotiation: Conditions for second language development. In B. Swierzbin, F. Morris, M. E. Anderson, C. A. Klee & E. Tarone (Eds.), *Social and cognitive factors in second language acquisition: Selected proceedings of the 1999 second language research forum* (pp. 345–371). Somerville MA: Cascadilla Press.

Spada, N., & Lightbown, P. M. (1993). Instruction and the development of questions in L2 classrooms. *Studies in Second Language Acquisition, 15,* 205–224.

Tinker Sachs, G. (2007). The challenges of adopting and adapting task-based cooperative teaching and learning in an EFL context. In K. Van den Branden, K. van Gorp, & M. Verhelst (Eds.), *Tasks in action: Task-based language education from a classroom-based perspective* (pp. 253–264). Newcastle upon Tyne: Cambridge Scholars.

Weaver, C. (2007). Willingness to communicate: A mediating factor in the interaction between learners and tasks. In K. Van den Branden, K. van Gorp, & M. Verhelst (Eds.), *Tasks in action: Task-based language education from a classroom-based perspective* (pp. 159–194). Newcastle upon Tyne: Cambridge Scholars.

Willis, J. R. (1996). *A framework for task-based learning.* London: Longman.

Willis, J., & Willis, D. (1996). *Challenge and change in language teaching.* Oxford: Macmillan Education.

Yan, J. X., & Horwitz, E. K. (2008). Learners' perceptions of how anxiety interacts with personal and instructional factors to influence their achievement in English: A qualitative analysis of EFL learners in China. *Language Learning, 58,* 151–183.

Appendix A

Tasks

Checking your notes

You are studying at a university in the U.K. and you are taking a course on Environmental Issues. You are working on a group project with 5 other students: 4 British students who are native speakers of English and 1 Korean student (Yun, who sometimes worries that she doesn't understand what the British students are saying).

After the group meeting Yun asks you to check her notes. You do find some differences in her notes and your notes. You are quite confident that your notes are accurate so you ask Yun some questions (politely) to point out the differences.

Compare the notes below. Find differences between your notes and Yun's notes. Brainstorm at least five questions to ask Yun to help her with the important points from the meeting.

My (Kyoko's) Notes from Group Meeting: Friday, May 23, 2008

Presentation Title: Nuclear Energy as a Solution to the Energy Crisis
Tasks:

1.	Find useful articles:	John
2.	Summarize articles:	Emily and Frank
3.	Make appointment for interview:	Yun
4.	Identify useful websites:	Kyoko and John
5.	Make copies of recent TV documentary:	Frank
6.	Reserve meeting room for next meeting:	Yun

Next meeting: Friday May 30, 2008 at 4:00pm in the library meeting room

---

Yun's Notes from Group Meeting: Friday, May 24, 2008

Presentation Title: Nuclear Energy as a Solution to the Energy Crisis
Tasks:

1.	Find useful newspapers:	John
2.	Summer articles:	Emily
3.	Make appointment for interview:	???
4.	Identify useful websites:	John
5.	Make copies of recent TV:	Frank
6.	Get pizza for next meeting:	Yun

Next meeting: Friday May 30, 2008 at 4:30pm in the ???

Appendix B

Grammar presentation handout example: Negative Questions

Example: <u>Didn't we decide</u> that you would reserve the meeting room

Structure: [auxiliary verb + n't + subject + main verb]

Isn't it true that...?

A negative question can ask for confirmation of a positive belief. In this case the question expects the answer YES, and means "I believe that/ I am pretty sure that"

Didn't you go and see Helen yesterday? How is she?
      (= I believe you went and saw Helen yesterday)

Practice:
Let's practice questions that confirm the following beliefs.

Example: I am pretty sure Mary lives in a dormitory → Doesn't Mary live in a dormitory?
   1. I am pretty sure that your plane leaves in the afternoon →
   2. I am pretty sure that I deserve an A in this class. →
   3. I am pretty sure that they know about the party →
   4. I am pretty sure that the restaurant is still open →
   5. I am pretty sure that his dog is at least three years old now →
   6. I am pretty sure that your parents are angry with my brother →
   7. I am pretty sure that Ellen has taken the test →
   8. I am pretty sure that they went swimming. →
   9. I am pretty sure my brother brought his computer along →
  10. I am pretty sure that the rainy season has started in Kyushu →
  11. I am pretty sure that was our hotel → Wasn't that our hotel?

*** Negative questions can also ask for confirmation of a negative belief (i.e. "Is it true that ....not...?").
It is usually clear from the situation and context whether negative questions are asking for confirmation of positive or negative beliefs.
E.g. Don't you feel well? (= Am I right in thinking you don't feel well?)

Acknowledgments

This project was funded by two grants: the Spencer Foundation small research grants program # 200800092 and the International Research Foundation for English Language Education (TIRF) Priority Research Grant, both to Alison Mackey.

Chapter 5

Building explicit L2 Spanish knowledge through guided induction in small-group and whole-class interaction

Elvis Wagner and Paul Toth
Temple University

This chapter explores interactions among American high school learners of L2 Spanish during three lessons on the pronominal clitic *se* which were designed to promote grammatical consciousness-raising through guided induction. Following Adair-Hauck, Donato, and Cumo-Johanssen (2010), each lesson first presented a property of *se* within a narrative text, with learners then inductively "co-constructing" rules in small groups, followed by a whole-class discussion where the teacher guided learners toward a consensus. Analyses of the small-group and whole-class discussions focused on the amount of analytic talk produced by individual learners and the types of interactions among learners. The results suggest that although the amount of analytic talk varied considerably across individuals, the tasks promoted consciousness-raising of the target form.

Introduction

Current second language (L2) pedagogy favors work in pairs or small groups to promote language learning through communicative interaction. Such interaction is seen as useful and even necessary because it (1) promotes the negotiation of meaning among participants (Gass 2003); (2) allows learners to test hypotheses about the L2 (Swain 1998); and (3) allows them to notice gaps between their interlanguage and the forms used by others (Doughty 2001). Similarly, much research has focused on the role of explicit knowledge in L2 teaching and learning. Many researchers (e.g., Ellis 2002; Paradis 2009) have argued that the explicit knowledge of a particular grammatical form indirectly promotes acquisition because it facilitates noticing and attention to the target form in subsequent input, and can be accessed during output when time constraints allow, such as during writing or planned speech. The present study examines an L2 classroom task that was designed to promote explicit knowledge of a target form through analytic talk among learners.

Although most current interaction research focuses on L2 use, this chapter examines how interaction in the L1 about L2 structures can promote explicit L2 knowledge.

Peer interaction in language learning

Much research has investigated the effects of peer interaction on language learning. Of particular relevance for this study are studies of small-group versus whole-class interaction, interaction patterns among learners, and L1 use in small-group tasks.

Small-group versus whole class interaction

The obvious allure of implementing small-group classroom tasks is that they provide more opportunities for learner interaction and involve more discourse turns than whole class discussions (Lee 2000; Long & Porter 1985). Researchers have also suggested that learners in small groups receive more comprehensible input and have more opportunities to produce output and negotiate meaning than in whole-class interaction (Long & Porter 1985; Long 1996; Mackey, Oliver, & Leeman 2003; Pica 1994). Small groups can also yield a more positive affective environment, which may increase learner motivation and encourage turn-taking from shy students who hold back in whole-class discourse (Cao & Philp 2006; de Saint Leger & Storch 2009; Long & Porter 1985). However, other studies have found that while small-group interactions might also lead to greater analysis by language learners, whole-class interactions can produce more expert guidance from the teacher (Toth 2008; Van den Branden 1997).

Patterns of interaction

Researchers have also investigated patterns of interaction within small groups to document how these dynamics influence the effectiveness of L2 tasks and L2 learning outcomes. Lockhart and Ng (1995) identified "collaborative" and "probing" interactions between learners that resulted in effective outcomes on an L2 writing task. Similarly, Swain (1998) described interaction in small group tasks as consisting of "collaborative dialogue," while Donato (1994) found that learners working in a small group were able to assist each other in accurately selecting vocabulary and grammar in an L2 French writing task through "collective scaffolding."

Storch (2002) meanwhile described patterns of dyadic interactions among ESL learners based on the degree of equality and mutuality involved. The former represented the extent to which each learner had equal control over the task, while the latter stood for each learner's level of engagement with the other's contributions. The intersection of high and low degrees of these two variables yielded four different types of dyadic interaction: "collaborative" (high equality, high mutuality); "dominant/dominant" (high equality, low mutuality); "dominant/passive" (low equality, low mutuality); and "expert/novice" (low equality, high mutuality). Of 10 dyads that Storch (2002) studied during one semester, five were classified as collaborative, two were dominant/dominant, two were dominant/

passive, and one was expert/novice. Those that had collaborative or expert/novice patterns were most likely to "scaffold" the other learner's performance. She also found that these patterns of interaction were fairly stable over the course of the semester. Watanabe (2008) used Storch's (2002) dyadic categories and reported similar results: dyads composed of high- and low-ability learners were able to learn from their interactions when working collaboratively.

The use of the L1 in small-group tasks

Numerous researchers have described how learners often use the L1 when engaged in challenging L2 language learning tasks, for a variety of reasons. Two studies that are particularly relevant are reviewed here. Swain and Lapkin (2000) examined how English-speaking learners of French used the L1 to complete a dictogloss and a jigsaw task while working in pairs. They found that the learners used the L1 for three main purposes: (1) to manage task procedures and move the task along; (2) to focus attention during vocabulary searches and when analyzing L2 form; and (3) for interpersonal interaction, usually during off-task conversations or disagreements (Swain & Lapkin 2000: 257). While there was more L1 use than the researchers had anticipated, they argued that using the L1 was beneficial in that it "served both cognitive and social functions" needed to complete the L2 task (p. 268). Similarly, Scott and de la Fuente (2008) examined how the L1 and L2 were used in form-focused, consciousness-raising tasks by pairs of American college students learning French or Spanish. They found that learners who were allowed to use the L1 had more fluid and balanced interactions, and used more metalinguistic terminology to complete the task. Conversely, learner pairs that were required to use only the L2 always involved one learner dominating the conversation, and the unbalanced interactions made true collaboration difficult to achieve. Scott and de la Fuente (2008) concluded that prohibiting students from using the L1 in these tasks was counterproductive.

Consciousness-raising tasks in developing explicit L2 knowledge

The role of grammar teaching in L2 learning has long been a contentious issue, and the effectiveness of explicit grammar teaching continues to be debated. There is disagreement about the possibility that explicit grammatical knowledge can be transformed into implicit L2 knowledge for communication. However, researchers such as Hulstijn (2002) and Ellis (2002) have argued that even if explicit knowledge does not become implicit knowledge, as some have argued (Krashen 1985; Paradis 2009), explicit grammatical knowledge can still facilitate acquisition. Ellis (2002) holds that explicit instruction raises learners' conscious awareness of grammatical forms, which contributes to the acquisition of implicit knowledge during utterance perception, planning, and production. This justification for explicit instruction is consistent with both cognitive and sociocultural views on the role of consciousness and consciousness-raising in language learning, as well as DeKeyser's work which provides support for the benefits of instruction in the development of explicit procedural knowledge as a more realistic goal for L2 learners (c.f., DeKeyser 1998, Lantolf & Thorne 2006; Rutherford & Sharwood Smith 1985; Schmidt 2001). For example, Swain (2000, 2006) has argued that employing explicit knowledge to make L2 form-function mappings is a vital component of proficiency development, and that when learners engage in such "metatalk" or "languaging," information that was originally mediated externally can become internalized as a deeper understanding.

The present study

The current study examines a consciousness-raising task where learners used the L1 to analyze an L2 target structure. Consciousness-raising occurred within a larger inductive task sequence, called PACE, where learners collaboratively constructed and applied explicit L2 knowledge for communication. As described by Adair-Hauck, Donato, and Cumo-Johanssen (2010), PACE is rooted in sociocultural concepts of collaborative learning (Vygotsky 1987) and Tharp and Gallimore's (1988) call for "instructional conversations" that develop verbal skills through inductive, dialogic interaction. PACE's four lesson phases involve first "Presenting" a target structure within a short, culturally-authentic narrative, drawing learners' "Attention" to the structure, and then "Co-constructing" explicit grammar rules based on patterns in the text. Rule formulation is then followed by "Extension" tasks that employ the structure for communication. Although this transition from presentation to production bears some resemblance to traditional pedagogy, PACE differs markedly from earlier approaches in that it tightly links explicit grammatical knowledge to text- and discourse-level L2 communication, and develops this knowledge among learners inductively. During Co-construction in this study, learners first worked in small groups and then reported their grammatical analyses during a teacher-led, whole-class follow-up. This two-step process was designed to first promote analytic talk and consciousness-raising among learners, followed by opportunities to clarify misunderstandings or incomplete analyses with the teacher. The analytic talk that is the focus of this study was defined as explicit statements about the relationship between L2 form and meaning, deemed to represent learner consciousness-raising.

The following research questions were addressed:

Research Question 1:   How is analytic talk distributed among participants during the small-group and whole-class segments of Co-construction? How does participants' analytic talk differ during the small-group and whole-class Co-construction?

Research Question 2:   How did participants contribute to each others' metalinguistic knowledge through inductive consciousness-raising, both in small-group and whole-class interactions?

Method

Participants

The 17 learners in this study comprised an intact class of third-year L2 Spanish in a public suburban U.S. high school. They included 4 females and 13 males, all Caucasian, ranging from ages 15 to 18. The instructor for the class was a 23 year-old female non-native Spanish speaker, who was finishing her third semester as a student-teacher intern. In this capacity, she prepared and taught the class every day herself, with the permanent, mentor teacher sitting quietly in the classroom, as commonly occurs with highly competent student teachers. The student teacher's Spanish proficiency had been assessed as "Advanced Low" on the scale of the American Council for the Teaching of Foreign Languages during her first internship semester[1].

The data were collected 8 weeks after the student teacher began her full-time internship with this class. Classes met every other school day for 90 minutes. Instruction was in Spanish about 60% of the time prior to data gathering, and most often consisted of explicit, deductive grammar presentations followed by mechanical and communicative exercises. During data gathering, however, the Presentation, Attention, and Co-construction lesson phases were almost entirely in Spanish. Nonetheless, as per Adair-Hauck et al.'s (2010) guidelines, the Co-construction phase was conducted in English so that learners could analyze the target structure without facing L2 proficiency limitations. To familiarize learners with inductive consciousness-raising and the overall increased use of Spanish, the teacher taught three PACE lessons on unrelated grammar topics in the week prior to data collection.

Lesson materials

The target structure for this study was the Spanish verbal clitic *se*, which seemed ideal for consciousness-raising given the syntactic consistency that underlies its polyfunctional semantics. It was reasoned that if explicit, inductive consciousness-raising could make the systematicity of *se*'s syntax-semantics correspondences more salient, learners might better comprehend its communicative value.

Spanish *se* is difficult for English-speaking learners because similar sequences using *se* with a verb and noun phrase (NP) correspond to varying English equivalents (Bruhn de Garavito 1999; Toth 2000). Nonetheless, linguists have identified the "absorption" of NP arguments implied by verb meanings as a common syntactic operation that underlies most of *se*'s uses (Reinhart & Siloni 2005). Often, this absorption allows a normally transitive verb to be used intransitively with impersonal or passive meaning, or with reflexive meaning, as (1)–(3) show. When *se* absorbs the agent, as in (1b) and (2b), the patient

---

1. The statewide requirement for all public school L2 teachers was 'Intermediate-High', which is one step lower than this instructor's proficiency on the 10-step ACTFL scale.

becomes the subject, which undergoes the event. Depending on the meaning of the verb, this "non-agentive *se*" could imply that an agent was present but simply omitted as in (1b), yielding a passive or impersonal interpretation, or that that the event took place spontaneously (i.e., "inchoatively") without an agent as in (2b). In contrast, when *se* absorbs a patient argument as in (3), a reflexive or reciprocal meaning is derived, so that the lone agent NP is understood to perform the action upon itself (Reinhart & Siloni 2005). Thus, for English-speaking learners, the similar structures "NP *se* verb" and "*se* verb NP" appear to yield inconsistent meanings with numerous English equivalents.

(1) a. *Juan   lavó   los suéteres*
         AGENT   3rd sing.   PATIENT
         'Juan washed the sweaters'
     b. *Se lav<u>aron</u>   los suéteres*
         3rd pl.   PATIENT
         'One washed sweaters'
         'The sweaters were washed'

(2) a. *Juan   secó   los suéteres*
         AGENT   3rd sing.   PATIENT
         'Juan dried the sweaters'
     b. *Los suéteres   se sec<u>aron</u>*
         PATIENT   3rd pl.
         'The sweaters [Ø] dried'

(3) a. *Los niños **se** lavaron.*
         'The children washed themselves /each other'
     b. *Los niños **se** secaron*
         'The children dried themselves /each other'

Se with impersonal, passive, and inchoative meaning, as in (1b) and (2b), was introduced at about the same time that it would have been in the regular curriculum, one year after the presentation of its reflexive functions. Three consecutive 90-minute lessons were designed to focus on these non-agentive aspects of *se*, with each including all four phases of PACE. Table 1 provides a general outline of the tasks used in each lesson, with the Co-construction phase. In Lesson 1, learners were to formulate a rule for *se* in impersonal expressions based on a reviewer's description of two Costa Rican restaurants, where *se* sentences stating what one ordinarily expects were contrasted with the reviewer's actual experiences. For Lesson 2, learners then articulated a rule for *se* in passive expressions, based on a story where the main character followed recipe instructions for Mexican *chiles rellenos*. Finally, Lesson 3 had learners explain the lack of external causation when *se* described inchoative, "spontaneous" events in a news report about a Chilean earthquake and rainstorm.

Following Table 1, the Presentation phase of each lesson involved learners listening twice to a recording while following along on a printed handout. After each pass through

Table 1. Outline of the three PACE lessons

Activity	Goal	Time
1. Warm-up / pre-reading	Orientation to reading topics	5 min
2. Presentation	Comprehension of text meaning, exposure to *se*	15 min
3. Attention	Draw learners' attention to sentences with and without *se*	5 min
4. Co-construction a. small-group hypothesizing b. whole-class follow-up	Guide students to develop rules for *se*	15–20 min

5. Extension
a. whole-class guided speaking with teacher feedback and support
b. small group interaction
  i. pretask: individuals plan language
  ii. task: small-group information exchange
  iii. posttask: whole-class comparison of results
	Use *se* to perform communicative tasks similar to that of the Presentation text	15 min
		
		25 min

6. Optional filler activities	Meaningful use of Spanish without further practice of *se*.	Time remaining

the text, learners completed meaning-based comprehension tasks. For the Attention phase, learners then worked in groups to sort selected sentences from the text into those representing a cause and effect (i.e., transitives without *se*) and those representing "general" events (i.e., *se*-derived impersonal intransitives). For example, in Lesson 1, learners considered underlined sentences in the text and sorted them into one column representing the restaurant reviewer's direct experience, and another describing restaurants in general. The results for most groups looked like Figure 1, with all the *se* sentences on the right.

La experiencia de la autora	Los restaurantes en general
1. No lo encontré así	1. Se dice que los dos restaurantes son iguales
2. Me gustó mucho la comida	2. Se come bien en los dos lugares
3. Encontré problemas con la cuenta	3. Se llega en carro o autobús
4. Me dijo que costaba 3,000 colones	4. Se sirve comida tradicional
5. Me sentaron inmediatamente	5. Se necesita una reservación

English translation

The author's experience	The restaurants in general
1. I didn't find it that way	1. They say the restaurants are the same
2. I liked the food a lot	2. One eats well in both places
3. I found problems with the check	3. You arrive by car or bus
4. He told me it cost 3,000 colones	4. They serve traditional food
5. They seated me immediately	5. You need a reservation

Figure 1. Sentences with and without *se* in Lesson 1's Co-construction

For Co-construction, learners then worked in groups of 2 or 3 to explain the contrasts between the two columns. After 5–10 minutes of small group discussion, the teacher led a whole-class follow-up in each lesson for another 5–10 minutes to guide learners toward a rule consensus. The Extension phase then occupied the remaining 40 minutes of each lesson, where learners performed 3–4 whole- and small-group tasks involving *se* in communicative functions like those of the original texts, such as comparing restaurants, or giving recipe instructions.

Data collection

During small-group Co-construction, the 17 learners were divided into 8 small groups, with 4 groups of 9 total learners volunteering to record their interactions with a digital audio recorder. These 9 learners are the focus of the small group component of this study. Likewise, all whole-class interactions were recorded with a digital camcorder set on a tripod at the back of the room. The data set thus consisted of 15 recordings: 4 small-group interactions and 1 whole-class follow-up in each of 3 lessons.

In order to quantify the amount of analytic talk produced by each participant, interaction during both small-group and whole-class Co-construction was recorded and transcribed. All learners were given Spanish alias names. The two researchers examined the transcripts independently and coded all instances of analytic talk, defined as propositions explicitly addressing L2 form or meaning. By contrast, non-analytic talk consisted of turns not focused on L2 form or meaning, including both off-task comments and comments intended to promote task completion without addressing the L2 itself. The researchers then compared their coding analyses, and reconciled the few differences, ultimately reaching 100% agreement. The analytic and non-analytic talk segments were identified and linked to their speakers using Transana 2.42 software (Fassnacht & Woods 2009), which linked the audio and video recordings to the transcripts and measured the amount of talk for each individual learner.

Analyses

For research question 1, which explores how analytic talk was distributed among participants, the percentage of time that each learner engaged in analytic talk during small-group and whole-class Co-construction was computed. A correlation analysis was then conducted comparing individual rates of analytic talk for the 9 learners from which data were collected for both the small-group and whole-class Co-construction interactions. (The teacher and the 8 other learners in the class were excluded from the correlation analysis). Because both variables were continuous, a Pearson product-moment correlation analysis was used, and the test of significance was set at $p < .05$.

For research question 2, which investigates how the individual participants contributed to each others' metalinguistic knowledge through inductive consciousness-raising, the transcripts of the small-group and whole-class interactions were reviewed and summarized, with attention given to how analytic talk developed over the three lessons.

A qualitative summary will be presented here, with excerpts provided to illustrate how learners' explicit knowledge developed through the interactions.

Results

Research Question 1

The percentage of time that individuals engaged in analytic talk during small-group Co-construction over the three lessons varied from a low of .1% for Luis, to a high of 22.9% for Pepe. The other seven learners' rate of analytic talk ranged from 3.5% to 10.6%. Three of the four small groups were fairly similar in their percentages of time in analytic talk, with Group 1 at 14.1%, Group 3 at 10.9%, and Group 4 at 15.6%. Although Group 2 had the highest percentage of analytic talk (29.5%), even this group spent more than 70% of the allotted small-group time over three lessons not engaged in analytic talk[2]. The learners in all of the small groups seemed to work to complete the task as quickly as possible; when they felt that they had completed the task (i.e., formulated a grammatical rule), they moved on to unrelated topics and generally did not explore possible alternatives. Because of the complexity of the target structure, however, there were often difficulties in interpreting and explaining the input that remained unresolved. Rather than explore these issues, learners generally used the remaining time to interact socially on unrelated matters.

For the whole-class discussion, the teacher performed the most analytic talk, speaking 28.2% of the time. As during the small-group phase, Pepe had the highest rate of analytic talk during the whole-class follow-ups, speaking 9.9% of the time. Three learners – Jesus, Luis, and Alberto – contributed virtually no analytic talk during whole-class interactions, while the analytic talk contributed by Diego, Raquel, Jose, Clara, and Lucas varied from 1.5% to 5.8%. The five other learners in the class who were not the focus of this study combined to contribute 4.3% of the total analytic talk in whole-class discussion. These figures appear in Table 2.

The correlation analysis that was conducted to compare the amount of individuals' analytic talk in the small-group and the whole-class Co-construction interactions indicated a strong and statistically significant relationship ($r = 0.883$; $p < .01$, 1-tailed). In other words, those learners that engaged in analytic talk during the small-group work also tended to engage in analytic talk during the whole-class discussion. This correlation is apparent in observing the histogram in Figure 2. Pepe was the learner who had the highest rate of analytic talk in both the small-group Co-construction (22.9%) and the whole-class discussion (9.9%). Luis had a negligible rate of analytic talk in both the small-group

---

2. Three of the four groups (groups 1, 3, and 4) consisted of two learners each, while group 2 consisted of 3 learners. This might have affected the dynamics of the group, and it is difficult to directly compare the rates between group 2 and the other groups.

Table 2. Percentage of available time in analytic talk

Group	Participant	Small-group co-construction	Whole-class discussion
1	Diego	5.8%	2.5%
1	Raquel	8.3%	2.6%
2	Jesus	6.5%	0%
2	Luis	0.1%	0.2%
2	Pepe	22.9%	9.9%
3	Alberto	3.5%	0%
3	Jose	7.4%	5.8%
4	Clara	5.0%	1.5%
4	Lucas	10.6%	2.8%
	Others	n.a.	4.3%
	Teacher	n.a.	28.2%

Co-construction and the whole-class discussion. The only learners that seemed to differ in their rate of analytic talk were Jesus and Alberto. While they engaged in moderate levels of analytic talk in the small-group Co-construction (6.5% and 3.5% respectively), neither of them engaged in any analytic talk during the whole-class discussion.

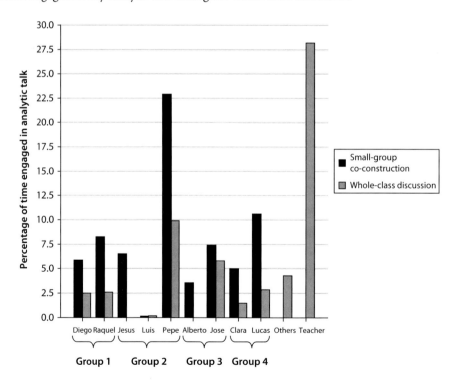

Figure 2. Histogram of individual participants' rate of analytic talk in the small-group Co-construction and the whole-class discussion

Research Question 2

As reported in the results for Research Question 1, there was a widespread tendency among small groups to conclude the Co-construction task as early as possible and turn to other topics. However, there was also ample transcript evidence of dialogic interaction among learners involving analytic talk. Indeed, while Figure 2 shows that all groups tended to have one participant who produced more analytic talk than the other, there was considerable evidence of the participants often revising and incorporating each other's contributions into their analytic thinking.

Meanwhile, the whole-class follow-ups demonstrated both the potential and limitations of teacher contributions to learner analyses. Across the gamut of learner and teacher contributions, a picture emerged of participants drawing on, and at times stretching the limits of, existing metalinguistic knowledge to interpret new data. When existing metalinguistic concepts reached their limit, informal language was often used to fill any gaps. At times, however, the limits of both the learners' and the teacher's existing metalinguistic knowledge made it difficult to achieve a descriptively adequate metalinguistic rule, particularly in the case of inchoative *se*. Still, through Co-construction, new knowledge of an unfamiliar grammatical structure emerged as extended existing knowledge combined with novel uses of informal language. The examples that follow in the lesson-by-lesson summaries illustrate this process.

Lesson 1

The goal of the first Co-construction task was to derive an explanation for *se* based on a comparison of sentences describing the restaurant reviewer's direct experiences with those describing "restaurants in general." As Figure 1 showed, sorting the sentences in this way resulted in transitive sentences with direct and indirect object pronouns being put in the left column and *se* sentences being put on the right. While working toward an explanation for *se*, the data showed the starting point in most small groups to be existing metalinguistic knowledge about past-tense (preterit) verb suffixes, object pronouns, and reflexives, all of which had been the focus of prior explicit instruction. In a manner consistent with Vygotsky's (1987:49) view of words and their meanings as tools for both thinking and social interaction, these known concepts mediated learners' interpretation of the data in the two columns. To illustrate, (4) shows how Clara and Lucas in Group 4 began by focusing on the pronouns *me* and *se* in both columns and the preterit verb suffixes.

(4)   a.   Clara: Well it seems to be that that's like, *me –aron* and *me –ier, me –ieron*. Cuz that's like –

      b.   Lucas: All are in preterit anyway. All are just preterit. Right?

      c.   Clara: Yeah but it's not like the *yo* form… Just kidding. I don't know what I'm talking about.

      d.   Lucas: That's cuz they're saying 'they,' 'they offered me.'

      e.   Clara: Yeah, yeah.

      f.   Lucas: I think that's just the…pronoun

      g.   Clara: Cuz she's like talking about her experience.

Thus, Clara in line (a) suggested a relationship in the reviewer's direct experiences between the appearance of the first-person object pronoun *me* with the third-person plural subject suffixes *-aron* and *-ieron*. After Lucas focused on the past-tense verb features in (b), Clara in (c) then appeared to imply that the sentences could not be reflexive, given that the object pronoun *me* did not correspond with a first-person subject suffix on the verb, which would agree with the first-person subject pronoun, *yo*. It seems that she intended to draw a contrast between the non-reflexive sentence with *me* and those with a possibly reflexive *se* in the next column. Clara then followed with a hedge of uncertainty, and Lucas in (d) gave a correct interpretation of the transitive sentences, to which Clara made a semantic link in (g) to their common function of describing the reviewer's direct experience. Their analysis ended shortly after this excerpt with a conclusion that *se* simply referred to the restaurants in general, while *me* referred to the author's experiences. The other groups' recordings show a similar focus on past tense, pronoun meaning, and reflexivity, none of which appeared to fully account for the presence of *se* in the impersonal sentences.

During the whole class follow-up illustrated in (5), the teacher first solicited summaries of the small group discussions and then followed with questions designed to lead learners toward a rule linking *se* with impersonal expressions. After noting that the transitive sentences were in the past tense while the *se* sentences were in the present, she prompted learners to identify the subject of the *se* sentences. Here and throughout the data, it was apparent that the descriptive adequacy of the resulting metalinguistic rules was limited by the teacher and learners' conflation of the syntactic term *subject* with the semantic term *agent*. Nonetheless, the teacher's prompt in line (a) to identify the "subject" of one of the impersonal *se* sentences, which was clearly not "María" the restaurant reviewer, appeared to bring learners' experience outside the classroom to bear on the analysis.

(5) a.   T: So do we have any ideas on who's the subject of "*se dice….que los dos restaurantes?*³" Diego?

    b.   Diego: Is it just some other person?

    c.   Raquel: Narrator.

    d.   T: So, it's kind of like – [sigh] Do you – so, like is there a subject?

    e.   José: So is she acting like Julius Cesar?

    f.   T: Is it possible –

    g.   Oscar: Julius Cesar has ID.

    h.   T: Do you think it's possible that there's no sen – that there's no subject?

    i.   José: Talks abut himself in the third person

    j.   Several: No

    k.   Raquel: That's not a sentence

    l.   Pepe: Maybe she means this just in like the sense of, like, "they say" or like "people say" or something like that.

    m. T: [smiling] What do you guys think?

---

3.   *Se dice que los dos restaurantes…* = "they say that the two restaurants…"

Thus, Diego suggested in (b) that the impersonal subject might be "some other person"; Raquel speculated in (c) that it might be a narrator; and José, possibly drawing on prior experience with classical literature, wondered in (f) and (j) whether, like Julius Caesar, the reviewer might be referring to herself in the third person. Interestingly, Oscar, who frequently made off-task comments during whole-class interactions, appeared to refute that analysis in line (g) with the observation that Julius Caesar has ID, possibly implying that such a referent would be too concrete. When the teacher asked in (h) whether it was possible that the sentence might have no subject, again the influence of prior metalinguistic knowledge appeared, as several learners' gave negative responses in (j) and Raquel referred in (k) to a common prescriptive grammatical rule that every sentence must have a subject. Finally, in (l), Pepe suggested an interpretation for impersonal *se* that quite closely aligned with the teacher's goals for the task. She signaled her assent in (m) with a smile and an appeal to others for approval.

Lesson 2

The goal of the second Co-construction task was to explain the differing subject-verb agreement patterns in the *chiles rellenos* story, where transitive, active-voice sentences depicting the cook's actions contrasted with impersonal, passive *se* sentences in the recipe. Specifically, the cook's actions were always depicted with third person singular verb agreement, and the *se* sentences varied between third person singular and plural verbal suffixes, depending on the ingredients being used. Again, the transcripts showed creative applications and extensions of prior metalinguistic knowledge to complete the task.

In Group 2, the learners coped with the task by saying that the "subject" was "general" or "unspecified," and that the verb therefore agreed with the direct object. Pepe developed this idea, and then a group-wide debate ensued over how best to interpret the *se* sentences. Jesús and Olivia, a classmate from a neighboring group, claimed that they were a kind of command, whereas Pepe disagreed, but admitted that he was not sure how best to interpret *se* other than as a signal that the verb was "in general form" and therefore agreed with the direct object. The conclusion of their analysis is shown in (6).

(6) a. Pepe: I'm just calling it like "in general" because it's always in third person. No matter what, this general form and the conjugation, whether it's singular third person or –

　　 b. Olivia: plural –

　　 c. Pepe: plural third person, depends on the direct object. The actual like, *narración*, the narration, what they're saying here, it could be, as I said, um, "*Tú pones los chiles*[4]" but here [referring to the recipe] it would still be "*se ponen.*"

　　 d. Jesús: Right cuz the recipe it's not, it doesn't care who's making it.

---

4. *Tú pones los chiles* = "You (specific) put the peppers."

(6) e. Pepe: Yeah. Exactly. And it just changes based on the direct object.
    f. Jesús: But what it's like, talking about over here [referring to the recipe], the direct object or whatever, does matter.

The informal terminology used to codify the non-agentive semantics of sentences with *se*, coupled with the conflation of the terms *subject* and *direct object* with *agent* and *patient* was further reinforced during whole-class follow-up. After prompting the class to identify precisely the subject of the sentences in the recipe, as in (5) from Lesson 1, the interaction concluded with Pepe offering his direct object analysis and the teacher affirming it. Thus, while successfully guiding learners through an explicit rule for a complex L2 structure, the teacher did not push a distinction between the syntactic and semantic terms that would have enhanced the descriptive adequacy of the rule.

Lesson 3

In the third lesson, the Co-construction task required learners to find 14 sentences containing 7 different verbs in the report on a rainstorm and earthquake in Chile. Half the sentences used *se* to depict inchoative, "spontaneous" events during the disaster – such as breaking, dropping, closing, and opening – while the other half used the same verbs transitively to depict the actions of individuals. Learners had to identify the "doers" of the actions in both lists and explain the use of *se*. This time, however, many turned to improvised, informal terminology to account for non-agentive, spontaneous events rather than the previously-known metalinguistic terms used earlier. Groups 1 and 4 proposed that *se* was used when a thing rather than a person caused the event. However, Lucas and Clara in Group 4 were confused by a transitive sentence describing how the inanimate rain had soaked one character's house. Meanwhile, in Group 2, Pepe built on his earlier analysis by suggesting that, because the verb agreed with the direct object when *se* was used, this was a kind of reflexive, where the direct object acted upon itself. Finally, in Group 3, José and Alberto likewise echoed conclusions from the previous lesson, using informal language to assert that when the verb is "specified" or "defined," it agrees with the subject, but when it is not, *se* is used and the verb "follows the direct object."

    In the whole class follow-up, the teacher again directed learners to compare the two lists of sentences, this time identifying the "doer" in each case. When the teacher inquired about the transitive sentences, Lucas alluded to his confusion over the absence of *se* when the inanimate rain caused one of the events, but the topic was not taken up. After the teacher turned to inchoative *se* as shown in (7), Pepe again offered an analysis in line (b) that demonstrated not only how previous knowledge and improvised terminology may be stretched to account for unfamiliar phenomena, but also how such formulations of new knowledge may or may not be accessible to other discourse participants.

(7) a. T: What's going on in the other column with the verbs *sin* – , the verbs that have se?

   b.   Pepe: Um, even though technically you could say that what did it is the storm, in all cases if we're just looking to find subjects and verbs. We're saying that the thing that, the doer is, like the thing it happened to. So like the win – *las ventanas se abieron* – so like the windows opened. It's the *windows* that opened, like they didn't do it of their own volition, but that's still what we're saying, *the windows opened.*

   c.   Several: [laughing and giggling]

   d.   T: What, did, does that make sense to you guys?

   e.   Several: Yeah, yeah. Uh-huh.

   f.   T: Does that, Are you sure? No?

   g.   Raquel: Student talk.

   h.   T: Does that make sense? Can anyone – I think you're on to a good idea. Can anyone, does anyone think they get what he's saying but have a different way of saying it?

   i.   Olivia: No [laughter]

   j.   Batista: Yeah, Pepe why don't you dumb it down a little bit?

   k.   T: Cuz I – No, I mean, it hardly makes sense to me. [laughs, students continue giggling] I just wanna make sure that everyone gets it. Shhhhhhh. Okay let's hear what he says

   l.   Pepe: The object is verbing itself

   m.   T: The object is verbing itself?

   n.   Jesús: Ah that makes sense

   o.   T: [chuckling] Okay well maybe we should –

   p.   Raquel: Actually, I understood that one.

Clearly, in line (b), Pepe utilized what Kozulin (1995) calls "everyday" concepts to articulate a fairly accurate, non-technical description of inchoativity as a non-volitional event, even though he labeled a window flung open during the storm as the "doer" of the event. When both the teacher and other learners responded in lines (c)–(k) with impressed laughter and appeals for a more accessible explanation, Pepe's response in (l) again casts the semantics of inchoativity informally, as an object that is "verbing" itself. With his classmates then expressing comprehension in lines (n) and (p), it is apparent that the application of informal language to account for a novel concept varied considerably in its accessibility to others. As both the teacher and learners marshaled existing metalinguistic knowledge and informal language to explain *se*, it can be said that their formulations of explicit knowledge were at times only *subjectively accessible* to others who shared similar background knowledge and could understand the sense in which it and the informal terminology were being stretched to cover this unfamiliar linguistic phenomenon.

Discussion

Research question 1

Regarding research question 1, the results suggest that there was considerable variability in the amounts of analytic talk among individuals during both small-group and whole-class Co-construction. The learners in Group 2 spent a much larger percentage of the time considering alternatives and exploring different grammatical rule possibilities than the learners in Groups 1, 3, and 4. Storch (2002) categorized dyadic interaction patterns based on degrees of "equality," or the extent to which each learner had control over the task, and "mutuality," or how engaged each learner was with his or her partner. In the current study, another dimension could be added to Storch's classification: commitment to task. The learners in Group 2 exhibited a much deeper commitment to fulfilling the task demands than the learners in Groups 1, 3, and 4.

In the whole-class discussions, the data again showed great variability in the amount of analytic talk. Not surprisingly, the teacher had the highest amount. The teacher's role here was to engage the students in the task, push them to actually construct a rule through guided induction, and provide expert assistance. Of the nine learners studied, six engaged in a substantial rate of whole-class analytic talk, while three engaged in virtually none.

In addition, there was a high correlation ($r = .883$) between the amount of an individual's analytic talk in both small-group and whole-class interactions. Thus, learners who engaged in extensive small-group analytic talk also engaged in extensive analytic talk during whole-class follow-ups. On the one hand, it is logical that there would be a strong correlation between the two steps of Co-construction: It seems likely that talkative and assertive students would be so in both small-group and whole-class settings. On the other hand, such a high correlation can be interpreted as surprising since one core belief of communicative and task-based language teaching is that working in small groups, as opposed to teacher-centered class discussions, allows shy or less assertive learners the chance to speak and interact in a safer and less face-threatening context. Yet the "quiet" learners in this study did not verbally contribute to the small-group Co-construction more than they did in the whole class discussion. This supports the findings of Cao and Philp (2006) and de Saint Leger and Storch (2009), who found that while learners were more comfortable interacting in small-groups than in whole-class settings, the personalities, assertiveness, and language competence of individuals that shaped the small-group dynamic strongly affected interactional patterns and learners' willingness to communicate (see also Batstone & Philp, this volume).

The data also indicate that using the L1 during the consciousness-raising task was useful for these learners. Swain and Lapkin (2000) found that even when learners were expected to use the L2 in small-group interactions, they often resorted to the L1 when interactions focused on form. These learners were expected to use their L1 during Co-construction, and it seems unlikely that they would have been able to analyze the target form at the same level in the L2, as shown in Scott and de la Fuente's (2008) study, as well as numerous others (e.g., Brooks & Donato 1994; Brooks, Donato & McGlone 1997), where learners' use of the L1 for L2 grammatical analysis proved advantageous for learning.

Research question 2

Regarding research question 2, which examined how participants contributed to each other's metalinguistic knowledge through inductive consciousness-raising in both small-group and whole-class interactions, the data provided strong evidence that this task promoted useful interactional patterns among learners for developing explicit metalinguistic knowledge of the target form. From a cognitive perspective, the data shows that small group interactions promoted and even required learners to discuss the linguistic examples and construct a rule for the target form in a manner consistent with the aims of instructional consciousness-raising. The data clearly indicate that the task was challenging for all of the learners, and required that they utilize intellectual effort in constructing a grammatical rule.

Interpreting the data from a socio-cultural perspective, there is also ample evidence that the task was useful for learners. In the small-group task, and to a lesser extent in the whole-class discussion, it is evident that learners were "thinking aloud" to interpret the characteristics of the target form. To use Swain's (2000, 2006) terminology, the learners were "languaging," or verbalizing their metalinguistic thinking, in order to resolve a complex task in a manner consistent with Vygotsky's (1987) view of language as a cognitive tool that mediates learning. As van Lier (1996) notes, by explaining the form to someone else, the learner is presumably constructing a more coherent and clear representation of his or her own L2 knowledge. But what is particularly interesting here is the extent to which one learner's languaging may or may not be helpful for other learners in the group. There were numerous instances in the data where one learner gained a clearer understanding of the target form because of the verbalized analytic talk of his or her partner, which corresponds to Storch's (2002) "collaborative" and "expert/novice" dyadic patterns. However, there were also numerous instances in the data where one learner did not benefit from the analytic talk of his or her partner, whether due to a lack of commitment to the task, the cognitive complexity of the task, or a lack of descriptive adequacy in the partner's metalanguage when characterizing the target form. While there were instances of one learner claiming to benefit from another's non-technical explanation for a rather complex linguistic form, (e.g., the "verbing itself" example from (7), lines (n) and (p)), there were also numerous instances of learners not benefitting from the languaging of his or her partner. Again, although languaging seemed to be beneficial for the learner actually performing it, its usefulness for the partner seemed to vary. Hence, we conclude that one consequence of inductive, metalinguistic consciousness-raising is that improvised explanations may be only "subjectively accessible" to discourse participants who can understand the sense in which existing knowledge or novel applications of informal terms are being stretched to account for the new phenomenon.

In contrast, many of the learners did seem to benefit from the analytic talk of the teacher during the whole class discussion. In socio-cultural terms, the teacher was attuned to the less able learners' needs, and worked to make the information accessible by scaffolding. According to Vygotsky (1987), for these interactions to be effective, the teacher, as the more able discourse participant, has to be aware of the individual learner's needs and tailor her assistance to meet them. The teacher was able to provide expert guidance during the whole class discussion that was useful for the learners, similar to the findings of Toth (2008) and Van den Branden (1997). In contrast, in the small group Co-construction, learners engaging in analytic talk might not be competent enough in the language, or might not be attuned to their partner's particular learning needs, and thus were not able to provide the scaffolding necessary for maximal learning to occur.

Limitations and implications

The most obvious limitation of the present study is the small sample size, which included only one class of learners and one teacher. In addition, only three consecutive class periods were examined. Thus, the results cannot be generalized to a larger context. Another limitation of the study is that while the observations did take place in an intact classroom, only 9 of the 17 learners agreed to have their interactions recorded, and thus there is the possibility that the self-selection may have skewed the results. In addition, while efforts were made to minimize the intrusiveness of the data collection, learners knew that they were being audio- and video-recorded, and thus the results of the study may have been affected by the observer's paradox.

Nevertheless, the results of this study are informative and illuminating for interactional patterns among high school learners of Spanish. The types of consciousness-raising tasks suggested by Ellis (2002), designed to promote explicit knowledge of the target forms by the learners, are indeed similar to the languaging tasks advocated by Swain (2000, 2006), in which learners engage in verbalizing their thoughts during a complex task in order to internalize the information. The results of this study suggest that these types of tasks can promote useful and meaningful interaction among language learners.

References

Adair-Hauck, B., Donato, R., & Cumo-Johanssen, P. (2010). Using a story-based approach to teach grammar. In J. Shrum & E. Glisan (Eds.), *Teacher's handbook: Contextualized foreign language instruction* (4th edn., pp. 216–244). Boston: Heinle Cengage Learning.

Brooks, F., & Donato, R. (1994). Vygotskyan approaches to understanding foreign language learner discourse during communicative tasks. *Hispania, 77*, 262–274.

Brooks, F. B., Donato, R., & McGlone, J. V. (1997). When are they going to say "it" right? Understanding learner talk during pair-work activity. *Foreign Language Annals, 30*, 524–541.

Bruhn de Garavito, J. (1999). Adult SLA of SE constructions in Spanish. *Spanish Applied Linguistics, 3*, 247–296.

Cao, Y., & Philp, J. (2006). Interactional context and willingness to communicate: A comparison of behaviour in whole class, group and dyadic interaction. *System, 34*, 480–493.

Dekeyser, R. (1998). Beyond focus on form: Cognitive perspectives on practicing and learning second language grammar. In C. Doughty & J. Evans (Eds.), *Focus on form in classroom second language acquisition*. Cambridge: Cambridge University Press.

de Saint Leger, D., & Storch, N. (2009). Learners' perceptions and attitudes: Implications for willingness to communicate in an L2 classroom. *System, 37*, 269–285.

Donato, R. (1994). Collective scaffolding in second language learning. In J. Lantolf & G. Appel (Eds.), *Vygotskian approaches to second language learning*. Norwood, NJ: Ablex.

Doughty, C. (2001). Cognitive underpinnings of focus on form. In P. Robinson (Ed.), *Cognition and second language instruction* (pp. 206–257). Cambridge: Cambridge University Press.

Ellis, R. (2002). Grammar teaching–practice or consciousness-raising? In J. Richards & W. Renandya (Eds.), *Methodology in language teaching: An anthology of current practice* (pp. 167–174). Cambridge: Cambridge University Press.

Fassnacht, C., & Woods, D. (2009). Transana (Version 2.42) [Software]. Madison, WI: Wisconsin Center for Education Research, School of Education, University of Wisconsin-Madison.

Gass, S. (2003). Input and interaction. In C. Doughty & M. Long (Eds.), *The handbook of second language acquisition* (pp. 224–256). Malden, MA: Blackwell.

Hulstijn, J. (2002). Towards a unified account of the representation, processing and acquisition of second language knowledge. *Second Language Research, 18*, 193–223.

Krashen, S. (1985). *The input hypothesis: Issues and implications*. New York, NY: Longman.

Kozulin, A. (1995). The learning process: Vygotsky's theory in the mirror of its interpretations. *School Psychology International, 16*, 117–129.

Lantolf, J., & Thorne, S. (2006). *Sociocultural theory and the genesis of second language development*. Oxford: Oxford University Press.

Lee, J. (2000). *Tasks and communicating in language classrooms*. New York, NY: McGraw-Hill.

Lockhart, C., & Ng, P. (1995). Analyzing talk in ESL peer response groups: Stances, functions, & content. *Language Learning, 45*, 605–655.

Long, M. (1996). The role of the linguistic environment in second language acquisition. In W. Ritchie & T. Bhatia (Eds.), *Handbook of second language acquisition* (pp. 413–468). San Diego, CA: Academic Press.

Long, M., & Porter, P. (1985). Group work, interlanguage talk, and second language acquisition. *TESOL Quarterly, 19*, 207–228.

Mackey, A., Oliver, R., & Leeman, J. (2003). Interactional input and the incorporation of feedback: An exploration of NS-NNS and NNS-NNS adult and child dyads. *Language Learning, 53*, 35–66.

Paradis, M. (2009). *Declarative and procedural determinants of second languages*. Amsterdam: John Benjamins.

Pica, T. (1994). Research on negotiation: What does it reveal about second language learning conditions, processes and outcomes? *Language Learning, 44*, 493–527.

Reinhart, T., & Siloni, T. (2005). The lexicon-syntax parameter: Reflexivization and other arity operations. *Linguistic Inquiry, 36*, 389–436.

Rutherford, W., & Sharwood Smith, M. (1985). Consciousness-raising and universal grammar. *Applied Linguistics, 6*, 274–292.

Schmidt, R. (2001). Attention. In P. Robinson (Ed.), *Cognition and second language instruction* (pp. 3–32). Cambridge: Cambridge University Press.

Scott, V., & de la Fuente, M. (2008). What's the problem? L2 learners' use of the L1 during consciousness-raising, form-focused tasks. *Modern Language Journal, 92*, 100–113.

Storch, N. (2002). Patterns of interaction in ESL pair work. *Language Learning, 52*, 119–158.

Swain, M. (1998). Focus on form through conscious reflection. In C. Doughty & J. Williams (Eds.), *Focus on form in classroom second language acquisition* (pp. 64–81). Cambridge: Cambridge University Press.

Swain, M. (2000). The output hypothesis and beyond: Mediating acquisition through collaborative dialogue. In J. Lantolf (Ed.), *Sociocultural theory and second language learning* (pp. 97–114). Oxford: Oxford University Press.

Swain, M. (2006). Languaging, agency and collaboration in advanced language proficiency. In H. Byrnes (Ed.), *Advancing language learning: The contribution of Halliday and Vygotsky* (pp. 95–108). London: Continuum.

Swain, M., & Lapkin, S. (2000). Task-based second language learning: The uses of the first language. *Language Teaching Research, 4*, 251–274.

Tharp, R., & Gallimore, R. (1988). *Rousing minds to life: Teaching, learning, and schooling in social context.* Cambridge: Cambridge University Press.

Toth, P. (2000). The interaction of instruction and learner-internal factors in the acquisition of L2 morphosyntax. *Studies in Second Language Acquisition, 22*, 169–208.

Toth, P. (2008). Teacher- and learner-led discourse in task-based grammar instruction: Providing procedural assistance for L2 morphosyntactic development. *Language Learning, 58*, 237–283.

Van den Branden, K. (1997). Effects of negotiation on language learners' output. *Language Learning, 47*, 589–636.

Van Lier, L. (1996). *Interaction in the language curriculum: Awareness, autonomy and authenticity.* London: Longman.

Vygotsky, L. (1987). Thinking and speech. In R. Reiber & A. Carton (Eds.), *The collected works of L. S. Vygotsky, Volume 1, Problems in general psychology* (pp. 39–288). New York, NY: Plenum Press.

Watanabe, Y. (2008). Peer-peer interaction between L2 learners of different proficiency levels: Their interactions and reflections. *The Canadian Modern Language Review*, 605–635.

Chapter 6

Classroom interaction and learning opportunities across time and space

Rob Batstone and Jenefer Philp
University of Auckland

Our data for this chapter comprises recordings of 12 advanced adult language learners within a single English for Academic Purposes (EAP) classroom as they work collaboratively over repeated cycles of teacher fronted and related group work tasks. Our interest is in classroom interactions as they evolve across time and in both public and private spaces. As such, our approach owes much to recent ecological accounts of the role of interaction, emphasizing the complex and situated nature of learning (van Lier 2004). In doing so, we wish to pick up on aspects of classroom interaction that are missed in more taxonomic approaches to interaction analysis, but which are nevertheless important components of how classroom interaction contributes to learning.

Introduction

The idea that some form of negotiation is a particularly useful means through which the processes of second language learning are driven forward has been a major source of empirical research amongst second language acquisition scholars for at least the past 40 years (for review see Gass 2003; Long 1996; Mackey to appear; Pica to appear; and for a recent meta-analysis of this research see Mackey & Goo 2007). Notwithstanding the important contributions that experimental studies have made to our understanding of negotiation, we argue that there is a strong need for more studies which are classroom-based. As Spada and Lightbown (2009: 170) note, "interactional features (…) contribute to L2 use and development *when combined with* the multitude of linguistic (and other) behaviours in real classroom settings" (emphasis added). In our view, the nature of negotiation (like any form of interactive discourse) changes depending on the contexts in which it is situated. Classroom negotiation will inevitably be shaped by its social and pedagogic context in fundamental ways. In order to better understand interaction-driven learning, we need to pay more attention to the complexity of classroom interaction and its many facets.

We see the classroom as a place where interactions of many sorts are continually (as well as purposefully) ongoing. The data we examine in this chapter were recorded through the use of multiple lapel microphones, and as a result we had access to a great deal of 'chatter' which would not normally find its way to the researcher's published transcriptions. For example, we found instances of learners involved in negotiations that often overlapped with other peer conversations, and with the more public teacher-led work. And within these patterns, we found repeated cases where something said by the teacher would act as a trigger, indirectly leading one or more learners to notice something of personal significance, and to turn to another learner in order to voice their uncertainty. Most interesting to us was the fact that related negotiation sequences were repeated, with local variations, over time and across sequences of both teacher-led discourse and group work.

Two aspects of classroom interaction

Interaction across time

There are two themes which we use to focus our discussion of these data. The first theme has to do with time. Very often, the same learner will seek out repeated opportunities to elicit help from peers once a particular learning issue has been identified, a process which on occasion straddled two or three cycles of teacher-led discourse followed by group work followed by teacher-led discourse and so on. This was something of a contrast with much of the SLA work on negotiation and corrective feedback. A few experimental or quasi-experimental studies of task based interaction acknowledge the provision of recurrent intensive feedback on particular forms (Mackey & Philp 1998; McDonough 2004; Doughty & Varela 1998). The majority, however, depend heavily on the identification of single episodes within a task (e.g. Ellis, Basturkmen, & Loewen 2002; Loewen & Philp 2006; Lyster 2004; Oliver & Mackey 2003). In such studies, trigger and response follow one another in quick succession, so that the same participants tend to be involved (either receptively and/or productively) throughout the episode. Our data, in contrast, involve recurring episodes which build upon one another, often with a considerable time-lag between the initial trigger and subsequent re-encounters with the same language related problem, and with different participants coming into play at different times.

Interaction across public and private spaces

The second theme has to do with space. By 'space' we mean the physical and interpersonal contexts within which different kinds of talk occur. We distinguish two kinds of interaction: interaction that takes place in public spaces, and interaction that takes place in private spaces. Interaction in public spaces involves talk which is understood to be heard by everyone in the class (in the case of teacher-led discourse) or by all members of the group (in the case of group work). Interaction in private spaces involves talk that is intended only for a sub-set of the group, and in some cases this is made obvious by the use of L1. In our data we found many instances where private and public spaces were in use simultaneously, both in teacher-led discourse and in group work. In the case of teacher-led discourse, one learner may quietly request clarification of something the teacher has said from another learner sitting nearby, whilst the rest of the class presses ahead with the more public business at hand. In the case of group work a similar process occurs: two learners may turn aside from the other group members momentarily in order to resolve a problem before re-joining the whole group interaction. This aspect of classroom interaction is seldom discussed in descriptions of classroom discourse within applied linguistics. As Koole (2007: 487) notes, there is a tendency to:

> analyse classroom interaction as a *single* interactional activity with only *two* participating parties, the teacher and the class (…) classroom interaction is analysed not as a multi-party interaction, but as two-party interaction. Interaction between the teacher and any student is treated as interaction with 'the' student, and this interaction is tacitly treated as the only activity that is going on at that moment.

Yet, as Koole (2007: 488) points out, a number of studies (e.g. Bloome & Theodorou 1988, cited in Koole, Jones & Thornborrow 2004) recognize that classroom interaction is not binary, but is characterized by "simultaneously occurring activities, in particular, simultaneous talk." In a descriptive study of one lesson in a grade 6 mainstream classroom in New Zealand (Alton-Lee, Nuthall, & Patrick 1993), the authors contrast the "official and public" with the "unofficial and private" utterances of four children in the class. They found that private talk, which included both talk to self (i.e. private speech, see Ohta 2001), and talk to a peer, accounted for 86 percent of all utterances made by these children. Interestingly, little of the private talk was "off-task"; it predominantly involved engagement with curriculum content. One finding of this study was that private talk can serve to support engagement and learning during teacher-led discourse through strategies such as making associative links with prior knowledge, evaluating and validating emerging understandings and developing and extending knowledge constructs.

Looking at classroom interaction in terms of time and space helps us to reflect something of the emergent nature of learning (Larsen-Freeman 2006), and the complex, multi-participant nature of classroom interaction. In the data presented here, we find that learning opportunities are distributed both over time and in the numerous shifts between interaction in public space and interaction in private space.

Setting the scene

The data reported on in the current study were drawn from a class in a university-based language school in New Zealand. All data were collected by Yiqian Cao as part of her doctoral research on willingness to communicate (see Cao 2009). The students, after successful completion of the programme, attained a Foundation Certificate in English for Academic Purposes and those with conditional offers could gain entry to a tertiary degree. Prospective degrees included undergraduate and postgraduate programmes in Science, Commerce, Architecture and Arts faculties. The 12 participants were advanced proficiency learners who had studied English for over seven years and scored between 5.5 and 7 on IELTS. The majority of the class spoke Mandarin (8), other L1s represented were Korean (2), Cantonese (1), French (1), Thai (1) and German/Czech (1). Class members had lived in New Zealand from a month to over a year. At the time of the data collection, students were in the final module of the 20–30 week course. The classes were audiotaped two hours per week through the use of individual digital recorders with a lapel microphone, and observed by Yiqian Cao. Data for the current study consisted of all recordings and transcripts together with field notes of weekly observations for 17 weeks. The information given in Table 1, (adapted from Cao 2009:79), concerns the key participants that appear in the data extracts in this chapter. A team of four teachers taught the class, but the teacher in the extracts was a Russian woman who spoke several other languages including English. She had extensive experience in teaching English for Academic Purposes and was, at the time of the data collection, enrolled in a Masters degree programme in applied linguistics. Prior to teaching in New Zealand, she had been living in English speaking countries for over 15 years.

Table 1. Biodata for participants in the extracts

Code	Pseudonym	L1	Gender	Age	Time in NZ	Time studying English
J	Jun	Korean	Male	25	1–3 months	8 years
SH	SH	Arabic	Male	mid 20s	unknown	8 years
S	Sirikit	Thai	Female	25	1–3 months	15 years
Y	Yi-yun	Mandarin	Male	25	7–12 months	8 years
X	Xiao-qing	Mandarin	Female	23	4–6 months	10 years
C	Cai-Wei	Mandarin	Female	26	7–12 months	10 years

We examined all 17 hours of data, but, for the sake of clarity and economy of space, have chosen to present extracts taken from one lesson in week 4. We chose this lesson because it provided rich examples of patterns represented across the data set. Participants had been working together for some time and were used to working with the teacher and vice versa. The lessons were very largely theme-based. The extracts come from a lesson on immigration, involving a critical reading task on author voice preceded by pre-reading tasks, including extended discussions of humanitarian and economic migration.

Recurring opportunities to focus on form

Introduction

One pertinent difficulty with quasi-experimental approaches to the description of classroom negotiation, as noted earlier, is the tendency to code and present occurrences of negotiated interaction or corrective feedback atomistically, thereby losing any sense of how individual episodes might interrelate in the context of a particular lesson, and for whom.

In this section we want to redress this tendency by suggesting that individual episodes of negotiation build one upon another. We make this argument in two stages. We first present examples of how (at least for some learners) the process of learning specific form/function links has its origins. We demonstrate how these same learners re-encountered the same forms (and had opportunities to call for further explanation) numerous times, first with a lexical focus on form (where they puzzle through the meaning of terms such as 'immigration' and 'refugee') and subsequently by attempting to draw upon the forms appropriately as communicative resources as they join in classroom discussion about immigration.

The notion of learning as a process, which requires re-engaging with linguistic forms of one sort or another over time, is one that many scholars would subscribe to. Schmitt (2008: 338), for example, speaking of vocabulary acquisition notes that 'the more a learner engages with a new word, the more likely they are to learn it' and cites Craik and Lockhart's (1972) hypothesis: "the more attention given to an item, and the more manipulation involved with the item, the greater the chances it will be remembered."

Teacher-led interaction

We begin right at the start of the lesson. In (1), we see teacher-led work in which, as a pre-reading task, the teacher (T1 in the extracts) introduces the theme and works to establish some of the basic features and key lexical items related to it, largely through elicitation. Transcription conventions are provided in the Appendix.

(1) 1. T1: What I'd like to do is XX what are the differences between XX
    2. Y: And the page?
    3. J: Immigrant, refugee
    4. T1: Refugee, and what are the differences ((boards up immigrant, emigrant and refugee))
    5. S: ° Emigrate, immigrate °
    6. X: Immigrant is come to this country and immigrant (emigrant) is going out to another country, refugee means somebody couldn't stay at their country and this country receive their people with some=
    7. T1: =OK if I moved from the UK to NZ five years ago, so who am I in NZ?
    8. SS: Immigrant
    9. T1: I'm an immigrant
    10. J: Yes immigrant
    11. T1: OK, New Zealand take I think 180 people every year from UN's um camps, from troubled spots of the earth so who are these people?
    12. X: Refugee
    13. J: Refugee
    14. T1: Refugees, from the point of view of Britain, who am I?
    15. J: Emigrant
    16. T1: Yeah I emigrated, good, excellent

From lines 7 through to 15 we see the teacher working systematically through a series of concept questions designed to present to the class the difference between the terms 'immigrant' and 'emigrant' and the term 'refugee'. A cursory glance at this extract might lead us to think that the interaction between teacher and class is working according to plan: the teacher has no difficulty in finding ready answers to her questions, so that the 'public business' is brought to a successful conclusion with the teacher's positive feedback in line 16 ("Yeah I emigrated, good, excellent") suggesting that she takes these terms as understood.

What happened immediately afterwards is shown in (2). Contrary to the teacher's positive tone in line 16, student S privately expresses uncertainty about the distinction between these two lexical items. She receives an assurance from J that he will deal with her issue later on (as we shall see, J is often called upon as a resource in this way). Two lines later (20), SH indicates to the teacher a lack of familiarity with the term 'refugee'.

(2) 16. T1: Yeah I emigrated, good, excellent.
17. S: What's the differences ((asks J))
18. J: I'll talk I'll talk to you later
19. T1: We're going to talk about immigration
20. SH: What is refusion (refugee)?
21. T: Pardon?
22. SH: I didn't understand refusion (refugee)

A few turns later we find first J and then SA responding to SH's query (lines 39 and 40 in 3), and this is quickly followed by a separate four-turn exchange between ST and S where S also signals uncertainty about the term 'refugee' and ST attempts to clarify.

(3) 39. J: Because there's a war so they cannot live in there ((to SH))
40. SA: XX refugee is people can leave the country
41. S: What is it? ((to ST))
42. ST: What's that?
43. S: Refugee
44. ST: They come from XX some problem XX

Clearly there are different degrees of understanding here. J, SA and ST appear to have a prior understanding of the meaning of the term 'refugee'. S and SH, on the other hand, are struggling. Nonetheless there is some evidence that they have at least registered its existence as a form. In terms of learning, they have noticed this lexical item, but they have not yet begun to understand its meaning (Schmidt 2010).

As the teacher-led discourse continues, S finds further opportunities to call for assistance. In lines 55 and 56 of (4) we find her turning once again to J. Notice how this interaction between S and J takes place whilst the teacher is simultaneously asking the class as a whole "why do they leave their country, if they're refugees?" (line 46). Notice, too, how J's response straddles a total of eight turns, so that this whole elicitation/response sequence between S and J takes the form of a kind of elaborated aside which is interwoven with the more public business being pursued by the teacher:

(4) 46. T1: So why do they leave their country, if they're refugees, why do they XX
      47. A: Poor
      48. SH: The war
      49. J: The war or
      50. R: War yeah
      51. A: They're poor or
      52. J: For evades from the war
      53. T1: (writing on whiteboard) yes yes maybe …. But apart from war? ….. War
            XX here here maybe ….. crimes against humanity maybe …
      54. A: [Not enough food
      55. S: [Refugee? ((asks J))
      56. J: [Refugee is a person who escape from war or
      57. T1: What else can be a reason?
      58. J: So
      59. T1: for them to become refugees?
      60. A: Their country and
      61. T1: for them to become a refugee?
      62. SL: Political reasons
      63. J: (continuing his response to S) If if there a war in your country [you
            cannot live in your country
      64. T1: [political reasons yes, apart from political reasons, what else?
      65. J: So you want to go to another country ((to S))
      66. SL: Religion

Moments later, we find that S has shifted the focus of her attention. Whereas in Extracts (2), (3) and (4) she was focussing first on hearing the word refugee and then on eliciting a working definition, in (5) we find her moving ahead, addressing the same issue which the teacher is pursuing with the class as a whole: why refugees leave their country of origin and (of particular concern to S) the consequences if they should return:

(5) 68. T1: Yes and also economic reasons so if there's famine somewhere or
            drought no water
      69. S. [If you come back to your country, you will be catched you
            cannot go to another country
      70. A: [no food
      71. J: (To S?) Have to go other country because your country is very dangerous
      72. T1: Yep and also economic reasons X
      73. SH: And the second word is it different from the first one?
      74. S: [for that for the people if they go back they will die (to J)
            (a few turns later)
      75. S: I think we were talking about that? (quietly, to J)
      76. J: Yes boat people [in Vietnam is Refugees (responding to S)

S makes her first 'out loud' contribution (line 69), focusing on the dangers for refugees if they return to their countries of origin ("If you come back to your country, you will be catched"), before reiterating the same point moments later in an aside directed at J (75). It's possible that S's reiteration in line 74 is devised as a more 'private' move to elicit confirmation from J that she was on the right track when she 'went public' with her utterance in line 69 (largely ignored by the teacher). These excerpts reflect teacher-led discourse characterized by layers of related conversations in the dual spaces of public and private, rather than a single strand.

Group work interaction

Soon after the end of (5), the teacher draws this phase of whole-class interaction to a close and gives the class a theme to explore in group work concerning immigration: "a good thing or a bad thing?" It is in this group discussion task, where S works with three other learners, that she actively uses the term "refugee" (line 9), appearing to understand it.

(6) 1. R: I think half and half
     2. SK: XX but I think we should argue
     3. S: Why?
     4. SK: XX leader you know
     5. S: You close the country?
     6. SK: Close close, XX ((inaudible))
     7. S: Yeah communist, they're communist, I don't want to XX in that country
     8. SK: Yeah yeah yeah
     9. **S: Refugee, to be refugee, to be refugees from North Korea, why?**
    10. SK: It is not good to XX because
    11. R: No we just talk about [it is good or bad to um to immigrate the country because in ancient times

Meanwhile, in another group, student Y takes the opportunity to clarify a problem encountered in teacher-led discourse, a context in which Y had made no comment. Even now, during the comparative 'safety' of group work, Y chooses to express his uncertainty in an aside directed solely to C, and to do so in L1 (lines 6–12):

(7) 1. J: Think about what?
     2. SH: About immigration
     3. J: Immigration
     4. SH: I think it's a bad thing?
     5. SH: Like they're they're very intelligent people and their country need them, they leave their country and go somewhere
               [SH and J continue their discussion]
     6. Y: Which one, E-M-M, *dan ci* (word)?
     7. C: *Cha Zi Dian* (look it up in your dictionary)

8. Y: *zhe shi shen me yi si?* (What does this mean?)
9. C: *Di er ge shi, bi ru ni yi ming dao xin xi lan ma, yi ming guo lai, ran hou ni dui xin xi lan lai shuo, dui xin xi lan de guo jia lai shuo ni jiu shi* immigrate immigrate, *ran hou ni dui zhong guo yi min chu lai de hua, dui zhong guo na ge guo jia lai shou ni jiu shi* emi er emigrate.
10.   (The second one is, for extract, you migrated to NZ, you migrated, then from NZ's point of view, you immigrate immigrate, then from China's point of view, you emigrate)
11. Y: *Yi chu de* (emigrate)
12. C: *Dui dui dui* (Yes yes yes)
13. SH: And you what do you think?
14. **Y: What are you talking about?**
15. **SH: Immigration**
16. **J: Immigration**
17. Y: I think immigration is er a big thing for the for the country, for extract, for NZ, lots of immigration immigrate take lots of money to this country and make the NZ much more stronger

It's clear in line 6 that Y has still not come to terms with the lexical items 'emigration' and 'immigration'. Consequently, while J and SH continue a discussion about possible downsides to immigration, C provides – again sotto voce – a lengthy explanation in L1 which leads Y to provide the appropriate Mandarin for emigrate (line 11), a contribution which C strongly supports (line 12), suggesting perhaps that the penny has dropped. These interactions have an informal quality about them – they are somehow less 'on the record' than, say, interactions during teacher-led discourse where learners respond to teacher elicitations. And as was noted in the transcriptions, they are often said quietly in a whisper and are typically directed to just one learner rather than being cast for more general consumption. As such, the interaction between C and Y (just like the earlier examples we saw in Extracts 2 and 3) occurs in a more private space which is related to but also detached from the more public level of interaction (such as lines 1 to 5 in Extract 4) where learners' talk appears to be available for the whole group.

Extract (8) comes from the end of the group work between C, Y, SH and J. Here the four summarise their ideas on immigration. All four are now active in the discussion, and continue to manipulate the key terms, struggling somewhat with the form "get immigrant" (C, line 40), "call them immigration" (SH, line 41). They negotiate the idea of immigration, clarifying what *they* mean by the term: the potential to claim a passport.

(8) 40. C: So it's easy or hard for people to get immigrant
     41. SH: They are not they don't call them immigration because they don't come and see oh their XX a lot of them XX their life their working, they most go back after maybe ten years
     42. J: Not immigrate not immigrated

(8) 43. Y: Which mean which means we can't get your country's passport
     44. SH: Yeah
     45. J: Yeah that is immigration

Discussion

There are three key issues arising from this exploration of the data, each of which contributes to the complexity of classroom interaction: the use of public and private spaces, the emergence of learning over time; and the multi-participant nature of classroom interaction. In this final section we discuss each of these in turn.

Public and private spaces

Having examined numerous examples of interaction in both public and private spaces, in this section we first provide more elaborated definitions of each, then move on to consider learners' motives for constructing private spaces.

Defining public and private space

Interaction in public space is conducted openly. It is intended to be heard by everyone in the class (in the case of teacher-led discourse) or by everyone in the group (in the case of group-work). Public discourse has a regulatory function. It creates and maintains a sense of coherence. In teacher-led discourse it is used to explain, present, reinforce, set up and provide feedback. In group work, it serves to define the task and it involves learners working together to pursue the task goal (or their interpretation of it).

Interaction in private spaces, in contrast, is intended only for a sub-group, so that whilst public discourse is open, private discourse is closed. In our data, private talk deals with subject matter that arises incidentally in relation to matters initially presented through public talk. When private talk arises in the context of teacher-led discourse, it has a *compensatory* function in the sense that it enables learners to refer aspects of the more public discourse to their own learning needs. Teacher-led discourse is notoriously unreliable as a tool for engaging all learners in a class. Young (1992: 108) for example, in discussing how teachers may interpret one learner's contribution as representative of all, cites Edwards and Furlong (1978): "the interaction then proceeds *as though* the other pupils either knew or already shared the same and now *corrected* inadequacies as those who spoke (…) the interaction can be seen as the managed product of one of its participants." Private asides provide a tool by which learners can compensate for this rather 'hit and miss' quality to teacher-led discourse, enabling them to take and adapt from the teacher's public discourse material of relevance to their own immediate needs.

Reasons for seeking private space

There appear to be a number of reasons why participants chose private over public spaces to voice their uncertainties. Public discourse necessarily involves being heard by everyone present, and thus can be face-threatening (Carter & McCarthy 1994; Cortazzi & Jin 1996; Peng 2007), or culturally inappropriate if it interrupts the class. Yi-yun (Y), for example, in an interview following this Week 4 lesson, reflects a reticence to disturb the class for his own needs: "if the word is special word it's OK, I ask the teacher is OK, but some words is my is my problem, it's not, if I ask lots of words in class, I waste other students' time" (Cao 2009: 159). Private asides may offer a "safer" space, and the possibility of greater clarity if L1 is involved. Yi-yun reports reliance on L1 translation (see 7 above):

> If something I don't know for example I didn't pay attention to teacher's speaking, and I misunderstand something yeah I ask I ask classmates in Chinese, yeah because... I know it's quite bad but but it's Chinese can help me to understand it completely."
>
> (Cao 2009: 128)

Possibilities for future research: Private space and private speech

There are evident similarities between the ways in which learners in our data co-construct and make use of private spaces, and the ways in which learners exploit private speech in sociocultural theory. Private speech occurs when a learner uses language that is not intended for an addressee (Ohta 2001: 16). Typically produced in a quiet voice or a whisper, classroom-based private speech (like much of the talk occupying private spaces in our data) occurs whilst the rest of the class remain engaged on some more public activity. Private speech can take the form of a number of strategic actions, including mental rehearsal, imitation, and vicarious response. More broadly, private speech plays an important role in the internalization (i.e. learning) of a language in the broader sense, because it helps the learner to become more self-regulated. Drawing on the work of McCafferty (1994) and Appel and Lantolf (1994), Smith (1996, cited in Donato 2000: 31) defines private speech as "a verbal attempt to gain self-regulation during problem-solving tasks: distinguishable from the interpersonal communication into which it is often interwoven."

Clearly there are differences between private speech and our use of the term private space. One very noticeable difference is that private speech is most often directed at the self (and so intrapersonal), whereas all the examples in our data involve one learner asking another learner for guidance, and is therefore interpersonal. Nonetheless there is an interesting question here about whether private speech might usefully be seen as one (but not the only) form of language which takes place in private spaces and which is often triggered by something said in a more public space. If this is so, then we could argue that the kind of interpersonal 'puzzling through' in private spaces seen in our data may have a similar status in regard to learning that private speech does in sociocultural theory. In other words, interpersonal talk in a private space may also be a form of talk which is being 'worked through' in a facilitating context en route to being further internalized and becoming 'inner speech'. We clearly do not have the space here to pursue such arguments, but we would like to suggest that issues of privacy and (less explicitly) of public spaces already raised by work on private speech might usefully be extended to encompass other forms of language which nonetheless perform a similar overall learning function.

Time, emergence and learning trajectories

The second issue concerns the emergent nature of learning. Learning opportunities in our data are created through a kind of 'learning trajectory' where particular learners re-engage with particular forms over time, often with different interlocutors. A learning trajectory often has its roots in teacher-led discourse, when a form introduced in public talk triggers related negotiation in private space, as happened, for instance, in (2). As the lesson proceeds the same form recurs; initial puzzling over forms and their meanings gradually gives way to the more complex task of applying this knowledge in language use (through the discussion of social and political issues raised by talk of immigration and emigration).

Defining emergence

Speculatively, we suggest that the ways in which learning opportunities in our data recur across time and space might be seen as instances of emergence in action.

van Lier (2004:80) draws on ecological theory in order to explain how "emergence happens when relatively simple organisms or elements reorganize themselves into more complex, more intelligent systems", and he notes how emerging systems can be seen to take "different trajectories [which] can come about in different ways" (81).

Evidence of emergence in our data

Examples in our data of learners' re-engagements with language might be manifestations of emergence in progress for two reasons: because they recur over time, and because (at least for some learners) their recurrence goes hand-in-hand with a growing complexity. One example of this growing complexity has to do with the struggle to clarify the difference in perspective between talking about immigration and talking about emigration that is illustrated in (1) to (3). Recall that the issue of perspective was first introduced by the teacher in (1), then questioned and examined by individual students in (2) and (3). Subsequently, these same learners turned their hand to a more complex task – that of putting the terms to communicative use in discussion and debate. This transition, from first focusing more on specific forms and form/function pairs, then moving on to apply these terms through language use, can be seen in (7). Here we find SH – who has previously struggled to understand the term 'immigration' – trying to draw on this language as a communicative resource in response to the teacher's task: 'is immigration a good thing or a bad thing?'. But SH's comment in line 5 ("like they're very intelligent people and their country need them, they leave their country and go somewhere") suggests he is erroneously taking the perspective of 'emigrant departure' rather than of 'immigrant arrival'.

Y follows a similar learning trajectory through the L1 private interaction in (7), but she seems better able to apply the form (and hence to control and to regulate more effectively) in the ensuing discussion. Note, for example, how her L1 check (conducted in private space) is followed immediately by her call to re-enter the group's public space in line 15 ("what are you talking about?"), and then just two turns later we find her correctly using the term whilst also making her own critical point ("I think immigration is er a big thing for the for the country, for example, for New Zealand, lots of immigration immigrate take lots of money to this country and make the New Zealand much more stronger").

Both in the case of SH and of Y, we see evidence of how exploiting a private space (primarily to focus on individual forms and meanings) then becomes a resource for engaging in a more complex exchange of views. This kind of trajectory (from focusing on form to tentatively applying it as a resource in the more elaborate and coordinated process of language use) jibes well with the notion that emergence evolves gradually. One can readily discern Y's experience of first focusing on form and then incorporating these forms into the much more complex processes of language use in van Lier's (2004: 5) discussion of emergence. He describes language learning:

> not as gradual, linear acquisition, but as emergence. Emergence happens when relatively simply elements combine together to form a higher-order system. The whole [*in our case, managing all the interrelated skills required for effective performance in language use*] is not only more than the sum of its parts, it is of a different nature than the parts. The new system is on a different scale, and has different meanings and patterns of functioning than the simpler ingredients [*in our case, the form and meaning of key lexical items such as 'immigrant' and 'emigrant'*] from which it emerged (italicized comments added).

Multiple participation

The third issue concerns the contribution of different participants within the class to learning. Language classrooms involve multi-participant interaction, with not one but layers of related interactions working in parallel. What happens in teacher-led discourse may trigger questions or deliberations for an individual who, not ready to publically expose his or her confusion, or to interrupt the teacher-led discourse, will seek instead the help of a neighboring peer. Thus problematic forms, lexical or syntactic, appear again and again in conversations in different spaces and among different participants, and continue to be re-negotiated before evidence of clear understanding begins to appear. In order to understand processes of learning through interaction, we need to recognise the interrelated contributions of participants (teachers, peers, friends) over time, and that public talk and private asides, teacher-led discourse and group work, each play a part in the kinds of affordances provided.

In our data we see a range of ways in which learners assist one another. In (2), (4) and (5), S asks J, then ST, for help in private asides. In (7), Y, who is Chinese, asks a fellow

Chinese for help and they work it out in Mandarin. Just as public and private talk function in complementary ways, it appears that learners make choices about who to ask help from and when. Thus when it comes to learning through interaction, classroom participants (teacher, peers, friends) provide particular and distinctive types of contributions: a peer may be a safe sounding board for ideas yet in draft, or for answers to questions that are too embarrassingly obvious to ask a teacher, while the teacher can provide an authoritative answer when needed. In this classroom we see participants contributing in different ways: the teacher may provide "seeding" in teacher-led discourse through the use of target forms, whether lexical or grammatical, but it is in the private safer space of peer interaction that some learners take the opportunity to query new forms and try them out. This may be (as we have suggested) because it affords less public exposure and threat to face, or because it allows time to work things out without bothering the teacher or fellow class members. It is likely that participants make the contributions they do because of their particular relationship to one another (Philp, Walter & Basturkmen 2010). The social nature of peer interaction and its significance for L2 learning is an aspect of interaction seldom investigated in adult classrooms (for work among child L2 learners in mainstream and reception classrooms, see e.g. Cekaite 2008; Philp & Duchesne 2008; Toohey 2000; Willett 1995).

Conclusion, limitations and future research

In this chapter we have sought to reflect upon the complexity of classroom interaction, and particularly upon aspects of this complexity that are seldom considered within an interactionist framework. Through a qualitative approach to analysis of extended stretches of classroom interaction, we considered the nature of this interaction across space and time. We identified continuities in interaction between teacher-led discourse and group work and across public and private spaces. A more comprehensive picture of classroom discourse was realized through use of individual lapel microphones for participants, enabling us to follow the emergence of learning between individuals, and providing a useful departure from the quantitative practice of coding individual episodes within a task. A drawback to this study is low generalisability, given that only one classroom was examined, and although 17 weeks of data were available to us, for the sake of clarity and economy of space, we chose to illustrate with data from just one class (albeit rich and representative of the whole). In the excerpts, learners chose to focus on lexical form, yet the data also contained examples of learners engaging with grammatical forms, not reported here due to space. Perhaps the main limitation of this study has to do with introspective data. Although we made use of stimulated recall interview and student journal data, these data were originally intended for a study on willingness to communicate, and were insufficient for our purposes. Further research on the role of teacher and peer interaction in L2 learning could profit from the use of such introspective techniques, specifically directed at exploring the relationships between participants and their perceptions of self and others' contributions to learning (Batstone 2010; Ortega 2007; Philp & Mackey 2010).

A multitude of factors work in tandem in the process of classroom interaction (N. Ellis & Larsen-Freeman 2006; van Lier 2004), and any one methodology or perspective necessarily presents only a partial view, highlighting some aspects to the exclusion of others. It is our hope that further longitudinal descriptive work on classroom interaction and learning, across time and space, will add to the developing picture created over years of interaction research.

References

Alton-Lee, A., Graham, N., & Patrick, J. (1993). Reframing classroom research: A lesson from the private world of children. *Harvard Educational Review, 63,* 50–83.

Appel, G., & Lantolf, J. P. (1994). Speaking as mediation: A study of LI and L2 text recall tasks. *The Modern Language Journal, 78,* 437–452.

Batstone, R. (2010). Issues and options in sociocognition. In R. Batstone (Ed.), *Sociocognitive perspectives on language use and language learning* (pp. 3–23). Oxford: Oxford University Press.

Bloome, D., & Theodorou, E. (1988). Analyzing teacher-student and student-student discourse. In J. I. Green & J. O. Harker (Eds.), *Multiple perspectives in classroom discourse* (pp. 217–248). Norwood, NJ: Ablex.

Cao, Y. (2009). *Understanding the notion of interdependence, and the dynamics of willingness to communicate.* Unpublished PhD dissertation, University of Auckland, New Zealand.

Carter, R., & McCarthy, M. (1994). *Language as discourse: Perspectives for language teaching.* London: Longman.

Cekaite, A. (2008). Developing conversational skills in a second language: Language learning affordances in a multiparty classroom setting. In J. Philp, R. Oliver, & A. Mackey (Eds.), *Second language acquisition and the younger learner. Child's play?* (pp. 105–130). Amsterdam: John Benjamins.

Cortazzi, M., & Jin, L. (1996). Cultures of learning: Language classrooms in China. In H. Coleman (Ed.), *Society and the language classroom* (pp. 169–206). Cambridge: Cambridge University Press.

Craik, F. I. M., & Lockhart, R. S. (1972). Levels of processing: A framework for memory research. *Journal of Verbal Learning and Verbal Behaviour, 11,* 671–684.

Donato, R. (2000). Sociocultural contributions to understanding the foreign and second language classroom. In J. Lantolf (Ed.), *Sociocultural theory and second language learning* (pp. 27–50). Oxford: Oxford University Press.

Doughty, C., & Varela, E. (1998). Communicative focus on form. In C. Doughty & J. Williams (Eds.), *Focus on form in classroom second language acquisition* (pp. 114–138). Cambridge: Cambridge University Press.

Edwards, A. D., & Furlong, V. J. (1978). *The language of teaching: Meaning in classroom interaction.* London: Heinemann Educational.

Ellis, N. C., & Larsen-Freeman, D. (2006). *Language emergence: Implications for applied linguistics –* Introduction to the Special Issue. *Applied Linguistics 27,* 558–589

Ellis, R., Basturkmen, H., & Loewen, S. (2002). Doing focus on form. *System, 30,* 419–432.

Gass, S. (2003). Input and interaction. In C. Doughty & M. Long (Eds.), *The handbook of second language acquisition* (pp. 224–255). Malden, MA: Blackwell.

Jones, R., & Thornborrow, J. (2004). Floors, talk and the organization of classroom activities. *Language in Society, 44,* 399–423.

Koole, T. (2007). Parallel activities in the classroom. *Language and Education, 21,* 487–515.

Lantolf, J. P., & Thorne, S. L. (2006). *Sociocultural theory and the genesis of second language development.* Oxford: Oxford University Press.

Larsen-Freeman, D. (2006). The emergence of complexity, fluency, and accuracy in the oral and written production of five Chinese learners of English. *Applied Linguistics, 27,* 590–619.

Loewen, S., & Philp, J. (2006). Recasts in the adult L2 classroom: Characteristics, explicitness and effectiveness. *Modern Language Journal, 90,* 536–556.

Long, M. (1996). The role of the linguistic environment in second language acquisition. In W. C. Ritchie & T. K. Bhatia (Eds.), *Handbook of second language acquisition* (pp. 413–468). San Diego, CA: Academic Press.

Lyster, R. (2004). Differential effects of prompts and recasts in form-focused instruction. *Studies in Second Language Acquisition, 20,* 51–81.

Mackey, A. (Forthcoming). *Input, interaction and corrective feedback in L2 learning.* Oxford: Oxford University Press.

Mackey, A. & Goo, J. (2007). Interaction research in SLA: A meta-analysis and research synthesis. In A. Mackey (Ed.), *Conversational interaction in second language acquisition: A collection of empirical studies* (pp. 407–452). Oxford: Oxford University Press.

Mackey, A., & Philp, J. (1998). Conversational interaction and second language development: Recasts, responses, and red herrings? *The Modern Language Journal, 82,* 338–356.

McCafferty, S. G. (1994). The use of private speech by adult ESL learners at different levels of proficiency. In J. P. Lantolf & G. Appel (Eds.), *Vygotskian approaches to second language research* (pp. 117–134). Norwood, NJ: Ablex.

McCarthy, M., & Carter, R. (1994). *Language as discourse: Perspectives for language teachers.* New York, NY: Longman.

McDonough, K. (2004). Learner-learner interaction during pair and small group activities in a Thai EFL context. *System, 32,* 207–224.

Ohta, A. (2001). *Second language acquisition processes in the classroom: Learning Japanese.* Mahwah, NJ: Lawrence Erlbaum Associates.

Oliver, R., & Mackey, A. (2003). Interactional context and feedback in child ESL classrooms. *The Modern Language Journal, 87,* 519–33.

Ortega, L. (2007). Second language learning explained? SLA across nine contemporary theories. In B. VanPatten & J. Williams (Eds.), *Theories in second language acquisition: An introduction* (pp. 225–250). Mahwah, NJ: Lawrence Erlbaum Associates.

Peng, J. (2007). Willingness to communicative in the Chinese EFL classroom: A cultural perspective. In J. Liu (Ed.), *English language teaching in China: New approaches, perspectives and standards* (pp. 33–59). London: Continuum.

Philp, J., & Duchesne, S. (2008). When the gate opens: The interaction between social and linguistic goals in child second language development. In J. Philp, R. Oliver, & A. Mackey (Eds.), *Second language acquisition and the young learner. Child's play?* (pp. 83–104). Amsterdam: John Benjamins.

Philp, J., & Mackey, A. (2010). Interaction research: What can socially informed approaches offer to cognitivists (and vice versa)? In R. Batstone (Ed.), *Sociocognitive perspectives on language use and language learning* (pp. 210–228). Oxford: Oxford University Press.

Philp, J., Walter, S., & Basturkmen, H. (2010) Peer interaction in the foreign language classroom: what factors foster a focus on form? *Language Awareness, 19,* 261–280.

Pica, T. (to appear). From input, output and comprehension to negotiation, evidence, and attention: An overview of theory and research on learner interaction and SLA. In M. P. García Mayo, J. Guierrez

Mangado & M. Martínez Adrián (Eds.), *Contemporary approaches to second language acquisition*. Amsterdam: John Benjamins.

Schmidt, R. W. (2010). Attention, awareness, and individual differences in language learning. In W. M. Chan, S. Chi, K. N. Cin, J. Istanto, M. Nagami, J. W. Sew, T. Suthiwan, & I. Walker, *Proceedings of CLASIC conference* (pp. 721–737). Singapore: National University of Singapore, Centre for Language Studies.

Schmitt, N. (2008). Review article: Instructed second language vocabulary learning. *Language Teaching Research, 12*, 329–363,

Smith, J. (1996). A seven-minute slice of chaos I'm puzzling through now. Unpublished research report. University of Pittsburg, Pittsburg, PA.

Spada N., & Lightbown, P. (2009). Interaction research in second/foreign language classrooms. In A. Mackey & C. Polio (Eds.), *Multiple perspectives on interaction in SLA; research in honor of Susan M. Gass* (pp. 157–175). Mahwah, NJ: Lawrence Erlbaum Associates.

Toohey, K. (2000). *Learning English at school*. Clevedon: Multilingual Matters.

van Lier, L. (2004). *The ecology and semiotics of language learning: A sociocultural perspective*. Norwell, MA: Kluwer.

Willett, J. (1995). Becoming first graders in an L2: An ethnographic study of L2 socialization. *TESOL Quarterly, 29*, 473–503.

Young, R. (1992). *Critical theory and classroom talk*. Clevedon: Multilingual Matters.

Appendix

Transcription conventions (from Cao 2009: 237)

[	Indicates overlap with portion in the next turn that is similarly bracketed
→	Line to be discussed in text
CAPS	Small caps in discourse are used to show the speaker's emphasis
?	Rising intonation
'	Slight rise in intonation
.	Falling intonation
(( ))	Comments enclosed in double parentheses
:	Elongation of a syllable
(.)	Brief pause
(…)	Longer pause
(#)	Times pause
° °	Reduced volume – soft voice
°° °°	Reduced volume – whispered
°°° °°°	Reduced volume – very soft whisper, with consonant sounds articulated and certain vowel sounds difficult to determine

Part II

Interactions involving technology

Chapter 7

The cyber language exchange
Cross-national computer-mediated interaction

Shannon Sauro
Malmö University

This study examines the text-chat interaction of second language learners and teacher trainees engaged in an online exchange linking classes in two countries: Sweden and the United States. During the semester, students met online for 6 sessions using the chat program Live Messenger. As part of the exchange, each U.S. student served as a tutor and chat partner for Swedish students on four writing tasks. These tasks were designed in accordance with language features (i.e. the zero article, agreement, possessives) and topics (i.e. human rights, environmental issues, Swedish and US culture) relevant for both classes. Chatscripts from focal participants' interactions were analyzed to explore the potential to foster attention to form in text-chat based telecollaboration that emphasized L2 writing.

Introduction

This chapter explores the language learning potential of computer-mediated interaction that occurred as part of an international partnership linking students in classrooms in two countries (Sweden and the United States). This international network-based partnership or telecollaboration represents an educational context increasingly relevant to language classrooms that incorporate computer-enhanced, blended or online instruction (see Goertler 2011 for an overview of these class types). In this chapter, the use of text-chat, a form of written synchronous computer-mediated communication (SCMC) reflects a modality of interaction most often explored in form-focused studies of second language acquisition under controlled laboratory conditions. In the context of this telecollaboration, however, text-chat served as the medium of interaction in an authentic educational context driven by curriculum standards, course goals, teacher preference, and student agency as opposed to research objectives. As such, this paper explores the potential for an authentic classroom-based telecollaboration to support the delivery of corrective feedback to facilitate attention to form and second language writing development by analyzing a cross section of chatscripts generated during the fall 2008 semester.

Foreign language telecollaboration as authentic educational context

Foreign language telecollaboration is defined here as an organized network-supported partnership linking language learners in one part of the world with people in other parts of the world for the purpose of language or culture learning through the completion of communicative activities or tasks (Ware & O'Dowd 2008). A rich body of research on foreign language telecollaboration in computer-assisted language learning (CALL) extends to the late 1990s when the proliferation of synchronous and asynchronous networked technologies (e.g. e-mail, discussion boards, text-chat) made it possible for language instructors to put their students in contact with other learners or target language speakers around the world for the purpose of communicating in the target language or learning about the target language culture.

One of the earliest telecollaborative projects, *Cultura* (Furstenberg, Levet, English, & Maillet 2001), which partnered a US university French class with a French university English class for the purpose of intercultural awareness, served as a model for later telecollaborative exchanges that had a strong cultural emphasis. Studies on intercultural telecollaborations have explored the type of cultural understandings and conflicts that can occur in such technology-mediated partnerships (e.g. Belz 2002; 2003; O'Dowd 2003; 2005).

Telecollaborative projects have also emphasized language in addition to cultural learning. These include partnerships that incorporate tandem learning (O'Rourke 2005), telecollaborations that rely on mutual language exchange between partner language classes and therefore incorporate interaction in both target languages (e.g. Vinagre & Muñoz 2011), as well as partnerships that emphasize a monolingual exchange (e.g. Ware & O'Dowd 2008). Learner language development during or as a result of foreign language telecollaborations have been documented in several areas. This includes, for instance, the corpus-based work of Belz and Vyatkina (2008) who used microgenetic analysis to document the longitudinal development of modal particles and the *da*-construction by English learners of German in a telecollaborative partnership with German learners of English. Studies examining learner language development as a result of a telecollaboration are relatively few but include Dussias's (2005) comparative study of the oral development of L2 learners of Spanish, which found evidence of increased gains in fluency and accurate use of certain morphosyntactic features among learners who participated in an e-mail telecollaboration compared to those who did not.

Still other telecollaborative projects have focused on specific features of interaction during telecollaborations to explore the potential for language learning. This includes examination of the amount and focus of feedback provided during partnerships as well as learners' willingness to attend to form (Ware & O'Dowd 2008), the particular focus of peer-feedback (Vinagre 2005), and the efficacy of feedback on subsequent written discourse (Vinagre & Lera 2008; Vinagre & Muñoz 2011). Unifying these studies is a particular focus on feedback generated during e-mail-based telecollaborations. However, while e-mail remains a foundational tool in telecollaborations, especially in contexts with substantial time-zone differences and more limited technology, other key tools in telecollaborations do support real-time synchronous computer-mediated communication (SCMC), which more closely approximates the demands of real-time spoken interaction. In particular, text-chat, or instant-messaging, represents a tool familiar to many foreign language learners that supports real-time interaction and has a nearly 20-year history as a context for research on second language development (Sauro 2011).

Text-chat for foreign language telecollaboration

Several characteristics of text-chat have made this an interactional medium of interest for both language educators and researchers. Much like asynchronous technologies such as e-mail and discussion boards, text-chat can be used by learners outside of class and at a time convenient to telecollaboration partners. However, unlike asynchronous technologies, text-chat enables real-time interaction and can be used to link learners with their interlocutors in synchronous interactions both during and outside of class meetings. From a pedagogical perspective, in language classrooms with networked computers and the necessary chat applications (e.g. Yahoo!Messenger, Skype), online partnerships that take place during class time can take advantage of on-hand teachers and technical support staff to help clarify instructions, to ensure that all students are in communication with a partner, and to manage technical problems. Such on-site pedagogical support can be particularly helpful in cases where language learners may be unfamiliar with the technology, or, in the case of lower proficiency learners, may not have yet developed the discourse level skills to read or write longer texts as found in e-mails and discussing board postings.

The synchronous and written nature of the text-chat medium poses both advantages and disadvantages for language learning. Relative to e-mail, text-chat provides learners with the opportunity to interact in real-time, requiring learners to both comprehend and produce the target language more rapidly than in asynchronous interaction. This real-time interaction also allows for more immediate feedback and opportunities for interactional modification, which may allow for noticing and uptake. Although conducted in real-time, turn-taking in text-chat is substantially slower than turn-taking in spoken discourse (Beauvois 1992; Sauro & Smith 2010). The slower pace of text-chat conversations affords learners more time to read and process their partners' turns and to monitor and edit their own discourse. This can have the advantage of allowing learners using text-chat to look up specific words or to modify and enhance what they have typed (see, for example, Sauro & Smith 2010). In addition, the visual nature of text-chat presents learners with a written record of what they and their partners have typed, enabling them to scroll back through the discourse to reread what has been said. This durable written record can be particularly useful in the case of corrective feedback, allowing learners the time and opportunity to compare the feedback they receive with their own prior output. This particular use of the enduring nature of text-chat is illustrated in (1), which is an exchange from Sauro (2009). In this example, at 10:12, Christie provides Monika9 corrective feedback regarding article use. After some discussion of the zero article, Monika9 continues with the task of describing elements of Swedish culture to Christie. Then, at 10:25:47, Monika9 returns to the issue of the zero article, realizing what was meant and reformulating her initial utterance more than 3 minutes after the corrective feedback was first supplied. The enduring nature of the text-chat interaction enabled her to return to her initial utterance to quote and then reformulate the targeted noun phrase.

(1)   1.   Monika9 Malmo: I'm thinking about what I know about the Swedish
       2.   culture. It's in many ways not very different from the American culture I
       3.   think. Feb 26, 2007 10:21:56 AM EST
       4.   Christie Penn: Monika9, be sure to use the zero artice. Feb 26, 2007
       5.   10:22:18 AM EST
       6.   Monika9 Malmo: What is the zero artice? Feb 26, 2007 10:22:31 AM EST
       7.   Christie Penn: It means no article. Feb 26, 2007 10:22:43 AM EST
       8.   Monika9 Malmo: Hmm, I asked my teacher what it means, but she said I
       9.   had to ask you again. Can you explain what it means to me? Feb 26, 2007
      10.   10:23:27 AM EST
      11.   Christie Penn: That's okay. Don't worry about it for now. Can you write
      12.   the next sentence? Feb 26, 2007 10:23:55 AM EST
      13.   Monika9 Malmo: Okay, I'll continue. Feb 26, 2007 10:24:11 AM EST
      14.   Monika9 Malmo: I think some Swedish literature is known in other
      15.   countries. Feb 26, 2007 10:24:43 AM EST
      16.   Monika9 Malmo: Do you know anything about Swedish literature? Feb
      17.   26, 2007 10:24:56 AM EST
      18.   Christie Penn: Good. I don't know much I'm afraid. What can you tell me
      19.   about it? Feb 26, 2007 10:25:24 AM EST
      20.   Monika9 Malmo: Ah, I think I know what you mean with zero article
      21.   now. You meant I shouldn't write "The American culture", it should be
      22.   only "American culture", right?" Feb 26, 2007 10:25:47 AM EST

(Sauro 2009: 111)

At the same time, text-chat interaction may also present disadvantages for language development, particularly with respect to certain features of formal L2 writing. The enduring visual nature of text-chat may reduce the need for learners to produce full sentences, allowing them to instead piggyback off the language of prior turns captured in the chat window. This can result in shorter more spoken-like utterances that lack the syntactic complexity found in academic writing. In the case of text-chatting in character-based languages, learners may also rely on copying and pasting their interlocutors' prior utterances if they are uncertain of how to type a particular character, thereby gaining no further practice with actually producing the character. In addition, other common features of text-chat discourse include the omission of sentence final punctuation and the avoidance of capital letters. These orthographic simplifications stem in part from avoidance of additional keystrokes (e.g. use of the SHIFT key when typing in English) which chatters may forgo in the interest of transmitting messages more rapidly (see, for example, discussions in Baron 2008). Excerpt (2), which was generated during the telecollaboration described in this study, illustrates this tendency towards brevity and selective punctuation and capitalization.

(2) 1. lexibrown says: Well my name is Lexibrown…so what year of school are you in?
2. zara says: first year in high school
3. lexibrown says: oh ok…well that's cool this is my last semester of college
4. lexibrown says: I will be graduating in December
5. lexibrown says: What do you do for fun?
6. zara says: ok thats nice

In this text-chat session, zara, a high school EFL student, omits all capital letters and punctuation (commas, periods, apostrophes) in responses to her chat partner's questions. Lack of capitalization is also found in the chat identity zara uses during this session. Like several free chat clients, Windows Messenger allows chatters to modify their identities for each chat session. While lexibrown relies on the default ID, her e-mail address, to identify herself, zara uses her first name uncapitalized. Although lexibrown, a university student pursuing teaching certification, begins by using formal capitalization and punctuation in her initial turn, she is less consistent in subsequent turns. Sentence final punctuation appears in a follow-up question but periods are omitted following statements. This tendency towards brevity and omission of formal orthographic features may be particularly prominent among learners who are frequent users of text-chat for informal communication with friends and family.

Research questions

As a result of the characteristics of text-chat interaction, telecollaborations that incorporate this form of SCMC as the primary tool for communication may not be thought of as ideal for supporting attention to form or the development of L2 writing. This study, therefore, examines actual classroom interaction in a text-chat based telecollaboration with a specific focus on L2 writing to explore the potential for this medium to foster attention to form in an authentic classroom and non-laboratory based context. The following question guided this study: Can text-chat based telecollaboration be used to foster opportunities for corrective feedback and attention to form in an authentic classroom environment?

Method

Context and participants

The data are drawn from the chatscripts of two focal participants and their chat partners during a telecollaborative exchange embedded in the fall semester of two participating classes: a university linguistics for educators course located in the United States and a secondary school English class located in Sweden. Over a period of eight weeks (September–November) 11 teacher-trainees and 34 English students met online in real-time for six sessions. In keeping with the different learning objectives of the two separate classes, three overarching aims guided this telecollaboration: (1) for teacher trainees to apply their developing linguistics knowledge to the evaluation of certain morphosyntactic features of their partners' English, (2) for English students to receive feedback on certain aspects of their English writing, and (3) for both groups to exchange opinions on major educational and social issues.

The US-based participants in the linguistics for educator course included both graduates and undergraduates enrolled at a Hispanic serving institution (HSI)[1] that drew a majority of its student body from the local area. This course was offered in the evenings (5:30–8:15pm) to accommodate the work schedules of the students, most of whom were completing their graduate or undergraduate degrees on a part-time basis while working full-time. Participants were self-selected and completed the telecollaboration in fulfillment of the final project for the course. Due to the real-time nature of the online sessions which occurred outside of class time (described below) only 11 of the 33 students enrolled in the linguistics for educator course were available to participate in this exchange[2]. These participating teacher trainees had various levels of prior experience teaching or tutoring in English, but none had prior experience participating in a telecollaboration or working with English learners from Sweden. US-based participants included speakers of Spanish, Korean, English, Mandarin Chinese, and Taiwanese.

The Sweden-based participants were in their first year of gymnasium (approximately equivalent to grade 10 in a US high school) and in the process of completing their final year of compulsory English instruction. The particular emphasis of their English course was on formal written English grammar and writing. The scheduled online meetings were held during their class time, and all 34 students enrolled in the English course were required to participate. Sweden-based participants included speakers of Swedish and Arabic. Although no specific assessment was used to determine proficiency, analysis of chatscripts and informal assessment by the course instructor revealed varying levels of English speaking and writing ability. Despite this range in proficiency, all possessed sufficient English to engage in real-time text-based interaction in English.

While a common model in language-based telecollaborations involves tandem-learning (O'Rourke 2005) which relies on a mutual language exchange and supports multilingual interaction, communication in this telecollaboration was exclusively in English. This was due in part to the different course aims outlined above as well as to the fact that English was the only common language among students in both partner classes.

---

1. According to the US Department of Education (2011), a HSI is a non-profit college or university with an undergraduate enrollment equivalent to at least 25% Hispanic students. http://www.ed.gov/programs/idueshsi/definition.html

2. Because the scheduled time for the telecollaboration (7:00–8:30 am) conflicted with the majority of US students' class or work schedules, those who could not participate in the telecollaboration were able to complete an alternative project.

Interaction took place in real time during six 90-minute class sessions held during scheduled class meetings for the Swedish partner school. Real-time sessions were held using the text-chat client Windows!Live Messenger, which was selected because it was the preferred free chat client of a majority of the Swedish participants and was already installed in the computer lab at the gymnasium. To support dyadic interaction between the different sized partner classes, each student in the US class was partnered with three students in the Swedish class and spent 25 minutes of the class session with each partner.

The chatscripts used in this analysis were drawn from two US based participants, one undergraduate and one graduate, and their Swedish chat partners. These two focal participants represented opposite ends of the spectrum in the linguistics for the educator course with respect to prior training in language instruction, language background, and formal instruction in English grammar. Both focal participants also had the most complete recorded chat involvement, having maintained chat logs with all chat partners over all 6 sessions. lexi-brown, a native speaker of US English, was an undergraduate pursuing her degree in teacher education. As part of her teacher training, she had completed one prior course on sheltered instructional techniques for working with English language learners in content-based classes but had had no additional coursework in linguistics, language pedagogy or language acquisition. TIN@, a second language speaker of English from Taiwan, was a graduate student who had completed several courses in second language acquisition, sociolinguistics, and language teaching methods. In addition, her own prior formal English language learning experience in both Taiwan and the United States had provided her with extensive training in formal English grammar and exposure to multiple varieties of English.

Telecollaboration tasks and feedback

To meet the three overarching aims of this project and to align with the complimentary objectives of each partner class, five different tasks or activities were carried out during the six sessions. These five activities were developed or modified through consultation between the partner class instructors and included an introductory activity, two form-focused tasks initially designed for research and modified for classroom implementation (Sauro 2009), and two writing tasks developed in accordance with the Swedish school's curriculum. Table 1 describes the topic, schedule and linguistic or writing focus for each of these activities (see the Appendix for detailed instructions).

Table 1. Topic and focus of telecollaboration sessions

Session	Topic	Function or linguistic focus
1	Getting to Know You	Introduction to partners and technical trouble-shooting
2	Swedish Culture	Zero article
3	Environmental Issues	Zero article
4	Human Rights	Opinion exchange and brainstorming for the following week
5	Human Rights continued	Subject-verb agreement
6	Newspaper Article	Apostrophe use for possessives

The first session served as an opportunity for collaborators to get to know their partners and to trouble-shoot any potential technical problems that arose. The second and third sessions incorporated two tasks designed to elicit productive use of the English zero article around the broad topics of Swedish culture and environmental issues, which allowed for the provision of form-focused corrective feedback as well as the sharing of personal opinion. For these two tasks, the Swedish partners were responsible for devising sentences that incorporated key nouns from a word bank related to the specific topic. This also provided the opportunity for the Swedish participants to share information and opinions on cultural and environmental issues in Sweden, which the US participants were unfamiliar with. Weeks four and five were cumulative activities based around the topic of human rights. In the first of these two sessions, partners explored possible global topics about which both were familiar and selected a specific focus for the following week. During the fifth week, the Swedish participants shared their writing on the pre-determined human rights topic and received feedback on subject-verb agreement from their US partners while exchanging opinions on their positions. For the sixth and final sessions, the Swedish participants shared their take on a story written as if for a newspaper to receive feedback on apostrophe use.

In preparation for each session, the US participants received an overview regarding the target form and instructions on how to provide metalinguistic feedback which identified the nature of the error but did not entail reformulation of the error. Instructions also included stock phrases for feedback that could be used: remember to use the zero article; check the verb; or you forgot the apostrophe. The decision to direct the US teacher trainees to rely on set phrases to provide focused corrective feedback was driven in part by findings from other studies on telecollaboration that identified the formulation of feedback as focal point of frustration arising from different cultural norms of interaction. For instance, Guth and Marini-Maio's (2010) Italian participants were frustrated by their US partners' unclear or nonspecific feedback while the US participants were offended by their Italian partners' directness and lack of hedging when providing feedback. These stock phrases were selected through consultation between both partner class instructors as containing language that would be familiar to both groups of students and direct enough to be sufficiently helpful for the goals of the Swedish class.

Results

In order to answer the guiding research question, chatscripts of text-chat sessions 2, 3, 4, and 6 were analyzed for feedback episodes and evidence of attention to form.

Corrective feedback and textual enhancement

Analysis of the focal chatscripts revealed feedback from the US partners was often more elaborate and deviated from the scripted feedback moves in several ways. This included use of special characters to enhance the feedback, incorporation of conversational continuants or commentary on the content of the prior turn in addition to the feedback, and, in some cases, feedback elaboration which resulted in multiple feedback moves. The first two of these modifications, the incorporation of special characters and conversational commentary is illustrated in (3):

(3) 1. Drew says: Today the wind energy is a big international industry
     2. TIN@ says: yes, people need different energy, and please use "zero
     3. article" of "wind energy"
     4. Drew says: alright
     5. Drew says: I will remember it from now on

In this example, TIN@ begins with a response to Drew's statement in line 1 and concludes with feedback on his use of the definite article with wind energy. She abbreviates the wording of the scripted "Remember to use the zero article" to "please use" and highlights both the target form as well as the specific noun phrase requiring the zero article with quotation marks thereby visually enhancing the feedback as well as the location of the error. By prefacing her feedback move with a response to the content of Drew's initial turn, TIN@ mediates the directness of her feedback with a conversational continuant and then relies on textual enhancement to direct Drew's attention to the nature and location of the error.

TIN@'s use of textual enhancement only occurred in two types of turns, those in which her feedback followed a conversational response such as the one highlighted here or in response to confusion or a question from her partner regarding the feedback. The latter is illustrated in (4) taken from chat session 5 in which the Swedish students had been instructed to write a letter to the editor on a human rights topic to share with their US partners. In this example, Haanz has copied several sentences from his letter into one turn (lines 1–5) to which TIN@ responds by acknowledging his argument and then offering feedback.

(4)   1. Haanz says: But the problem is that you can never know if a company use child
      2. labor or not. If I had a company should I go out at my homepage
      3. with that we don't use child labor. I think more people should buy
      4. from us if they know that we not using child labor even if the take
      5. a higher price on exact same product.
      6. TIN@ says: good point, and check the verb agreement
      7. Haanz says: were shall I look?
      8. TIN@ says: what do you mean "were shall I look"
      9. Haanz says: witch verb agreement should I looked on
     10. TIN@ says: you said "a company" so you have to use "uses"
     11. Haanz says: 0okey

Due to the length of his turn and the various instances of agreement, in line 7 Haanz asks TIN@ to elaborate on her feedback, which remained close to the scripted feedback students had been advised to use. TIN@ does so in lines 8 and 10 by using textual enhancement to highlight the location of the agreement issue as well as the recast she provides. In doing so, she provides Haanz with more information than initially contained in the simple metalinguistic feedback move earlier: information on the nature of the error, its location, and an acceptable reformulation.

Textual enhancements in feedback moves were also used by lexibrown but in slightly different contexts. She too used quotation marks to highlight the location of errors in longer turns that contained multiple clauses. However, while TIN@ almost exclusively provided feedback on only the target forms for each lesson, lexibrown gave feedback on multiple additional features including spelling, sentence final punctuation, verb tense, preposition choice, and agreement. When giving feedback on these non-target features, lexibrown alternated between recasting the error and providing explicit correction in combination with metalinguistic feedback. Isolated recasts such as the one in (5) were usually accompanied by one or several * to signify a reformulation.

> (5) 1. Janni says: in the town everybody were sad because everybody felt sorry for
> 2. the Johnsons.
> 3. lexibrown says: *was sad*

lexibrown as well as several of the Swedish participants also used * when performing self repair on prior utterances, indicating that this was an understood technique for marking a reformulation. Ernesto! employs this strategy in (6) when he self-corrects capitalization of the pronoun I during session 1 with lexibrown and before she beings using it in the chat.

> (6) 1. Ernesto! says: oh, spelled wrong there, i think
> 2. Ernesto! says: I*

This use of special characters for the purpose of self- and other repair highlights one manner in which participants in a text-chat enabled telecollaboration may choose to enhance the salience or corrective intent of certain feedback moves in an authentic computer-mediated classroom context. As discussed above, not all turns elicited such textually enhanced feedback and such enhancement was most likely to occur the longer and more writing-like (as opposed to speech-like) the turns were. However, in using such a technique, partners increased the salience of the corrective feedback during writing and communication focused interaction in which the corrective feedback may be buried in surrounding discourse. This naturally occurring textually enhanced feedback represents a diversion from the corrective feedback types explored in several experimental studies of computer-mediated interaction and SLA (e.g. Loewen & Erlam 2006; Sauro 2009) which have focused primarily on unenhanced recasts and metalinguistic comments (however see Sachs & Suh 2007 for a study that uses enhanced recasts and Doughty and Varela 1998 for corrective recasts enhanced by stress). However, in classroom-based longitudinal interaction such as that found in a full or half-semester telecollaboration, brief and precisely scripted feedback moves may appear overly terse and under-informative. In addition, this use of special characters for textual enhancement may reflect a natural tendency in authentic classroom interaction where attention to form is anticipated in longer turns that reflect written as opposed to speech-like chat turns.

Attention to form and limited uptake in a visual environment

The guiding research question also asked whether text-chat based telecollaboration can be used to foster attention to form, particularly with respect to target forms relevant for L2 writing. Here attention to form is operationalized as uptake, learners' responses that acknowledge in some way their partners' attempts to provide information on linguistic form. In keeping with the work of Smith (2005) who also explored uptake in text-chat contexts, uptake as operationalized here includes both immediate responses and delayed responses to the corrective feedback. Smith's (2005) adaptation of Ellis, Basturkmen and Loewen's (2001) uptake coding categories were used to determine uptake: recognition and application. The former included learners' use of linguistic tokens (e.g. Okay, thanks) or questions and statements that acknowledge the corrective intent of their partners' feedback move. Drew's and Haanz's responses to TIN@ in Excerpt (3) line 4 and Excerpt (4) line 11 are examples of this type of uptake. The latter category of uptake consisted of productive attempts to use the target form either in isolation or in context in a subsequent turn. Excerpt (7) contains an example of productive application of the feedback move.

(7) 1. Lotte says: child abuse have increased in Sweden the past years
    2. TIN@ says: check the verb
    3. Lotte says: has

Lotte's response to TIN@'s feedback move in line 2 is an isolated reformulation of the verb. This isolated production of the targeted language feature was the most common type of application uptake and tended to occur following feedback on agreement and possessive constructions but not for feedback on the zero article. However, across all chat sessions, recognition uptake was much more common than application uptake and most often took the form of a simple acknowledgment such as that illustrated in (8) between Janni and lexibrown.

(8) 1. Janni says: 7. Mankind have to open there eyes for the problems before it gets
    2. to late.
    3. lexibrown says: Remember use has instead of have
    4. Janni says: okey

Janni's acknowledgment (line 4) of the feedback reflects a similar trend found in laboratory studies of corrective feedback in text-chat environments (e.g. Smith 2005; Sauro 2009) in which application uptake that resulted in attempted reformulation of all or part of the initial utterance was rare. The tendency toward acknowledging as opposed to applying the feedback in this classroom context can be attributed to several factors. This included the format of the feedback and the discourse context in which it occurred. In cases where feedback took the form of a recast, the enduring nature of text-chat interaction, in which prior turns remained visible in the chat window, made repetition of the recast redundant as a form of acknowledgment. This is illustrated in (9). lexibrown's textually enhanced isolated recast in line 2, "*threatened" remains on the screen immediately below zara's initial sentence, obviating any need for zara to retype the recast as acknowledgement.

(9)   1.   zara says: Mankind feels treaten by the global warming.
      2.   lexibrown says: *threatened
      3.   lexibrown says: ok!
      4.   lexibrown says: Can you make a sentence using Space?
      5.   lexibrown says: or nature?
      6.   zara says: I can try

Afterwards, leixbrown generates three transmissions immediately following the recast (lines 3–5). Taken together, these three transmissions function to close the feedback sequence and prompt the next stage of the activity with a request. It is to this sequence that zara responds and not to the preceding isolated recast. It is likely, therefore, that zara's lack of response to the recast lexibrown provides is not due to the ambiguity of the recast but rather to the redundancy of an acknowledgement move in the chat context as well as the new shift in conversation that lexibrown has introduced in a series of multiple transmissions.

The particular focus on writing level issues and the writing-type activities used during the chat sessions resulted in frequent use of multiple consecutive transmission units (Baron 2008) by the same partner which mitigated the amount of uptake that occurred. Swedish students who prepared for their chat sessions by writing sentences in advance (as directed by their instructor) would copy and paste sentence after sentence in the chat window resulting in their partners responding with multiple sequential feedback moves. This is illustrated in (10) in which Janni transmits five full sentences.

(10) 1.   Janni says: 1. Space is a hugh mistory
      2.   Janni says: 2. global warming is a ig problem all over the world
      3.   Janni says: 3. nature is a thing we humans have to take care of and treat well
      4.   Janni says: 4. wind energy have become a big energy saurce here in sweden
      5.   Janni says: 5. the pollution have to stop if we want to save the Earth
      6.   lexibrown says: Ok…hold on.. give them to me one by one.. I want to help
      7.   you with some mechanical issues you are having with your sentences
      8.   Janni says: oh okey, I tought I would just give them to you and then you
      9.   will correct them
      10. Janni says: but I will wait no
      11. Janni says: sorry
      12. lexibrown says: It's okay… for the first one it was a good sentence but
      13. you spell hugh huge and mistory mystery
      14. lexibrown says: The second sentence was good too except you forgot to
      15. put the period
      16. lexibrown says: The third sentence was good too but same thing, you
      17. forgot to put the period
      18. lexibrown says: Your fourth one should read, Wind Energy has instead of
      19. have and saurce is spelled source

20.   Janni says: I always forget to put a period when I'm chatting, it's on my
21.   papers

After negotiating with Janni to transmit only one sentence at a time (line 6), lexibrown then provides explicit feedback. Although the linguistic target of this particular chat session was the zero article, lexibrown replies with multiple consecutive turns (lines 12–19) containing feedback on spelling and punctuation in the first four sentences. In response, Janni acknowledges only the feedback on sentence final punctuation (lines 20–21). It is likely that the writing-focused nature of this telecollaboration encouraged the sending of multiple sequential transmission units that elicited multiple feedback moves for which only select feedback, the most frequent or the most recent, generated uptake during the chat sessions.

Discussion

Analysis of chatscripts from focal participants highlighted preferences and strategies for the provision of corrective feedback in this textual and discourse rich environment. Specifically, textual enhancement of the feedback through special characters was used to signify a feedback move and to increase the salience of the target form in longer chat transmissions. However, feedback consistency varied depending on the nature of the form and the background of the focal participant. lexibrown's preference in offering explicit feedback on specific writing-level features (e.g. punctuation and spelling) may reflect her own prior educational training and comfort with giving feedback on common-writing level issues well as the frequency that such errors occurred. In contrast, TIN@'s consistent provision of focused feedback that addressed only the target form may have reflected her greater familiarity with focused error correction through prior training and her own English language learning background.

   Although the selection of forms to target through feedback was driven by the linguistic and curriculum goals of the Swedish partner class, the variation in feedback provided by the US partners suggest that the needs of the one class may not map on to the linguistic knowledge or preference of students in the other class. Thus, although this project was an example of a language class and teacher trainee telecollaboration (e.g. Fuchs 2007; Müller-Hartmann 2006) it too faced linguistic challenges similar to those found in telecollaborations that link partner language classes for tandem exchanges (see for example, Belz 2002; O'Dowd 2005). While there was evidence of uptake in authentic telecollaboration-based text-chat interaction, it was limited by the format and target of the feedback, the writing intensive nature of the text-chat activity, and the discourse immediately surrounding the feedback move. In particular, the nature of the writing activities, which many of the Swedish students prepared in advance of the chat sessions, did not provide an optimal opportunity for uptake since students relied on copying and pasting of pre-composed text.

This study set out to examine interaction in a telecollaboration with an L2 writing focus to explore whether such a text-chat based classroom environment could be a productive context for fostering attention to form. Although beyond the scope of the current chapter, the participants' orientation to culture was also a relevant and ubiquitous component of this international educational exchange. As discussed previously, a common motivation for the establishment of international telecollaborations is intercultural-learning (O'Dowd 2003). While the telecollaboration described here was specifically form-focused and not culture-oriented, the partnering of two remote classes and the inherent curiosity of participants elicited frequent discussion and comparison of cultural norms and practices. However, the curriculum and assignment objectives for both partner classes did not reference intercultural learning or cultural development, and there was no guidance provided for discussing cultural topics. Future studies that are designed specifically to explore the role of tellecolaborations in facilitating attention to form might benefit from providing participants with opportunities to discuss and reflect on the cultural assumptions that were raised during the chat interaction.

Recommendations for form-focused telecollaborations

Analysis of the focal participants' chatscripts was useful in identifying ways to structure and support future text-chat based telecollaborations between learners and teacher trainees to foster both attention to form and more productive engagement with content and culture. For fostering attention to form in a synchronous written exchange, pre-determined feedback moves should be familiar to both groups of participants and used consistently. In particular, feedback moves that incorporate textual enhancement strategies that participants are already familiar with and which occur organically in text-chat based interaction (e.g. *) or which serve to highlight the target feature in longer stretches of discourse (e.g. "") may be most effective in this visual, written type of interaction. In addition, to provide opportunities for uptake of feedback in this written environment, indirect feedback (Ferris 2006) such as textual enhancement appears more productive than recasts or reformulations of errors, which remain on screen. Finally, allowing participants time to prepare sentences in advance of the chat session may be effective for lower level participants, but designing writing activities that also require spontaneous writing can ensure opportunities for feedback to be incorporated in subsequent discourse.

References

Beauvois, M. H. (1992). Computer-assisted classroom discussion in the foreign language classroom: Conversation in slow motion. *Foreign Language Annals*, 25, 455–464.

Baron, N. S. (2008). *Always on*. Oxford: Oxford University Press.

Belz, J. A. (2003). Linguistic perspective on the development of intercultural communicative competence in telecollaboration. *Language Learning & Technology, 7*(2), 68–117.

Belz, J. A. (2002). Social dimensions of telecollaborative foreign language study. *Language Learning & Technology, 6*(1), 60–81.

Belz, J. A., & Vyatkina, N. (2008). The pedagogical mediation of a developmental learner corpus for classroom-based language instruction. *Language Learning & Technology, 12*(3), 33–52.

Doughty, C., & Varela, E. (1998). Communicative focus on form. In C. Doughty & J. Williams (Eds.), *Focus on form in classroom second language acquisition* (pp. 114–138). Cambridge: Cambridge University Press.

Dussias, P. E. (2005). Telecollaboration and lexical and morphological development in Spanish L2. In J. A. Belz & S. L. Thorne (Eds.), Internet-mediated intercultural foreign language education (pp. 121–146). Boston, MA: Heinle & Heinle.

Ellis, R., Basturkmen, H., & Loewen, S. (2001a). Learner uptake in communicative ESL lessons. *Language Learning, 51*, 281–326.

Ferris, D. (2006). Does error feedback help student writers? New evidence on the short- and long-term effects of written error correction. In K. Hyland & F. Hyland (Eds.), *Feedback in second language writing: Contexts and issues* (pp. 81–104). Cambridge: Cambridge University Press.

Fuchs, C. (2007). Pre-service teachers as intercultural learners in CMC-based collaboration: The case of the literature group. *Journal of Intercultural Communication, 13*. Available at http://www.immi.se/intercultural/nr13/fuchs.htm (28 July 2011).

Furstenberg, G., Levet, S., English, K., & Maillet, K. (2001). Giving a virtual voice to the silent language of culture: The *Cultural* project. *Language Learning & Technology, 5*(1), 55–102.

Goertler, S. (2011). Blended and open/online learning: Adapting to a changing world of language teaching. In N. Arnold & L. Ducate (Eds.), *Present and future promises of CALL: From theory and research to new directions in language teaching* (pp. 471–501). San Marcos, TX: CALICO.

Guth, S., & Marini-Maio, N. (2010). Close encounters of a new kind: The use of skype and wiki in telecollaboration. In S. Guth & F. Helm (Eds.), *Telecollaboration 2.0: Language, literacies, and intercultural learning in the 21st century* (pp. 413–426). Bern: Peter Lang.

Loewen, S., & Erlam, R. (2006). Corrective feedback in the chatroom: An experimental study. *Computer Assisted Language Learning, 19*(1), 1–14.

Müller-Hartmann, A. (2006). Learning how to teach intercultural communicative competence via telecollaboration: A model for language teacher education. In J. A. Belz & S. L. Thorne (Eds.), *Internet-mediated intercultural foreign language education* (pp. 63–84). Boston, MA: Thomson Heinle.

O'Dowd, R. (2005). Negotiating sociocultural and institutional contexts: The case of Spanish-American telecollaboration. *Language and Intercultural Communication, 5*(1), 40–57.

O'Dowd, R. (2003). Understanding the "other side": Intercultural learning in a Spanish-English e-mail exchange. *Language Learning & Technology, 7*(2), 118–144.

O'Rourke, B. (2005). Form-focused interaction in online tandem learning. *CALICO Journal, 22*, 433–466.

Sachs, R., & Suh, B. (2007). Textually enhanced recasts, learner awareness, and L2 outcomes in synchronous computer-mediated interaction. In A. Mackey (Ed.), *Conversational interaction in second language acquisition: A collection of empirical studies* (pp. 197–227). Oxford: Oxford University Press.

Sauro, S. (2011). SCMC for SLA: A research synthesis. *CALICO Journal, 28*, 369–391.

Sauro, S. (2009). Computer-mediated corrective feedback and the development of L2 grammar. *Language Learning & Technology, 13*(1), 96–120.

Sauro, S., & Smith, B. (2010). Investigating L2 performance in chat. *Applied Linguistics, 31*, 554–577.

Smith, B. (2005). The relationship between negotiated interaction, learner uptake, and lexical acquisition in task-based computer-mediated communication. *TESOL Quarterly, 31*, 33–58.

U.S. Department of Education (2011, March 4). *Title V developing Hispanic serving institutions program – Definition of an HSI.* Available at http://www2.ed.gov/programs/idueshsi/definition.html (14 July 2011).

Vinagre, M. (2005). Fostering language learning via e-mail: An English-Spanish exchange. *Computer-Assisted Language Learning, 18*(5), 369–388.

Vinagre, M., & Lera, M. (2008). The role of error correction in online exchanges. In F. Zhang & B. Barber (Eds.), *Handbook of research on computer-enhanced language acquisition and learning* (pp. 326–341). Hershey, PA: IG Publishing.

Vinagre, M., & Muñoz, B. (2011). Computer-mediated corrective feedback and language accuracy in tele-collaborative exchanges. *Language Learning & Technology, 15*(1), 72–103.

Ware, P., & O'Dowd, R. (2008). Peer feedback on language form in telecollaboration. *Language Learning & Technology, 12*(1), 43–63.

Appendix

Activity 1: Getting to know your partner

The purpose of the first chat session is for you to get to know your chat partner(s) and to troubleshoot any possible technical problems. Be sure to use proper capitalization, spelling and punctuation during the chat. As always, feel free to share as much or as little personal information as you feel comfortable with. If you're so inclined, you can also use Live Messenger to send your partner(s) a photo of yourself or to provide links to the university, this city, your hometown, etc. You will have 25 minutes to complete this activity:

In preparation: Write down at least 5 questions to ask your partner(s). Topics may range from the personal (age, family, interests, travel) to the professional (career goals, education) to the political and social (favorite movies, the environment, upcoming holidays, favorite foods, etc.).

Activity 2: Introduction to Sweden for Americans

You will be writing sentences about the mentality, the values, and the culture of Sweden for an American audience. (Think of it as writing an essay sentence by sentence.) Your partner will be helping you. You each have a different word bank of 10 words (10 verb phrases or 10 noun phrases) which you must use in your sentences. First share your words with your partner; then begin writing. You will have 25 minutes to complete this activity:

Word bank: unemployment, Swedish culture, Swedish history, Swedish literature, nationalism in Sweden, Swedish architecture, alcohol, immigration to Sweden, education in Sweden, Swedish society

Activity 3: Environmental issues

You will be writing sentences about the environment. (Think of it as writing an essay sentence by sentence.) Your partner will be helping you. You each have a different word bank of 10 words (10 verb phrases or 10 noun phrases) which you must use in your sentences. First share your words with your partner; then begin writing. You will have 25 minutes to complete this activity.

Word bank: nature, space, mankind, carbon dioxide, wind energy, global warming, nuclear power, industrial waste, pollution, industry

Activities 4 & 5: Letter to the editor on human rights

During the next two sessions, you and your partner will work on composing a letter to the editor of a local newspaper on a human rights issue. On October 13th, you and your partner will share your opinions on several human rights topics and select one to write about in a letter to the editor. On October 27th, you and your partner will work together to write a letter to the editor expressing your opinion on the human rights topic you selected. To prepare for your chat, brainstorm and write down 3–5 human rights issues that you are interested in talking with your partner about.

Activity 6: What happened to the Johnsons

For the final chat session, you will help your partner write an article for tomorrow's edition of "Dagens Nyheter", Sweden's leading newspaper, about what happened to the Johnson family on a summer's day in June when they went on a 3 weeks´ holiday to Spain – a 300 kilometers´ long journey by car. Topics will include the following: What happened to James's (or James') parents´ house; what happened to the children's toys, bikes etc.; and what happened in the village (at the hairdresser's, the butcher's, the baker's etc.).

Chapter 8

Using eye tracking as a measure of foreign language learners' noticing of recasts during computer-mediated writing conferences

Bryan Smith and Claire Renaud
Arizona State University

This study used eye tracking to explore the relationship between second-language recasts, noticing, and learning during computer-mediated communication. Learners' eye fixations were used as a measure of noticing. We examined the relationship between occurrence, number, and duration of fixations and posttest success and between the nature of the recasts and fixation duration. Intermediate learners of Spanish and German (*N* = 16) engaged in chat conferences with their instructor, taking posttests one week later. Results showed a relationship between noticing of lexical and grammatical form and posttest success. Suggestive effects were found for fixation number and posttest success and for number of targets in complex recasts and fixation duration. Eye tracking can be a useful tool for exploring attention to form.

Introduction

This exploratory study asks whether employing eye-tracking technology can offer insights into what learners attend to and/or notice in the corrective feedback (specifically recasts) provided by their teacher during interaction in a synchronous computer-mediated communicative (SCMC) environment. Although eye tracking has been employed in educational research since the 1960s, it has only very recently been used to explore the nature of learner interaction in second-language (L2) learning.

Recasts, the basic unit of analysis focused on here, may be defined as discourse moves (by an interlocutor) that, within the context of a communicative activity, correctly restate or rephrase (modify) all or part of a learner's utterance to be more target-like by changing one or more sentence components while still retaining its central meaning (Lyster & Ranta 1997; Nicholas, Lightbown, & Spada 2001; Sheen 2006; Trofimovich, Ammar, & Gatbonton

2007). Recasts have been widely examined in L2 acquisition (SLA) research in the context of meaningful interaction (see Ellis & Sheen 2006; Long 2007; Mackey & Goo 2007) and are generally theorized to be a powerful form of corrective feedback because they simultaneously provide negative feedback and positive input (Leeman 2003). They may occur in reaction to a breakdown in communication – in which case they may be embedded in a negotiation routine of some sort – or they may be provided (in response to a learner's non-target-like utterance) without any true non-understanding having occurred. Teachers often prefer recasts because they are a relatively non-threatening, mitigated, unobtrusive, and implicit feedback type (Seedhouse 1997).

On the nature and effectiveness of recasts

Research to date shows recasts to be generally facilitative for SLA, with their effectiveness more pronounced in lab over classroom settings (see Li 2010; Long 2007; Lyster & Saito 2010; Mackey & Goo 2007). Recasts have been shown to be a dynamic and multifaceted construct (e.g., Sheen 2004), consisting of many different types including corrective, non-corrective, intensive, explicit, implicit, full, partial, simple, complex, adjacent, and non-adjacent recasts. It is this dynamic nature (i.e., its form and presentation) that partially contributes to debates regarding the efficacy of recasts. However, most SLA studies show their developmental effectiveness, (Goo & Mackey, in press), with a few showing limited or no effects of recasts on L2 learning (e.g., Ellis, Loewen, & Erlaum 2006; Lyster & Ranta 1997; Sauro 2009). In exploring the effectiveness of recasts from an interactionist perspective, the assumption is that learners are able to attend to and make use of the positive input and negative feedback recasts provide. Gass (2010) suggests that, "if there is no attention to a particular part of language during an interaction, then it is difficult to attribute the source of change to the interaction itself" (226; e.g., Schmidt 2001). Further, Carroll (2001) suggests that, to take advantage of recasts, learners need to notice their corrective intent. This notion finds support in a recent computer-assisted language learning (CALL) study (Sachs & Suh 2007). Exploring whether recasts involving textual enhancements (in a SCMC environment) applied to arguably non-salient and communicatively redundant target forms impacted learners' subsequent accuracy in selecting and using these forms, they found that higher levels of reported awareness showed stronger correlations with posttest performance. Factors that may affect the noticing and, therefore, the effectiveness of recasts include the form targeted by the recast (e.g., Mackey, Gass, & McDonough 2000; Trofimovich et al. 2007), its structural composition (Ellis et al. 2006; Loewen & Philp 2006; Sheen 2006) as well as its linguistic context (Tarone & Bigelow 2007). Additional factors may be related to the pedagogical and social context such as learner familiarity with the type of feedback provided and the setting.

Methodologies measuring learner attention to feedback

An adequate measure of what learners attend to and when is crucial to exploring the relationship between attention and SLA (Trofimovich et al. 2007). Three methods have been employed most widely in an instructed SLA context: the analysis of immediate uptake in the discourse (e.g., Lyster & Ranta 1997; Mackey & Philp 1998), the use of concurrent (e.g., Alanen 1995; Lai, Fei, & Roots 2008; Leow 2000) and retrospective (e.g., Gass & Mackey 2000; Mackey, Philp, Egi, Fujii, & Tatsumi 2002) verbal reports. Other approaches have been occasionally used including instances of private speech (Ohta 2000), cued immediate recall (Philp 2003), learners' comments via online journals (Mackey 2006), written questionnaires following the treatment (Mackey 2006; Robinson 1996), and the use of some sort of immediate or delayed productive measure (e.g., Ammar & Spada 2006; Mackey & Philp 1998). Each of these approaches has its advantages and flaws.

SCMC: A good avenue for exploring learner attention to form

The potential benefits of text-based SCMC for SLA, consistent with the interactionist approach adopted here, have been elaborated in detail elsewhere and include an increased participation among students, an increased quantity and heightened quality of learner output, an enhanced attention to linguistic form, and an increased willingness to take risks with their L2 (Pellettieri 1999; Smith 2004). The slower speed of typing as well as a software- and network-induced lag time between turns, coupled with the heightened salience of input and output afforded by the permanence of the written message on the screen means that interlocutors have more time to both process incoming messages (Pellettierri 1999) and produce and monitor their output (Smith 2008). Essentially, then, the potential advantages afforded SLA by text-based SCMC comes down to the construct of attention and noticing – especially the noticing of non-target-like input and output (Salaberry 2000; Smith 2004). More specifically, text-based SCMC affords more online planning time, which is argued to contribute to L2 performance by freeing up attentional resources (Yuan & Ellis 2003). Sauro and Smith (2010) showed that learners appear to use the increased online planning time afforded by chat to engage in careful production that results in more complex language. This finding echoes that of Yilmaz and Yuksel (2011) that learners scored significantly higher on oral production tasks when receiving recasts through text-based SCMC than through the face-to-face mode. Recasts in a SCMC environment, then, might be expected to be especially salient to learners, though this research is just emerging (Lai et al. 2008; Sauro 2009).

Eye tracking

Eye-tracking technology, an important tool in psychological (reading) research, consists of a suite of techniques whereby an individual's eye movements are measured so that the researcher knows both where a person is looking at any given time and the sequence in which their eyes are shifting from one location to another (Poole & Ball 2005). Eye-movement measures, such as gaze duration, occurrence of regressions, and search time provide a dynamic trace of where a person's *attention*[1] is being directed in relation to a visual display (Just & Carpenter 1976) and are considered empirical correlates of processing complexity. This can allow us to make precise moment-by-moment inferences about the nature and *amount* of processing being applied without significantly altering the normal characteristics of either the task or the presentation of the stimuli (Dussias 2010). Eye-movement patterns have been used to explore the cognitive processes of pronoun resolution and co-reference, word frequency, lexical ambiguity, syntactic ambiguity, and discourse factors (see Rayner 1998, for a review). Longer fixations are widely argued to indicate either difficulty in extracting information or that the object is more engaging in some way (Just & Carpenter 1976). Up to now, eye-movement records in L2 research have been used to investigate two major areas: (a) the way in which L2 speakers recognize words when they are spoken in each language; and (b) the question of whether monolingual and L2 speakers process various syntactic sub-processes similarly during sentence comprehension tasks (see Dussias 2010, for an overview).

The overarching research question for the current study asks whether employing eye-tracking technology can offer insights into what learners attend to and/or notice in the corrective feedback (specifically recasts) from their teacher and whether this noticing leads to learning. Eye-tracking technology was chosen to examine the degree to which learners attend to recasts in a SCMC context to answer earlier calls for SCMC researchers to reach beyond output logs alone (O'Rourke 2008, 2012; Smith 2008, 2010). The assumption here is that this technique will not interfere with the participants' cognitive processing (Godfroid, Housen, & Boers 2010) and, thus, is a potentially powerful ancillary to other, more established, methodologies (such as verbal reports) for tracking learner attention (Smith 2010, 2012) and may provide detailed insight into individual linguistic-cognitive strategies. Here, we interpret a higher quantity of fixations as well as longer fixations on the same target as indicative of increased processing demands.

Given their currency in the SLA literature, we chose to examine recasts. More specifically, we wanted to examine whether learners seem to attend to aspects of the target language embedded in the corrective feedback – especially those aspects that are quite difficult for first-language (L1) English speakers to learn. Among these aspects, grammatical gender in particular, has been the focus of a great deal of L2 research (e.g., Hopp 2011 for German; Franceschina 2005; McCarthy 2008; White, Valenzuela, Kozlowska-Macgregor,

---

1.   The eye-tracking literature on reading and that from L2 studies use the terms attention and noticing in different ways. In the former, the term attention reflects an increased amount of processing effort. In the latter, the constructs of attention and noticing can be said to be key in all cognitively-oriented approaches to SLA and is widely viewed in these circles as a critical factor that mediates L2 input and interaction driven learning (Gass 1997; Gass & Varonis 1994; Long 1996).

& Leung 2004 for Spanish), and is particularly difficult for L1 English learners because it is absent from their native language, which only marks natural gender on pronouns. Grammatical gender involves not only the correct assignment of gender to nouns but also agreement between nouns and determiners and adjectives. Indeed, DeKeyser (2005) suggests that those aspects of morphosyntax, such as gender and subject-verb agreement, are strongly resistant to instructional treatments because learners are faced with recognizing and learning a complex underlying system of syntactic, semantic, morphological, and phonological rules.

We address two research questions in the present study: (1) what eye gaze behavior and recast features are associated with posttest performance? and (2) what is the relationship between recast features and eye gaze? For the first research question, we considered the posttest performance in terms of three recast features (the number of targets, the type of targets, the linguistic difficulty of the targets) and two eye gaze behaviors (number and duration of eye fixations). For the second research question, we considered the relationship between the three recast features and two eye gaze behaviors.

Method

Participants

Participants were all volunteers from one low-intermediate-level Spanish class and one low-intermediate-level German class at a major university in the U.S. A total of eight participants from each language group completed all phases of the study and had usable records for each phase. Only these participants ($n = 16$) are considered in the analysis. All 16 participants were native English speakers, and none were majors in the target languages under consideration.

Instructional context

As part of the regular curriculum, the instructors involved in this study typically held one-on-one student conferences as needed during the course of the semester. They reported that these conferences vary in number and duration and may occur in the form of face-to-face meetings, text-based chat meetings using, for example, Google Talk, or meetings using the chat function of Facebook. Participants in this study volunteered to participate and elected to use the text-based chat mode for the conference. We are therefore confident that all participants were comfortable interacting via synchronous chat. There are typically three writing assignments for this level, so learners would normally have the opportunity for six conferences of roughly 30 minutes each (one each for a rough and final draft). For this study the instructors agreed to hold online chat conferences for each participant focusing on one specific assignment late in the semester. Learners who chose not to participate held their conferences in one of the other formats.

Instructors, known personally to one of the researchers, were experienced L2 teachers who typically employed computer technology as a regular part of their curriculum
and had engaged in online conferences with students in past semesters. The timeline and
assignments that seemed compatible with our study were negotiated with the instructors
the semester before. The instructors requested to conduct the actual recruiting of participants and they were thus provided with all the IRB approved forms necessary.

Design and materials

Figure 1 shows the different tasks that the participants completed. The pre-treatment
tasks were completed a week before the writing conference, and the post-treatment tasks
approximately a week after.[2]

Phase	Activities
Pre-treatment	Questionnaire
Treatment	Calibration of eye tracker
	Writing conference
Post-treatment	Post-test

Figure 1. Overview of data collection

The pre-treatment questionnaire was used to establish comparability among students in
terms of their experience with the target language. As the treatment task, learners engaged
in a 15-minute one-on-one writing conference with their instructor about a draft of a
written assignment due the following week. This online conference took the place of the
face-to-face conference that non-participants attended that same week. The instructors,
who were familiar with using recasts in the classroom, were asked to provide full recasts
when it seemed natural to do so. To allow for a span of recast difficulty to emerge from
the interaction, instructors were asked to pay special attention to errors on morphosyntax
such as grammatical gender (more difficult), with errors involving word choice or spelling
at the less difficult end of the continuum. Instructors provided recasts at the earliest possible point in the chat interaction after they noted a problematic utterance. Many of these
consisted of complex recasts, where one recast targets more than one linguistic item in the
participant's previous message. Even though partial recasts that target a single linguistic
item have been argued to be easier for learners to attend to, we might expect the increased
processing time and message permanence afforded by the chat interface to mediate these
variables in the text-based SCMC environment.

Learners took a delayed posttest about one week after the treatment, with a few students completing this part one day later than most. The posttests were created to match

---

2. A cloze test was administered after each phase of the data collection for use as a general proficiency measure in a different study.

to their specific chat interaction (see Appendix A for an example), by using the actual chat interaction transcript produced for each participant. First, we identified each teacher recast and paired it with the non-target-like utterance that prompted the recast. Second, each recast was verified as being target-like. Non-target-like recasts were not considered in the data. Next, the non-target-like student utterances were copied onto the individualized delayed posttest sheet with any accompanying contextualizing text from the transcript that was required. These items were then randomized and presented along with several distractor items taken from various German or Spanish language sources. Learners were required to first determine whether each item was target-like as written or not; if not, they were required to rewrite the sentence in a target-like fashion. In this way, we could determine if learners were able to productively use the information found in the instructor's recast during the writing conference. No outside sources were allowed in completing the delayed posttest.

Data collection and analysis

Calibrating the eye tracker and capturing the interaction

A portable eye-tracker from EyeTech Digital Systems (model TM3) was used along with the Gaze Tracker 9.0 Data Analysis Software. This remote eye-tracker is fastened to the bottom edge of any computer screen and thus did not interfere with participants' normal range of head movements. Such an eye-tracker needs to be fine-tuned to the particularities of each person's eye movements by a "calibration" process. To ensure accuracy, the software requires data collected from learners following a green ball on the screen with their eyes for about 30 seconds prior to the actual task. Once the calibration process is complete, participants use the computer as they normally would, and their eye-movements are captured remotely. The software creates a video file similar to a screen capture record but with the participant's eye movements superimposed on the screen; it also records the location and duration of each eye fixation. Learners engaged with their instructor using the chat program Google Talk. Spelling and grammar "check as you go" were disabled, and the font size was set at 36 to allow for easier interpretation of eye fixations and targets.

Coding the interaction

There were multiple steps to coding. First, learner chat transcripts were evaluated, and each recast was coded for the number of targets embedded in the recast. This variable, referred to as *target number*, comprises four levels: Recasts that contained a single target were coded as 1, those with two targets as 2, three targets as 3, four targets as 4, and five or more targets as 5. Next, each of the targets within a given recast was coded for linguistic focus, hereafter, *target type*. The specific categories for coding each of the targets were lexical, agreement, tense, spelling, and other (i.e., missing word). Most categories had several sub-categories, but these are not differentiated in the statistical analysis given the modest data presented here. Since one of our goals was to explore whether English L1 speakers were able to attend to aspects of the recasts that are markedly different from their native language, each target type was also coded for projected difficulty. For example, recasts that targeted aspects related to grammar (the agreement and tense categories) were hypothesized to be difficult for English L1 speakers to attend to, whereas recasts of the wrong lexical item were not (see Example 1). The researchers made all coding decisions jointly. Initial discrepancies (about 5%) were discussed until 100% agreement was reached. This also resulted in the removal of three data points (2 for Spanish and 1 for German) because it was impossible to identify a category for those items.

(1) *Recast showing a single target and linguistic focus*
      me: ok gracias, y tengo preguntas acerda de <u>las problemas</u> con mis gramatica
      L2InstructorA: ok. ¿cuáles son **los** problemas de tu gramática que tienes?
                              agreement
                              difficulty = 1

Coding the eye gazes

After having identified each instructor recast, the eye-tracking record was evaluated. Although the eye-gaze software is typically designed to record one's eye movements on a static target, the so-called area of interest in the current study was constantly shifting due to the task at hand (i.e., chatting with the instructor). Therefore, at least one separate eye-gaze record (in the form of still images of the computer screen) for each recast had to be created. Each eye-gaze record is based on the time immediately following the appearance of the recast on the learner's computer screen (post pane) and runs until just before there is a shift in the post pane, such as when another incoming (or outgoing) message is posted (or in the rare case, scrolling up). Since we were not concerned with what learners were composing, the movement in the compose window did not affect the salient aspects of the eye-gaze record. The exception to this was in the case of lengthy messages, whereby each pressing of the return (enter) key by the writer would cause a shift in the post pane. In this case, the eye-gaze clip would stop immediately before this shift occurred. In several cases it was necessary to create multiple eye-gaze records for a single recast item to accommodate these shifts.

      Two variables were created from the eye-gaze records. First, the total number of eye fixations (fixation number) on each target, including the first fixation on the target and any subsequent regressions (i.e., fixations) back to the target, was recorded. The eye-tracking software was set to create screen shots of the chat interface that show each eye fixation (see Figure 2). Fixation numbers ranged from 0–4+ with this last number reflecting four or more separate fixations on the same target. For example, a fixation number of 3 would mean that the learner's eye gaze fixated that target a total of three separate times. Fixation duration, the second eye-gaze variable, corresponds to the total time or total duration of the learner's eye gaze(s) on a specific target. A fixation was operationalized as being greater than 200 milliseconds in duration. In cases where there was only one fixation on a target, this number reflects the duration of that single fixation. However, when there were two or more fixations on a target the total time reflects the sum of all fixations on that target.

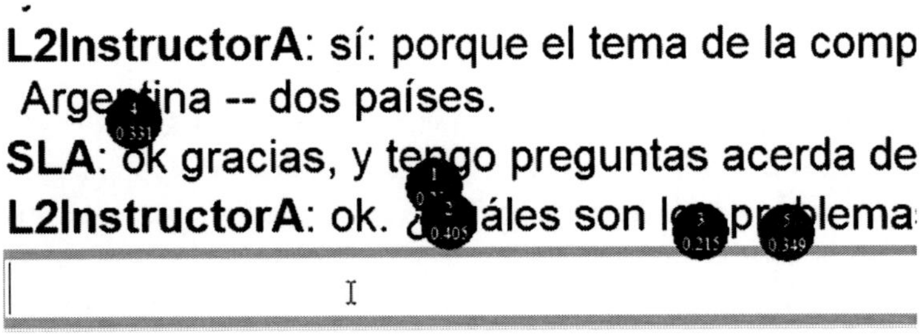

L2InstructorA: sí: porque el tema de la comp Argentina -- dos países.
SLA: ok gracias, y tengo preguntas acerda de
L2InstructorA: ok. ¿Cuáles son los problema:

Figure 2. Enlarged section of a screen-shot indicating number, sequence (the whole number in the circles), and duration of eye fixations

The delayed posttest

The posttest score for each targeted item was calculated such that if learners failed to correct a sentence that was recast in the treatment phase or if they made non-target-like changes to a recast item, then this item was scored 0 (incorrect). Changes (correct or incorrect) made to the distractor items were ignored. Only those recast sentences that were rewritten to follow the form suggested by the interlocutor in the recast were scored as 1 (correct). This is an admittedly strict threshold for correctness, but it allows the data to remain in binomial form.

Results

There were a total of 72 recasts in the data reflecting 127 specific linguistic targets. This translates into about 1.76 targets per recast. Of these 127 targeted items, learners fixated on the appropriate target 92 times. Table 1 shows the descriptive data of eye fixations and posttest scores for all recast items. On the delayed posttest, learners cumulatively got 23 of 122 items correct.[3] Viewed another way, although learners typically fixated on the intended targets, they were able to produce only about one in five of these correctly on the posttest taken about one week after the chat interaction.

---

3. There were five empty cells for posttest due to the occasional failure by learners to address all posttest items.

Table 1. Descriptive data of recasts, eye fixations, and posttest score

Fixation	Posttest incorrect	Posttest correct
No	33	2
Yes	66	21

Learners' posttest performance

Our first research question concerned the factors that impact learners' performance on the delayed posttest. Since the number of correct items in the delayed posttest seems quite low, we first explored the relationship between eye fixation and posttest success. Accordingly, a Generalized Estimating Equation for Logistic regression (*GEE logit*)[4] was used (with exchangeable working matrix). Here, we are concerned only with the extent to which eye fixation predicts posttest success. Results show that the estimated odds of learners scoring a "1" on the posttest for a particular target item are 4.99 times higher when they fixated on that target item than when they did not ($\chi^2 = 7.16$, df $= 1$, $p < .01$). When the repeated subject was participant (taking into account the non-independence of these observations), the estimated within-subject correlation between the binary responses (0 or 1 on the posttest) was 0.022. This extremely small value suggests that the non-independence issue is not a major factor with these data. When a simple one-way ANOVA is run with these same data (with fixation only as a predictor variable and assuming independence of observations), it results in a significant difference in favor of fixation=yes, $F(1, 120) = 5.58$, $p < .02$. The Cohen's d value is 0.46, indicating a moderate effect.[5]

Because of the exploratory nature of this study, we ran this basic comparison another way. Only those learners ($n = 11$) who had both fixations and no fixations on targeted items in the recasts were considered. This second analysis yielded posttest scores of just over 30% and 3% for fixation=yes and fixation=no, respectively. A paired samples *t*-test examining the effect of fixation (yes/no) on posttest score revealed that posttest scores were significantly higher for those items that learners fixated on *(M = .30, SD = .32)* than for those where they did not *(M = .03, SD = .08)*; $t(10) = 2.63$, $p < .025$. The Cohen's d yielded a border-line strong effect *(d = .79)*. These results suggest that learners focus their attention at some level on the salient aspects of the teacher's recast and that fixation on a targeted item predicts a significantly higher posttest score than no fixation.

---

4. The *GEE logit* estimates the same model as a standard logistic regression but GEE logit allows for dependence within clusters (participants).

5. Since we hypothesized that target difficulty may play an important role in this study, an ANCOVA was run on the same data with difficulty as the covariate. Whereas difficulty was not shown to be a mediating factor ($p = .126$), fixation remained a strong predictor of posttest success $F(1, 120) = 5.437$, $p < .021$.

We next considered the factors that were predicted to possibly affect posttest success, including the two eye gaze measures (number and duration of fixations to a target) and the three recast features (number of targets, the type of targets, and target difficulty). To examine the relationship between these variables and posttest performance more closely, a *GEE logit* procedure was used (see Appendix B for the descriptive data). None of the variables reached a .05 level of significance; however, there was a trend toward a positive relationship between the number of fixations and posttest success ($\chi^2 = 9.03$, df = 4, $p = .06$). As the number of fixations increases, there seems to be an increase in the likelihood that learners will get that target correct on the posttest (see Table 2). None of the other factors appeared to predict posttest performance.

Table 2. Score statistics for type 3 *GEE logit* analysis

Variable	df	Chi-square	p
Target language	1	0.88	.347
Fixation duration	1	0.60	.438
Number of fixations	4	9.03	.060
Target difficulty	1	0.17	.681
Target type	4	3.89	.421
Target number	4	3.71	.446

A *GEE logit* procedure was run to examine the relationship between number of fixations and posttest success further.[6] The results were once again suggestive ($\chi^2 = 9.14$, df = 4, $p = .057$), with a fixation number of 3 carrying most of the weight in this difference. The estimated odds of a learner scoring a "1" on the posttest were thus about 16 times greater when a learner fixated on a target item three times than when the learner did not fixate on the item. Learners were also more likely to get the posttest item correct with three fixations as compared with one, two, and four or more fixations at a rate of 3.8, 4.0, and 3.5 times, respectively.

Recasts and eye gaze

Our second research question asked about the relationship between the characteristics of the recasts and the learners' eye gaze. Learners fixated on the appropriate target 92 (out of 127) times. It is possible that some targets were fixated on more than other targets were, and, if so, we wonder what affects whether a target is fixated. It seems reasonable to expect the target number, type, and difficulty might affect learners' fixations. A *GEE logit* procedure examining these relationships reveals that, even though learners typically fixate on the target items, none of these variables have any significant effect (see Table 3).

---

6. In this analysis the variable "number of fixations" *only* was included in the model.

Table 3. Effects of target focus, target difficulty, and target number
on fixation (yes/no)

Variable	df	Chi-square	p
Target difficulty	1	0.32	.573
Target type	4	2.29	.682
Target number	4	3.57	.467

We may also expect the projected difficulty[7] of the target and the number of embedded targets to affect the duration of fixations. A two-factor ANOVA was run with length of fixation as the dependent variable. To make the normality of residuals assumption plausible, a transformation of the original fixation length data was required so that the square root of each fixation length measure was used in the analysis.[8] Participant as a variable was included in the model as a blocking effect.[9] There was a suggestive main effect for target number, $F(4, 102) = 2.05$, $p = .09$, with no effect for target difficulty, $F(1, 102) = 0.01$, $p = .91$, and there was no interaction effect, allowing us to interpret the suggestive effect for target number unambiguously. The number of targets, then, may have an effect on the fixation length. This finding seems to indicate that, as the number of targets in the recast increases, so does the duration of any one fixation associated with that recast.

Discussion

The results from this exploratory study suggest that using eye-tracking methodology as a measure of noticing of recasts in a SCMC context offers insights into micro-aspects of individual SCMC behavior. Indeed, SCMC appears to enable learners to pay careful attention to not only lexical but also grammatical recasts. Since corrective feedback in SCMC is provided through a written medium, students are able to linger on the recast as well as refer back to it, to make sure they assimilate its content. The eye-tracking methodology, without interfering with the task at hand, clearly demonstrates that this is so.

Research question 1 asked what eye gaze behavior and recast features impact learners' performance on the delayed posttest. We saw that learners fixated on corrective recasts of

---

7. The variables within target focus and difficulty were highly correlated with Agreement and Tense coded as "difficult" 100% of the time and Spelling, Lexical, and Other coded as "not difficult" 100%, 92%, and 82%, respectively. With this in mind, we did not run target focus to keep the model as simple as possible.

8. A histogram of residuals did not indicate any sever departure from normality for the transformed (square root) data.

9. The variable "participant" had a significant effect on fixation length indicating that there are large participant-to-participant differences.

their initially non-target like utterances about 72% of the time, and that they often looked at the salient features in the recasts more than once. About one-fifth to one-third of these targets was scored correct on the subsequent posttest. Although this may seem low, recall the strict coding threshold mentioned above and also that this posttest occurred about one week after the interaction with no explicit follow-up on these targets by the instructor. Considering that there was no additional pedagogical intervention, we feel that these results are encouraging. Learners are clearly focusing on formal aspects of the recast item relative to the rest of the text produced by the interlocutor. Additionally, although we did not directly examine the correlation between the complexity of the recasts and the posttest scores, the text-based SCMC may also alleviate some of the processing costs associated with complex recasts simply because learners can fixate a target for a longer period of time and to refer back to it later, if needed. This possibility seems supported by the fact that learners fixated targets independently of their complexity.

The eye-tracking record convincingly showed that the strongest predictor of posttest success of all of the variables considered is when learners fixated on a targeted item for at least 200 milliseconds. Methodologically, this may be viewed as an advance in that we are able to pinpoint where learners direct their attention after receiving corrective feedback and show that this is beneficial for short-term language development as measured by the posttest. This finding is made even more compelling as both target language groups showed the same pattern. The linguistic focus of the recast as well as how complex the recast was did not seem to affect how well one recalled the targeted items, nor did the difficulty of the targeted items. This is interesting because, by design, there were a significant number of recasts targeting an area notoriously difficult for English L1 speakers to learn. We might expect the more difficult targets to be accurately recalled at a significantly lower rate than the easier targets. Yet, this was not the case. Because we could interpret this finding in various ways, a more focused and controlled study of this specific area may be in order to explicitly test the notion that the nature of 'the' SCMC interface itself makes these difficult targets more salient and noticeable. It is also possible that the unrefined coding for difficulty (with lexical and spelling issues coded as easy but agreement and tense as difficult) may be the cause for the lack of significant result. Nonetheless, it appears that any type of recast has an equal chance of being noticed and fixated by the learners in this environment.

The eye-tracking methodology also allowed us to explore not just whether, but also how long learners attended to the corrective targets. Although the duration of the fixation did not seem to be a factor in posttest success, the number of fixations showed a suggestive effect, in that three separate fixations on a targeted item seemed to be the 'sweet spot' in terms of predicting posttest success. However, these results must be interpreted cautiously, as the numbers of items were rather small.

Research question 2 asked about the relationship between the recast features and the learners' eye gaze. The nature of the recast, whether it was a multiple item recasts or a single recast or whether it was a difficult or an easy target, did not seem to affect whether or not learners fixated on it. Finally, the linguistic focus of the target did not seem to matter. The statistical analysis chosen to explore these possible effects took into account variation across participants, so these findings are quite strong for these particular learners. Looking at the descriptive data (see Appendix B), we find some patterns that beckon a closer look, perhaps in the form of replication. For example, in terms of the target focus, we noticed that lexically-based errors/recasts resulted in fixations 22% more often than spelling-based errors/recasts. Although this difference was not significant, it would be interesting to set the fixation threshold (for analysis) lower, since it could be that learners fixate just as often on spelling-based recasts, but that these fixations are under the 200 milliseconds threshold. The almost identical fixation rate for difficult versus easy items is interesting. Due to our coding, we may consider projected difficulty highly co-indexed with target focus, with the categories agreement and tense coded as difficult, and lexical, spelling, and other as not difficult. However, the rather large difference between spelling and other (and between spelling and lexical) suggests a problem with one or more of those categories. Indeed, the mean across these two categories spanned 24%, whereas the difficult categories spanned only 5%. Another coding-related explanation is that functional words have been shown (in L1 research) to be fixated less often than content words (Carpenter & Just 1983). Furthermore, word length strongly affects fixation, with two-to-three letter words being skipped 75% of the time (Rayner & McConkie 1976). Note that within our agreement category, some of the words were determiners, both functional words and short. Therefore, it is possible that these target words were skipped simply because of the nature of the words themselves and not because of their inherent difficulty.

The interlocutor-controlled number of targets within each recast showed no effect on fixation, even though in raw numbers, single recasts occurred most frequently, and recasts containing five or more targets occur least frequently. However, the fact that the 'five plus' recasts category has a fixation rate of almost 30 percentage points lower than the highest rate (target number=two recasts) suggests that too many embedded targets in a recast (even in SCMC) may be counter-productive if the goal is to draw learners' attention to this type of corrective feedback. Again, more research is required before any strong conclusions can be reached.

When considering the relative fixation length on targets, we saw no difference for more or less difficult targets. The fact that target number showed a suggestive effect on fixation length, with the more complex recasts on the shorter side also warrants a closer look. It may be that we see a drop off in the ability to attend to recasts as well as in the relative length of fixation as the number of embedded targets increases past a certain point. Alternatively, this may simply reflect the sense of urgency to respond to one's interlocutor in the SCMC environment. That is, when reviewing a recast packed with multiple targets, one simply has less time to devote to its various components.

Given our findings, it may be that the SCMC recasts, while still 'intruding minimally,' are a bit more salient to learners than oral/aural recasts as evidenced by the fact that

(a) learners fixated on the targeted items in the recasts 92 (of 127) times, with fixation being the sole predictor of posttest success; (b) there was 'no effect' (on posttest success) for the single/multiple error variable (i.e., target number) suggested in Loewen and Philp (2006); and (c) the difficulty of the targeted items did not seem to be a factor in posttest success. Indeed, the nature of the recast and its targets did not seem to affect fixation at all. The divergent findings may be due to the mode of the recasts, specifically whether they were provided orally or in writing.

Limitations

One obvious limitation of this study is the attempt to apply an existing technology in a new way to explore phenomena for which the technology was not necessarily created. For example, it is not clear how tracking learners' eye movements while engaged in synchronous L2 text chat compares to research where learners are viewing a static record. Though precautions were taken to make this new setting/application more accommodating to the eye-tracking system, such application is virtually uncharted territory (cf. Kuhn 2012; O'Rourke 2008, 2012; Smith 2010, 2012).

Finally, the small sample size resulted from our focus on intact groups of language learners engaged in authentic and relevant tasks in a classroom setting. Given the suggestive findings discussed here, any conclusions will need to be confirmed. Additional tokens would allow a firmer assertion of the relationship between eye fixations and posttest scores across the various categories examined. Also, it would be interesting to investigate immediate posttest scores, as only delayed measures of gains were obtained here.

Final words

Eye-tracking data, though precise and revealing in many ways, is by nature limiting as we are required to make inferences about attention and noticing based on the learners' eye movements. Additionally, given its novelty, it is not really clear that we can speak of an eye-tracking "methodology" in a SCMC L2 context at this time. Indeed, if eye-movement analysis is in its infancy in human-computer interaction and usability research as suggested by Poole and Ball (2005), then applying this technique in SCMC/instructed SLA research is at best "embryonic" (O'Rourke 2012). Nevertheless, it seems that eye tracking is potentially an attractive technique for examining learner attention to form in ways that more common methods cannot do – especially due to its online, non-intrusive nature. Indeed, this approach may work well in conjunction with data from other more established concurrent or retrospective data elicitation measures.

References

Alanen, R. (1995). Input enhancement and rule presentation in second language acquisition. In R. Schmidt (Ed.), *Attention and awareness in foreign language learning and teaching* (pp. 259–302). Honolulu, HI: University of Hawai'i Press.

Ammar, A., & Spada, N. (2006). One size fits all?: Recasts, prompts, and L2 learning. *Studies in Second Language Acquisition, 28,* 543–574.

Carpenter, P. A., & Just, M. A. (1983). What your eyes do while your mind is reading. In K. Rayner (Ed.), *Eye movements in reading: Perceptual and language processes* (pp. 275–307). New York, NY: Academic Press.

Carroll, S. (2001). *Input and evidence: The raw material of second language acquisition.* Amsterdam: John Benjamins.

DeKeyser, R. M. (2005). What makes learning second language grammar difficult? A review of issues. *Language Learning, 55*(S1), 1–25.

Dussias, P. (2010). Uses of eye-tracking data in second language sentence processing research. *Annual Review of Applied Linguistics, 30,* 149–166.

Ellis, R., Loewen, S., & Erlam, R. (2006). Implicit and explicit corrective feedback and the acquisition of L2 grammar. *Studies in Second Language Acquisition, 28,* 339–368.

Ellis, R., & Sheen, Y. (2006). Reexamining the role of recasts in second language acquisition. *Studies in Second Language Acquisition, 28,* 575–600.

Franceschina, F. (2005). *Fossilized second language grammars: The acquisition of grammatical gender.* Amsterdam: John Benjamins.

Gass, S. M. (1997). *Input, interaction, and the second language learner.* Mahwah, NJ: Lawrence Erlbaum Associates.

Gass, S. M. (2010). Interactionist perspectives on second language acquisition. In R. Kaplan (Ed.), *The Oxford handbook of applied linguistics* (pp. 217–231). Oxford: Oxford University Press.

Gass, S. M., & Mackey, A. (2000). *Stimulated recall methodology in second language research.* Mahwah, NJ: Lawrence Erlbaum Associates.

Gass, S. M., & Varonis, E. M. (1994). Input, interaction, and second language production. *Studies in Second Language Acquisition, 16,* 283–302.

Godfroid, A., Housen, A., & Boers, F. (2010). A procedure for testing the noticing hypothesis in the context of vocabulary acquisition. In M. Pütz & L. Sicola (Eds.), *Cognitive processing in second language acquisition* (pp. 169–197). Amsterdam: John Benjamins.

Hopp, H. (2011). Internal and external factors in the child L2 development of the German determiner phrase. *Linguistic Approaches to Bilingualism, 1,* 238–264.

Just, M. A., & Carpenter, P. A. (1976). Eye fixations and cognitive processes. *Cognitive Psychology, 8,* 441–480.

Lai, C., Fei, F., & Roots, R. (2008). The contingency of recasts and noticing. *CALICO Journal, 26,* 70–90.

Leeman, J. (2003). Recasts and second language development: Beyond negative evidence. *Studies in Second Language Acquisition, 25,* 37–63.

Leow, R. P. (2000). A study of the role of awareness in foreign language behavior: Aware vs. unaware learners. *Studies in Second Language Acquisition, 22,* 557–584.

Li, S. (2010). The effectiveness of corrective feedback in SLA: A meta-analysis. *Language Learning, 60,* 309–365.

Loewen, S., & Philp, J. (2006). Recasts in the adult English L2 classroom: Characteristics, explicitness, and effectiveness. *Modern Language Journal, 90,* 536–556.

Long, M. H. (1996). The role of the linguistic environment in second language acquisition. In W. Ritchie & T. Bhatia (Eds.), *Handbook of second language acquisition* (pp. 413–463). San Diego, CA: Academic Press.

Long, M. H. (2007). *Problems in SLA*. Mahwah, NJ: Lawrence Erlbaum Associates.

Lyster, R., & Ranta, L. (1997). Corrective feedback and learner uptake: Negotiation of form in communicative classrooms. *Studies in Second Language Acquisition, 19,* 37–66.

Lyster, R., & Saito, K. (2010). Oral feedback in classroom SLA: A meta-analysis. *Studies in Second Language Acquisition, 32,* 265–302.

Mackey, A. (2006). Feedback, noticing and instructed second language learning. *Applied Linguistics, 27,* 405–430.

Mackey, A., Gass, S. M., & McDonough, K. (2000). How do learners perceive interactional feedback? *Studies in Second Language Acquisition, 22,* 471–497.

Mackey, A., & Goo, J. (2007). Interaction research in SLA: A meta-analysis and research synthesis. In A. Mackey (Ed.), *Conversational interaction in second language acquisition: A collection of empirical studies* (pp. 407–451). Oxford: Oxford University Press.

Mackey, A., & Philp, J. (1998). Conversational interaction and development and second language development: Recasts, responses, and red herrings? *Modern Language Journal, 82,* 338–356.

Mackey, A., Philp, J., Egi, T., Fujii, A., & Tatsumi, T. (2002). Individual differences in working memory, noticing of interactional feedback and L2 development. In P. Robinson (Ed.), *Individual differences and instructed language learning* (pp. 181–208). Amsterdam: John Benjamins.

McCarthy, C. (2008). Morphological variability in the comprehension of agreement: An argument for representation over computation. *Second Language Research, 24,* 459–486.

Nicholas, H., Lightbown, P. M., & Spada, N. (2001). Recasts as feedback to language learners. *Language Learning, 51,* 719–758.

Ohta, A. (2000). Rethinking recasts: A learner-centered examination of corrective feedback in the Japanese classroom. In J. K. Hall & L. Verplaetse (Eds.), *The construction of second and foreign language learning through classroom interaction* (pp. 47–71). Mahwah, NJ: Lawrence Erlbaum Associates.

O'Rourke, B. (2008). The other C in CMC: What alternative data sources can tell us about text-based synchronous computer mediated communication and language learning. *Computer Assisted Language Learning, 21,* 227–251.

O'Rourke, B. (2012). Using eye tracking to investigate gaze behaviour in synchronous computer-mediated communication for language learning. In M. Dooly & R. O'Dowd (Eds.), *Researching online interaction and exchange in foreign language education: Methods and issues,* pp. 305–341. Frankfurt: Peter Lang.

Pellettieri, J. (1999). *Why-talk? Investigating the role of task-based interaction through synchronous network-based communication among classroom learners of Spanish.* Unpublished PhD dissertation, University of California, Davis.

Philp, J. (2003). Constraints on "noticing the gap": Nonnative speakers' noticing of recasts in NS-NNS interaction. *Studies in Second Language Acquisition, 25,* 99–126.

Poole, A., & Ball, L. (2005). Eye tracking in human-computer interaction and usability research. In C. Ghaoui (Ed.): *Encyclopedia of human-computer interaction* (pp. 211–219). Hershey, PA: Idea Group Reference.

Rayner, K. (1998). Eye movements in reading and information processing: 20 years of research. *Psychological Bulletin, 12,* 372–422.

Rayner, K., & McConkie, G. W. (1976). What guides a reader's eye movements? *Vision Research, 16,* 829–837.

Robinson, P. (1996). Learning simple and complex second language rules under implicit, incidental, rule-search and instructed conditions. *Studies in Second Language Acquisition, 18,* 27–67.

Sachs, R., & Suh, B. (2007). Textually enhanced recasts, learner awareness, and L2 outcomes in synchronous computer-mediated interaction. In A. Mackey (Ed.), *Conversational interaction in second language acquisition: A collection of empirical studies* (pp. 197–227). Oxford: Oxford University Press.

Salaberry, M. R. (2000). L2 morphosyntactic development in text-based computer mediated communication. *Computer Assisted Language Learning, 13,* 5–27.

Sauro, S. (2009). Computer-mediated corrective feedback and the development of L2 grammar. *Language Learning and Technology, 13*(1), 96–120.

Sauro, S., & Smith, B. (2010). Investigating L2 performance in text chat. *Applied Linguistics, 31,* 554–577.

Schmidt, R. (2001). Attention. In P. Robinson (Ed.), *Cognition and second language instruction* (pp. 3–32). Cambridge: Cambridge University Press.

Seedhouse, P. (1997). The case of the missing "no": The relationship between pedagogy and interaction. *Language Learning, 47,* 547–583.

Sheen, Y. (2004). Corrective feedback and learner uptake in communicative classrooms across instructional settings. *Language Teaching Research, 8,* 263–300.

Sheen, Y. (2006). Exploring the relationship between characteristics of recasts and learner uptake. *Language Teaching Research, 10,* 361–392.

Smith, B. (2004). Computer-mediated negotiated interaction and lexical acquisition. *Studies in Second Language Acquisition, 26,* 365–398.

Smith, B. (2008). Methodological hurdles in capturing CMC data: The case of the missing self-repair. *Language Learning and Technology, 12*(1), 85–103.

Smith, B. (2010). Employing eye-tracking technology in researching the effectiveness of recasts in CMC. In F. M. Hult (Ed.), *Directions and prospects for educational linguistics* (pp. 79–97). London: Springer.

Tarone, E., & Bigelow, M. (2007). Alphabetic print literacy and oral language processing in SLA. In A. Mackey (Ed.), *Conversational interaction in second language acquisition: A collection of empirical studies* (pp. 101–122). Oxford: Oxford University Press.

Trofimovich, P., Ammar, A., & Gatbonton, E. (2007). How effective are recasts? The role of attention, memory, and analytical ability. In A. Mackey (Ed.), *Conversational interaction in second language acquisition: A collection of empirical studies* (pp. 171–195). Oxford: Oxford University Press.

White, L., Valenzuela, E., Kozlowska-Macgregor, M., & Leung, Y.-k. I. (2004). Gender and number agreement in nonnative Spanish. *Applied Psycholinguistics, 25,* 105–133.

Yilmaz, Y., & Yuksel, D. (2011). Effects of communication mode and salience on recasts: A first exposure study. *Language Teaching Research, 15,* 457–477.

Yuan, F., & Ellis, R. (2003). The effects of pre-task planning and on-line planning on fluency, complexity and accuracy in L2 oral production. *Applied Linguistics, 24,* 1–28.

Appendix A

Example of a delayed posttest

Directions:

Some of the sentences below are correct and grammatical the way they are written and some are not. For each of the sentences below, please write "OK" directly under the sentence if it is correct the way it appears and "No" if it is not correct. If you write "No" then please rewrite the sentence correcting any mistakes the original sentence contains.

1. Ich lese und koche gern und ich arbeite gern aus
2. Ich muss viel arbeiten, also ich kann geld genug für deutschland haben
3. Ich will Latein, Franzosisch, Chineisisch lernen
4. Ich wöllte viel spracher lernen.
5. Soziologe ist sehr general, damit kann ich viel problem ein bisschen lernen
6. A: Welche Berufsplaene haben Sie?
    B: Idealisch will ich ein soziologist werden
7. A: Wie sehen Sie aus?
    B: Ich bin sehr hoch mit blandenes haar
8. A: Wie sollte Ihre ideale Partnerin sein?
    B: Sie sollte klein und kurz aussiehen, mit dunkeles haar
9. A: Wohinn wollen Sie reisen?
    B: Nach deutschland, über all europa, griechland

Appendix B

Descriptive data on the effects of target type, target difficulty, and target number on the response variable fixation (yes/no)

Recast features		N	Mean fixation rate	SD	SEM
Target type	Adjective	33	.70	.47	.08
	Lexical	38	.79	.41	.07
	Other	21	.81	.40	.09
	Spelling	23	.57	.51	.11
	Tense	12	.75	.45	.13
Difficulty	Not difficult	75	.73	.45	.05
	Difficult	52	.71	.46	.06
Target number	1	42	.76	.43	.07
	2	30	.83	.38	.07
	3	28	.61	.50	.09
	4	16	.75	.45	.11
	5+	11	.55	.52	.16

Chapter 9

A corpus approach to studying structural convergence in task-based Spanish L2 interactions

Joseph Collentine and Karina Collentine
Northern Arizona University

Having established that interaction positively affects acquisition, research is expanding the theoretical frameworks and methodological tools with which it studies how interactional processes promote L2 development. This chapter uses corpus-linguistic tools to study Spanish L2 learners' interaction in tasks involving a 3D world and synchronous computer-mediated communication (SCMC). We study the learners' use of complex syntax from the theoretical perspective of structural alignment, which posits that language acquisition is enhanced when two learners' output essentially "converges" (Branigan, Pickering, Pearson & McLean 2010) on the use of the same or comparable linguistic structures. The present study provides evidence that Spanish L2 learners align their syntactic production during communicative interaction by converging on the use of complex sentences containing nominal clauses.

Introduction

An important first question investigated in interaction research was whether interactional processes promote second language (L2) development. Having established that such is the case (cf. Mackey & Gass 2006), the current goal of interaction research to attain an understanding of how it brings about L2 development (see Mackey 2007) challenges researchers to strive for greater ecological validity, such that we can improve our practical recommendations to educators about instructional practices and learning conditions where interaction can foster L2 development.

Generalizing the beneficial effects of interactional processes from the laboratory to the classroom is not straightforward. Nicholas, Lightbown, and Spada (2001) suggest that learners may be especially sensitive to certain interactive features (e.g., feedback) in laboratory settings, where feedback is not mitigated by the potential distractions of the classroom. Recent meta-analyses comparing the effects of interactional processes in laboratory and classroom settings underscore how difficult it is to generalize laboratory findings to the classroom. Russell and Spada (2006), focusing on the effects of corrective feedback, found no differences between classroom and laboratory settings. Mackey and Goo (2007) in their meta-analysis of the effects of interaction on the acquisition of grammatical and lexical items showed that laboratory settings have consistently larger effects than classroom settings. Similarly, Li's (2010) meta-analysis about the effects of corrective feedback on L2 acquisition indicated that laboratory settings have a larger effect than classrooms. He conjectured that in classroom settings, teachers tend to provide feedback to whole groups of learners rather than individuals. While it is debatable whether feedback given to whole groups of learners constitutes interaction, Li's (2010) assessment does illustrate obstacles researchers face when trying to increase the ecological validity of interaction research. Lyster and Saito's (2010) meta-analysis, which focused exclusively on classroom-based studies, suggested that the research setting may interact with the types of corrective feedback that impact acquisition (e.g., classroom learners are especially sensitive to prompts). Similar to Li (2010), Lyster and Saito (2010) surmised that classroom settings may provide corrective feedback with less intensity and consistency than the feedback provided in laboratory settings. This observation is interesting given that Li (2010) found that, even though classroom settings have less impact on acquisition, classroom studies entail longer treatment periods than laboratory settings.

Mackey and Gass (2006: 171–172) pointed out that the shift to researching how interactional processes affect L2 development has entailed a "broadening of the research methods employed" which calls for the utilization of "novel types of data collection." They observed an expansion in the types of coding systems researchers use to study interaction effects, such as analytical schemas measuring fluency, accuracy, and complexity. Broadening the methodological tools and theoretical frameworks with which we study interaction may provide "a more detailed and nuanced picture of the mechanisms of the interaction-learning relationship" (Mackey & Gass 2006: 72).

The empirical study reported in this chapter, involving foreign-language (FL) learners of Spanish at the third year of university instruction, seeks to enhance the ecological validity of interaction research and demonstrate ways of broadening the field's methodological tools and theoretical frameworks. To contribute to our understanding of the practical benefits of interactional processes in L2 learning, we study learner interaction in a task-based, 3D environment where dyads communicate to achieve their goals through synchronous computer-mediated communication (SCMC) (for additional SCMC studies see Smith & Renaud, this volume and Sauro, this volume). The study utilizes corpus-linguistic tools, methods that are rarely employed in interaction research. We study the learners' use of complex syntax from the theoretical perspective of structural alignment (Pickering & Garrod 2004), which posits that language acquisition is enhanced when two learners' output essentially "converges" (Branigan, Pickering, Pearson & McLean 2010: 2355) on the use of the same or comparable linguistic structures.

Task-based synchronous computer-mediated communication

Research shows that SCMC is effective at encouraging L2 interaction (Beauvois 1997; Warschauer 1996, 1997). As Smith (2008) noted, since L2 communication in chat technologies is not simply a written form of oral discourse, SCMC is a valid and valuable context for conducting L2 interaction research. SCMC interaction can be thought of as data that represent learners' abilities in the absence of the pressures that 'unfilled pauses' can place on the need for spontaneity in oral, face-to-face interactions. These pressures can lead to incomplete processing of complex linguistic elements due to processing challenges (Kern 1995; Warschauer & Kern 2000). SCMC may even lead to more complex language than oral, face-to-face interaction (Kern 1995; Salaberry 2000).

Doughty and Long (2003) suggest that SCMC activities should follow task-based language-teaching (TBLT) principles. Tasks involve holistic language use such that learners must focus on meaning because the reason for their interaction is non-linguistic (e.g., find the lost keys; Samuda & Bygate 2008). Robinson (2001) and Yuan and Ellis (2003) argue that an important product of tasks is that they can push output. Tasks can move learners from pragmatic processing, which is characterized by single-clause sentences and simple word formation, to syntactic processing, such as complex sentences and complex word formations (Foster & Skehan 1996).

One way to increase the meaningfulness of task-based SCMC interaction could be to place the task within a 3D virtual environment, where learners accomplish their non-linguistic goal by reading or listening to information found in the virtual world (e.g., a letter found on the floor) and by obtaining information from avatars. Virtual environments can provide learners with situationally authentic experiences (Jones, Squires & Hicks 2007; Peterson 2006; Sykes 2009; Toyoda & Harrison 2002; Zheng, Young, Brewer & Wagner 2009). SLA researchers are just beginning to study L2 development in 3D environments. Most research has focused on whether learners can be autonomous in these settings. Nonetheless, Collentine (2011) demonstrated that certain design features of 3D worlds involving a task (e.g., the lexical density of avatars' statements and sentences that learners read) predicted learners' use of syntactic complexity in SCMC.

FL practitioners have shown interest in identifying the potential benefits of emerging technologies. Instant messaging, with which SCMC shares many features, and 3D environments, an extension of gaming, could well become popular in future instructional settings. Thus, we suggest that framing an interaction study within a 3D task, as we do in this chapter, will add to the ecological validity of interaction research.

Corpus-linguistic tools and techniques

In addition to studying interaction in SCMC based on tasks situated in a 3D world, this chapter demonstrates how interactionist research can utilize corpus-linguistic tools. Myles (2005) and Myles and Mitchell (2005) lament that SLA research has not been quick to embrace new technologies for collecting and analyzing data, especially considering the important insights that corpus linguistics has provided in first-language (L1) research. They argued that corpus linguistics can complement current SLA research by examining large amounts of data with relative ease, thus increasing the generalizability of finding (Rutherford & Thomas 2001).

Corpus linguistics uses digitized text to answer research questions (Reppen & Simpson-Vach 2010). Concordance applications and scripting languages (e.g., Python) allow researchers to tabulate the frequencies of both general (e.g., word classes) and very specific (e.g., inflectional properties of verbs) information in learner production. When investigators need to search for morphosyntactic information (e.g., all adjectives, all verbs whose infinitive is either *ser* or *estar*), they often use a part-of-speech (POS) tagger: a series of software modules that, based on a dictionary and word-guessing algorithms, annotates every word with information about its major word class (e.g., adjective, noun, verb, determiner, preposition), basic morphological features (e.g., plural, preterit), and its lemma (i.e., its unmarked, dictionary root, such as a verb's infinitive or a noun's masculine, singular form). An increasingly popular technology to search for patterns across a tagged corpus is regular expressions, a wild-card and variable-based text-search system (e.g., \w{3,} symbolizes words of three letters or more; \w+ing symbolizes words of any length ending in -*ing*). Searching a tagged corpus with regular expressions provides a powerful means of studying a number of lexical and/or grammatical phenomena. For instance, the pattern \w+\^v[^`]*`[^`]*`[^`]*`(?:ser|parecer)` (?:obvio|evidente)\^j\w+ que\^\w+ is one way to search for every verb whose lemma is either *ser* 'to be' or *parecer* 'to seem' followed by the adjectives *obvio* 'obvious' or *evidente* 'evident' followed by the conjunction *que*.

POS tagging and analysis can answer important SLA questions. Collentine and Asención-Delaney (2010) used a POS tagged corpus of L2 Spanish of three instructional levels to examine the extent to which a total of 37 lexical and grammatical properties predicted copula + adjective use. The analysis produced a description of the different associations that learners make with both of Spanish's copulas (in attributive sentences) and how those associations might change from one level of instruction to the next. Asención-Delaney and Collentine (2011) employed a tagged corpus to conduct a multidimensional (factor) analysis of a written Spanish corpus from FL learners at the second and third years of university instruction. Their study showed the multiple ways that learners generate stylistic sophistication and linguistic complexity, demonstrating that learners generate discourse types that are not reflective of the models that they study in their FL curriculum.

Corpus-linguistic tools are uncommon in interaction research. Reinhardt (2008), for instance, used corpus techniques to identify and analyze 'negotiations for meaning' in Telekorp (Telecollaborative Corpus of German and English). K. Collentine (2010) used corpus techniques to study linguistic complexity in learner chats, showing that the extent to which constellations of complexity features appear in task-based SCMC is dependent on task features such as the amount of time learners interact.

A corpus-based approach can increase the ecological validity of studies on classroom interaction and address frequency issues. It allows the researcher to be inconspicuous since highly naturalistic data (e.g., SCMC transcripts) can be analyzed *post facto*. Of course, moving interaction research from the laboratory to the classroom can make it difficult to study interaction's effects on grammatical structures that occur infrequently in learner interaction. As noted above, one of the challenges to promoting interactional processes in classroom settings is that classroom learners inconsistently focus their attention on targeted structures (Lyster & Saito 2010). Additionally, some structures are infrequent even in the interactions of proficient speakers. J. Collentine (2010:49), for instance, provided evidence that the Spanish subjunctive (a central construct in the Spanish FL curriculum) is infrequent in native-speaker dialogues and it tends to have a low "communicative value" because it is often semantically redundant; the modality it conveys is normally marked lexically within the same sentence. This presents an immense challenge to materials designers attempting to promote the subjunctive's use in communicative interaction. Corpus-based research can be very useful in studying low-frequency structures in classroom-based interaction since, if a large corpus is available, corpus tools' computational power can provide a sufficiently large sample for a researcher to make generalizable conclusions. Finally, corpora can be tagged for all sorts of information important to interactionist researchers. Learner data can be annotated with information such as where turns begin and end, permitting us to readily examine how learners affect each other's output in communicative interaction.

The present study takes advantage of the fact that the SCMC data it uses is digitized, thus lending itself to corpus linguistic analysis. We focus on a grammatical structure that, for developmental reasons, is not likely to be frequent in Spanish learner interaction, namely, sentences with nominal clauses (see below). And, since we can easily study the relationship between the content of learners' (adjacent) turns, we analyze the extent to which learners implicitly encourage each other to use nominal clauses, a cognitive process known as *convergence*.

Priming and syntactic convergence in interaction

The present chapter analyzes learners' use of complex syntax from a structural alignment perspective (Garrod & Clark 1993), a framework for studying cognition and learning during interaction that draws on priming theory. Priming research attempts to explain how a speaker's use of, say, a grammatical structure leads his interlocutor to use the same structure. Cognitively speaking, a learner processing a sentence with complex syntax (from an input or output perspective) activates the rules associated with the construct. Syntactic activation does not decay quickly. Priming is said to occur when the persistence of the activated structure increases the likelihood that it will appear again, either in one's own production or in the production of an interlocutor (Pickering & Ferreira 2008). Priming appears to be an interactional process that promotes language learning. For example, L2 learners of English appear to be sensitive to whether an interlocutor produces a prepositional dative (e.g., *Mary gave the ball to him*) rather than a double-object dative (e.g., *Mary gave him the ball*). McDonough and Mackey (2008) provided L2 learners of English with scripted *wh*-questions, and learners who generated similar *wh*-questions in response to the scripted questions showed greater subsequent usage of native-like *wh*-questions. McDonough and Kim (2009) showed that syntactic priming materials prompting English L2 learners to produce *wh*-questions with a variety of lexical verbs increased the likelihood that they would produce the structure in subsequent testing. The present study focuses on an aspect of priming that promotes learning during communicative interaction known as structural alignment.

Structural alignment refers to a mental state whereas two interlocutors adopt comparable mental representations of the information about which they are communicating. Structural alignment occurs when interlocutors instantiate and draw on similar mental representations of syntactic structures and inflectional morphology during interaction (Pickering & Garrod 2004). Structural alignment is, in fact, an important language-learning mechanism, since it can reduce processing demands. Garrod and Clark (1993) surmise that alignment is children's default behavior, and mature language users will suppress the tendency to align linguistic behaviors (cf. Branigan et al. 2010).

Convergence is a production behavior that is indicative of (the mental state of) alignment. It manifests itself at various levels of representation, such as lexical choice – e.g., two interlocutors using *sofa* throughout a conversation even if one normally uses *couch* – or syntax – e.g., two interlocutors favoring restrictive clauses like *the cow that's brown* over adjectives such as *the brown cow*. Pickering and Garrod (2004) refer to this as interactive alignment, and it affords processing advantages to less proficient speakers of a language. According to Pickering and Garrod (2004), convergence permits interlocutors to use fewer attentional resources than if they were to use different structures. For example, when speakers converge, one does not need to activate both the structures that s/he wants to use (to process output) as well as (to process input) the ones that his or her interlocutor might use. High levels of convergence may be an indicator of less overall L2 proficiency. In contrast, more proficient language users such as native speakers have automatized the processing of a larger repertoire of linguistic structures, which likely will lead to less convergence.

It is thus reasonable to predict that L2 learners will demonstrate relatively more structural convergence than native speakers under similar conditions of interaction. To that end, the study presented below uses corpus-linguistic techniques to compare learners' and native speakers' convergence with nominal-clause syntax. The study's tasks (described below) required learners to interact in SCMC to solve a mystery with information they obtain from a 3D virtual environment. During their SCMC interaction, they needed to share information about the whereabouts of persons and objects in the 3D world. They also needed to conjecture about the truthfulness and reliability of the information they obtained. Spanish epistemic syntax – that is, sentences containing a main and a nominal clause – is quite useful for such conjecturing (J. Collentine 2010). Spanish epistemic syntax relates the source of information that one shares with an interlocutor as well as the confidence an interlocutor has in the truth value of some information that s/he shares. For instance, Example (1) contains a main-clause verb of communication.

(1) *Elena dice que el criminal es Juan.*
      'Elena says that the criminal is Juan.'
      V (finite; epistemic verb) + que (that complementizer) + V (finite; any state/event)

The structure *decir que* 'to say that' attributes the truthfulness of the proposition 'the criminal is Juan' to someone in the 3D world named Elena. Example (2) includes main-clause verbs of knowledge or belief, which indicate the extent to which the main-clause subject is dedicated to the truth value of the subordinate-clause proposition.

(2) *Yo creo/pienso/sé que el criminal es Juan.*
      'I believe/think/know that the criminal is Juan.'
      V (finite; epistemic verb) + que (that complementizer) + V (finite; any state/event)

Collentine (1995) presented evidence that epistemic structures emerge late in Spanish FL development. J. Collentine (2010) provided a comprehensive review of the research relating to the acquisition of complex syntax in Spanish FL acquisition, considering semantic, morphological, and syntactic factors as well as cognitive ones. He concluded that information-processing issues largely account for why structures such as nominal clauses have a protracted period of development in Spanish FL learning. For instance, even advanced learners struggle to share information between clauses because Spanish has intricate morphological and pronominal agreement rules. Nevertheless, to our knowledge, no research to date has examined Spanish FL learners' use of epistemic syntax from an interactionist perspective.

Research questions

This study investigates interaction in task-based SCMC situated in a 3D virtual environment. Furthermore, it uses and demonstrates the utility of corpus-linguistic methods for studying structural convergence in these language-learning conditions. Advanced FL learners of Spanish participated in two tasks consisting of a 3D exploration segment followed by an SCMC chat segment (see Tasks below). Dyads were instructed to interact in the SCMC segments to solve a crime related to the virtual world, where they were to gather clues. We compare the learner data with a native-speaker baseline to provide an understanding of the extent to which L2 and L1 convergence are different. Finally, to explore the ways that Spanish proficiency might interact with syntactic convergence, we compare the types of structures that learners and native-speakers employ in utterances where they did not demonstrate convergence. We thus ask:

1. Does nominal-clause convergence occur amongst Spanish L2 dyads in SCMC when learners interact to accomplish a task?
2. Is Spanish L2 nominal-clause convergence greater than Spanish L1 convergence under similar interactional conditions?
3. If they do not demonstrate convergence, what syntactic structures do L1 and L2 Spanish speakers use?

Method

Participants

A total of 53 third-year university-level learners at a medium-sized university in the United States from intact Spanish classes participated in the study. They were enrolled in a junior-level course designed to review major grammatical structures and in a junior-level course focusing on developing conversational fluency. All participants had met or exceeded the learning outcomes from the previous course, a fourth-semester Spanish course. The classes were traditional, face-to-face courses employing group activities as well as a variety of multimedia activities (e.g., watching videos, Internet exploration/research). While the courses required writing, speaking, and inductive/exploration activities, they did not entail any chat or instant messaging beyond the segments of this study. One of the researchers was the instructor of these classes but did not participate in the experimental tasks. The tasks were integrated into two lesson plans lasting two class periods of 1.5 hours, for a total of 3 hours. No grades were awarded for participation.

Tasks

Learners participated in two tasks designed by the present authors, each containing a 3D exploration segment and a subsequent SCMC segment. The 3D segments were developed with the Unity suite of tools (http://unity3d.com/). The SCMC segments occurred in a local area network with the dyads using iChat. The laboratory where both segments took place was equipped with individual Mac laptops placed on conference tables arranged in a semicircle.

Each task first took learners to a 3D island containing non-player characters and objects relevant to some crime. They explored the island to collect clues as first-person characters, queried non-player characters, and collected clues from objects in the environment (e.g., notes, letters). The first task asked learners to find clues to solve a missing-persons case, while the second task required learners to solve a murder-mystery. The 3D tasks contained two user interfaces within which to gather clues and information, one interface involving non-player characters and another interface involving objects. Participants moved individually and freely within the 3D environment, choosing who or what to approach and how often.

When learners approached non-player characters, they saw three possible questions that they could 'ask' by clicking on any of the three buttons with questions written in Spanish, whereupon they received a written answer in Spanish (see Figure 1).

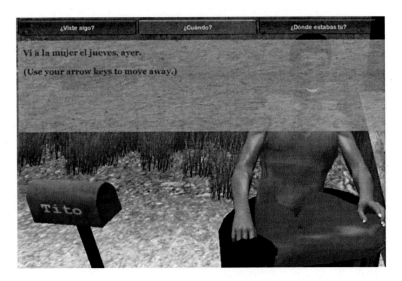

Figure 1. Sample non-player character question dialog

If they approached an object (e.g., a diary), they saw a written message in Spanish containing information to read, as shown in Figure 2.

Figure 2. Sample message dialog

Learners were told to explore the 3D environment all they wanted to solve the task. In both 3D segments, learners were told to close the application after 10 minutes of gathering clues.

After each task, students were paired up into predetermined, randomly assigned dyads to carry out SCMC interactions. Dyads were instructed to arrive at a consensus relating to the relevant crime. For the missing-persons task, dyads needed to determine the reason(s) for the person's disappearance, and for the murder-mystery, they needed to determine the reason(s) for the murder. Each SCMC phase lasted 25 minutes.

To familiarize the learners with both the 3D technology and iChat, the day before the experiment the learners navigated a sample 3D world (not employed in the present analyses) containing examples/instances of the technologies described here. Subsequently, the participants practiced chatting about the sample 3D world.

Dataset: Learner chatscripts

Each dyad's iChat transcript was archived to a text document, allowing the measurement of various aspects of a dyad's lexical and syntactic output. The corpus totaled 34,395 words with 2063 turns, for an average of 16.7 ($SD = 27.5$) words per turn. A turn could be composed of more than one message (i.e., any line of output extending up to where a learner hit RETURN/ENTER), and there were a total of 3538 messages in the sample. Each turn averaged 1.7 ($SD = 2.8$) messages, with each message averaging 10.3 ($SD = 7.0$) words. In any measure, the variation is quite high. The mode per message was 4.0 and the median 8.5. It is thus not surprising that the distribution of words per message was positively skewed at 2.1, whereas some messages were quite long: a total of 167 messages (4.7%) contained 20 or more words.

Every word of every dyad's transcript in each task was tagged for lexical and part-of-speech information. The tagger employed a training set from the *Corpus del español* (Biber, Davies, Jones, & Tracy-Ventura 2006) and a part-of-speech dictionary with words tagged for various lexical and inflectional properties. The tagger also entailed probabilistic routines from the python-based Natural Language Toolkit (http://www.nltk.org/) as well as routines specifically designed for tagging L2 corpora. Tagging routines also marked the start of all messages and turns. The researchers composed search routings with Python and regular expressions to tabulate the counts per turn of the target structure.

Dataset: Native speaker interaction

To obtain baseline native-speaker data to provide an understanding of the extent to which L2 convergence is different from L1 convergence with nominal-clause syntax, we compiled a subcorpus of the *Corpus del español*, a 20 million-word Spanish corpus with written and oral data from a variety of registers with each word tagged for part-of-speech features (Biber et al. 2006). To obtain a subcorpus consisting of robust native-speaker Spanish interactional discourse, we selected documents that were categorized as an interview or a conversation, that had between 250 and 600 words, and that had between 10 and 40 words per turn. This yielded 129 candidate documents, 126 of which had at least one instance of nominal-clause syntax. Since there were 53 chats in the learner corpus, we then used a random sampling algorithm to select 53 native-speaker baseline documents, producing a corpus of 24,048 words.

Analyses

To study nominal-clause syntactic convergence amongst Spanish L2 dyads and to compare such convergence with L1 Spanish production under comparable conditions, we employed an analysis of variance (ANOVA) to compare the learners' and native speakers' production of targets in response to primes, or lack thereof. We first designed a regular expressions pattern to search for instances of: V (finite; verb) + *que* (that complementizer) + V (finite; any state/event). Before conducting a complete analysis, we analyzed qualitatively the reliability of the pattern with samples of the learner and native-speaker corpora that indicated they were accurate in identifying sentences with nominal-clause syntax. We then constructed Python scripts to count the occurrences of primes and targets in any given turn (cf. Gries 2005). Primes were the occurrence of nominal-clause syntax in a turn where the previous turn lacked such syntax; targets were the occurrence of nominal-clause syntax where the previous turn had such syntax. No target was counted as a prime. Thus, if three consecutive turns had nominal-clause syntax, the third turn's data could only be classified as a (potential) prime. Following Gries (2005), this analysis yielded four distinct counts per document illustrated in (3) and (4).

(3) Interlocutor A uttered the prime, whereupon…
    a.   interlocutor B produced the target.
    b.   interlocutor B did not produce the target.

(4) Interlocutor A did not utter the prime, whereupon…
    a.   interlocutor B produced the target.
    b.   interlocutor B did not produce the target.

For both the learner and native-speaker documents, we calculated two types of target proportions to measure the potential effects of one interlocutor's syntactic structure on the other. The first was target-prime proportions, which was the proportion of targets produced by interlocutor B when interlocutor A uttered a prime, which corresponds with (1a). The second was target-no-prime proportions, which was the proportion of targets produced by interlocutor B when interlocutor A did not utter a prime, which corresponds with (2a). To assess the learners' propensity for syntactic priming while considering normal priming effects that native speakers realize, we employ a repeated-measures ANOVA with one between-groups factor and one within-groups factor. The dependent variable is target proportion. The between-groups factor is interlocutor type (2 levels: learner dyad, native-speaker dyad) and the within-groups factor is priming relationship, for which each interlocutor type provided (i) a target-prime proportion and (ii) a target-no-prime proportion.

To compare the types of syntactic structures that the learners and the native speakers produced when they do not demonstrate nominal-clause convergence, we employ a discriminant analysis to see whether learners and native speakers react similarly or differently when they do not produce a target in response to a prime. To conduct this analysis, we first wrote a Python script with regular expressions that tabulated the occurrence of 16 complex syntactic structures in the learner corpus and the native-speaker subcorpus in turns where the preceding turn had no nominal-clause syntax.[1] Essentially, the analysis looked at differences between learners and native speakers in terms of subordinate clauses other than nominal clauses, Spanish's various passive constructs, and clitic usage. Specifically, the structures involved seven types of adverbial clauses (mode, place/place preceded by preposition, time, causality, conditional, and purpose), four types of adjectival/relative clauses (on the subject, objective, prepositional position, and appositives), three passive types (*ser* 'to be' passives; *se* 'middle-voice' passives, unplanned *se* passives), so-called psych verbs, which like passives place experiencers (typically subjects) in an object (i.e., dative) position (e.g., *Me molesta la pereza* 'Laziness bothers me'), and other preverbal clitics. Since the learner corpus averaged 648 words, to control for the amount of Spanish produced by dyads in non-target responses (e.g., dyads with more frequent counts may simply have produced more words per response), we normed the counts of each of the 12 complex syntactic variables to 650 words. The discriminant analysis uses the complex syntactic structures as predictors of membership in two groups, namely, learners or native-speakers. Like multivariate regression, discriminant analysis produces a set of coefficients that (i) describe each of the complex syntactic structures' ability to discriminate between the learners and the native speakers and (ii) the association of each structure with either group of interlocutors. This permits us to triangulate which complex syntactic structures each group of interlocutors favors.

Results

The repeated-measures ANOVA comparing nominal-clause convergence between the learners and the native speakers indicates that, whereas the learners exhibited structural convergence, the native-speaker baseline did not. Since the ANOVA identified a significant within-subjects interaction between priming relationship and interlocutor type, $F(1,104) = 2.24$, $p = 0.015$, $\eta^2 = 0.055$, any significant main effects are effectively of no interest (see Table 2). The partial eta squared value of 0.055 indicates that the interaction effect was medium in strength, suggesting an important interaction although a more fine-grained analysis might uncover additional factors explaining instances of convergence. The significant interaction effect (illustrated in Figure 3) is thus attributable to the learners' propensity to exhibit nominal-clause syntactic convergence. Whereas the native

---

1.   Asención-Delaney and Collentine (2011) use these features as indicators of complex syntax in their multidimensional analysis of L2 Spanish.

Table 1. Mean target proportions by interlocutor type and priming relationship

Interlocutor type	Priming relationship	M	n	SD	95% Confidence interval	
					Lower bound	Upper bound
learner	target-prime	0.37	53	0.21	0.32	0.42
	target-no-prime	0.29	53	0.12	0.26	0.33
native-speaker	target-prime	0.29	53	0.17	0.24	0.34
	target-no-prime	0.30	53	1.72	0.27	0.33

Table 2. ANOVAs for within-subjects and between-subjects effect

Effect	Source	SS	df	MS	F	p	η^2
Within-subjects	Priming relationship	.058	1	.058	3.469	.065	.032
	Priming relationship × Interlocutor type	.101	1	.101	6.085	.015	.055
	Error	1.733	104	.017			
Between-subjects	Intercept	20.795	1	20.795	602.952	.000	.830
	Interlocutor type	.077	1	.077	2.240	.137	.021
	Error	3.587	104	.034			

speakers were as likely to produce the target when a prime was present in the preceding turn, $M = 0.29$, $SD = 0.17$, as they were when the prime was absent, $M = 0.30$, $SD = 1.72$, the learners were much more likely to produce the target in response to a prime, $M = 0.37$, $SD = 0.21$, than in response to a turn lacking the prime, $M = 0.29$, $SD = 0.12$ (see Table 1).

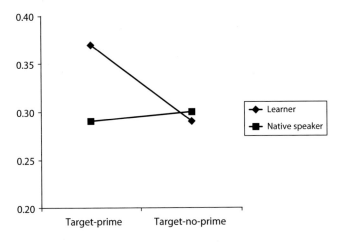

Figure 3. Mean target proportions by interlocutor type and priming relationship

The discriminant analysis comparison of the learners' and the native-speakers' syntactic behaviors when they did not receive a prime in the preceding turn indicates that the native speakers tended to use syntactic structures that are decidedly more complex than those used by the learners. Of the 16 complex syntactic structures included in the analysis, we included eight, all of which had at least 13 counts.

Table 3. Mean counts of complex syntactic structures in turns not preceded by prime

Structure	Native speakers		Learners		Wilk's Λ mean comparison (df = 1,104)
	M	SD	M	SD	p
Adverbial clause: causality	0.81	1.57	2.15	2.60	0.00
Adverbial clause: purpose	0.25	0.76	0.00	0.00	0.02
Adverbial clause: conditional	0.25	0.68	1.11	2.14	0.01
Adverbial clause: time	0.38	0.79	0.17	0.73	0.16
Appositive	0.68	1.42	0.13	0.68	0.01
Preverbal clitic	5.79	4.38	4.28	4.56	0.09
Se passive	1.87	3.43	1.00	2.14	0.12
Psych verbs	0.15	0.41	0.28	1.06	0.40

Tests of equality indicate that four pairs of means differed significantly at $\alpha = .05$. The learners averaged more causality adverbial clauses (e.g., *Fue Juan porque no estaba en la fiesta* 'It was Juan because he wasn't at the party') and conditionals (e.g., *Si es María, hay poca evidencia* 'If it's María, there's little evidence') than the native speakers. On the other hand, the native speakers averaged more purpose adverbial clauses (e.g., *Trabajo allí para que tengamos lo necesario* 'I work there so that we have enough') and appositives (e.g., *Mi amigo, quien no trabaja, está frustrado* 'Mi friend, who doesn't work, is frustrated').

The eight variables significantly differentiated between the learners and the native speakers, Wilk's Λ (8) = .755, $p < 0.00$. The four structures with significant differences between the learners and native speakers were precisely those that combined together in the discriminant function to distinguish the interlocutor groups.

Table 4. Standardized canonical discriminant function coefficients

Syntactic structure	Coefficient
Adverbial clause: purpose	0.41
Appositive	0.36
Preverbal clitic	0.30
Adverbial clause: time	0.23
Se passive	0.13
Psych verbs	−0.10
Adverbial clause: conditional	−0.41
Adverbial clause: causality	−0.51

Although the direction of the sign is merely an artifact of the order in which data were introduced to the discriminant analysis, coefficients with a positive sign are those that most distinguish the native speakers and negative coefficients most distinguish the learners. That is, whereas learners use causality adverbial clauses and conditionals in the absence of a prime, the native speakers use adverbial clauses of purpose and appositives. The native-speaker behaviors are more complex syntactically and functionally. For the most part, native speakers appear to have greater abilities to maintain discursive and situational reference. Adverbial clauses of purpose in Spanish require that the main and subordinate clauses have different subjects, which requires binding considerations (e.g., *Juan$_i$ trabaja para que *Juan$_i$/Paco$_j$ coma* 'Juan works so that *Juan/Paco might eat'). No such restriction is placed on Spanish causality adverbial clauses (e.g., *Juan trabaja$_i$ porque él$_{i,j}$ necesita comer* 'Juan works because he needs to eat) or conditionals (e.g., *Si Juan$_i$ trabaja, él$_{i,j}$ come* 'If Juan works, he eats'). Additionally, appositives involve complex syntactic reference because they are extraposed from the sentence to which their relative pronoun is bound (*Juan$_i$, quien$_i$ trabaja mucho, no tiene nada* 'Juan, who works a lot, doesn't have anything'). Finally, it is important to note that, while both the learners and the native speakers used preverbal clitics often and they did not differ significantly in their average use, preverbal clitics trended towards being more associated with the native speakers. This is reflected in the fact that preverbal clitics were the third most distinguishing feature identifying native-speaker behaviors in the discriminant function. Functionally speaking, the learners' distinctive structures are arguably two different ways of conveying cause-and-effect relationships. The native speakers' structures constitute, in the case of purpose adverbials, ways of showing one person's effect on another, and, in the case of appositives, descriptive elaboration.

Discussion

The first two research questions require an affirmative answer in light of (i) the repeated-measures ANOVA comparing nominal-clause convergence between the learners and the native speakers and (ii) a comparison of the learner and native-speaker target-proportion means. Regarding the first research question, while interacting in SCMC, the learners demonstrated nominal-clause convergence, with learners being 1.28 (0.37/0.29) times more likely to produce a nominal clause in a turn immediately following a turn where their fellow interlocutors produced the same structure. Concerning the second question, comparing the learners and the native speakers under similar interactional conditions, the learners demonstrated more nominal-clause convergence than the native speakers. Indeed, even though the learners were more likely to produce nominal-clause syntax when (presumably) primed to do so, the native speakers produced such syntax with the same frequency whether the previous turn contained that structure (0.29) or it lacked the structure (0.30). As noted above, the difference between the two types of interlocutors may be that the learners' lower Spanish proficiency led them to favor convergence much more than the native speakers. Structural alignment –and so convergence – is conjectured to be a learning strategy that facilitates interaction because, when dyads align their mental representations of their communicative goals/demands, they conserve precious processing resources (Garrod & Clark 1993; Pickering & Garrod 2004).

A qualitative inspection of the corpus data suggests that the learners converged on nominal clauses using a very small set of epistemic verbs in the main clause. McDonough and Kim (2009: 386) suggested that sensitivity to syntactic structure may be caused by "residual activation of the morphosyntactic information stored within individual lexical items." For the native speakers, approximately 80% of the main-clause verbs followed by a nominal clause involved 22 different verbs (tabulated according to all verb forms' lemma). For the learners, approximately 80% of the main-clause verbs followed by a nominal clause entailed only four different verbs, namely, *creer* 'to believe' (30.3%), *pensar* 'to think' (22.9%), *decir* 'to tell' (22.3%), and *saber* 'to know' (6.9%). Thus, it is likely that these four verbs are highly associated with nominal-clause syntax. To be sure, an examination of a different Spanish learner corpus – utilized in Asención-Delaney and Collentine (2011), containing samples of second, third, and fourth year learners – reveals that 59% (1474/2501) of the time these four lemmas are followed by the complementizer *que* 'that', which in such a syntactic context would invariably head a nominal clause.

An example of structural alignment is illustrated in (5), which occurred between two students who – according to the instructor – had high levels of Spanish proficiency. S1 produces three epistemic sentences with a nominal clause, utilizing the verb of belief *creer* and the verb of communication *decir*. S2 responds with S1's nominal-clause syntax but uses a different verb of communication, *escribir* 'to write that.' What supports the notion that this example evidences structural alignment is that the main-clause verb *escribir* is rarely employed as a verb of communication licensing a nominal clause. The native speakers never used *escribir* with a nominal clause (* denotes a lexical or grammatical error).

(5)   S1: El muchacho *dijo que* la llevó a la isla grande hace 4 días, pero Juan *dijo que* la vio hoy. *Creo que* el muchacho es mentiroso.
      'The boy said that he took her to the big island four days ago, but Juan said that he saw her today. I think that the boy is a liar'

      S2: Pero ella *escribió que* va al otro lado de la isla.
      'But she wrote that she was going to the other side of the island'

Additional evidence of L2 structural convergence where the main-clause verb is *decir* is provided in (6).

(6)   S3: *Pienso que* ella *encontré un tesoro y tiene *una mapa. no sé si Angela fue a isla *nuevo pero Tito *digo que* vio * Angela y *otro mujer hablando de dinero doña Ana ?
      'I think she found a treasure and has a map. I don't know if Angela went to the new/other island but Tito said that he saw Angela and another woman talking about money. Doña Ana?'

> S4: no, Tito *dice que* vio * una mujer en *el frente de la casa de Angela *en jueves.
> no *dice que* habló con Angela.
> 'No, Tito says that he saw a woman in front of the house of Angela on Thursday. He doesn't say that he spoke with Angela.'

Learner S3 produces *decir* followed by a nominal clause. S4 subsequently produces the same nominal-clause syntax with the same main-clause verb. Interestingly, the inflected form of *decir* that S3 produces is erroneous – S3 produced *digo* '< decir; 1st person singular, present' instead of the necessary form *dijo* '< decir; 3rd person singular, preterit' – and yet S4 produces nominal-clause syntax without any error. This suggests that S4 is not simply reproducing the lexical features of S3's turn. The residual activation of nominal-clause syntax from the previous utterance, coupled with the fact that L2 learners of Spanish associate *decir* with nominal clauses, may have increased the likelihood of convergence.

The last research question asked what syntactic structures do L1 and L2 Spanish speakers use when they do not demonstrate convergence on nominal clauses. The discriminant analysis indicated that the native speakers have more complex means of expressing themselves. When the native speakers did not demonstrate convergence, they employed complex syntactic structures that require careful attention to referential and binding properties. In other words, the native speakers made long-distance (e.g., interclausal) relationships. When the learners did not demonstrate convergence, they made extensive use of cause-and-effect constructs that have no referential/binding considerations, which implies that the learners did not necessarily have to make long-distance relationships. Perhaps more importantly, clauses headed by the conjunctions *porque* 'because' and *si* 'if …' are not strictly bound syntactically to their main clause, meaning they can be uttered by themselves, in which case the conjunction serves as a type of discourse marker.

The discursive function of the learners' constructs is probably causality, which may reflect the task demand that learners conjecture about a crime mystery based on clues found in the 3D world. Both conditionals and causative adverbials are commonly employed in languages for causality purposes (Sweetser 1990). Both constructs can often have an evidential purpose such that the clauses headed by *si* 'if' or *porque* 'because' describe the evidence or motivation for some conclusion. Interestingly, Branigan et al. (2010) noted that interlocutors converge at multiple levels of linguistic representation, ranging from phonology to pragmatics. The functional similarity of these two distinguishing features may indicate that, during their communicative interaction, the learners aligned not only at the level of syntax but also at the level of discourse, such that causality constructs were exposed in the data set when nominal-clause priming did not. What remains unclear in this study is whether the task demands motivated the use of causality constructs or convergence, or both.

With respect to the mystery tasks, most expressions of causality in the learner corpus took the form of: proposition A serves as evidence for conclusion/assertion B. In (7) we see that S5 asserts something about the mystery, whereupon S6 uses the *porque* 'because' conjunction to note evidence that might motivate S5's assertion that the girl left to find the treasure. S6's syntax is nonetheless simple because it is elliptical. S5's final assertion uses the causative adverbial in a much more prototypical causal manner rather than an evidential manner.

(7) S5: estoy de acuerdo (que ella fue a encontrar el tesoro)
   'I agree (that she left to find the treasure)'

   S6: porque *la papel *acerca de la casa de nora
   'Because of the paper near Nora's house.'

   S5: la doña ana dijo que angela le pidió dinero porque alguien *la había robado.
   'Doña Ana said that Angela asked her for money because someone had robbed her.'

In (8), S8 uses a *si* 'if' clause as a way to question a conclusion or observation. That is, the *si* 'if' clause is presented as if its propositional content is incompatible with some other conclusion or observation.

(8) S7: sabes *que *un otra persona *encontré *la tesoro o angela?
   'Do you know whether another person found the treasure or Angela?'

   S8: no sé. si Angela sabe dónde está la tesoro, por qué necesitaba el dinero de doña Ana ?
   'I don't know. If Angela knows where the treasure is, why does she need the money from doña Ana?'

   S7: es posible que ella *necesita dinero para llevar *la Tesoro
   'It's possible that she needs money to take the treasure away.'

This exchange also suggests that the learners have rather simple syntactic devices at their disposal beyond nominal clauses. The *si* 'if' clause does not appear to be embedded to a main clause. Finally, even though S7 produces a main clause followed by a nominal clause in both of her turns, she struggles with long-distance relationships since she does not produce the required subjunctive in the subordinate-clause, producing *necesita* [indicative] rather than *necesite* [subjunctive] following the dubative phrase *es posible* 'it is possible'.

Conclusions

The present study examined the extent to which L2 learners of Spanish exhibit structural convergence on nominal-clause syntax in task-based SCMC interactions with corpus-linguistic methods. The analysis provided evidence that L2 learners align at the level of syntax. Key support for this assertion is that the learners were significantly more likely to converge on this structure than native speakers interacting under similar conditions. The analysis also suggested that, when learners did not converge on nominal-clause syntax, they used cause-and-effect structures to connect evidence to conclusions. We thus have good reason to suspect that the learners were aligning linguistic aspects of their interactions, which researchers conjecture to be a learning strategy for less proficient speakers of a language (Branigan et al. 2010; Garrod & Clark 1993). The study also indicates that FL learners of Spanish interact in ways that are productive when tasks involve technologies such as a 3D virtual world and instant messaging, specifically SCMC. There is reason to suspect that these sorts of conditions promoting communicative interaction can encourage the use of complex syntax and the development of certain discourse strategies.

Future research should consider that there are limitations to generalizing the present analysis. We do not know the effects of the task demands on learners relative to the native speakers. The learners were told to conjecture about two mysteries and to interact to come to some conclusion. This task feature, as opposed to proficiency level, may have indirectly ensured that convergence with nominal clauses and causality constructs might occur. The native-speaker corpus did not reflect task-based conditions, as it consisted of interviewers and transcribed conversations. The modality of the two corpora was different as well: while both involved spontaneity, one involved speaking and the other texting. Future research could compare the learner data to a native-speaker baseline whose participants utilized the same tasks studied here.

The study raises intriguing questions about communicative interaction in tasks and structural convergence as a learning mechanism. If it can be established that certain task demands and features encourage the use and learning of particular structural elements, communicative interaction may even increase in importance in the L2 curriculum. The propensity for less proficient language learners to converge could be exploited by language professionals to explicitly promote certain aspects of learners' L2 development.

References

Asención-Delaney, Y., & Collentine, J. (2011). A multidimensional analysis of a written L2 Spanish corpus. *Applied Linguistics, 32*, 299–322.

Beauvois, M. (1997). High tech, high touch: From discussion to composition in the networked classroom. *Computer Assisted Language Learning, 10*, 57–69.

Biber, D., Davies, M., Jones, J., & Tracy-Ventura, N. (2006). Spoken and written register variation in Spanish: A Multi-dimensional analysis. *Corpora, 1*, 1–37.

Branigan, H., Pickering M., Pearson J., & McLean, J. (2010). Linguistic alignment between people and computers. *Journal of Pragmatics, 42*, 2355–2368.

Collentine, J. (1995). The development of complex syntax and mood-selection abilities by intermediate-level learners of Spanish. *Hispania, 78*, 123–36.

Collentine, J. (2010). The acquisition and teaching of the Spanish subjunctive: An update on current findings. *Hispania, 93*, 39–51.

Collentine, J., & Asención-Delaney, Y. (2010). A corpus-based analysis of the discourse functions of ser/estar + adjective in three levels of Spanish as FL learners. *Language Learning, 60*, 409–445.

Collentine, K. (2010). Measuring complexity in task-based synchronous computer-mediated communication. In M. Thomas & H. Reinders (Eds.), *Task-based language learning and teaching with technology* (pp. 105–130). New York: Continuum.

Collentine, K. (2011). Learner autonomy in a task-based 3d world and production. *Language Learning & Technology, 15,* 50–67.

Doughty, C., & Long, M. (2003). Optimal psycholinguistic environments for distance foreign language learning. *Language Learning & Technology, 7,* 50–80.

Foster, P., & Skehan, P. (1996). The influence of planning and task type on second language performance. *Studies in Second Language Acquisition, 18,* 299–323.

Garrod, S., & Clark, A. (1993). The development of dialogue co-ordination skills in schoolchildren. *Language and Cognitive Processes, 8,* 101–126.

Gries, S. (2005). Syntactic priming: a corpus-based approach. *Journal of Psycholinguistic Research, 34,* 365–399.

Jones, G., Squires, T., & Hicks, J. (2007). Combining speech recognition natural language processing with 3D online learning environments to create distributed authentic and situated spoken language learning. *Journal of Educational Technology Systems, 39,* 375–392.

Kern, R. (1995). Restructuring classroom interaction with networked computers: Effects on quantity and characteristics of language production. *Modern Language Journal, 79,* 457–476.

Li, S. (2010). The effectiveness of corrective feedback in SLA: A meta-analysis. *Language Learning, 60,* 309–365.

Lyster, R., & Saito, K. (2010). Interactional feedback as instructional input: A synthesis of classroom SLA research. *Language, Interaction and Acquisition, 1,* 276–296.

Mackey, A. (2007). Interaction as practice. In R. DeKeyser (Ed.), *Practice in second language learning: Perspectives from linguistics and psychology* (pp. 85–110). Cambridge: Cambridge University Press.

Mackey, A., & Gass, S. (2006). Introduction. *Studies in Second Language Acquisition, 28,* 169–178.

Mackey, A., & Goo, J. (2007). Interaction research in SLA: A meta-analysis and research synthesis. In A. Mackey (Ed.), *Conversational interaction in SLA: A collection of empirical studies* (pp. 408–452). New York, NY: Oxford University Press.

McDonough, K., & Kim, Y. (2009). Syntactic priming, type frequency, and EFL learners' production of wh-questions. *The Modern Language Journal, 93,* 386–398.

McDonough, K., & Mackey, A. (2008). Syntactic priming and ESL question development. *Studies in Second Language Acquisition, 30,* 31–47.

Myles, F. (2005). Interlanguage corpora and second language acquisition research. *Second Language Research, 21,* 373–391.

Myles, F., & Mitchell, R. (2005). Using information technology to support empirical SLA research. *Journal of Applied Linguistics, 1,* 169–196.

Nicholas, H., Lightbown, P., & Spada, N. (2001). Recasts as feedback to language learners. *Language Learning, 51,* 719–758.

Peterson, M. (2006). Learner interaction management in an avatar and chat-based virtual world. *Computer Assisted Language Learning, 19,* 79–103.

Pickering, M., & Ferreira, V. (2008). Structural priming: a critical review. *Psychological Bulletin, 134,* 427–459.

Pickering, M., & Garrod, S. (2004). Toward a mechanistic psychology of dialogue. *Behavioral and Brain Sciences, 27,* 169–225.

Reinhardt, J. (2008). Negotiating meaningfulness: An enhanced perspective on interaction in computer-mediated foreign language learning environments. In S. Magnan (Ed.), *Mediating discourse online* (pp. 219–244). Amsterdam: John Benjamins.

Reppen, R., & Simpson-Vach, R. (2010). Corpus linguistics. In N. Schmidt (Ed.), *Introduction to applied linguistics* (pp. 89–105). London: Hodder Education.

Robinson, P. (2001). Task complexity, task difficulty, and task production: Exploring interactions in a componential framework. *Applied Linguistics, 22,* 27–57.

Russell, J., & Spada, N. (2006). The effectiveness of corrective feedback for the acquisition of L2 grammar. In J. Norris, & L. Ortega (Eds.), *Synthesizing research on language learning and teaching* (pp. 133–164). Amsterdam: John Benjamins.

Rutherford, W., & Thomas, M. (2001). The Child Language Data Exchange System in research on second language acquisition. *Second Language Research, 17*, 195–212.

Salaberry, R. M. (2000). L2 morphosyntactic development in text-based computer-mediated communication. *Computer Assisted Language Learning, 13*, 5–27.

Samuda, V., & Bygate, M. (2008). *Tasks in second language learning*. Hampshire: Palgrave Macmillan.

Smith, B. (2008). Methodological hurdles in capturing CMC data: The case of the missing self- repair. *Language Learning & Technology, 12*, 85–103.

Sweetser, E. (1990). *From etymology to pragmatics*. Cambridge: Cambridge University Press.

Sykes, J. (2009). Learner requests in Spanish: Examining the potential of multiuser virtual environments for L2 pragmatics acquisition. In L. Lomicka & G. Lord (Eds.), *The next generation: Social networking and online collaboration* (pp. 199–234). San Marcos, TX: Texas State University: CALICO.

Toyoda, E., & Harrison, R. (2002). Categorization of text chat communication between learners and native speakers of Japanese. *Language Learning & Technology, 6*, 82–99.

Warschauer, M. (1996). Motivational aspects of using computers for writing and communication. In M. Warschauer (Ed.), *Telecollaboration in foreign language learning: Proceedings of the Hawai'i Symposium* (pp. 29–46). Honolulu, HI: University of Hawai'i, Second Language Teaching & Curriculum Center.

Warschauer, M. (1997). Computer-mediated collaborative learning: Theory and practice. *Modern Language Journal, 81*, 470–481.

Warschauer, M., & Kern, R. (Eds.). (2000). *Network-based language teaching: Concepts and practice*. Cambridge: Cambridge University Press.

Yuan, F., & Ellis, R. (2003). The effects of pre-task planning and on-line planning on fluency, complexity, and accuracy in L2 monologic oral production. *Applied Linguistics, 24*, 1–27.

Zheng, D., Young, M., Brewer, R., & Wagner, M. (2009). Attitude and self-efficacy change: English language learning in virtual worlds. *CALICO Journal, 27*, 205–231.

Chapter 10

Preemptive feedback in CALL

Trude Heift
Simon Fraser University

This study compared the effectiveness of two types of preemptive feedback in a CALL environment. As part of their regular course assignments throughout the fall 2009 semester, L2 learners of German ($N = 185$) performed a sentence completion task. For each individual exercise, the CALL system generated preemptive feedback based on the error profiles from 5000 users who previously used the CALL system between 2003 and 2008. Two types of preemptive feedback with varying specificity were designed to draw attention to the most common errors associated with each item. Results indicate that both types of preemptive feedback were significantly more effective than not providing any task assistance. In addition, differences with respect to proficiency levels and error types were found.

Introduction

Over the past years, computer-assisted language learning (CALL) systems have placed an increased focus on pedagogical, user-centered designs by emphasizing, among other aspects, learner assistance for task completion. One way to assist learners with a task is to provide help options, and/or hints and reminders that coach learners as they perform a language task. Indeed, CALL programs have placed a notable emphasis on reactive feedback whereby learner errors are first analyzed by the CALL system and then error-specific feedback is generated and communicated to the learner.

One area of task assistance in CALL, however, that has not yet received due attention is that of preemptive feedback. In contrast to reactive feedback, preemptive feedback initiates a focus-on-form phase so that learners receive relevant meta-linguistic information before difficulties come up. This may not only lead to more successful task completion but also reduce potential frustration by marking critical features in the language task (see Ellis, Basturkmen, & Loewen 2001). However, at this point, the effects of preemptive feedback in CALL have not yet been studied and are thus speculative and deserve closer investigation.

One reason for this apparent lack of research might be due to the efforts involved in generating preemptive feedback in a CALL environment. For this, the CALL system must first decide on the type of information that learners should receive when attempting a language task. In a face-to-face classroom, teachers commonly highlight linguistic forms which, based on their experience with previous learners, have shown to be difficult and problematic for most learners. For a CALL environment, however, this requires a learner corpus that consists of the input of previous users for all exercises and activity types contained in the system so that the problematic grammatical constructs and forms can be identified and communicated to the learner.

In an effort to shed more light on the effects of preemptive feedback in a CALL environment, we conducted a study with 185 beginner and early intermediate learners of L2 German who performed a sentence completion task which was embedded in a conventional university language course (13 weeks of instruction) as opposed to a laboratory, thus reflecting learners' actual performance. For each individual exercise, the CALL system generated preemptive feedback based on a learner corpus that consists of the error profiles of 5000 previous users who had used the CALL system between 2003 and 2008. The study focuses on two types of preemptive feedback of varying specificity, both drawing attention to the most common errors unique to a given activity type and exercise.

Interactions in the language classroom

By now, it is unquestionable that the interactions which L2 learners engage in provide one of the main sources for L2 acquisition data. Allwright (1984: 156), for instance, refers to the role of interaction as "the fundamental fact of pedagogy" and according to Ellis (1991: 5), "teaching can be profitably viewed as interaction that supplies learners with opportunities for learning." Accordingly, research that examines the relationship between interaction and SLA helps inform language learning pedagogy. In brief, Long (1983, 1996) argues in the interaction hypothesis that (1) comprehensible input is necessary for SLA, and (2) modified interaction, namely through negotiation of meaning, assists in making input comprehensible to the L2 learner. Moreover, in investigating the conditions that promote negotiation of meaning, Long (1981, 1983) found that tasks that require information exchange are significantly more effective in producing negotiation than decision-making tasks. Moreover, closed tasks are also more successful than open tasks in this regard (see also Pica, Young, & Doughty 1987). Finally, in drawing on Swain's (1985) output hypothesis, Long (1996) further acknowledges that interlanguage development can take place when learners are 'pushed' to organize and restructure their output by means of negative, or corrective feedback (see also, e.g., Gass 1997; Long 1983, 1996; Ellis 1991 for a more detailed discussion of the interaction hypothesis such as the distinction between its strong and weak version).

The interaction hypothesis has received ample attention in SLA and related research has provided evidence that interaction is important for SLA in face-to-face interactions. As pointed out in the preface to this volume, in some educational settings learners may not have many opportunities for face-to-face interactions, but may have access to technology (see Serafina, this volume, for another example of learner-technology interaction). This raises an important question as to whether the interactions that learners engage in through technology are also beneficial for language learning. Clearly, learners' use of technology involves various forms of interaction, between the learner and the computer, and between the learner and other people in computer-mediated communication. Ellis (1999) takes a broad view of the ways in which interaction might benefit language learners by examining cognitive and social benefits of both interpersonal and intrapersonal interaction, and Chapelle (2003) extends that framework to include human-computer interaction as well. Of all of the types of interactions that occur, the instances where learners are able to get help with or feedback on their language are particularly interesting in CALL research because these studies not only inform us about aspects of SLA but also about issues surrounding human-computer interaction and software design, more generally.

Reactive and preemptive focus on form

Long and Robinson (1998) identify two kinds of negative evidence in response to learner input: reactive and preemptive. Reactive focus on form has also been referred to as error correction, corrective feedback, or negative evidence/feedback (Long 1991, 1996) and it supplies learners with either explicit or implicit negative evidence. Accordingly, reactive focus on form occurs in reaction to learner errors which are then addressed by, for instance, the teacher. In contrast, preemptive feedback can either be student or teacher-initiated and it draws attention to form before a problem has occurred. Interestingly, Williams (1999) as well as Poole (2005) found that learners initiate focus on form less often than teachers (see also e.g., Farrokhi & Gholami 2007; Loewen 2003; Farrokhi, Ansarin, & Mohammadnia 2008) while differences in the extent to which teachers initiate focus on form were also found (see e.g., Borg 1998; Mackey, Polio & McDonough 2004).

According to Ellis et al. (2001:414), however, both reactive and preemptive focus on form are problem-oriented and the difference lies in the nature of the problem that is addressed.

> Whereas reactive focus on form involves negotiation and is triggered by something problematic that an interactant has said or written, preemptive focus on form involves the teacher or learner initiating attention to form even though no actual problem in production has arisen.

This notion of attention is closely related to Schmidt's (1990, 1994) Noticing Hypothesis which stipulates that language learners are limited in what they are able to notice and the main determining factor is attention. Schmidt (1994:176) argues that attention is not only necessary for acquisition to take place but noticing is also a conscious process in that "attention also controls access to conscious experience thus allowing the acquisition of new items to take place". Accordingly, form-focused instruction that induces learners to pay conscious attention to forms in the input can assist interlanguage development.

A large body of research both in face-to-face settings as well as in CALL environments has provided evidence of the benefits of reactive focus on form (e.g., Bowles 2005; Heift 2002, 2004, 2010; Murphy 2007; Nagata 1993, 1996; Nagata & Swisher 1995; Petersen

2010; Pujolà 2002; Rosa & Leow 2004; Sauro 2009; Vinther 2005; Ware 2008), while far less research has studied preemptive interventions or feedback. Preemptive feedback draws attention to potentially problematic areas in the task and thus one might speculate that providing relevant meta-linguistic information before difficulties arise may encourage more successful task completion and reduce potential frustration (see Ellis et al. 2001). Moreover, preemptive feedback may aid in providing learners with explicit knowledge, which, as Ellis (1993) has argued, constitutes a valid goal for instruction because it helps improve performance through monitoring and facilitate acquisition through noticing. Indeed, while the existing research on preemptive feedback is scarce, two studies highlight some of the benefits of preemptive feedback in the face-to-face classroom.

In the first study, Ellis et al. (2001) investigated preemptive feedback with two ESL classes at two intermediate levels. The authors found that in 12 hours of meaning-focused instruction, there were as many preemptive focus-on-form episodes (FFEs) as reactive FFEs. The majority of the preemptive FFEs dealt with vocabulary and were initiated by students rather than the teacher. Students were also more likely to use the form in a subsequent utterance if the FFE was student-initiated. In the second study, Farrokhi et al. (2008) investigated teacher-initiated preemptive focus-on-form episodes (FFEs) by observing five teachers in ten EFL classes of two levels of proficiency, beginner and advanced. The authors found that the proficiency of the learners was not a factor in the type or quantity of FFEs that teachers produced. More specifically, vocabulary had the highest rate of preemptive FFEs at both proficiency levels. Grammar and pronunciation had higher reactive FFEs with no major differences in the use of FFEs between beginner and advanced learners.

When it comes to CALL environments, however, no studies to date have investigated preemptive feedback. Moreover, the two classroom-based studies above focus on sponta-neous productions of preemptive feedback (i.e., FFEs), which is not a feasible possibility for a CALL environment where preemptive feedback is more likely to be pre-planned (i.e., coded into the system), particularly in the absence of a dialogue module which allows learners to interact with the CALL system in a more sophisticated manner. Given these differences, the goal of our study is to investigate two types of preemptive feedback of varying specificity with beginner and early intermediate L2 learners of German in a CALL environment. The current study focuses on the following two research questions:

1. What are the effects of different types of preemptive feedback on learner performance at the beginner and early intermediate levels of German?
2. What are the effects of different types of preemptive feedback on learner performance for different error classes?

Method

Participants

The data were collected from 185 L2 learners of German from two Canadian universities in the fall semester 2009. The participants were 149 beginner learners, who were enrolled in their first German university course (GERM 100), and 36 students in their third semester of German language instruction (GERM 200). At the beginning of the semester, the participants consented to a possible anonymous analysis of their data for research purposes. Table 1 displays some background information about the participants, which they provided as part of a questionnaire at the beginning of their respective course. There were 98 female and 87 male participants and the average age across both courses was 20.2 years. In addition, most participants were native speakers of English (164 students) and 14 students had a German parent.

Table 1. Participant profiles

	GERM 100	GERM 200	Total
Gender	79 females & 70 males	19 females & 17 males	98 females & 87 males
Mean age	19.1	21.3	20.2
L1	132 English, 9 Chinese, 1 Croatian, 1 Farsi, 1 Greek, 2 Polish, 2 Spanish	32 English, 2 Chinese, 1 Farsi, 1 French	164 English, 11 Chinese, 1 Croatian, 3 Farsi, 1 French, 1 Greek, 2 Polish, 2 Spanish

The participants also indicated in the questionnaire that they were comfortable using computers and generally enjoyed the use of computers for foreign language practice. Moreover, given that the participating universities have no language requirement for undergraduates, students who choose to learn German do so for reasons of heritage, travel, business or general interest and are thus assumed to be highly motivated.

E-tutor program

E-Tutor (*www.e-tutor.org*), an online CALL program for L2 German, is a comprehensive language learning environment which provides a multitude of activities for learners at all levels, from beginner to advanced. The activity types cover pronunciation, vocabulary, grammar, writing, listening and reading comprehension as well as cultural information about Germany (for a more detailed description of the system, see Heift 2010). E-Tutor was first integrated into the curriculum of the first three semesters of German language instruction at the author's institution in 2003. However, the CALL program has been continuously expanded and, as a result, while the activity types initially focused mainly on grammar acquisition, they now cover a vast range of skills beyond those typically provided in a workbook. E-Tutor contains a total of 15 chapters and their grammatical sequence corresponds to the chapters in Deutsch: Na klar! (Di Donato, Clyde, & Vansant 2008), which is a textbook commonly used in university German L2 programs throughout North America. The system also contains a pronunciation unit that allows students to practice individual sounds, word stress and intonation.

As part of the curriculum, students complete the 11 activity types for each chapter of E-Tutor as part of their homework assignments. At the beginning of the semester, students watch a 15 minute video tutorial about E-Tutor which explains the different exercise types and illustrates the functionality of the system. Prior to assigning the E-Tutor homework, the relevant parts in the course book (e.g., grammar constructs, vocabulary) are commonly introduced in class. The 11 activity types contain approximately 90–100 individual items in addition to an essay task that students must complete. Moreover, the system contains flash cards for vocabulary practice, as well as grammar and cultural notes and pictures that students can browse as part of the chapter exploration and homework completion. On average, a book chapter is covered in about 8–10 hours of class instruction (2–2.5 weeks) and students spend an additional 2–3 hours to complete the activity types of a chapter in E-Tutor. For some activities, for example those that contain an audio component, students may be initially exposed to the audio portion as a class activity in a computer laboratory. However, students then generally complete the listening comprehension activity, such as answering questions about the dialogue, independently as part of E-Tutor homework.

E-Tutor is primarily designed as an opportunity for students to practice their German in a non-threatening and flexible environment. For this reason, students are graded on task completion and not on their linguistic performance, that is, the number of errors they make is not taken into consideration for their course grade. E-Tutor, however, records when students skip an exercise and/or look up the correct answer and this information is part of the report that is submitted to their instructor. This largely ensures that students engage in exercise completion rather than clicking through an exercise by either skipping it and/or looking up the answer without giving it a try. For instance, Figure 1 provides an example of the report of a sentence completion activity type that students mail to their instructors.

Figure 1, for example, shows that the student did not skip or look up an answer (*peek*) for any of the ten items, had a correct initial response for four items, and achieved a correct response after multiple attempts for six items. Due to its underlying parsing technology, E-Tutor provides a break-down of the errors the student committed.

The data for this study is from the E-Tutor fill-in-the-blank activity, which focuses on the grammar topics covered in each chapter. For this activity type, students are required to provide a single word in a blank field to complete a sentence (see Figure 2). Along with all other E-Tutor activity types, the fill-in-the-blank activity was part of the regular homework assignments and thus was not designed especially for this experiment. Students completed the fill-in-the-blank activities independently and outside class time by the stipulated deadline for each chapter.

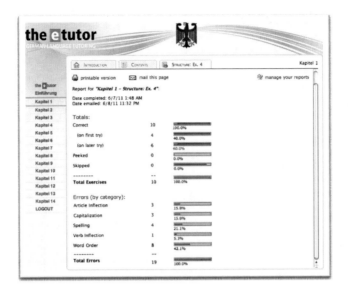

Figure 1. E-Tutor error report

Preemptive feedback

Creating preemptive feedback

To create the preemptive feedback for the E-Tutor fill-in-the-blank activity, we compiled a learner corpus consisting of several million responses submitted by roughly 5000 students who had completed E-Tutor between 2003 and 2008. We conducted an extensive statistical analysis for these millions of entries and, for each item, activity type and chapter, we produced a ranked list of errors based on prior student performance. For each error profile, we then generated preemptive feedback for the system to display when students start an item. For instance, Example (1) displays the item given in Figure 2, which is from a fill-in-the-blank activity. Here, students are asked to provide the correct form of the adjective *gut*.

(1)   Klaus kocht immer ein _____ Abendessen.
       Klaus always makes a good dinner.

Based on our statistical analysis of the previous submissions, 52% of the roughly 5000 student responses for this particular item were correct while 48% contained an error. Of the incorrect responses, 39.1% contained a wrong adjective inflection (e.g., *gute* instead of *gutes*), followed by the provision of an extra word (7%), incorrect spelling (1.8%) and, finally, wrong capitalization (0.1%). Based on these error files, preemptive feedback was created to reflect the most common errors for each item.

Preemptive feedback types

For the purpose of this study, the participants completed the fill-in-the-blank activity corresponding to three chapters in the course textbook (10 items per chapter). For each chapter, students were randomly assigned to receive one of the two preemptive feedback types or no feedback (control condition). The first type of preemptive feedback, 3-hints, provided one hint for each of the top three errors associated with each item. In contrast, the second type of feedback, 1-hint, provided a single hint for the most frequent error only. In the control condition, 0-hints, the program did not provide any hints about specific error types, but instead generated a generic message.

Figure 2 provides a typical fill-in-the-blank item in the *3-hints condition*. For this particular item, the system generated preemptive feedback that displays an alert for the three most common errors (1. adjective inflection (*gut*); 2. spelling of 'gut', 3. capitalization). In the *1-hint* condition, the system would show the top error only (1. adjective inflection (*gut*)). Whenever a hint refers to a grammar point, then a link to the relevant inflectional paradigm is provided. The paradigm allows students to access the various inflections of a verb or a determiner, for instance. In contrast, the control condition *0-hints* provides no hints about error types but displays a generic message: "This is where the *E-Tutor* displays feedback to your input. It also gives you tips that will assist you in completing an exercise." In all other respects, the E-Tutor interface was identical for all three study conditions.

Figure 2. Preemptive feedback 3-hints

Data collection

Data logs

Because E-Tutor is an online CALL program, students can complete the homework from any computer with an internet connection. E-Tutor maintains a record for each user which tracks exercise completion by collecting and retaining information on the learner's progress and performance. This student record is saved between visits and, for this reason, students do not have to complete the exercises of the activity types in one sitting but instead can resume their work at any time and from any location (see Heift 2010). For the purpose of this study, the participants' interaction with E-Tutor was recorded throughout the entire semester in order to examine their responses to different types of preemptive feedback of varying specificity. Besides a unique student ID and a time stamp, the data log records the entire interaction between the computer and the student. This includes the activity type, the student input, the system feedback, and navigation patterns.

Retrospective interviews

In addition to the questionnaire and the E-Tutor log data, retrospective interviews were carried out one week after the semester had ended to elicit information about the students' impressions of the CALL program in general and of preemptive feedback in particular. Retrospective interviews were carried out rather than administering online questionnaires because our prior data collection and analyses revealed significant discrepancies between learner self-reports of system use and log files of their software use (see also Fischer 2004; Hubbard 2005). In other words, the responses that students provided in the questionnaires contradicted what they actually did. Although carrying out interviews rather drastically reduced the quantity of responses received, it provided more insightful and elaborate than responses than could be achieved through an online questionnaire.

The retrospective interviews were conducted with a subgroup of 15 volunteer participants from one of the institutions. Each interview lasted for about 15 minutes. A research assistant met with each of the 15 students individually and, with their consent, recorded and subsequently transcribed their responses. Each student was asked the same questions and, in all instances, the same visual aids were employed. For instance, one of the questions referred to the preemptive feedback that the system provided and students were shown a screenshot and asked to comment on its usefulness and explain their answer. These visual aids ensured that students understood the questions.

Data analysis

With respect to data analysis, E-Tutor logged student interaction with the CALL system, keeping track of each submission and saving it for research purposes (e.g., student ID, activity type, student input, time submitted, etc.). We employed both descriptive and inferential statistics. For the descriptive statistics, we counted the total number of correct and incorrect responses for each student and feedback type. The inferential statistics required a calculation of the average rate of correct and wrong responses for each student and feedback type. To allow for cross-comparisons among learners, we first normalized the working style data by dividing for each student the number of correct responses by the total number of items (e.g., 10 per chapter). For an investigation of different error types, we divided for each student the number of incorrect responses for each error type (i.e., capitalization, grammar, and spelling) by the total number of items. For the inferential statistics, we applied Repeated Measures ANOVA tests with an alpha level set to 0.05 to determine statistical significance.

Results

Effects of preemptive feedback: Correct responses

The data displayed in Table 2 indicate that the participants achieved the highest number of correct responses with preemptive feedback type *1-hint* (63.0%) which displays only the top error, followed by *3-hints* (62.5%) which shows tips for the top three errors and, finally *0-hints* (57.4%) which displays no hints. When considering the responses by each level of German separately, students in GERM 100 performed best and almost identical with *3-hints* (63.8%) and *1-hint* (63.7%) while students in GERM 200 achieved higher scores with *1-hint* (60.3%) than with *3-hints* (57.2%) and *0-hints* (49.4%).

Table 2. Descriptive statistics for correct responses

Feedback type	Level	Mean	SD	N
3-hints	GERM 100	.64	.19	49
	GERM 200	.57	.28	6
	Total	.63	.21	85
1-hint	GERM 100	.64	.19	49
	GERM 200	.60	.23	6
	Total	.63	.20	85
0-hints	GERM 100	.59	.23	49
	GERM 200	.49	.32	6
	Total	.57	.25	85

Results of the Repeated-Measures ANOVA indicated that preemptive feedback type had a significant main effect on correct responses (F (2,182) = 6.354; p = .002). Pairwise comparisons revealed that both preemptive feedback types, *3-hints* and *1-hint*, led to significantly more correct responses than *0-hints* (p = .026 and .005, respectively), but there was no significant difference in their effectiveness (p = 1.00). There was also a main effect for proficiency level [F (1,183) = 4.415; p = .037], with GERM 100 students performing significantly better than GERM 200 students. Finally, there was no interaction effect between preemptive feedback and proficiency level (p = .370).

Effects of preemptive feedback by error types

The effect of preemptive feedback was also considered separately for three error types: capitalization, grammar, and spelling. For capitalization errors, there were no significant main effects for feedback type ($p = .410$) or for proficiency ($p = .151$). However, statistically significant results were found for both grammar and spelling errors.

Grammar errors

For grammar errors, the descriptive data displayed in Table 3 indicate that the students committed the fewest grammar errors following 1-hint preemptive feedback, with this finding applying to each level independently (GERM 100: 31%; GERM 200: and 29%) as well as to the two levels combined (31%). Grammar errors were most frequent following 0-hints (GERM 100: 34%; GERM 200: 37%; both courses: 35%).

Table 3. Descriptive statistics for number of grammar errors

Feedback type	Level	Mean	SD	N
3-hints	GERM 100	.32	.18	49
	GERM 200	.35	.25	6
	Total	.32	.19	85
1-hint	GERM 100	.31	.18	49
	GERM 200	.29	.21	6
	Total	.31	.19	85
0-hints	GERM 100	.34	.20	49
	GERM 200	.37	.26	6
	Total	.35	.22	85

Results of the Repeated Measures ANOVA indicated that preemptive feedback type had a significant effect on grammar errors [$F (2,182) = 3.164$; $p = .044$]. Pairwise comparisons revealed that *1-hint* resulted in significantly fewer grammar errors than *0-hints* ($p = .019$), but none of the other comparisons were significant. Moreover, proficiency level has no significant effect on grammar errors ($p = .596$) indicating that the difference of grammar errors made by our beginner and early intermediate learners of German is not significant. Finally, no significant interaction effect between preemptive feedback and proficiency level was found ($p = .387$).

Spelling errors

With respect to spelling errors, Table 4 indicates that the students committed the fewest spelling errors following preemptive feedback types 3-hints and 1-hint (4.0%), while they made the most spelling errors when receiving the 0-hints feedback (6.4%). However, in considering each course independently, students in GERM 200 preformed better with 3-hints (6.0%) than with 1-hint (9.0%) or 0-hints (13.3%) while GERM 100 committed the same number of spelling errors with 3-hints and 1-hint (3.0%), followed by 0-hints (4.8%).

Table 4. Descriptive statistics for number of spelling errors

Feedback type	Level	Mean	SD	N
3-hints	GERM 100	.03	.05	49
	GERM 200	.06	.08	6
	Total	.04	.06	85
1-hint	GERM 100	.03	.06	49
	GERM 200	.09	.10	6
	Total	.04	.07	185
0-hints	GERM 100	.05	.074	49
	GERM 200	.13	.13	6
	Total	.06	.09	85

The results of the Repeated Measures ANOVA indicated that preemptive feedback type has a significant main effect on spelling errors [$F(2,182) = 11.286$; $p = .000$]. Pairwise comparisons revealed that both preemptive feedback types, *3-hints* and *1-hint*, resulted in significantly fewer spelling errors than *0-hints* ($p = .000$ and $p = .017$, respectively). Moreover, proficiency level had a significant effect on spelling errors [$F(1,183) = 51.223$; $p = .000$], with GERM 200 students making significantly more spelling errors than the GERM 100 students. Finally, a significant interaction effect between preemptive feedback and proficiency level was also found ($F = 3.777$; $p = .028$) indicating that, for both proficiency levels, there is an increase in spelling errors if no preemptive feedback is provided.

Discussion

The first research question focused on the effect of preemptive feedback for students from two proficiency levels, beginner (GERM 100) and early intermediate (GERM 200). The findings revealed that the students generally benefitted from the preemptive feedback provided by the CALL program, thus supporting previous classroom-based studies (Ellis et al. 2001; Farrokhi et al. 2008). More specifically, the results show that the students performed significantly better with preemptive feedback than without it. Moreover, the beginner students performed significantly better than the early intermediate learners.

These findings are indirectly supported by research that found that learners at lower proficiency levels frequently direct their attention to processing meaning rather than placing an emphasis on form (e.g., VanPatten 1990, 1996, 2003). For instance, Williams (1999) found that lower proficiency learners focused less on form until they became more proficient (see also Farrokhi et al. 2008). In these studies, however, student attention was not intentionally drawn to form. In contrast, the preemptive feedback displayed by the E-Tutor program may have assisted students by drawing their attention away from meaning toward form. The beginner students seemed to benefit from the intentional focus on form of the preemptive feedback even more than the early intermediate learners thus suggesting that the lower the students' proficiency the more they benefit from an intentional focus on form. However, the performance difference between the two proficiency levels might also be partially due to issues related to task complexity.

In support of previous research (see, e.g., Adamson 2009: 139–140), simple grammar rules can be "monitored" successfully in form-focused tasks whereas difficult rules, if monitored in a form-focused task, might result in decreased accuracy. This increase in difficulty for our early intermediate learners is reflected in at least two ways. First, there is a general increase in sentence length from the beginner to the intermediate level for the form-focused activity types (i.e., fill-in-the-blank) in E-Tutor, which is one indicator of task complexity (see Ortega 2003). More specifically, text length (e.g., words per sentence) is commonly employed to assess fluency which, in addition to accuracy and complexity, forms part of a learner's proficiency measure (e.g., Chander 2003; Larsen-Freeman 1978, 2006, 2009; Leal 2005). Second, the grammatical constructions that the early intermediate students are required to use are more complex than those required at the beginner level given that the grammar topics are to some extent cumulative and thus graded. For instance, in Chapter 1 students need to know only the conjugation of the verb in the present tense while in a later chapter they must know the inflections of the verb in several tenses as well as when to use each tense appropriately.

It is interesting, however, that no significant differences between the two types of pre-emptive feedback, *1-hint* and *3-hints,* were found. Nonetheless, our descriptive data show that with respect to correct responses, students in GERM 100 performed almost identical with preemptive feedback type *3-hints* (63.8%) and *1-hint* (63.7%) while GERM 200 achieved higher scores with *1-hint* (60.3%) than with *3-hints* (57.2%). To interpret these results, we need to first have a closer look at the content of the preemptive feedback that E-Tutor provided, which is discussed in the following section.

Different error types

The second research question investigated the effect of preemptive feedback on different error classes. Although there were no significant differences between the two preemptive feedback types, *1-hint* and *3-hints,* the descriptive results provide interesting insights. For instance, beginner learners achieved nearly the same number of correct responses with *1-hint* and *3-hints* while early intermediate learners performed better with *1-hint.*

Table 5. Number of errors by error type and feedback type

Error type	GERM 100		GERM 200	
	3-hints	1-hint	3-hints	1-hint
Grammar	30	27	30	27
Spelling	30	2	30	3
Capitalization	30	1	30	0
Total	90	30	90	30

Table 5 indicates that for *1-hint*, which displays an alert for the top error only, the tip referred to a grammar mistake in 27/30 instances and rarely targeted a spelling or capitalization error. In German 100, *1-hint* referred only twice to a spelling error and only once to a capitalization error. In contrast, because *3-hints* displays the top three errors, the preemptive feedback always contained all three error types: the error type displayed for the *1-hint* feedback and the two remaining error types. Accordingly, and at least for grammar errors, there was little advantage in receiving preemptive feedback type *3-hints* over *1-hint*. The tips on the two additional errors contained in *3-hints* might have been rather distracting, or at least had no positive effect, given that both our beginner and early intermediate learners performed better with *1-hint*.

In considering the difference in the two preemptive feedback types for spelling errors, beginner learners scored identically with *1-hint* and *3-hints* while early intermediate learners performed better with *3-hints* (see Table 4). Given that only 10% of the *1-hint* preemptive feedback contained a tip on spelling, one would assume that there was an advantage in receiving *3-hints* over *1-hint*. While this is reflected in the performance of our early intermediate learners in that they performed better with *3-hints*, for our beginner learners this is not the case. It is possible that the differences found with the two proficiency levels might be due to an increase in task complexity, that is, spelling might become more demanding at a more advanced level and thus fewer tips are needed at a beginner level. Another likely explanation might be one of working memory capacity and/or cognitive load in that beginner learners might only pay attention and/or be able to process the top error no matter which feedback type is displayed. Thus if the spelling error is not ranked first for *3-hints*, the tip is ignored. This then also might provide an explanation for why beginner learners achieved almost identical scores for the number of correct responses with the two feedback types, *1-hint* and *3-hints*, given that the additional information contained in *3-hints* might simply not be processed.

Although in a different context, Plass, Chun, Mayer and Leutner (2003: 240) concluded that rather than displaying all available information by default, multimedia environments should be tailored to learners by taking their individual differences into account. Their conclusion is based on the learner performance on a vocabulary posttest which demonstrated "that multiple representations of information do not always help learning. Indeed, they may hinder learning in low-ability students when they experience high cognitive load as it is imposed by the requirement to process visual information". Regarding multimedia learning more generally, the individual differences principle states that "design effects are stronger for low-knowledge learners than for high-knowledge learners, and for high-spatial learners than for low-spatial learners" (Mayer 2001: 161) thus emphasizing the importance of individual differences. In the absence of an eye-tracking device that records whether students indeed read the preemptive feedback, however, it remains a speculation whether our beginner learners paid attention only to the top error. However, it is likely that individual differences play a role here, too.

Learner perceptions of preemptive feedback

In addition to investigating the two research questions, we were also interested in learners' perceptions about the preemptive feedback that the CALL program provided as reported during the retrospective interviews. These interviews consisted of a number of questions with the following as the most relevant to the discussion at hand: *Before you started an exercise, the E-Tutor provided you with tips on the most common error(s) for that exercise. Did you think that the tips were useful? Why?* Table 6 provides a sample of the responses from five students.

Table 6. Learner perceptions about preemptive feedback

Student	Responses
1	Yeah, definitely. There are so many things that you can do wrong when doing the E-Tutor exercises, so when you look at the tips, it kind of prevents you from some of the mistakes, some things that you might have forgotten or are just not aware of.
2	It was useful, yeah. Especially like some things were saying capitalization and I did miss a couple and I was getting them wrong until I realized: Okay, I need to read this a little bit more carefully.
3	Yes, I always looked at them but sometimes I already knew the tips I got.
4	Yeah, it was useful because otherwise I might have made something wrong. It helped me a lot of times to get it right on the first try. And it was kind of presetting too, so it was kind of helpful.
5	Well, I would always look at them, but a lot of the time it was things I already knew, but every once in while there was something useful. It really depended on how much I had been studying beforehand.

According to the learner responses displayed in Table 6, the learners generally found the preemptive feedback of the CALL system useful. Moreover, and at least for those five students, it seems that they generally read and paid attention to the preemptive feedback. Finally, it is interesting to note that, although students knew that they were not being graded on their mistakes, they nonetheless seemed quite concerned about making errors. This might be due to the fact that when students submit their work, E-Tutor will not only show that the work has been completed but also the number of errors (see Figure 1). Thus learners are aware that their teacher will see the number of their mistakes which might influence their study behavior although it has no effect on their course grade. In a previous study investigating language learning behavior in CALL, Heift (2005) found that the mere fact that students had to submit their results motivated them to repeat items that, according to their judgment, contained too many mistakes. Similarly, it seems that students will pay close attention to preemptive feedback, if they feel that it will reduce the number of errors they are making. Naturally, students could also be intrinsically motivated in that they want to learn German and thus want to perform well for their own sake.

Issues for further research

Although the findings highlight the potential value of preemptive feedback in CALL, more research is clearly needed before any generalizations about its efficacy can be made. For instance, the current study can make no claims as to whether the preemptive feedback was indeed read by all of the students. Those students who volunteered to take part in the retrospective interviews may have been more conscientious about looking at all the help options available. As previously mentioned, an eye-tracking device might provide clearer insight into learner behaviour in this regard. In addition, this study did not explore whether preemptive feedback was more effective when students followed the link to the inflectional paradigm following a hint for a grammar error. Moreover, the data was collected from only one activity type in which grammar errors far outnumbered other error types. Subsequent research might investigate other error types. In this context, motivational aspects of preemptive feedback as well as individual differences also deserve further investigation.

Finally, the study considered learner performance with respect to correct and incorrect responses. Another interesting topic related to feedback is that of uptake, which was not considered in this study given that every item required a learner response. However, one of the findings of Lyster's research into reactive feedback (Lyster 1998; Lyster & Ranta 1997) was that explicit rather than implicit feedback was more likely to lead to learner uptake. Given that preemptive feedback is more explicit, one might speculate that preemptive feedback will also result in an increase in uptake which, however, at this point needs further research.

Conclusion

This chapter investigated the effectiveness of preemptive feedback for L2 learners of German in a CALL environment. Results indicated that for both beginner and early intermediate learners, both types of preemptive feedback were significantly more effective than not providing any feedback. Moreover, the beginner learners significantly outperformed the early intermediate students. Finally, by considering the two distinct types of preemptive feedback in relation to different error types, the findings suggest that at an intermediate level, students are more likely and/or seem more able to pay attention to multiple pieces of information contained in the preemptive feedback.

From a computational perspective, the preemptive feedback in our CALL program is based on extensive statistical analyses of a learner corpus. A manual analysis of error profiles for each exercise is impossible due to the substantial number of instances needed to make the feedback reliable. However, a language teacher with sufficient experience can probably predict the most likely errors for an exercise although the error rankings may not be as reliable as statistical analyses. Thus, the implementation of preemptive feedback can certainly be achieved and implemented without a learner corpus.

From a pedagogical perspective, our study suggests that preemptive feedback not only leads to more successful task completion but it may also reduce frustration. As expressed by our learners during the retrospective interviews, students seem quite concerned about making errors regardless of whether or not the errors contribute to their course grade. Preemptive feedback cuts down on the number of errors and this may lead to a more positive learning experience. The CALL environment reported here created opportunities for learners to access feedback individually through technology, which may be beneficial for learners who feel uncomfortable receiving feedback orally in group settings.

More generally, CALL programs like E-Tutor provide a rich learning environment which enable learners to focus on form and meaning independent of time and place by, at the time, allowing them to explore their interlanguage in a non-threatening learning setting which does not penalize them for making errors. This is particularly so if the CALL program is integrated into the language learning curriculum, thus giving learners a chance to explore and get to know the CALL program over time. More importantly, however, these kinds of learning environments are learner-centered in that they place a strong emphasis on the interaction between the learner and the computer. In the end, it is less crucial whether a meaningful interaction is achieved by means of error-specific feedback or any other task assistance. It is central, however, that the CALL program aims at a rich interaction by reflecting sound teaching pedagogy and by also taking advantage of currently available technology if deemed appropriate. Despite the fact that computers have become ubiquitous in our daily lives, there is still very little justification to integrating a CALL program into the language learning curriculum unless there is an obvious benefit to it. Our study suggests that the preemptive feedback in E-Tutor might form part of that meaningful interaction we are seeking by minimizing learner errors from the start, thus reducing learner frustration and enhancing SLA.

References

Adamson, H. D. (2009). *Interlanguage variation in theoretical and pedagogical perspective.* New York, NY: Routledge.

Allwright, R. (1984). The importance of interaction in classroom language learning. *Applied Linguistics, 5,* 156–171.

Borg, S. (1998). Teachers' pedagogical systems and grammar teaching: A qualitative study. *TESOL Quarterly, 32,* 9–38.

Bowles, M. (2005). *Effects of verbalization condition and type of feedback on L2 development in a CALL task.* Georgetown University, Washington, DC.

Chander, J. (2003). The efficacy of various kinds of error feedback for improvement in the accuracy and fluency of L2 student writing. *Journal of Second Language Writing, 12,* 267–296.

Chapelle, C. A. (2003). *English language learning and technology: Lectures on applied linguistics in the age of information and communication technology.* Amsterdam: John Benjamins.

Di Donato, R., Clyde, M. D., & Vansant, J. (2008). *Deutsch: Na Klar! – An introductory German course.* New York, NY: McGraw Hill.

Ellis, R. (1991). The interaction hypothesis: A critical evaluation. Paper presented at the *Regional Language Centre Seminar*, Singapore, April 22–28.

Ellis, R. (1993). The structural syllabus and second language acquisition. *TESOL Quarterly, 27*, 91–113.

Ellis, R. (1999). *The study of second language acquisition*. Oxford: Oxford University Press.

Ellis, R., Basturkmen, H., & Loewen, S. (2001). Preemptive focus on form in the ESL classroom. *TESOL Quarterly, 35*, 407–432.

Farrokhi, F., Ansarin, A., & Mohammadnia, Z. (2008). Preemptive focus on form: Teachers' practices across proficiencies. *The Linguistics Journal, 3*(2), 7–30.

Farrokhi, F., & Gholami, J. (2007). Reactive and preemptive language related episodes and uptake in an EFL class. *Asian EFL Journal, 9*(2), 58–92.

Fischer, R. (2004). How do we know what students are actually doing? Monitoring students' behavior in CALL. *Computer Assisted Language Learning, 20*(5), 409–442.

Gass, S. M. (1997). *Input, interaction, and the second language learner*. Mahwah, NJ: Lawrence Erlbaum Associates.

Heift, T. (2002). Learner control and error correction in ICALL: Browsers, peekers and adamants. *CALICO Journal, 19*(3), 295–313.

Heift, T. (2004). Corrective feedback and learner uptake in CALL. *ReCALL, 16*(2), 416–431.

Heift, T. (2005). Inspectable learner reports for web-based language learning. *ReCALL, 17*(1), 32–46.

Heift, T. (2010). Developing an intelligent language tutor. *CALICO, 27*(3), 443–459.

Hubbard, P. (2005). A review of subject characteristics in CALL research. *Computer Assisted Language Learning, 18*(5), 351–368.

Larsen-Freeman, D. (1978). An ESL index of development. *TESOL Quarterly, 12*, 439–448.

Larsen-Freeman, D. (2006). The emergence of complexity, fluency, and accuracy in the oral and written production of five Chinese learners of English. *Applied Linguistics, 27*, 590–619.

Larsen-Freeman, D. (2009). Adjusting expectations: The study of complexity, accuracy, and fluency in second language acquisition. *Applied Linguistics, 30*, 579–589.

Leal, D. J. (2005). The word writing CAFE: Assessing student writing for complexity, accuracy, and fluency. *Reading Teacher, 59*, 340–350.

Loewen, S. (2003). Variation in the frequency and characteristics of incidental focus on form. *Language Teaching Research, 7*, 315–345.

Long, M. H. (1981). Input, interaction, and second language acquisition. *Annals of the New York Academy of Sciences, 379*(1), 259–278.

Long, M. H. (1983). Native speaker/non-native speaker conversation and the negotiation of comprehensible input. *Applied linguistics, 4*, 126–141.

Long, M. H. (1991). Focus on form: A design feature in language teaching methodology. In K. de Bot, R. Ginsberg, & C. Kramsch (Eds.), *Foreign languageresearch in cross-cultural perspective* (pp. 39–52). Amsterdam: John Benjamins.

Long, M. H. (1996). The role of the linguistic environment in second language acquisition. In W. C. Ritchie, & T. K. Bahtia (Eds.), *Handbook of second language acquisition* (pp. 413–68). New York, NY: Academic Press.

Long, M., & Robinson, P. (1998). Focus on form: Theory, research, and practice. In C. Doughty & J. Williams (Eds.), *Focus on form in classroom second languageacquisition* (pp. 15–63). Cambridge: Cambridge University Press.

Lyster, R. (1998). Negotiation of form, recasts, and explicit correction in relation to error types and learner repair in immersion classrooms. *Language Learning, 48*, 183–218.

Lyster, R., & Ranta, L. (1997). Corrective feedback and learner uptake: Negotiation of form in communicative classrooms. *Studies in Second Language Acquisition, 19*, 36–7.

Mackey, A., Polio, C., & McDonough, K. (2004). The relationship between experience, education and teachers' use of incidental focus on form techniques. *Language Teaching Research, 8*, 301–327.

Mayer, R. E. (2001). *Multimedia learning*. Cambridge: Cambridge University Press.

Murphy, P. (2007). Reading comprehension exercises online: The effects of feedback, proficiency and inter-action. *Language Learning & Technology, 11*(3), 107–129.

Nagata, N. (1993). Intelligent computer feedback for second language instruction. *Modern Language Journal, 77*, 330–338.

Nagata, N. (1996). Computer vs. workbook instruction in second language acquisition. *CALICO Journal, 14*(1), 53–75.

Nagata, N., & Swisher, M. V. (1995). A study of consciousness-raising by computer: The effect of metalin-guistic feedback on second language learning. *Foreign Language Annals, 28*, 337–347.

Ortega, L. (2003). Syntactic complexity measures and their relationship to L2 proficiency: A research synthesis of college-level L2 writing. *Applied Linguistics, 24*, 492–518.

Peterson, K. (2010). *Implicit corrective feedback in computer-guided interaction. Does mode matter?* PhD dissertation, Georgetown University.

Pica,T., Young, R., & Doughty, C. (1987). The impact of interaction on comprehension. *TESOL Quarterly, 21*, 737–758.

Plass, J. L., Chun, D. M., Mayer, R. E., & Leutner, D. (2003). Cognitive load in reading a foreign language text with multimedia aids and the influence of verbal and spatial abilities. *Computers in Human Behavior, 19*, 221–243.

Poole, A. (2005a). The kinds of forms learners attend to during focus on form instruction: A description of an advanced ESL writing class. *Asian EFL Journal, 7*(3), 58–92. Retrieved on July 14, 2011 from: http://www.asian-efl-journal.com/sept_05_ap.pdf

Pujolà, J.-T. (2002). CALLing for help: Researching language learning strategies using help facilities in a web-based multimedia program. *ReCALL, 14*(2), 235–262.

Rosa, E., & Leow, R. (2004). Computerized task-based exposure, explicitness and type of feedback on Spanish L2 development. *Modern Language Journal, 88*, 192–217.

Sauro, S. (2009). Computer-mediated corrective feedback and the development of L2 grammar. *Language Learning & Technology, 13*(1), 96–120.

Schmidt, R. (1990). The role of consciousness in second language learning. *Applied Linguistics, 11*, 129–158.

Schmidt, R. (1994). Deconstructing consciousness in search of useful definitions for applied linguistics. *AILA Review, 11*, 11–26.

Swain, M. (1985). Communicative competence: Some rules of comprehensible input and comprehensible output in its development. In S. Gass & C. Madden (Eds.), *Input in second language acquisition* (pp. 235–253). Rowley, MA: Newbury House.

VanPatten, B. (1990). Attending to form and content in the input: An experiment in consciousness. *Studies in Second Language Acquisition, 12*, 287–301.

VanPatten, B. (1996). *Input processing and grammar instruction in second language acquisition.* Norwood, NJ: Ablex.

VanPatten, B. (2003). *From input to output: A teacher's guide to second language acquisition.* Boston: McGraw Hill.

Vinther, J. (2005). Cognitive processes at work in CALL. *Computer Assisted Language Learning, 18*(4), 251–271.

Ware, P. (2008). Peer feedback on language form in telecollaboration. *Language Learning & Technology, 12*(1), 43–63.

Williams, J. (1999). Learner-initiated attention to form. *Language Learning, 49*, 583–625.

Author note

This research was supported by Social Sciences and Humanities Research Council (SSHRC), Canada, grant 632209.

Chapter 11

Learner perceptions of clickers as a source of feedback in the classroom

Ellen Johnson Serafini
Georgetown University

This chapter explores the use of learner response systems, or "clickers", as a source of immediate feedback in beginning Spanish foreign language classrooms. Learners in seven intact classes participated in clicker-based activities and received feedback that differed according to degree of explicitness (+/− metalinguistic information) and enhancement (+/− visual display). Learners then completed reflection questionnaires (N=37) based on their experience. Quantitative and qualitative analyses of questionnaire items revealed strengths and weaknesses of the clicker-based activities as well as similarities and differences with learner perceptions in other contexts (Cardoso 2011; Cutrim Schmid 2007, 2008). The chapter concludes with a discussion on individual differences as well as suggestions for teachers about the use of clicker-based materials.

Introduction

Even though the use of learner response systems, or "clickers", in higher education dates back almost forty years (Littauer 1972) the adoption of these systems has grown considerably in the past half decade, particularly in the sciences (Moss & Crowley 2011). Clickers are hand-held devices that collect learner responses. A software system then electronically tabulates the student response data, making it available for instant display on a computer monitor (Bush & McLester 2007). For example, in order to gauge student comprehension, an instructor might ask the class a multiple-choice question. Using their clickers, students "click in" their answer. Almost instantaneously, the instructor can show the responses from the entire class. Clickers can be used to ensure students understand the material, to encourage class voting, to provide immediate feedback, and to make course content more interactive.

It is estimated that one in every ten undergraduate students has been exposed to clickers (Sevian & Robinson 2011: 14), which is largely due to their prevalence in large introductory lecture courses. As is the case with most emerging technologies, research so far on clickers has explored both learner and instructor perceptions, as well as the way in which instructors use them in their courses. The majority of research on clickers has been in scientific disciplines (e.g., biology, chemistry, physics, psychology) and other general education classes (e.g., Cheesman, Winograd, & Wehrman 2010; Flynn & Russell 2008; Kenwright 2009; Lee, Ding, & Reay 2011; Mollborn & Hoekstra 2010; Moniz, Eshleman, Jewell, Mooney, & Tran 2010; Russell, McWilliams, Chasen, & Farley 2011; Salemi 2009; Shaffer & Collura 2009; Stagg & Lane 2010; Stowell, Oldham, & Bennett 2010; Woelk 2008; Wolter, Lundeberg, Kang, & Herreid 2011).

Most of this research has reported that learner perceptions of clickers are extremely positive. The perceived benefits of clickers include increased motivation, more involvement and interaction, opportunities for self-assessment and the ability to compare performance with peers. While classroom response systems have been used extensively in large courses to promote active, student-centered learning environments (Hake 1998), studies have reported similar benefits for use in small, upper-level science and laboratory sections (Milner-Bolotin, Antimirova, & Petrov 2010; Sevian & Robinson 2011). Although the literature on clicker use in scientific and general education disciplines is growing, there is so far very little research on the use of clickers in second and foreign language contexts. Some pedagogically oriented presentations exist (e.g., Cardoso 2010; Corder 2008; Tabak & Cardoso 2009; Yoder-Kreger 2009), but only two published studies have explored the benefits of using clickers in an English foreign language (EFL) context (Cardoso 2011) and an English for academic purposes (EAP) course (Cutrim Schmid 2007, 2008).

Cardoso (2011) investigated EFL learners' views ($N = 30$) about the use of clickers as part of an 8-week vocabulary learning study carried out in Brazil. He elicited learners' perceptions using Likert-style questionnaires and open-ended oral interviews. Results generally confirmed previous learner reports from academic lecture settings such as increased motivation, participation and involvement in the class as well as a positive view of the opportunity for self and peer assessment provided by the devices. However, learner responses were neutral with respect to fostering increased interaction with classmates and contributing to better course grades. Cutrim Schmid (2007, 2008) examined the use of clickers as a voting system in an English for Academic Purposes summer course for intermediate- and advanced-level learners ($N = 62$). Their perceptions about the clickers were elicited through questionnaires and interviews. Cutrim Schmid reported that they viewed the clickers as having several pedagogical benefits, including feedback and privacy, peer comparison, self-esteem and more collaboration (2007) as well as increased interactivity in the classroom (2008). However, some learners reported concerns about guessing and suggested that students be required to justify their answers.

Of most relevance to the current study is the frequently reported benefit of clickers as a valuable source of immediate and anonymous feedback by language learners in both studies. Given that feedback is a key component of the interaction hypothesis (Mackey 2012). Although most interaction hypothesis research has focused on face-to-face interaction as a source for feedback, researchers have extended claims about the benefits of feedback into technology-mediated communication. As described by Heift (this volume), technology creates opportunities for different kinds of interaction, ranging from communication between people using computers as well as between learners and computers. Similar to computers, clickers can be used as a source of feedback to L2 learners.

Carroll (2001:21), defines feedback as utterances that "are used by learners to derive positive and negative evidence about the second language." Although considerable debate remains about the relative effectiveness of explicit versus implicit types of feedback, several studies have reported general advantages for explicit feedback (Carroll & Swain 1993; DeKeyser 1993; Ellis, Loewen, & Erlam 2006; Nagata 1993; Norris & Ortega 2000; Rosa & Leow 2004), particularly for short-term development (Li 2010:29) and interaction research has found positive benefits as well (Mackey and Goo 2007). However, one recent meta-analysis reported the effects of explicit correction in classroom settings to be equivalent to those of implicit forms of feedback such as recasts and prompts (Lyster & Saito 2010:283). Nonetheless, this chapter focuses on explicit feedback based on the nature of the learner response system and short-term design of the study. Minimally, explicit feedback indicates to the learner that an error has been committed which can also be considered an implicit form of feedback (see Ellis et al. 2006:348). More extensively, explicit feedback provides the learner with detailed grammatical information, or metalinguistic explanation, about the nature of the error. Metalinguistic feedback has been shown to be particularly useful for second language (L2) generalization, being able to accurately apply a grammatical rule to new items (Carroll & Swain 1993; Rosa & Leow 2004).

The purpose of this study is to explore learners' perceptions about the use of clickers as a source of feedback in beginning Spanish foreign language classrooms, with the goal of expanding the small body of L2 classroom-based research that has investigated learner response systems in relation to feedback. More specifically, it explores learners' perceptions about the use of clickers as a way to obtain feedback about a complex morphosyntactic distinction in Spanish. As part of a larger study that compared the effectiveness of different types of feedback, this chapter explores (i) how university beginning foreign language learners of Spanish view the use and effectiveness of clickers in the foreign language classroom and (ii) how learner perceptions vary according to the type of feedback they receive.

Based on findings by Cardoso (2011) and Cutrim Schmid (2007, 2008), it was predicted that learners would report positive perceptions of clickers towards learning, while offering a more detailed view of the perceived benefits and weaknesses of clicker-based feedback by employing a bottom-up approach to qualitatively analyze open-ended learner responses using NVivo. NVivo is a software program that facilitates the identification, sorting, and arranging of unstructured data. The analysis aims to inform pedagogical practice involving learner response systems in L2 classrooms by focusing on the uses, benefits and limitations of this technology.

Method

Participants

A total of 63 students enrolled in beginner level Spanish as a foreign language courses at a private East coast university carried out the clicker activities, but only the subset of students who completed the reflective questionnaire ($N=37$) were included in the current study. They were native speakers of English with a mean age of 19.1 ($SD=1.4$) years who had no more than two years high school Spanish instruction and no reported study abroad experience. Seven Spanish classes were randomly assigned to different clicker activity groups following a convenience sampling method. Four instructors observed the class sessions while the researcher, who was also a teacher in the program, taught the designated syllabus topic for the day of instruction. This decision was made in order to control for individual differences in instructional style and to keep the lesson constant.

Instructional context

The participants' Spanish course met three days a week for fifty minutes each day. At the beginning of the semester, students were encouraged to consider three key components in their pursuit of learning Spanish for communicative purposes: (a) Vocabulary; (b) Language Awareness; and (c) Practice/Participation. The instructional materials were designed to address the third component, to increase the amount of practice and participation in a class targeting a difficult grammatical distinction. Based on informal communication with the four instructors who observed the clicker-based activities, they reported one of their biggest challenges was facilitating learner comprehension of the contextual differences between past tense forms in Spanish and their accurate use in oral and written activities. While the text-book served as their starting point for differentiating between the past tense forms, they had to design additional activities to target these goals. The clicker-based activity was one such activity, and it was specifically designed to facilitate comprehension. At the time the study was carried out, clicker use in Spanish foreign language classes varied by individual teachers, and a total of five instructors had reported using clickers for general test reviews.

Materials

Target structure

The target structure was the aspectual distinction between the past tense forms of the *imperfect* and *preterit* in Spanish. Native English-speaking learners at a novice proficiency level notoriously show problems with learning this complex distinction as it is realized through overt tense morphology in Spanish but not English (Montrul & Slabakova 2000: 536). Initial classroom exposure to the imperfect and preterit typically takes the form of a traditional list of rules with examples in a textbook. Below (1–2) are the functions of the imperfect and preterit as presented in *Vistazos* (VanPatten, Lee, & Ballman 2010), the textbook used at the introductory level within the Department of Spanish and Portuguese in the learners' home institution.

(1) *Uses of the Imperfect*
   a. Habitual action
   b. Event in progress
   c. Background information

(2) *Uses of the Preterit*
   a. Points in time
   b. Recurring event within specified time frame
   c. Sequence of completed actions
   d. Interrupting action
   e. Change in meaning predicates in the preterit

The textbook functions above, along with common cue words and phrases such as *ayer* 'yesterday' to cue perfective aspect (preterit) and *siempre* 'always' to signal the need for imperfective (imperfect), were used to inform the creation of classroom activities.

Clicker activities

Table 1 below displays three types of feedback that students received during the clicker activities. Learners in all seven classes received explicit feedback that highlighted the correct response after they clicked in their answers.

Table 1. Characteristics of feedback provided during clicker activities

Group	Correct response	Visual display	Metalinguistic explanation
Response only ($n = 11$)	Yes	No	No
Visual display ($n = 14$)	Yes	Yes	No
Metalinguistic explanation ($n = 12$)	Yes	No	Yes

However, learners in the metalinguistic explanation group also received an elaborated grammatical explanation of the reason underlying the correct response. Learners in the visual display group were provided with a histogram of class performance. In sum, learners in all groups had the opportunity to "notice the gap" (Schmidt & Frota 1986) in their linguistic knowledge within a crucial "window of opportunity" (Doughty 2001:257).

Nonetheless, the nature of feedback provided in these activities differs from Long's conception (1983, 1996, 2006) of interactional feedback. Learners did not actively negotiate for meaning and receive feedback as the need naturally arose as advocated in Focus on Form (FonF) (Long 1991) instructional approaches, but rather had the opportunity to make comparisons between their clicked answer and a preplanned correct response. Whether learners received positive or negative evidence thus depended on the nature of learners' individual answers. Therefore, the nature of the clicker classroom response system lent itself more to a grammar-focused, or focus-on-forms (FonFs) (Long 1991), intervention at this proficiency level. However, clickers are by no means limited to form-focused activities and a discussion of possible pedagogical applications at different proficiency levels is provided in the Discussion section. In other words, clicker activities of the types reported here are very adaptable to more communicative task-based activities. The current research represents one perspective on this very promising line of investigation for work in interaction in general.

The clicker activities were incorporated into the Spanish classroom following the syllabus and course textbook. A PowerPoint presentation was designed that first included a brief review of the verbal conjugations for both the preterit and imperfect tenses. Then, a series of slides presented three functions of the imperfect with examples and four functions of the preterit with examples. The final presentation slides illustrated a complex group of verbs that change meaning in the preterit (e.g., 'saber': *Yo sabía-* 'I knew'; *Yo supe-* 'I found out'). All materials were reviewed by a native Spanish-speaker to ensure that examples were contextually appropriate and accurate.

After the PowerPoint presentation, learners then answered forty-one multiple-choice questions, each of which had five options (a, b, c, d, e), by clicking in an answer displayed on the slides. Each use of the imperfect and preterit appeared at least once, and the questions took approximately 30 minutes to complete. Once the whole class clicked in after each question (usually within 15–20 seconds), the correct response appeared in red. In addition to the correct response, learners in the metalinguistic group received a 'reason' slide (illustrated in Figure 1), while the visual display group was shown a histogram of the class performance.

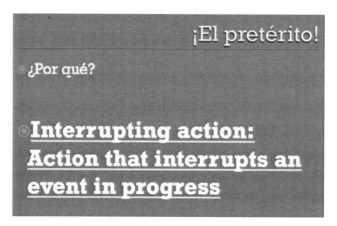

Figure 1. Example reason slide provided to the metalinguistic group

Reflection questionnaire

After participating in the clicker-based activities, the learners completed a reflection questionnaire designed to elicit both closed (*Yes, Somewhat, No*) and open-ended (*Why, or why not? Please explain*) responses about their experiences using clickers. An abbreviated version of the six questionnaire items is provided in (3).

(3) Q1: *Overall effectiveness.*
     Q2: *Relative effectiveness compared to other activities.*
     Q3: *Preference for immediate or delayed feedback.*
     Q4: Visual display group – *Helpfulness of viewing histogram*
          Metalinguistic group – *Helpfulness of viewing reason*
     Q5: *Overall enjoyment of the technology.*
     Q6: *Improved performance with continued use.*

Analysis

All closed-ended responses were coded numerically (1 – 'Yes'; 2 – 'Somewhat'; 3 – 'No') and entered into the statistical software program SPSS (19.0). The open-ended response data informed the bottom-up analysis carried out in NVivo9, which is a software program for analyzing qualitative data. As mentioned earlier, NVivo has the capacity to sort and extract meaningful themes from unstructured information so it is an ideal resource when working with qualitative data. Thirty-seven completed questionnaires were included in both the descriptive statistical analysis of close-ended items as well as in the bottom-up NVivo analysis of open-ended response trends. Results are discussed in turn below.

Results

Quantitative analysis

The first research question explored general student perceptions of the use and effectiveness of clickers in relation to their task of learning the uses of the preterit and imperfect in Spanish. Table 2 summarizes the descriptive statistics for overall learner responses (in percentages).

Table 2. All closed-ended responses

Question	Yes	Somewhat	No
Q1: Overall effectiveness	82	11	7
Q2: Relative effectiveness	63	13	24
Q3: Feedback preference	100	n/a	0
Q4: Helpfulness of display/reason	71/92	7/0	22/8
Q5: Overall enjoyment	89	0	11
Q6: Improved performance	60	24	16

Note: 'Yes' in Q3 represents a preference for immediate feedback whereas 'No' indicates a preference for delayed feedback

As Table 2 shows, the overwhelming majority of students (i) thought that clickers effectively prepared them for being tested on the preterit/imperfect (Q1), (ii) indicated a preference for immediate feedback (Q3) and (iii) enjoyed participating in the activity overall (Q5). In contrast, responses regarding the relative effectiveness of clickers compared to other classroom activities (Q2) were more varied; while 63% believed they were more effective, 13% said somewhat more effective, and 24% thought they were relatively less effective. Responses regarding continued improvement (Q6) are closer to fifty-fifty; 40% said they somewhat or don't believe that continuing to use clickers would help their performance in Spanish while 60% were optimistic in this regard. As will be seen in the bottom-up analysis of open-ended items, negative responses to Q2 were usually qualified in relation to student individual differences such as preferring oral interactive activities based on the belief that oral fluency was their greatest weakness. Time was also a frequently reported drawback as some students thought the activity went too fast to allow them to fully process the complex material. In relation to Q6, negative answers were modified by clarifying that clickers would help them develop grammatical concepts but not conversational skills and should be used only as a supplement in the classroom, not as a substitute for other communicative activities.

Interestingly, the majority of learners in the visual display group (71%) believed that viewing the histogram with their peers' responses was helpful for their own progress while around a quarter thought this aspect distracted or hindered their performance. Almost all of the learners in the metalinguistic explanation group (92%) believed viewing and discussing the reason why the answer was correct improved their understanding and subsequent performance. As the qualitative analysis will show, the learners' open-ended responses provided further useful information for the design of clicker activities.

The second research question considered learner perceptions by group, based on the type of feedback they received during the clicker activities: Correct response only, visual display or metalinguistic explanation. Table 3 provides descriptive statistics of learner response data by group (in percentages).

Table 3. Closed-ended responses by group in percentages

Question	Response only			Visual display			Metalinguistic explanation		
	Yes	Some	No	Yes	Some	No	Yes	Some	No
Q1: Overall effectiveness	91	0	9	79	14	7	83	0	17
Q2: Relative effectiveness	73	9	18	57	14	29	58	17	25
Q5: Overall enjoyment	91	0	9	93	0	7	83	0	17
Q6: Improved performance	64	18	18	72	14	14	41.5	41.5	17

As Table 3 indicates, responses to Q1 (*Overall effectiveness*) were uniformly positive across groups, ranging from 91% in the correct response only group to 83% and 79% in the metalinguistic and visual display groups, respectively. However, there is much more variance in responses to Q2, which probed the clicker system's relative effectiveness to other class activities. Almost three quarters (73%) of learners in the correct response only group believed the clicker-based activity was more effective than other class activities while only a little over half of learners in visual display (57%) and metalinguistic explanation (58%) groups agreed. Finally, Q6, which pertained to perceived improvement with continued use of clickers, revealed varied responses by group. The visual display and correct response only groups were the most positive (72% and 64% respectively) whereas only 41.5% of learners who received metalinguistic explanation believed their Spanish skills would improve or somewhat improve by continuing to use clickers in the classroom.

Qualitative analysis

To enrich the quantitative analysis, NVivo 9 was used to identify response patterns in the open-ended responses to "*Why or why not?*" and "*Please explain*" components of the six reflection questions. Twenty-seven coding categories, or nodes, emerged from the response data across all clicker activity groups with a total of 285 references. The most relevant categories are visually organized below in Figure 2.

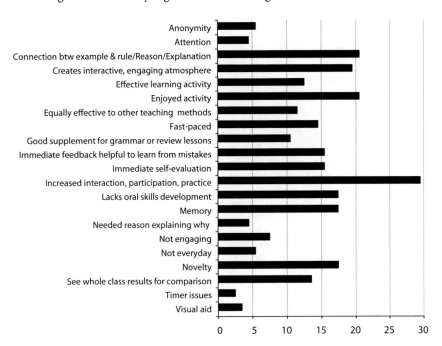

Figure 2. Number of references to NVivo categories across groups

Overall, nine categories were referenced fifteen times or more across clicker groups: (i) 'Immediate feedback helpful to learn' ($n = 15$); (ii) 'Immediate self-evaluation' ($n = 15$); (iii) 'Novelty' ($n = 17$); (iv) 'Lacks oral skills development' ($n = 17$); (v) 'Memory'

($n = 17$); (vi) 'Creates interactive, engaging atmosphere' ($n = 19$); (vii) 'Enjoyed activity' ($n = 20$); (viii) 'Connection between Example-Rule, Reason, Explanation' ($n = 20$); and (ix) 'Increased interaction, participation, practice' ($n = 29$). With the exception of the frequently reported weakness, 'Lacks oral skills development', all of the most pertinent categories were perceived *benefits* of using clickers. 'Increased interaction, participation, practice' was by far the most frequently referenced benefit across activity groups.

Sample written learner responses are provided in (4–10) which illustrate categories referenced over fifteen times.

(4) Novelty ($n = 17$)
"*It was something new and different.*"
"*It was a nice change.*"

(5) Memory ($n = 17$) (indicating a preference for immediate feedback)
"*It is better when it is fresh in my mind.*"
"*I may forget what I had answered.*"

(6) Lacks oral skills development ($n = 17$)
"*I feel that speaking the language is a better way to learn.*"
"*They may take away time from practice speaking.*"

(7) Creates interactive, engaging atmosphere ($n = 19$)
"*…kept me really engaged in the lesson.*"
"*… the clickers encourage an interactive atmosphere.*"

(8) Enjoyed activity ($n = 20$)
"*The clickers are fun and useful.*"
"*It made the class more fun.*"

(9) Connection between Example-Rule/Reason/Explanation ($n = 20$)
"*The specific examples and clear reasons for each really helped.*"
"*It was a great review & made me apply the rules to specific examples.*"

(10) Increased Interaction/Participation/Practice ($n = 29$)
"*It will force me to make a decision on every question rather than just the ones I am asked.*"
"*It makes me actively think, even when I'm not called on.*"
"*Everyone had to answer the questions instead of just one person.*"
"*You get to interact on every question.*"

Other relevant perceptions referenced ten times or more were 'Effective learning activity' (e.g., "*I felt that the clicker activity allowed me to learn quickly and more effectively*"), 'Equally effective to other methods' (e.g., "*I feel it was equally effective. It would help on a written test but less so during an oral exam*"), and 'See whole class results for comparison' (e.g., "*I knew that I was in the same place as my classmates*").

Despite the identified strengths of this instructional tool, perhaps even more important to the classroom practitioner are its weaknesses. Learners in this context referenced the categories '(Too) fast-paced' and 'Good supplement for grammar or review (only)' ten times or more. Sample responses are given in (11–12):

(11) (Too) Fast-paced
   "*I felt really rushed to get answers in, so I didn't always evaluate/understand my choices fully...*"
   "*I think if it went a little slower it would have been great.*"

(12) Good supplement for grammar or review (only)
   "*...it would help me learn grammar concepts more easily.*"
   "*...not as a substitute for verbal participation.*"

Additional learner perceptions that may help instructors design clicker activities for use in foreign language classrooms included 'Anonymity' (e.g., "*It took away the fear of not knowing the answer*"), 'Attention' (e.g., "*I was forced to pay more attention because I had to answer all of the questions*"), and 'Not everyday' (e.g., "*I really like the clickers and think they are great teaching resources, but I wouldn't want to use them everyday*").

Discussion

The findings of this classroom-based study employing both quantitative and qualitative methods shed light on both the potential effectiveness and limitations of learner-technology interaction though clicker-based feedback in a foreign language learning setting. Beginning Spanish learners' perceptions about the usefulness of clickers were highly positive overall with reported limitations mainly linked to individual differences and oral skills development. More importantly, learner perceptions differed among the clicker groups according to the way the clicker system provided feedback, which can improve the use of clickers in L2 classrooms.

Though positive responses strongly outweighed negative responses in all clicker groups regarding the *overall* effectiveness of the clicker-based activity, there was less uniformity in learner responses to questions about their *relative* effectiveness to other classroom activities. Likewise, learners were less certain about their future improvement if clickers were to be integrated as a daily part of classroom instruction. Contrary to what might be expected, learners who received metalinguistic explanations revealed a certain degree of doubt about its relative effectiveness and regular use in particular. Although this group was highly positive toward the usefulness of viewing the reason (92%), it is important to consider the frequently referenced disadvantage of the fast pace of the activity in the qualitative analysis. The activity went too quickly for some learners and didn't allow enough time for processing. The added element of connecting the rule to the right answer might have caused a cognitive overload for certain learners in this group. On the contrary, the visual display group was the most optimistic toward continuing to use clickers in their Spanish classroom. Viewing the class performance histogram could have promoted a more interactive, competitive atmosphere and fulfilled a desire for self-monitoring through access to peer comparison, an interpretation further confirmed in the qualitative analysis of open-ended responses.

Relevant similarities and differences emerged with learner perceptions in two English L2 contexts with a different target and duration of clicker-based activities. Compared to perceptions reported by advanced native Portuguese-speaking EFL learners (Cardoso 2011), three themes were echoed here: (1) Increased participation and involvement, (2) Opportunity for self-assessment and peer comparison, and (3) Overall contribution to learning. Furthermore, learners in this study and Cardoso's study were somewhat skeptical about whether using clickers would actually lead to achieving better course grades. With respect to perceived level of interaction promoted by clickers, learners in Cardoso's study were neutral whereas this was the most referenced category to emerge in this study's bottom-up qualitative analysis. The difference between learner perceptions could be due to the length of each study; in Cardoso's study clickers were used for eight weeks while this study implemented them for one day of classroom instruction. It is possible that perceived level of interaction decreases with a longer period of classroom usage as clickers become a common part of classroom instruction. Another plausible reason is that 'participation' and 'practice' were included in the 'interaction' category established by NVivo based on similarity of learner responses. The decision to include rather than separate these categories could have led to an inflated perception of increased interaction in this study.

In comparison to Cutrim Schmid's findings with EAP learners (2007, 2008), the perceived benefit of peer comparison was echoed here whereas anonymity was not as highly valued by learners in this context as it was only referenced five times. The more advanced nature of course content (i.e., topics related to academia) could explain why anonymity was viewed as a more valued benefit in an EAP program rather than in a beginning level course since learners are more likely to feel vulnerable sharing opinions about advanced and potentially controversial topics.

Overall, this study builds on and expands previous studies by demonstrating that learner perceptions are not uniform and can vary according to *how* learners interact with features of the clicker system. The nature of feedback provided in each classroom activity was varied in order to explore its impact on learner perceptions. The ability to view how the class performed as a whole seemed to have a positive effect as it seemed to promote a competitive, game-like atmosphere while the perceived benefits of metalinguistic explanation depended on individual differences. The qualitative analysis guided by NVivo also provided a more systematic approach for identifying themes in open-ended response data. In Cardoso and Cutrim Schmid, it is not clear under what criteria themes emerged based on learner reports. While both studies triangulate data from surveys and interviews, it is unknown whether a theme could be established based on one learner mentioning it once or if more references were required across data sources. Finally, this study provides a more detailed look at learner reported *weaknesses* such as the negative impact of the quick paced activity on learners' ability to process the material. Thus, clicker activities should be paced according to learner preferences and needs. Learners in this study also believed that clickers would serve best as a tool for practicing difficult grammatical concepts on a supplementary basis and should be varied along with a range of communicative activities to support oral fluency development. Overall, it seems that learner reported weaknesses of using clickers are arguably even more useful to language practitioners than their reported benefits.

Despite these advantages, interpretation of learner perceptions is somewhat limited considering the short duration of the clicker activities. Clicker use lasted over a longer instructional period in previous research, either over several weeks (Cardoso) or over the course of a summer program (Cutrim Schmid). Without a longer period of instructional duration, it is possible that the highly optimistic perceptions reported here were influenced by a "novelty effect", as warned by Cardoso (412–413, c.f. Clark 1983). Indeed "Novelty" was frequently referenced here as a perceived benefit in terms of being a change from the routine. If learner response systems were incorporated into the curriculum over a longer period of learning, a novelty effect would be less likely to influence learner perceptions.

Finally, other pedagogical applications with classroom response systems in language learning settings should be considered for learners at different proficiency levels. Bruff (2009) is a good resource to consult as he details clicker use in several universities across the US, including two examples of use in language instruction. One instructor teaching intermediate and advanced Spanish courses at James Madison University reports using clickers for oral exercises and with correct/incorrect or true/false questions as a warm-up activity. Students see a series of statements about a piece of artwork; then they must click correct/incorrect or true/false based on the accuracy of grammar and vocabulary. The instructor uses follow-up questions to prompt students to verbally explain the reasons for their answers, either in small groups or with the whole class. She believes that "missing a question motivates them to want to get the next one correct, so they are more engaged in the discussion" (p. 203). The instructor also incorporates clickers with a student-paced mode for exams by using multiple-choice questions to prepare students for free response writing.

An instructor at Boston University incorporates clickers in courses on academic writing in English for international students with a focus on grammar and sentence-level writing issues. However, clickers are used to gauge understanding and facilitate small group discussions. For example, in a grammar lesson, learners click 'yes' or 'no' to a series of questions (e.g., "Is this a run-on sentence?"). When results are mixed, students return to small groups to discuss their answers. Clickers are also used as a tool to encourage friendly competition among peer groups. Students win points for each correct individual response and the group with the most correct answers receives a small prize.

Conclusion

The present study has provided insight into the potential effectiveness of using clickers as a form of learner-technology interaction that provides explicit feedback in foreign language classrooms. Findings discussed here have expanded previous classroom-based evidence by further exploring the perceived benefits and weaknesses of this instructional tool. Learner self-reports generally confirm positive findings of the previously published studies, but reveal that the effectiveness of this technology depends on *how* the system is used, and more specifically, on how feedback is delivered. Namely, learners in all groups reported a 'net benefit' (i.e., the advantages outweighed the disadvantages), but perceptions varied according to delivery of feedback and learner individual differences. Learners' limited cognitive resources somewhat negatively affected learner reports in the metalinguistic explanation group while learners' desire for peer comparison positively affected reports in the visual display group.

In order to exploit the full potential of these technological devices as foreign language learning tools in language classrooms, clicker activities should be paced according to learner needs and used to practice difficult grammatical concepts on a supplementary basis rather than as a replacement for oral communication activities. Furthermore, future research should incorporate clickers into the curriculum on a long-term basis to avoid the potential influence of a "novelty effect." Finally, the effectiveness of clicker-based activities merits further evaluation according to learner individual differences (e.g., memory) and across a range of proficiency levels, particularly at more advanced levels as a tool to prompt oral discussion in content-based tasks.

References

Bush, S., & McLester, S. (2007). Clickers rule! *Technology & Learning, 28*(4), 10–11.

Bruff, D. (2009). *Teaching with classroom response systems – Creating active learning environments.* San Francisco, CA: Jossey-Bass.

Cardoso, W. (2011). Learning a foreign language with a learner response system: The student's perspective. *Computer Assisted Language Learning, 24,* 393–417.

Cardoso, W. (2010). Make your ESL students click: Classroom response systems in second language teaching. *Proceedings of INTED 2010 conference,* Valencia, Spain.

Carroll, S., & Swain, M. (1993). Explicit and implicit negative feedback: An empirical study of the learning of linguistic generalizations. *Studies in Second Language Acquisition, 15,* 357–366.

Carroll, S. (2001). *Input and evidence: The raw material of second language acquisition.* Amsterdam: John Benjamins.

Cheesman, E. A., Winograd, G. R., & Wehrman, J. D. (2010). Clickers in teacher education: Student perceptions by age and gender. *Journal of Technology and Teacher Education, 18,* 35–55.

Clark, R. E. (1983). Reconsidering research on learning from media. *Review of Educational Research, 53,* 445–459.

Corder, G. (2008). Using clickers to engage students and facilitate immediate feedback. Paper presented at the *American Council on the Teaching of Foreign Languages* (ACTFL) Convention, Orlando, FL.

Cutrim Schmid, E. (2007). Enhancing performance knowledge and self-esteem in classroom language learning: The potential of the ACTIVote system component of interactive whiteboard technology. *System, 35,* 119–133.

Cutrim Schmid, E. (2008). Using a voting system in conjunction with interactive whiteboard technology to enhance learning in the English language classroom. *Computers and Education, 50,* 338–356.

DeKeyser, R. (1993). The effect of error correction on L2 grammar knowledge and oral proficiency. *The Modern Language Journal, 77,* 501–14.

Doughty, C. (2001). Cognitive underpinnings of focus on form. In P. Robinson (Ed.), *Cognition and second language instruction* (pp. 206–57). Cambridge: Cambridge University Press.

Ellis, R., Loewen, S., & Erlam, E. (2006). Implicit and explicit corrective feedback and the acquisition of L2 grammar. *SSLA, 28,* 339–68.

Flynn, J., & Russell, J. (2008). Personal response systems: Is success in learning just a click away? *Educational Technology, 48,* 20–3.

Hake, R. (1998). Interactive engagement versus traditional methods: A sixty-thousand-student survey of mechanics test data for introductory physics courses. *American Journal of Physics, 66,* 64–74.

Kenwright, K. (2009). Clickers in the classroom. *TechTrends, 53,* 74–7.

Lee, A., Ding, L., & Reay, N. W. (2011). Single-concept clicker question sequences. *The Physics Teacher, 49,* 385–9.

Li, S. (2010). The effectiveness of corrective feedback in SLA: A meta-analysis. *Language Learning, 60,* 1–57.

Littauer, R. (1972). Instructional implications of a low-cost electronic student response system. *Educational Technology: Teacher and Technology Supplement, 12,* 69–71.

Long, M. H. (1983). 'Native speaker/non-native speaker conversation and the negotiation of comprehensible input, *Applied Linguistics, 4,* 126–41.

Long, M. (1991). Focus-on-form: A design feature in language teaching methodology. In K. de Bot, R. Ginsberg, & C. Kramsch (Eds.), *Foreign language research in cross-cultural perspective* (pp. 39–52). Amsterdam: John Benjamins.

Long, M. H. (1996). The role of the linguistic environment in second language acquisition. In W. C. Ritchie & T. K. Bhatia (Eds), *Handbook of second language acquisition* (pp. 413–68). New York, NY: Academic Press,

Long, M. H. (2006). Recasts in SLA: The story so far. In M. H. Long (Ed.), *Problems in SLA*. Mahwah, NJ: Lawrence Erlbaum Associates.

Lyster, R., & Saito, K. (2010). Oral feedback in classroom SLA. *Studies in Second Language Acquisition, 32,* 265–302.

Mackey, A. (2012). *Input, interaction and corrective feedback in L2 classrooms*. Oxford: Oxford University Press.

Mackey, A., & Goo, J. (2007). Interaction research in SLA: A meta-analysis and research synthesis. In A. Mackey (Ed.), *Conversational interaction in second language acquisition: A collection of empirical studies* (pp. 407–452). Oxford: Oxford University Press.

Milner-Bolotin, M., Antimirova, T., & Petrov, A. (2010). Clickers beyond the first-year science classroom. *Journal of College Science Teaching, 40,* 14–18.

Mollborn, S., & Hoekstra, A. (2010). A meeting of minds: Using clickers for critical thinking and discussion in large sociology classes. *Teaching Sociology, 38,* 18–27.

Moniz, R., Eshleman, J., Jewell, D., Mooney, B., & Tran, C. (2010). The impact of information literacy-related instruction in the science classroom: Clickers versus nonclickers. *College & Undergraduate Libraries, 17,* 349–64.

Montrul, S., & Slabakova, R. (2000). Acquiring semantic properties of Preterite and Imperfect tenses in L2 Spanish. *Proceedings of the Annual Boston University Conference on Language Development, 24*, 534–545.

Moss, K., & Crowley, M. (2011). Effective learning in science: The use of personal response systems with a wide range of audiences. *Computers & Education, 56*, 36–43.

Nagata, N. (1993). Intelligent computer feedback for second languageinstruction. *The Modern Language Journal, 77*, 330–339.

Norris, J. M., & Ortega, L. (2000). Effectiveness of L2 instruction: A research synthesis and quantitative meta-analysis. *Language Learning, 50*, 417–528.

Rosa, E., & Leow, R. P. (2004). Awareness, different learning conditions, and second language development. *Applied Psycholinguistics, 25*, 269–92.

Russell, J., McWilliams, M., Chasen, L., & Farley, J. (2011). Using clickers for clinical reasoning and problem solving. *Nurse Educator, 36*, 13–15.

Salemi, M. K. (2009). Clickenomics: Using a classroom response system to increase student engagement in a large-enrollment principles of economics course. *The Journal of Economic Education, 40*, 385–404.

Schmidt, R. W., & Frota, S. (1986). Developing basic conversational ability in a second language: A case-study of an adult learner. In R. Day (Ed.), *Talking to Learn: Conversation in second language acquisition*. Rowley, MA: Newbury House.

Sevian, H., & Robinson, W. E. (2011). Clickers promote learning in all kinds of classes-small and large, graduate and undergraduate, Lecture and Lab. *Journal of College Science Teaching, 40*, 14–18.

Shaffer, D. M., & Collura, M. J. (2009). Evaluating the effectiveness of a personal response system in the classroom. *Teaching of Psychology, 36*, 273–277.

Stagg, A., & Lane, M. (2010). Using clickers to support information literacy skills development and instruction in first-year business students. *Journal of Information Technology Education, 9*, 197–215.

Stowell, J. R., Oldham, T., & Bennett, D. (2010). Using student response systems ("clickers") to combat conformity and shyness. *Teaching of Psychology, 37*, 135–140.

Tabak, K., & Cardoso, W. (2009). Make your material click: Tweak your class with clickers. Paper presented at the meeting of the *Society for the Promotion of the Teaching of English as a Second Language* in Quebec (SPEAQ) Conference, Montreal, QC.

VanPatten, B., Lee, J., & Ballman, T. (2010). *Vistazos: Un curso breve* (3rd edn.). New York, NY: McGraw-Hill.

Woelk, K. (2008). Optimizing the use of personal response devices (Clickers) in large-enrollment introductory courses. *Journal of Chemical Education, 85*, 1400–5.

Wolter, B. H. K., Lundeberg, M. A., Kang, H., & Herreid, C. F. (2011). Students' perceptions of using personal response systems ("Clickers") with cases in science. *Journal of College Science Teaching, 40*, 14–19.

Yoder-Kreger, S. (2009). Clickers: Can they be used to facilitate communicative language learning? Paper presented at the *Missouri Modern Languages and Modern Technologies (MO3) Conference*, University of Missouri-Columbia, USA.

Part III

Interactions in other educational settings

Chapter 12

International engineering graduate students' interactional patterns on a paired speaking test

Interlocutors' perspectives

Talia Isaacs
University of Bristol

This study examines interactional patterns between English language learners from different first language backgrounds on a collaborative speaking task from the Business English Certificates, a standardized test often used to screen prospective employees for their English language proficiency at international companies. Peer interactions of 84 international engineering graduate students, categorized using Galaczi's (2008) interactional typology, were examined in relation to individual interlocutors' target language use in daily life, oral proficiency level, and perceptions of their performance on the task. Results showed that collaborative pairs were the most positive overall about the quality of their interactions. Conversely, dominant members of unevenly matched (asymmetric) pairs rated their interactional success and their ability to understand and be understood by their partner most negatively.

Introduction

Canada welcomes hundreds of thousands of immigrants each year, approximately 80% of whom speak neither official language (English or French) as their mother tongue (Corbeil & Blaser 2007). For many, the need to acquire a new language compounds the challenge of integrating into society and securing employment. Although the government finances language training courses to assist newcomers in overcoming language barriers and transitioning into the labor market, intercultural communication can pose difficulties in workplace settings. For example, "culturally different" job candidates' aims to obtain employment may be derailed at the interview stage by linguistic and/or nonlinguistic factors (Laroche & Rutherford 2007). Even when newcomers are recruited into jobs commensurate with their professional training, oral communication challenges may be prevalent, and those related to intelligibility, broadly defined as second language (L2) learners' ability to understand and be understood by their interlocutors (e.g., colleagues, clients), appear to be among the most pressing (Derwing & Munro 2009). For instance, Canadian-born employees often find it difficult to communicate with their foreign-born colleagues and may avoid interacting with them, with oral language barriers serving as a major deterrent (Derwing & Munro 2008). In companies that emphasize teamwork and collaboration, communication difficulties could impede employee motivation and productivity.

Problems with intercultural communication are not unique to corporate settings and extend to other contexts, including educational settings. The academic domain is of particular importance in Canada due to the influx of "visa students" on Canadian campuses (Belkhodja 2011) and the need for accessible language support in cases when the medium of instruction is different than the student's first language (L1). Engaging in social interactions with members of the host culture has been identified as a major adjustment challenge for international students and may have negative repercussions on intercultural adaptation, academic attainment, and social cohesion, particularly in cases where there is little mixing with members of different cultural or linguistic communities (Spencer-Oatey & Xiong 2006; Zimmerman 1995). In addition to requiring oral communication skills to perform their academic tasks, some international graduate students bear research or instructional responsibilities and, therefore, may need to communicate effectively with undergraduate students in addition to their professors and peers. Pronunciation is often identified as a prominent problem by multiple stakeholders including, in the case of international teaching assistants (ITAs), for example, L2 teaching and testing professionals, undergraduate students, and ITAs themselves (Cheng, Myles, & Curtis 2004; Hoekje & Williams 1994). Although L2 accents tend to be accorded disproportionate attention due to their perceptual salience, even occasionally serving as a scapegoat to veil discriminatory attitudes (Derwing & Munro 2009), in some cases, genuine pronunciation problems impede listener understanding (Isaacs 2008).

The literature on language and communication challenges in workplace and academic settings is relevant to the present study, which examines the nature of the interactions that arise among paired international engineering graduate students from different linguistic and cultural backgrounds on a collaborative L2 speaking test task. This target population arguably needs spoken English to perform their academic responsibilities, including, in some cases, instructional duties, to achieve their stated aim of securing employment in North America post-graduation, and to perform domain-relevant tasks, including interacting with various stakeholders (e.g., coworkers, clients) in their eventual jobs (Human Resources and Skills Development Canada 2011). The study also explores the link between the students' reported L2 use and proficiency, the overall interactional pattern of their co-constructed discourse, and their perceptions of the quality of the communicative exchange and of the role of pronunciation in shaping their interactions. Before describing the language needs and background characteristics of this target population, the remainder of the literature review will overview research on the paired speaking test format (i.e., peer interactions among L2 test-takers), including both language testing and SLA research on interactional patterns and interlocutor proficiency effects on dyadic interactions. This research is relevant to the present study, which makes use of a collaborative speaking task on a standardized international L2 proficiency test – the Business English Certificates (BEC).

The paired speaking test format and insights from SLA interaction research

There is a growing trend in L2 assessment research to examine the paired speaking test format, as is evidenced by the publication of a recent special issue in *Language Testing* on peer interactions in L2 assessment settings (Taylor & Wigglesworth 2009). Ducasse and Brown (2009) chart a concomitant movement away from the traditional oral proficiency interview in operational assessment settings, which has been the most common and preferred method for assessing L2 speech since the communicative era (Luoma 2004), to an increased focus on peer performance on interactional tasks (see Winke, this volume). This has come about as a result of influence from SLA research in support of the Interaction Hypothesis (Long 1996), which holds that interaction is beneficial for L2 learning, with several meta-analyses demonstrating the facilitative effects of interaction (e.g., mediated by corrective or interactional feedback) on the acquisition of target language forms (Li 2010; Lyster & Saito 2010; Mackey & Goo 2007). The increasing prominence of peer oral proficiency testing has been buttressed by claims that pair and group work in language classrooms reflect good teaching practice, promote positive washback, and have the advantage of not containing the power imbalance between interviewer and interviewee that is inherent in the traditional oral proficiency interview (Fulcher 1996; Winke, this volume), thereby enabling students to perform their best on the assessment (Egyud & Glover 2001; Taylor 2001). Further, in comparison with semi-direct (i.e., machine-mediated) nonreciprocal tasks, which involve the test-taker speaking into a recording device without a human audience (e.g., the TOEFL iBT speaking component), face-to-face interactions may contribute to more authentic assessments (i.e., if they resemble the collaborative tasks that test-takers are likely to perform in the real-world context being generalized to) and tend to appeal more to test-takers (Qian 2009).

The paired speaking test format was first adopted in the Cambridge ESOL Main Suite Exams in 1996 in response to advancements in L2 research and classroom practice coupled with the need to draw on a broader range of tasks to elicit different dimensions of the L2 oral proficiency construct (Saville & Hargreaves 1999). Collaborative tasks remain a staple of these tests today, including the BEC, which is the source of the task in the present study. However, test-taker parings at testing sites tend to be ad hoc, with little attention paid to interlocutor variables that could affect the nature of the interaction and unduly optimize or penalize test-taker performance. That is, involving a conversational partner in L2 oral assessments introduces a range of peer interlocutor variables (e.g., age, gender, personality characteristics, attitudinal variables, L1 background, L2 proficiency level, exposure to the interlocutor's accent) that are extraneous to the construct being measured and that could pose a threat to the validity of the assessment (Van Moere 2006). To mitigate concerns about test fairness due to haphazard peer pairing practices in operational assessment settings, different interactional patterns are elicited in the Cambridge Main Suite Exams. In addition to the collaborative task, candidates also respond to short interview questions from the examiner and perform a brief monologue. The resulting range of tasks offers opportunities for the use of more varied language than would be possible if all oral proficiency tasks were monologic or in oral interview format (Saville & Hargreaves 1999).

One of the most extensively researched interlocutor variables in both the language testing and SLA literature is the effect of peer proficiency on L2 learner performance and interactional patterns (e.g., Davis 2009; Kim & McDonough 2008), since this research has direct implications for optimizing peer pairing practices in both high-stakes assessment and lower-stakes classroom contexts. In language assessment research, the major focus has been on interlocutor proficiency effects on test-takers' attainment, as attested by raters' holistic or analytic scoring of learners' paired performances on collaborative L2 speaking test tasks (Davis 2009; Norton 2005). Conversely, the orientation in the SLA interaction literature has been on learners' attention to language in collaborative discourse, as attested by the occurrence and resolution of language-related episodes when performing tasks designed to gauge learners' attention to form in L2 classroom settings (e.g., dictogloss; Kowal & Swain 1994). Overall, findings from the language assessment literature have been inconclusive with respect to rated outcomes, with some studies revealing that test-takers tend to be rated more highly when paired with a higher proficiency interlocutor (Iwashita 1996), while others reveal no interlocutor proficiency effects on rated measures (Csépes 2002). However, the quantity of the oral discourse the dyad generates (e.g., total words produced, number of speaker turns) appears to be sensitive to differences in test-taker L2 proficiency level across assessment studies, with test-takers producing relatively more output when paired with a higher-level peer than with a lower-level peer (Davis 2009). Similarly, findings from SLA research have revealed that language-related episodes tend to occur and to be resolved with greater frequency in parings with a relatively more advanced L2 interlocutor than with a lower proficiency partner (e.g., Kim & McDonough 2008; Leeser 2004).

Recent language assessment and SLA interaction studies have additionally examined interlocutor proficiency in conjunction with the pattern of interaction that emerges between learner dyads on a collaborative task. Storch's (2002) typology of co-constructed discourse, which distinguishes four patterns of interaction in learner dyads' communicative exchanges, has been used to classify interactional discourse in classroom talk in the SLA literature (e.g., Watanabe & Swain 2007). It has also served as the basis of Galaczi's (2004, 2008) slightly adapted framework for analyzing collaborative speaking test data which, in turn, has been used in language assessment studies on the paired speaking test format (e.g., May 2009). In both Storch's (2002) and Galaczi's (2008) frameworks, categorization decisions about the nature of the interactions are made on the basis of the notions of equality (the extent to which the interlocutors contribute proportionally to and assume ownership of the task) and mutuality (the extent to which the interlocutors are engaged with each other's contributions and actively co-construct meaning). Taken together, studies which have employed either framework have shown that interactions which are collaborative in nature (i.e., involve the interlocutors' active interchange of ideas and engagement) foster greater opportunities for noticing form-meaning relationships (Kim & McDonough 2008; Watanabe & Swain 2007), are overall rated highly in terms of individual speakers' proficiency scores (Davis 2009), and pose fewer dilemmas for raters' scoring decisions than dyads in which one interlocutor engages in interactional dominance (May 2009).

In the language assessment literature, interactional patterns classified using Galaczi's (2008) typology have been investigated with respect to raters' perceptions of the paired interaction and views on whether test-taker performances should be subject to individual or joint scoring (May 2009). However, the relationship between interactional patterns and *interlocutors'* (i.e., L2 test-takers') perceptions of the communicative efficiency of the interactions and attitudes toward engaging with their partner have yet to be examined. Further, in reference to the engineering graduate student participants in this study, because international students' interactions with members of the target language community have been linked to academic attainment and because oral communication difficulties can act as a deterrent to learners' engagement in L2 oral interactions and as a barrier to social integration (Cheng et al. 2004; Zimmerman 1995), there is an need to examine whether interactional patterns on a collaborative L2 speaking test task relate to learners' use of and exposure to the L2 in the host country. Therefore, the goal of this descriptive study is threefold: to examine (1) the nature of the interactions that occur between international graduate students on a paired collaborative L2 speaking test task, (2) whether the identified interactional pattern for the dyads relates to individual interlocutors' reported L2 use and proficiency level, and (3) individual interlocutors' perceptions of the quality of their interaction (e.g., in terms of communicative efficiency) in relation to the identified interactional pattern.

Method

Description of context and participants' language needs and interactional practice

This study took place in the oil-rich province of Alberta, Canada, which has suffered from an acute shortage of engineers over the past several decades. Although considerable government resources have been allocated to attracting and retaining foreign engineers, the oral communication challenges that they face are considerable. The "Essential Skills Inventory" (Human Resources and Skills Development Canada 2011), developed in reference to the Canadian Language Benchmarks, suggests that engineers require L2 oral proficiency skills of up to '4' out of '5' on a language complexity scale, including interacting with numerous stakeholders (e.g., co-workers, clients, suppliers) to carry out their professional tasks. Studies conducted in the Alberta context specifically have demonstrated the detrimental effects of foreign-born engineers' pragmatically inappropriate responses on job recruiters' hiring decisions (Louw, Derwing, & Abbott 2010) and Canadian-born engineers' reported difficulties communicating with their foreign-born colleagues and avoidance of conversational exchanges with them (Derwing & Munro 2008). In addition to jeopardizing workplace and company productivity, oral communication challenges can lead to cultural segregation and a lack of social cohesion.

Fuelled by the belief that holding a Canadian degree makes them more employable than their foreign credentials, many engineers seeking to build a career in Canada pursue postgraduate degrees at higher education institutions in hopes of securing a job in industry or academia. This is the case for the 84 international graduate student engineers who participated in this study (57 males, 27 females; M_{age} = 26.75; 23–36), enrolled in electrical (49), chemical (32), civil (2), and mechanical engineering programs (1) at a research-intensive Alberta university. The participants, who all reported having normal hearing, were from numerous L1 backgrounds, including Mandarin (23), Farsi (23), Urdu (9), Bengali (8), Hindi (6), Spanish (4), Sinhala (3), Punjabi (2), and one L1 speaker of each of Cantonese, French, Hindko, Konkani, Pashto, and Portuguese. They were all "visa students" who had moved to Canada on average 1.5 years earlier to pursue graduate studies (range: 1 month–5 years, 5 months) with the exception of one participant, who had moved to Canada as an undergraduate student seven years earlier and had subsequently obtained citizenship. At least 12 research participants had been admitted to the university without any oral proficiency testing due to having taken versions of the TOEFL that did not include a speaking component (i.e., the paper-and-pencil or computer-based TOEFL). There was no additional language screening for the 40 participants employed as ITAs, including 21 with full instructional responsibilities (e.g., formal lecturing or running labs and tutorials). In addition, none of the participants had taken an English for Academic Purposes course at the university, which some reported was inaccessible due to the expense.

Over 75% of all graduate students at the Faculty of Engineering were foreign nationals at the time of admission, with the largest groups from Mainland China and Iran. Thus, in cases of interactions between peers or professors who did not share the same (or a mutually intelligible) L1, English was used as the lingua franca. Participants estimated interacting in English 44% of the time in their daily lives (SD=24) and 64% of the time at university (SD=25), with participants from Mandarin and Farsi L1 groups, the two largest L1 groups in the dataset and at the faculty, below average in their interactional engagement in English at university (61% and 51% of the time, respectively). Although the large standard deviations (25 for each) evidence considerable variability, with some participants pursuing opportunities to engage in L2 interactions more actively than others, patterns emerged in semi-structured interviews conducted at the end of the data collection session (see description of procedure below). As one L1 Mandarin speaker related,

"My supervisor is Chinese and he recruited student all from Chinese. All from China. So we, our laboratory, are all Chinese. Yeah, whole laboratory. So sometimes we do not have much chance to speak English because we all speak Mandarin." Like several of his peers, he revealed that his Chinese supervisor was the only one he ever conversed with in English due to her belief that English was professionally important. Similarly, several Iranian participants reported having no opportunities to speak English since moving to Canada. One Iranian student, for example, reported speaking English less in Canada than during the few hours a week she had worked as an IELTS trainer in Iran, due to peer pressure among Iranian students in the faculty to conform by speaking their L1 (although a few Farsi speakers resisted this). She related, "everyone [Iranian students] know that they had the better English, before they come here." Still other participants reported that their interview with the researcher was the first time they had ever conversed with a Canadian-born individual besides routine encounters. On the basis of participants' descriptions, a picture of a linguistically and culturally-segregated graduate student body emerges, particularly for students in predetermined cliques who come to the university specifically to work with a supervisor from their country and who are designated for work in a linguistically homogeneous lab from the outset. Challenges in cross-cultural communication emerged in anecdotes. For example, an L1 Bengali speaker described his experience attempting to get help solving an engineering problem from a classmate:

> After the class, I passed one of my classmate. He was from China. Firstly he told me can you please write it down, what you are asking. After the class, I asked him, can you please explain me how it [the problem] worked? He told me to write down in a paper what my question is. After writing the question, he told me ok, I know how it works, but I cannot explain it to you in English.

Clearly, the written medium was being used to compensate for poor oral/aural English skills or for reticence to communicatively engage with his peer. In a second anecdote, the participant described larger-scale compensatory strategies for understanding a professor:

> One instructor was a native Canadian. So, his English was very fluent and it was a little different. It was very fast and his accent was a little different than what we normally hear. So I could not follow some part of his lecture. So we had some uh Chinese classmate and they could not follow what he taught because he was speaking so fast. The next day of our class he [the teacher] found all the Chinese students, they brought the Chinese version of the textbook.

Apparently, none of the students in the class had asked the instructor to slow down or repeat. It is possible that the instructor was unaware of his students' comprehension difficulties (mostly international students who had recently arrived in Canada) and made little effort to adapt his speech. Regardless, these accounts reveal cross-cultural communication challenges at the faculty due to language barriers.

Instruments and data collection procedure

Because the majority of graduate students at the Faculty of Engineering are L2 English speakers and there is evidence of linguistic segregation, the intention here was to examine the interactions of dyads from different L1 backgrounds. To create pairings that were as linguistically and culturally different as possible, speakers from Indic languages (e.g., Urdu, Bengali, Hindi) and Romance languages (e.g., Spanish, Portuguese, French) were not paired with a peer from within the same L1 group. After completing a language background questionnaire, paired participants completed a series of L2 speaking tasks. Performance on the BEC collaborative task will be the focus of this manuscript. Cambridge ESOL's BEC is a standardized test used by major international engineering companies (e.g., Ericsson, Shell, Vodafone) to screen prospective employees for English language proficiency or for staff development (http://www.cambridgeesol.org). The sample collaborative speaking task for the "Vantage Level" test, aligned with level B2 of the Common European Framework of Reference, was used to elicit the peer dialogue. The two interlocutors were each provided with the written scenario of needing to make preparations for a business trip in a foreign country, with discussion points on making travel and accommodation arrangements and learning about foreign business customs. In accordance with exam procedures, participants were instructed to discuss and decide about these points together (University of Cambridge ESOL Examinations, 2008).

Speech samples were recorded in a quiet room using a multi-track digital recorder, with unidirectional lavalier microphones provided for each interlocutor. To simulate the BEC test procedure, which includes the presence of two examiners, the researcher and a research assistant (RA) were both present during data collection and undertook different roles. The researcher introduced the speaking tasks, operated the recording equipment, interjected if necessary to keep participants on track (e.g., to redress the communication balance if one participant was dominant, in accordance with guidelines described in the BEC handbook), and monitored time. The researcher was not a trained Cambridge rater but had served as examiner for speaking assessments for university entrance purposes and used the Cambridge ESOL standard oral scripts. The RA fulfilled the role of silent observer, recording details on body language and other features that emerged during the interaction in a research log. Although in an operational testing situation, the BEC examiner is instructed to stop the test-taker pair after the approximate 2 minute duration of the task if it does not come to a natural close, for the purposes of data collection in the present study, the time for task completion was not constrained beyond the 2 minute minimum and, thus, was longer and more variable ($M = 4$ min 42 s; $SD = 2$ min 5 s). After completing the speaking tasks, both participants filled out separate follow-up questionnaires items on the success of their interactions, how well they had understood and been understood by their partner, the role of pronunciation in their communicative exchange, and their willingness to engage with their partner on future professional projects on separate 5-point Likert-type scales. Finally, the researcher and RA interviewed the interlocutors in separate rooms about their impressions of the interaction with their partner, their oral communication needs and interactional engagement at the university, in their envisioned future job, and in life more generally. Participants were remunerated for approximately 1.5 hours of their time.

Data analysis

After normalizing interlocutors' speech samples on separate audio tracks, the L2 speech data were transcribed using conversational analysis conventions adapted from Atkinson and Heritage (1984; see Appendix). Next, three categories from Galaczi's (2004, 2008) typology of interactional patterns, derived from an analysis of the topical moves on the collaborative speaking task from another Cambridge test (the First Certificate in English), were used to classify the overall interactional orientation of the paired graduate student engineers' co-constructed discourse on the BEC. Galaczi's first category, the "collaborative" interaction type, which is equivalent to the "collaborative" pattern in Storch's (2002) framework for classroom work, is characterized by both interlocutors contributing creatively to the task and evidence of mutual engagement through peer topic extension and, occasionally, the completion of each other's thoughts. An example of collaborative discourse is shown in Hassan (L1 Iranian male) and Sanjay's (L1 Hindi male) 35 second conversational exchange in (1). Pseudonyms are used for all participants in this paper.

(1) H: where we stay should be close to (.) I'd rather- (.) it be li- (.) close to the, to the
         (.) to the m- to the meeting to the business mee[ting-],
     S: [yeah] we sh- we should look for [that]
     H: [bus]iness place=
     S: =yeah we should be close to the place and yeah. Traveling,
     H: that's easy. that's (.) google map.=
     S: =e- yeah that's google maps.
     H: yeah.
     S: and we have smart phones most of the people. [so]
     H: [yeah]
     S: company has given us that. ((laughter))=
     H: =yeah. we shou- we should buy a [company, um],
     S: [yeah we should] companie[s:]
     H: [we] should ask the company to buy us uh (.) new google ph[ones],
     S: [new] google pha. [yeah].
     H: [is it] android?=
     S: =an[droid].
     H: [or] droid? what is [it?]
     S: [android]. yeah.

Notably, both interlocutors propose novel content (Hassan: location of meeting; use of Google maps; Sanjay: company provision of smart phones for employees) and play off of each other's ideas. Their speech is characterized by frequent acknowledgment tokens to signal agreement (particularly in Sanjay's case) and numerous instances of overlapping or latched speech, resulting in little (if any) time between turns.

Galaczi's (2004) second category of interactional behavior, "parallel," is characterized by both interlocutors initiating novel ideas but not following up on each other's turns. This interactional pattern is construed somewhat differently from the "dominant/dominant" category in Storch's (2002) framework. In Galaczi's (2004) conception of the parallel interaction type and its application in the present study, the key notion is not conversational dominance or the inability of the pair to achieve consensus, as is emphasized in Storch's (2002) framework, but, rather, that there is little evidence of mutual engagement (Galaczi 2004), with few instances of supportive topic development or of the partners' ideas intertwining. For example, in Ayaz (L1 Urdu male) and Alda's (L1 Spanish female) 42 second conversational exchange in (2), both parties independently contribute ideas but do not build on their partner's contributions and do not appear to be responsive to the content of the partner's utterances.

> (2)   Ay: so we need to know how- many persons for how many person we are (.) booking, in a h- in a hotel? or any other place? (.6) so: uh tickets and: accommodations, and (.) uh, what else? should we: (.) you know take (.6) to that trip (.) with us (1.7)
>
>   Al: um: if they have some: um: special necessities? like um (.7) i:f some of them cannot eat certain type of food, if they are (.) some like- one of them could be in wheelchairs, and that kind of (1.0) [um: (.) different]
>
>   Ay: [ok th- important] documents? (1.2) and um (…) the documents we will be (1.0) needing in (.7) for meeting?

Ayaz's invitation to Alda to suggest items to bring on the trip is followed by Alda's input on the seemingly unrelated topic of accommodating special needs. Instead of continuing in her line of thought, Ayaz declines to expand her topic and, instead, advances his own idea about needing important documents. Although, in this pairing, there does not appear to be competition for holding the floor, each partner's focus is clearly on getting his/her own points across. Notably, both participants' contributions are marked by dysfluencies at awkward junctures (i.e., within clauses).

Galaczi's third interactional category, "asymmetric," which subsumes Storch's (2002) "expert/novice" and "dominant/passive" interactional patterns, is characterized by one interlocutor clearly dominating the conversation in terms of the amount of discourse produced and the contribution of content, and the other partner assuming a relatively passive role. These unequal contributions may be manifested in the dominant partner's reticence to cede the floor, in the passive partner's lack of initiative in assuming the floor and/or proposing new ideas, or in the dominant partner's collegial scaffolding of the passive partner to facilitate his/her participation in the interaction. Due to the imbalance inherent in this category, the individual interlocutors who made up the asymmetric parings in this study were further classified as "dominant speaker" and "passive speaker." A 29 second asymmetric conversational exchange between Faisal (L1 Urdu male), who assumed a dominant role in the interaction, and Walton (L1 Mandarin male), who assumed a passive role is shown in (3).

(3) F: so I will say that uh I have a Canadian boss and I am going with him to Pakistan and he's taking me to Pakistan because I am a Pakistani? [and] I know (.) about th-=

W: [yeah] = kay

F: their culture a:nd how things go over there?

W: okay.

F: so: (.) the first uh (.) thing we have to discuss like what travel and accommodation arrangements we have to make before the trip so:=

W: =uh huh=

F:. =the first and the most important thing is the ticket (.) [arrange]ment because=

W: [uh huh] =yup=

F: =usually [uh] there are some peak seasons?

W: [yeah] okay

F: in June and in November?

Faisal made it difficult for Walton to interject, with hardly any pauses between his turns, despite occasionally ending tone groups with rising intonation. He also unilaterally decided on a foreign country in which the BEC scenario would take place and chose a cultural context for which Walton presumably had no cultural reference. This arguably strengthened his position of power in the interaction as the purveyor of knowledge. Walton's contribution was relegated to backchannelling and he was unable to assert control over the task.

Galaczi (2004) refers to a final "blended" interaction type, which is a hybrid of two categories, presented in alteration within the same pairing. This category was not used in the present study because it was possible to categorize the overall interactional orientation of the dyadic discourse using one of the three main interactional patterns described above. In rare instances when the interactional orientation appeared to shift midway through the task and the predominant orientation was unclear, the interactional pattern that was most representative of the first minute of the conversation was selected.

Following initial classification of the data, an intercoder reliability check by a second RA yielded exact agreement on 88% of the category assignments for 60% of the data. In instances of disputes, a third coder (the author) independently recoded the data and made the final classification decision. Next, descriptive statistics were calculated for participant self-report data, grouped by interactional category, on their English language ability, use, and the quality of their interactions.

Results

Table 1 shows the number of pairs classified into the three interaction types based on their co-constructed discourse, with interlocutors in the asymmetric group further designated as dominant or passive. This breakdown is similar to Galaczi's (2008) study, where the number of collaborative versus parallel pairings was equal, with relatively fewer asymmetric pairings. Indicative patterns suggest a link between interaction type and participants' pre-task questionnaire responses on their language proficiency and use. First, the findings support the claim that asymmetric interactional patterns generally arise in pairings with uneven L2 proficiency profiles (May 2009). The dominant speakers in this study reported considerably higher English language proficiency, speaking and listening to English a higher proportion of the time, and engaging more with native English speakers than did their passive partners. Notably, these disparities in target language use did not extend to their interactions with L2 speakers from other L1 backgrounds. There is likely a linguistic and cultural component to this finding that needs to be unpacked. For example, although Mandarin speakers accounted for 27% of participants in this study, they were represented in 58% of the cases of individuals classified as passive within the asymmetric group. Similarly, speakers of Indic languages accounted for 27% of participants in this study but were overrepresented in the asymmetric dominant group at 83%. In one such asymmetric pairing, a dominant male L1 Hindko speaker produced 417 words 2.5 minutes into the task compared to his passive female L1 Mandarin speaking partner's 34 words. When the researcher intervened to ask the passive speaker about business customs in an attempt to redress the conversation, the passive speaker reflected on cultural differences in conversational norms, stating, "I think here [in Canada], people can speak in the meeting but in China, only the head while he's speaking no one can speak, so you have to respect the leader." Thus, interlocutors' views of the pragmatic acceptability of interrupting a partner's turns through overlapping speech and their pre-interactional perceptions of their partner as equal or unequal in status (i.e., through first impressions) are potential influences on turn-taking behavior that warrant further investigation.

Taken together, the highest reported English language proficiency and use for dominant speakers followed by collaborative, parallel, then passive speakers suggests that interactional type categorizations could efficiently predict individual speakers' L2 use and proficiency. However, May (2009) found that speakers classified as dominant based on their interaction with a lower proficiency learner may be categorized as collaborative when paired with an interlocutor of similar or higher L2 proficiency (see also Kim & McDonough 2008). Thus, the interactional pattern clearly depends on the *pairing* and not simply on the individual speaker.

Table 2, which presents descriptive statistics of the interlocutors' perceptions of the interaction obtained in a follow-up questionnaire after all L2 speaking tasks had been completed, also shows clear patterns. Participants whose discourse was collaborative had the most positive overall feeling about the quality of the interaction, reported the fewest

Table 1. Interlocutors' reported English language use and proficiency by interaction type

Interaction type	No. of pairs ($n = 42$) & proportion	Mean participant self-report data (*SD*) obtained prior to administering the L2 speech tasks				
		English speaking & listening proficiency[a]	English spoken in daily life[b]	English spoken at university[b]	Time speaking to native speakers[b]	Time speaking to L2 learners from other L1 backgrounds[b]
Collaborative	15 = 36%	3.8 (.6)	45.7 (27)	69.5 (25)	44.7 (23)	32.0 (22)
Parallel	16 = 38%	3.7 (.7)	34.3 (19)	56.5 (26)	44.3 (28)	33.0 (25)
Asymmetric	11 = 26%	3.9 (.6)	52.3 (22)	67.2 (23)	52.5 (26)	34.2 (22)
Dominant		4.3 (.5)	60.4 (24)	82.1 (14)	62.5 (23)	34.2 (26)
Passive		3.5 (.3)	44.2 (19)	52.5 (22)	34.2 (19)	34.2 (19)

Note: [a]Measured on a 5-point scale (*1 = extremely poor, 5 = extremely proficient*).
        [b]Measured on a 0–100% scale.

Table 2. Interlocutors' perceptions of their interaction and partner by interaction type

Interactional type (*n* pairs)	Mean participant self-report data (*SD*) obtained immediately after the L2 speech tasks had been completed				
	Overall success of the interaction	How well understand partner	How well understood by partner	Pronunciation an issue in the interaction	How well would collaborate with partner on a professional task
Collaborative (15)	4.3 (.6)	4.5 (.7)	4.1 (.5)	2.6 (1.3)	4.2 (.7)
Parallel (16)	4.1 (.7)	4.2 (.9)	3.9 (.8)	2.9 (1.2)	3.8 (.7)
Asymmetric (11)	3.8 (.8)	3.8 (1.0)	3.9 (.8)	3.0 (1.1)	3.8 (.6)
Dominant	3.5 (1.0)	3.4 (1.1)	3.8 (.6)	2.8 (1.4)	3.7 (.5)
Passive	4.1 (.5)	4.1 (.8)	4.1 (.9)	3.3 (.9)	3.9 (.7)

Note: [a]Measured on a 5-point scale (*1 = negative response/ no, 5 = positive response/ yes*).

gaps in understanding, felt that pronunciation detracted the least from their communicative exchanges, and were the most receptive to working with their partner on future professional projects. The parallel group scored less well on these metrics, albeit better than the asymmetric group, who was the least satisfied with their interactional experience.

Breaking down the asymmetric group further, the passive speakers were overall more positive than the dominant speakers about the success of the interaction. They also perceived higher mutual understanding and were more open to future collaborations with their partner, recording approximately the same levels of satisfaction as the parallel group. The dominant speakers appear to have been more frustrated with the interaction. However, the passive speakers identified pronunciation as being more problematic than did the dominant speakers, although the high standard deviation for the dominant speakers reveals considerable variability on this point. It could be that the passive speakers were overall more self-conscious about their pronunciation due to everyday communication difficulties that they experienced, even though they felt supported by their partner in the research setting and were possibly unaware of their partner's more negative perceptions.

Engaging in a collaborative interactional pattern thus appears to be the most positive for L2 learners and could lead to positive rapport-building and establishing solidarity that is important in human relationships (e.g., for job hiring decisions; Kerekes 2006). Parallel interaction, where there is little uptake on partners' turns, appears to be more preferable, from the interlocutor's perspective, to being paired with someone who struggles to contribute to the conversation and who plays a subordinate role in defining the creative direction of the task. In high-stakes assessments (e.g., operational administrations of the BEC), test-taker pairing practices could affect the quality of the co-constructed discourse and could, in turn, impact raters' scoring decisions. This issue is discussed further in the Discussion section.

Discussion

The goal of this descriptive study was, first, to examine the nature of the interactions that arise between international engineering graduate student dyads from different L1 backgrounds on the BEC collaborative speaking test task. Analysis of the co-constructed discourse generated by each of the pairs revealed that parallel and collaborative interaction types were the most prevalent in the dataset and occurred in approximately equal proportion (together, 3/4 of the time), whereas the asymmetric pattern, which occurred in the remainder of the cases, was less common. This closely corresponds with the proportion of interaction types observed in Galaczi (2008), although, in the present study, it was possible to reliably classify the overall interactional orientation of the dyadic discourse without resorting to a "blended" category (i.e., consisting of two distinct interaction types).

The second goal of the study was to examine individual interlocutors' estimates of their L2 speaking ability and the proportion of their time spent engaging in target language interactions in relation to the interaction type to which they had been assigned. Mean L2 speaking proficiency and language use measures, pooled over interaction type, were the highest for dominant speakers followed by collaborative and parallel speakers, with dominant speakers' passive partners reporting the lowest overall means. This finding supports evidence from the language assessment literature that asymmetric interactions tend to occur when there is a mismatch in paired test-takers' L2 proficiency level (May 2009) and echoes indications from SLA classroom interaction research that learner pairs with largely discrepant L2 proficiency levels are less likely to be collaboratively oriented in their discourse productions than when they are more evenly matched (Kowal & Swain 1994). Cultural issues that mediate interactional orientations and turn-taking strategies arose in some participants' qualitative accounts in the present study. These need to be systematically investigated in future research, particularly in relation to other interlocutor variables such as gender and interlocutors' perceptions of gender roles.

The final goal of the study was to examine individual interlocutors' perceptions of their joint performance (e.g., communicative efficiency) in relation to interactional type. Results revealed that interlocutors in the collaborative group were the most satisfied of all groups with the quality of their interaction, experienced the fewest pronunciation and communication problems, and were most receptive to the idea of participating in future professional collaborations with their partner. This suggests that collaborative interactions, which, in previous studies, were found to yield the highest ratings in the paired speaking test format (Davis 2009) and to be the most facilitative for creating opportunities for learning in classroom settings (Kim & McDonough 2008), also tend to be perceived the most positively by L2 interlocutors themselves. Further, the finding implies that being in a collaborative interactional situation with a peer is not only optimal in assessment and classroom settings from the perspective of external parties observing or evaluating the interactions (e.g., raters scoring their performance or researchers examining language-related episodes), but is also conducive to performance from the perspective of the L2 interlocutors who are directly involved in the interaction.

In comparison with the collaborative dyads, interlocutors classified in the parallel and asymmetric-passive groups were relatively less positive about the interactional outcome and their partner, likely due to poorer peer engagement (e.g., as signaled through a lack of topic extension). However, the asymmetric-dominant group appeared to experience the most frustration with the interaction, scoring the interactional indices and their ability to understand and be understood by their partner most negatively, although they ascribed a less important role to pronunciation in contributing to the difficulties than did their passive partners. The passive speakers may have been more concerned about their own pronunciation due to oral communication difficulties that they routinely experience and, therefore, to have weighted this factor more heavily than the speakers in the other interactional groups, although this is merely speculative. In sum, being a dominant speaker within an asymmetric paring appears to be the worst case scenario from the perspective of an interlocutor performing a collaborative L2 speaking test task. This aligns with May's (2009) contention that raters have the most difficulty arriving at scoring decisions for asymmetric pairings due to the imbalance inherent in the interaction. The issue of whether co-constructed learner performance on an interactional task should be singly or jointly scored, which has been the subject of considerable attention in the language assessment literature (Taylor & Wigglesworth 2009), was not examined here, since ratings based on the dyadic BEC performances were not obtained. Future research could elicit the ratings and perceptions of interviewers employed at an engineering company with a culturally diverse workforce, for example.

Notably, no objective measure of L2 proficiency was obtained in the present study. Reliance on participant self-report ratings of their L2 oral proficiency, exposure to the target language, and performance on the task, as was done here, has obvious limitations which need to be acknowledged. A further limitation is that, due to the use of descriptive rather than inferential statistics in the present study to examine interlocutors' reported L2 proficiency level, interactional encounters, and perceptions of their interaction, no group differences as a function of interaction type can be ascertained. These issues notwithstanding, the interlocutors' self-report indices yielded clear patterns when grouped by interaction type, to the extent that it was possible to rank order interactional groups on all indicators in a way that was consistent with what has been reported previously in the literature (e.g., that collaborative interactions are viewed most favorably from learning and assessment standpoints; Davis 2009; Storch 2002). Further, the value of test-taker self-assessments of their performance has been emphasized in the language assessment literature as an important part of learner awareness-raising (see Alderson 2005; Winke, this volume). Therefore, the relationship between interlocutors' perceptions of their contribution to the joint performance on the paired-speaking test format, including whether they viewed themselves or their partner to be interactionally dominant, the scores that they obtain, and the feedback that they receive about their performance in score reporting forms needs to be examined in future research.

Although Swain suggests that peer speaking tests may be a way of "biasing for best" (2001:298) in language assessments, asymmetric pairings appear to pose difficulties for key stakeholders in the assessment process, including the dominant speakers in this study, and raters, as shown in previous L2 assessment research (May 2009). Evidently, peer pairing could have the potential to alter the nature of the interaction (Kim & McDonough 2008) and to penalize scoring (Iwashita 1996). Although engineering test-taker pairings in operational assessment situations may be logistically difficult to implement, the relationship between interactional type, L2 proficiency, target language interactions, and interlocutors' (test-takers') perceptions of their performance needs to be more extensively researched in the interest of test fairness and in order to allay test-takers' concerns. To do this, multiple sources of evidence need to be examined in research settings in order to investigate the extent to which interlocutors' discourse productions, self-ratings of their joint performance, and interview comments about their interaction align. Although the present study represents a preliminary attempt to examine test-takers' perspectives and features a relatively large sample size (42 pairs), one of the limitations is that interlocutors' qualitative interview data and the analysis of their collaborative discourse were not directly mapped onto their quantitative self-report data. These data sources need to be more rigorously triangulated.

The population of engineering professionals in this study, including 1/4 who reportedly bore full instructional responsibilities as ITAs, were motivated to perform well academically and to integrate into the Canadian labor market post-graduation. Clearly, this population require L2 oral communication skills to successfully integrate into academic or workplace culture and to carry out their professional responsibilities. The use of the BEC in this study is ecologically valid inasmuch as it is used for screening or professional development purposes at major international engineering companies. However, the content of the task (organizing a business trip for a company) arguably does not simulate the domain-specific tasks that the international engineers in this study are likely to encounter in academic or workplace settings. Achieving greater authenticity in task design would likely entail enlisting the help of a domain expert (engineer) in the design of a joint problem-solving task, for example (Douglas 2000), although the implementation of such a task in the present study would have been challenging due to parings between engineers from different fields (e.g., electrical and chemical engineering). Therefore, the generalizability of the performances on the collaborative BEC speaking task used in this study to oral communication tasks that engineers are expected to perform in real-world contexts (Human Resources and Skills Development Canada 2011) is arguably limited.

One of the major challenges that international students on foreign campuses face is engaging in interactions with members of the host community (Cheng et al. 2004; Spencer-Oatey & Xiong 2006). Due to the high concentration of L2 graduate students and staff at the Faculty of Engineering from which the participants in this study were recruited, opportunities to interact in English in the academic domain are more likely to occur with other international engineers than with Canadian-born individuals. Thus, being paired with an international graduate student peer in this study reflects the grouping that might take place in the university setting if learners move beyond being entrenched in L1 cliques to engaging more broadly with L2 speakers from different linguistic and cultural backgrounds.

References

Alderson, J. C. (2005). *Diagnosing foreign language proficiency: The interface between learning and assessment*. London: Continuum.

Atkinson, J. M., & Heritage, J. (Eds.). (1984). *Structures of social action*. Cambridge: Cambridge University Press.

Belkhodja, C. (Ed.). (2011). International migration: The emergence of the mobile student. *Canadian Diversity, 8*.

Cheng, L., Myles, J., & Curtis, A. (2004). Targeting language support for non-native English-speaking graduate students at a Canadian university. *TESL Canada Journal, 21*, 50–71.

Corbeil, J. P., & Blaser, C. (2007). *The evolving linguistic portrait, 2006 census*. Ottawa, ON: Statistics Canada.

Csépes, I. (2002). Is testing speaking in pairs disadvantageous for students? A quantitative study of partner effects on oral test scores. *novELTy, 9*, 22–45.

Davis, L. (2009). The influence of interlocutor proficiency in a paired oral assessment. *Language Testing, 26*, 367–396.

Derwing, T. M., & Munro, M. J. (2008, June). *Engineering better communication in the workplace*. Paper presented at the Canadian Association of Applied Linguistics conference, Vancouver, BC.

Derwing, T. M., & Munro, M. J. (2009). Putting accent in its place: Rethinking obstacles to communication. *Language Teaching, 42*, 1–15.

Douglas, D. (2000). *Assessing languages for specific purposes*. Cambridge: Cambridge University Press.

Ducasse, A., & Brown, A. (2009). Assessing paired orals: Raters' orientation to interaction. *Language Testing, 26*, 423–443.

Egyud, G., & Glover, P. (2001). Oral testing in pairs: A secondary school perspective. *ELT Journal, 55*, 70–76.

Fulcher, G. (1996). Testing tasks: Issues in task design and the group oral. *Language Testing, 13*, 23–51.

Galaczi, E. D. (2004). *Peer-peer interaction in a paired speaking test: The case of the First Certificate in English.* Unpublished PhD dissertation, Columbia University, New York.

Galaczi, E. D. (2008). Peer-peer interaction in a speaking test: The case of the First Certificate in English examination. *Language Assessment Quarterly, 5*, 89–119.

Hoekje, B., & Williams, J. (1994). Communicative competence as a theoretical framework for ITA education. In C. G. Madden & C. L. Myers (Eds.), *Discourse and performance of international teaching assistants* (pp. 11–26). Alexandria, VA: TESOL.

Human Resources and Skills Development Canada. (2011). *Essential skills*. Retrieved July 6, 2011, from http://www10.hrsdc.gc.ca/es/english/all_profiles.aspx

Isaacs, T. (2008). Towards defining a valid assessment criterion of pronunciation proficiency in non-native English speaking graduate students. *Canadian Modern Language Review, 64*, 555–580.

Iwashita, N. (1996). The validity of the paired interview format in oral performance testing. *Melbourne Papers in Language Testing, 5*, 51–65.

Kerekes, J. A. (2006). Winning an interviewer's trust in a gatekeeping encounter. *Language in Society, 35*, 27–57.

Kim, Y., & McDonough, K. (2008). The effect of interlocutor proficiency on the collaborative dialogue between Korean as a second language learners. *Language Teaching Research, 12*, 211–234.

Kowal, M., & Swain, M. (1994). Using collaborative language production tasks to promote students' language awareness. *Language Awareness, 3*, 73–93.

Laroche, L., & Rutherford, D. (2007). *Recruiting, retaining, and promoting culturally different employees.* Oxford: Oxford University Press.

Leeser, M. J. (2004). Learner proficiency and focus on form during collaborative dialogue. *Language Teaching Research, 8*, 55–81.

Li, S. (2010). The effectiveness of corrective feedback in SLA: A meta-analysis. *Language Learning, 60*, 309–365.

Long, M. H. (1996). The role of the linguistic environment in second language acquisition. In W. C. Ritchie & T. K. Bhatia (Eds.), *Handbook of language acquisition.* San Diego, CA: Academic Press.

Louw, K. J., Derwing, T. M., & Abbott, M. L. (2010). Teaching pragmatics to L2 learners for the workplace: The job interview. *Canadian Modern Language Review, 66*, 739–758.

Luoma, S. (2004). *Assessing speaking.* Cambridge: Cambridge University Press.

Lyster, R., & Saito, K. (2010). Oral feedback in classroom SLA. *Studies in Second Language Acquisition, 32*, 265–302.

Mackey, A., & Goo, J. (2007). Interaction research in SLA: A meta-analysis and research synthesis. In A. Mackey (Ed.), *Conversational interaction in second language acquisition: A collection of empirical studies* (pp. 407–451). Oxford: Oxford University Press.

May, L. (2009). Co-constructed interaction in a paired speaking test: The rater's perspective. *Language Testing, 26*, 397–421.

Norton, J. (2005). The paired format in the Cambridge Speaking Tests. *ELT Journal, 59*, 287–297.

Qian, D. D. (2009). Comparing direct and semi-direct modes for speaking assessment: Affective effects on test takers. *Language Assessment Quarterly, 6*, 113–125.

Saville, N., & Hargreaves, P. (1999). Assessing speaking in the revised FCE. *ELT Journal, 53*, 42–51.

Spencer-Oatey, H., & Xiong, Z. (2006). Chinese students' psychological and sociocultural adjustments to Britain: An empirical study. *Language, Culture and Curriculum, 19*, 37–53.

Storch, N. (2002). Patterns of interaction in ESL pair work. *Language Learning, 52,* 119–158.

Swain, M. (2001). Examining dialogue: Another approach to content specification and to validating inferences drawn from test scores. *Language Testing, 18,* 275–302.

Taylor, L. (2001). The paired speaking test format: Recent studies. *University of Cambridge Local Examinations Syndicate Research Notes, 6,* 15–17.

Taylor, L., & Wigglesworth, G. (Eds.). (2009). Pair work in L2 assessment context [Special issue]. *Language Testing, 26.*

University of Cambridge ESOL Examinations. (2008). *Business English Certificates: Handbook for teachers.* Cambridge: UCLES.

Van Moere, A. (2006). Validity evidence in a university group oral test. *Language Testing, 23,* 411–440.

Watanabe, Y., & Swain, M. (2007). Effects of proficiency differences and patterns of pair interaction on second language learning: collaborative dialogue between adult ESL learners. *Language Teaching Research, 11,* 121–142.

Zimmerman, S. (1995). Perceptions of intercultural communication competence and international student adaptation to an American campus. *Communication Education, 44,* 321–335.

Appendix

Transcription conventions

[ ]	overlapping utterance
=	latched utterance, no intervening time between turns
?	rising intonation
.	falling intonation
,	level intonation
-	abruptly ended sound
(.)	brief silent pause < .5 seconds
(.5)	length of pause if ≥ .5 seconds
:	lengthening of sound
(( ))	nonlinguistic occurrence (e.g., laughter)
(?)	inaudible/incomprehensible utterance

Adapted from Atkinson & Heritage (1984)

Chapter 13

The effectiveness of interactive group orals for placement testing

Paula Winke
Michigan State University

In task-based language classes, teachers increasingly use interactive, peer-to-peer group orals to measure learners' communicative competence. This chapter examines the reliability and validity of placing learners into task-based ESL listening and speaking classes based on their performances during task-based, peer-to-peer, group oral interactions. ESL learners ($n = 128$) took a 30-item, listening and speaking self-assessment exam. The self-assessment scores were used to create groups of three to five learners who carried out two group-oral tasks. The listening test and group-oral test scores were used in a k-cluster analysis to place learners into seven classes. I conclude by suggesting how practitioners can employ interactive, group orals as part of placement testing and how they positively contribute to interactive and task-based learning.

Introduction

Researchers and teachers have long investigated the procedures, processes, and outcomes of oral assessment (e.g., A. Brown 2003; Chalhoub-Deville 1995; Douglas 1994; Douglas & Selinker 1992; Fulcher 2003; Iwashita, McNamara, & Elder 2001; Jenkins & Parra 2003; Upshur & Turner 1999). Many of these investigations have centered on one popular method for assessing oral proficiency – the face-to-face, Oral Proficiency Interview (OPI), made popular in the 1950s by the American Council on the teaching of Foreign Languages (ACTFL, http://www.actfl.org), the Interagency Language Roundtable (ILR, http://www.govtilr.org) and Educational Testing Service (http://www.ets.org), and which has been adapted to telephonic, tape-mediated, and computerized versions by researchers and testing programs worldwide (ACTFL 2004; Mikhailova 2007). (For comprehensive overviews of the OPI, see Johnson 2001; Malone 2003) The hallmark of any OPI is the non-participation of the test administrator in developing the test taker's speech. Rather, the test administrator is non-participatory and *interviews* the test taker – asking him or her to respond to questions and perform one-way role plays.

OPIs are frequently employed in foreign and second language (L2) classrooms by teachers who want to formally assess students' oral language gains (Harlow & Caminero

1990). OPIs are also commonly used for placement testing or selection criteria; for example, scores are often used to determine who is eligible for study abroad (Kenyon & Malabonga 2001). Nonetheless, the OPI has been criticized as producing speech that underrepresents the construct of speaking (Kasper & Ross 2007) and discourse that is problematically asymmetrical (Swain 2001; van Lier 1989), pseudosocial (van Lier 1989), and non-authentic (Johnson & Tyler 1998). The basis of the criticism is that the test taker just answers questions or performs one-way tasks. OPIs lack authentic two-way communication and opportunities for language learners to utilize strategies that help them negotiate for meaning and ultimately express themselves effectively. Such strategies, consequentially, may help the test takers sustain conversation at higher discourse levels. In other words, in an OPI context, test takers do not receive real feedback. With feedback (verbal and/or visual) speakers may come to understand that their messages was not understood, which may trigger speech modification and better message conveyance, hallmarks of true discourse. Additionally problematical, in an OPI the test administrator has a higher social status – that is, he or she, as the test taker's teacher (or as a member of the testing program) mandates the exam, regulates topics during the test, and determines the test score. This uneven power relationship may modulate test-taker performance and is not representative of most conversation varieties (Lazaraton 2002; Ross & Berwick 1992), especially those undertaken by students in task-based, L2 classrooms.

Recently, researchers and teachers have begun to look anew at the potential of paired or group orals for accurately measuring L2 oral performance (Davis 2009; Ducasse & Brown 2009; Gan 2008a, 2008b, 2010; Gan, Davison, & Hamp-Lyons 2009; Luk 2010; Negishi 2010; Ockey 2009). This is because, as explained by Luk and by Isaacs (this volume), testing programs and teachers are becoming more attuned to the importance of *communicative competency* (Bachman 1990; Canale 1983, 1987; Canale & Swain 1980; Hymes 1971; Swain 1985), the idea that knowledge of an L2 encompasses more than the language code (often represented in scores of linguistic accuracy, fluency, and complexity). Communication involves the mastery of sociolinguistic, pragmatic, discourse, and (verbal and non-verbal) strategic competencies (Swain 1985). L2 speakers must acquire these to appropriately participate in real conversations in the L2: that is, speakers must employ accurate and appropriate pragmatic and discourse strategies, respond appropriately to content, correctly form questions or comments, and negotiate in culturally-appropriate ways that are beneficial for sustaining conversation. As stated by Gan et al. (2009: 315), communicative competence includes discourse management and interpersonal dynamics, which include "the ability to stay on topic, to move from topic to topic and to introduce new topics appropriately." Liski (1983), Brown, Anderson, Shillcock and Yule (1985), and Day and Shapson (1987) described over two decades ago how task-based, group orals effectively and efficiently tap into communicative competence and as such were a promising alternative to classroom-based, OPI assessments. But at that time there were grave concerns about the administration, reliability, and fairness of such exams (van Lier 1989). Recent research has addressed such concerns and has assuaged them to a certain extent.

Current research on paired and group orals

In paired or group oral tests, test takers participate in task-based conversations with their peers or a peer, but each is assessed as an individual (Van Moere 2006). The rater observes and listens to the test candidates' interaction, but does not intervene. While listening, the rater evaluates the speech of each individual based on criteria outlined on a rubric. The rater provides the task directions to the test takers, provides planning time, and then listens and evaluates. The actual task-based conversations last about 8 to 15 minutes, depending on the test takers' proficiency levels, the amount of time the administrator is willing to give, and the task.

Bonk and Ockey (2003) described a group oral they administered to 2,427 test takers at a private university in Japan. The test was used to help place students into upper-level English language classes. After taking reading, grammar, listening, and writing tests, all test takers participated in group orals. The test takers first saw a video in Japanese (their L1) that explained what to do. The video also explained the criteria upon which their speech would be rated. The administrators assigned the students to groups of three or four, then gave each group a short written prompt and one minute to prepare. After the minute was up, two raters observed and listened to each group and assigned scores. Bonk and Ockey found variation in score assignment based on the rater (some raters were harsher than others), but *not* more variation than normally appears in other types of oral assessment. They concurred with Fulcher (1996) that group orals were a viable method of testing a large number of test candidates' speaking, but warned that raters need intensive training and monitoring, just as raters of any oral proficiency test do.

Researchers reported that test candidates regard the group oral as a valid form of oral testing and that examinees are more comfortable and confident when they are tasked to speak with peers instead of with a teacher (Folland & Robertson 1976; Fulcher 1996; Liski 1983; Robison 1992). For example, Fulcher administered OPIs and group orals to 47 English language learners in Cyprus. Afterwards, learners completed a questionnaire on their test-taking experiences. Learners indicated group orals were easier and more enjoyable and believed they were more valid indicators of their speech because group orals were not as scary (less anxiety-ridden) and allowed them to produce more natural speech. Other researchers found that paired or group orals promote positive *washback*: they positively influence learning leading up to the test (Messik 1996). Group orals encourage more classroom collaboration amongst peers (Saville & Hargreaves 1999) and promote teachers to teach using pair and group work more often (Együnd & Glover 2001).

Most recently, researchers have been concerned with the effects of pairing – that is, how who is paired with whom affects test takers' abilities or willingness to speak and, ultimately, their scores. Studies have found that test takers' scores differ slightly in relation to the proficiency of the partner, with lower-proficiency test takers producing more and/or better language when working with a higher-level language partner (Davis 2009; Iwashita 1996; Lazaraton & Davis 2008; Norton 2005). The general conclusion has been that it is important to pair or group learners with speakers who are at relatively the same proficiency level and to avoid paring test takers who have different levels of speaking, which may create asymmetric interaction (Davis 2009). Additionally, interlocutor familiarity (e.g., paired with a friend versus a stranger) and personality (i.e., assertive versus non-assertive) affects performance (Ockey 2009), and this is because, as explained by Van Moere (2006), test takers' performances may depend on the characteristics of the group members and the dynamics that come about within the group during their interaction.

Group orals in placement testing

Two of the studies reviewed above used group orals for placement testing – Bonk and Ockey (2003) and Van Moere (2006). Both were large-scale investigations into the validity and reliability of using group orals for oral assessment and placement purposes. Bonk and Ockey's study is described above. Van Moere (2006) studied the test, retest reliability of group orals by having 113 learners take group orals twice with 15 minutes between sessions. For the second test, administrators gave a second, counterbalanced task and grouped test takers with different peers and assigned new raters. Van Moere found that differing rater severity was not a source of score variations. The task appeared to be more responsible for test score variance. In sum, test takers reacted differently to different prompts, suggesting that group-oral test scores should not be based on the performance of a single task, a notion substantiated in research on writing prompts as well (Lee & Anderson 2007).

The studies on using group orals for placement testing leave some questions unanswered. In Bonk and Ockey and Van Moere's studies, all participants were higher-level learners of English. None were novice or low-level L2 learners. This raises the question as to whether group orals would work equally well in evaluating the speech of all levels of L2 learners. Furthermore, Bonk and Ockey did not explain how the combination of listening, speaking, reading, writing, and group-oral test scores were used for placing students in their study. While both Bonk and Ockey and Van Moere's studies demonstrated that group orals are useful tests of L2 oral ability, they did not reveal how group-oral test scores can be applied for placement. Therefore, this study examines the efficacy of group orals for placing all levels of students into conversational English language classes.

The context of the study

At Michigan State University, a large Midwestern university in the United States, the Department of Linguistics and Languages' MA TESOL Program offers free conversational English classes that focus on listening, speaking, and American culture. The classes are popular with recent immigrants and refugees living in the greater Lansing area where the university is located, as well as spouses and significant others of local graduate students and employees. The classes run for six weeks each semester, with four hours of instruction each week. Each semester, approximately 100 to 150 community members take the classes that are team-taught by 10 to 14 MA TESOL students enrolled in the TESOL practicum. Practicum supervisors are in charge of placing the learners into classes, coordinating the testing and instructional programs, and supervising the student teachers. Each semester the program offers anywhere from five to seven classes depending on how many student teachers are enrolled; placement is dependent on the learner population rather than course objectives – the classes are formed, and then the MA TESOL student teachers design task-based materials to match the specific task needs and proficiency levels of the learners assigned to their classes. Students in a graduate-level language testing class aid in the administration of the placement test.

In the past, a listening and reading test was used to make placement decisions, but this had drawbacks. The placement test constructs (listening and reading) did not match course objectives (listening and speaking), and the test relied heavily on literacy skills. Learners who could not read English but could speak well (for example, those who had lived in the area for many years and worked at area businesses, but who did not have prior formal education in English) were placed into lower-level classes with learners who could not speak well. Those who could read English (for example, international spouses of graduate students who had studied English formally in universities abroad, but who had not spoken English for decades) were placed into upper-level classes, even though they could not speak well. Misplacement was a common frustration, with 15 to 25% of students needing to change classes after classes began.

Language classes based on interactive, task-based syllabi should employ interactive, task-based assessments (Chalhoub-Deville 2001; Skehan 2001). In other words, teachers should test what they teach and should test in ways that reflect how they teach (Robison 1992). Likewise, placement tests designed to assign language learners to task-based classes should involve interactive tasks. Placement tests should foreshadow what will be done in the language classroom. Only then can they reliably and validly predict future in-class performance.

In sum, this study is a description of an action research project involving a redesign of the placement test to better reflect the goals of the conversation classes. As part of the redesign, the reading test was eliminated and replaced with a speaking test. Because technology was not an option for the administration of the speaking test (it could not be presumed that learners could use computers; a large-enough lab was not available) and because there was not enough time to assess the speaking of the learners one-by-one, group orals were implemented. This study describes the implementation of group orals in this context and examines its effectiveness in terms of relaibilty and validity as a measure of oral proficiency.

Method

Participants

One hundred and twenty-eight test takers and 28 raters participated. The test takers were from 35 different countries and spoke 26 native languages. Most were recent immigrants and/or refugees; some were spouses or significant others of university employees and/ or graduate students. The participants' English skills ranged from no apparent English skills whatsoever to working- or superior-level proficiency. Their motivation for enrolling varied. Many desired to better understand American culture; others needed vocabulary for attending to basic, daily needs. The 28 raters were graduate students enrolled in a graduate-level language testing class, the MA TESOL practicum, or both.

Materials

Self-assessment test

Because it is important to group test takers with partners that are similar in terms of language proficiency, (Davis 2009; Isaacs this volume; Iwashita 1996; Lazaraton & Davis 2008; Norton 2005), a self-assessment test was developed to place the test takers into groups based on their oral proficiency *before* the group-oral exams. Research has generally found self-assessment a poor predictor for placement purposes (Brantmeier 2006; Peirce, Swain, & Hart 1993). On the other hand, self-assessment has been shown to be a fairly reliable way for examinees to be assigned to the starting level of oral tasks (Malabonga, Kenyon, & Carpenter 2005). The self-assessment test contained 30, 5-point, Likert-scale items that were based on the Test of English for International Communication (TOEIC) "Can do" Guide (The Chauncy Group, 2000). The items related to listening, speaking, and interactive skills as outlined in the "Can do" statements. The self-assessment test, which included a short background questionnaire, can be found in Appendix A.

Oral test

Because task topic influences group-oral-test performance (Van Moere 2006), two tasks were devised. The tasks and their directions (given to the learners on paper) were based on those described in Bonk and Ockey (2003). The first was entitled "Packing for a desert island" and had the following directions:

> You and the people in your group are going on vacation to a deserted island for two weeks. There is enough food and water on the island. Your group can take five items from the following list to the island. What five things will the group take? What are the most important things? Please discuss as a group what you should take and what you should leave behind.

Next to the directions was a picture of a desert island, and below that was a list of 12 items that one might take on a trip to a desert island (a radio, matches, board games, some rope, sleeping bags, knives, beer and wine, etc.) and pictures of the items. The second task was entitled "Picking movies to watch." The directions were as follows:

> You and the people in your group are going to have a dinner party. After you have dinner, you will want to watch two movies. You have the following movies to choose from. What do you know about these movies already? What information do you need to know in order to choose the right movie? Decide which movies you should watch and decide in which order you will watch them.

Below the directions were six movie poster images from the internet. The movies exemplified different movie genres (romance, action, drama/suspense, horror, fantasy, and comedy). For both tasks, participants were instructed that they would have about 10 minutes.

Listening test

Test takers took a standardized, 50-item, multiple-choice, listening exam previously developed for this program's placement testing purposes. All directions for the listening exam were recorded and played over loud speakers during the test. For each audio file, a context of the file (why and/or where one would hear the audio in real life) was provided both in written and aural form before the audio file was played. Each audio file was followed by one to three multiple-choice questions. The audio files were either authentic audio from recorded campus announcements or broadcast radio programs (news programs, special interest programs), or non-scripted, recorded monologues or dialogs with the contexts created for examination purposes. An example of the latter is in (1). A copy of the placement test (audio files and exam booklet) can be obtained by emailing me.

(1) *Context: A friend tells you about how she decided what kind of pet to have.*

Transcript of audio (woman's voice): I really like dogs, and there are times that I wished that I had gotten a dog, ahm, as a pet. But I don't have any dogs. Part of the problem is that dogs cost so much money, ahm, and they take so much time. So, I have two cats because cats are much easier. You can leave for the weekend, and, ahm, they'll be okay. And especially since I am not home very much, that's a much better pet for me.

1. What does the woman have?
    A. 1 cat
    B. 2 cats
    C. 1 dog
    D. 2 dogs
2. What did you learn about the woman?
    A. She travels a lot.
    B. She wants another pet.
    C. She has a small apartment.
    D. She spends a lot of time with her pet(s).

Rating rubric

Raters used the rating rubric in Appendix B. The rubric is based on the ACTFL Speaking Guidelines (http://www.actfl.org/files/public/Guidelinesspeak.pdf), but incorporates communicative competency (communication skills) as outlined in the Council of Europe Framework of Reference (CEFR) for Languages (the global scale is provided in the Appendix of this volume).

Procedure

One week before the placement test, the 28 raters participated in a three-hour, rater-training program during which they took turns administering the group-oral tasks to non-native English speakers. The raters practiced using the rating rubric and discussed the scores they assigned to the individual test takers.

The placement test was administered over the course of two sessions a week before the six-week, listening and speaking (English conversation) classes began. During session one, the 128 test takers registered for the course by paying the course materials fee (10 dollars). After paying, participants took the self-assessment exam (Appendix A). Many of the lower-level English learners had come to the registration with translators; the test administrators informed the translators that they could assist the learners in filling out their self-assessment forms and corresponding bubble sheets. Scores from the self-assessment were used to place the learners into groups of three to five people of similar proficiency in terms of their composite self-assessment scores.

During session two, the test takers were presented with a seating chart that listed their names (in alphabetical order) along with their group assignment (A, B, C, etc.) They were also given a map of the testing room (a large auditorium) and told to sit with their group and the student teacher in charge of their group (see Figure 1). There were 28 groups, with each rater/test administrator being in charge of one group. The groups were organized in the auditorium in a spiral by self-assessment score. For example, those with the lowest scores were placed in the middle-front of the auditorium with Monica (Group A); the second lowest scorers were placed next to Monica with Nuria (Group B). The highest scorers were on the outer ring of the auditorium, with, for example, the best scorers on the self-assessment placed with Adam (Group BB).

After finding their groups and their seats next to their raters, the test takers took the 50-item, paper-and-pencil-based listening test. The listening test took approximately 45 minutes.

After a 15-minute break, the raters administered the first group oral. For example, Monica (see Figure 1) administered the first group-oral task to the test takers in Group A, and Nuria administered the first group oral to the test takers in Group B. For the second oral task, the test takers stayed at their desks but the raters moved to new groups. Raters were paired and switched with the rater with whom they were paired (as coded in Figure 1). For example, Monica and Nuria changed places, Ashtin and Chelsea changed places, and Fannie and Adam changed places. Thus, each learner group participated in

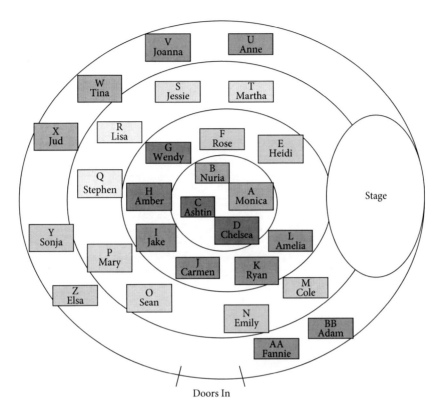

Figure 1. Seating chart for the group orals

two oral tasks, each with a different rater. By having the raters switch places with the rater directly nearby, the raters were tasked with rating similar speakers in terms of their speaking proficiency, which allowed them to focus on one portion of the rubric. For example, Fannie and Adam tended to only monitor their test takers' performance in terms of the scores on the upper-end of the rubric (scores of 3 or 4), while Monica and Nuria focused on the lower end of the scale (scores of 1 or 2). After the group orals were administered, the raters told the test takers the class lists would be posted in the hallways outside the classrooms on the first day of classes.

The rater pairs (for example, Monica and Nuria) then gathered their test takers' bubble sheets and bubbled in the oral scores they assigned, with, for example, Monica bubbling in the scores she assigned on Task A (the desert island task) on Group A's bubble sheets in the spaces provided. Nuria then bubbled in the scores she assigned on Task B (the movie task) on Group A's bubble sheets. The next day the listening tests were automatically scored by scanning bubble sheets. Scores from the raters were averaged so that each individual received a single speaking score that was an average of five speaking categories from two raters.

Results

The results section is divided into two parts. First, use of test scores (the self-assessment, listening, and group oral scores) to place the learners into seven classes is described. Second, the reliability and validity of using the group oral scores for placing learners into the seven classes is reported. The descriptive statistics of the three placement test measures are presented in Table 1.

Table 1. Descriptive statistics of the placement test measures

Test	n	M	SD	Cronbach's alpha	Range Potential	Actual	Skewness (Std. error)
SA	128	99.20	23.66	0.97	30–150	31–150	−.54 (.21)
Listening	128	27.71	9.20	0.89	1–50	4–45	−.25 (.21)
Oral	128	3.08	0.91	0.96	1–5	1–4.9	−.53 (.21)

Note. SA = self-assessment.

Using test scores for placement

To place the learners into seven classes, k-cluster analysis in IBM SPSS 19 was used to cluster the *cases* (that is, the individuals) in terms of their listening and speaking skills. K or *kernel* cluster analysis is a type of data reduction that uses Euclidean distances from kernels (central data points) to identify relatively homogenous groups within the data set (Everitt, Landau, Leese, & Stahl 2011). Cluster analysis and factor analysis are much the same, but with cluster analysis one can set the number of clusters to be identified. The goal was to identify seven groups of language learners that were relatively homogeneous with respect to their listening and speaking test scores because the learners needed to be organized into seven classes. In a nutshell, k-cluster analysis sorted through my two sets of (listening and speaking) test data (which I standardized into Z-scores beforehand) and partitioned the data points into disjoint groups such that data points belonging to the same cluster were similar, while data points belonging to different clusters were dissimilar (Ding & He 2004). This is different from averaging learners' listening and oral test scores and organizing those averages along a single, linear scale to place learners into classes. Doing so would ignore the concept that listening and speaking are related but not equally, incrementally-acquired skill sets, which is particularly true for the learner population at hand – many did not learn English in academic contexts or learned English in instructed settings long ago when speaking skills were not a primary focus. Indeed, in this data set, listening and speaking scores were only weakly related; Pearson's $r = .63$.

The results of the k-cluster analysis are in Figure 2. Seven clusters were formed with seven learners in the lowest-level cluster in terms of English ability (cluster 7) and 14 to 31 learners in the other six (20 in cluster 1, 18 in cluster 2, 14 in cluster 3, 24 in cluster 4, 31 in cluster 5, and 14 in cluster 6). As can be seen in Figure 2, cluster 4 comprised learners with the highest levels of English. Clusters 1 and 5, on the other hand, were equal on average in terms of English listening ability, but cluster 1 had higher speaking abilities. Clusters 2, 3, and 6 had similar listening test averages, but differed markedly on speaking.

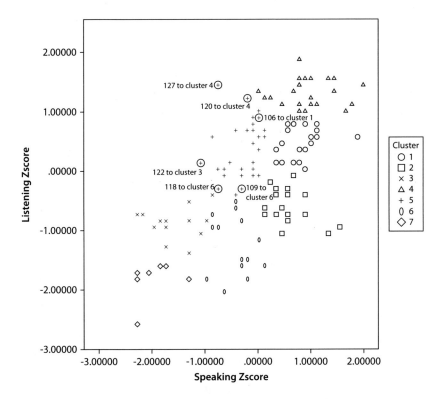

Figure 2. Results of the k-cluster analysis. Individuals who are circled are those assigned to a different cluster based on their large distances from cluster 5's center and their proximity to other clusters so the class comprised of individuals from cluster 5 would not be too large

Problematic with k-cluster analysis for placement testing purposes is that the cluster centers do not align themselves such that there are equal numbers of cases within each cluster. This is good in that if a few learners have skill patterns that differ markedly from the others (such as the seven low-level learners in cluster 7), they are set off from the others as their own cluster. Class size, determined by k-cluster analysis, is determined purely according to the traits measured, and not by other factors teachers need to consider, such as class size. Thus, to better balance the clusters in terms of class size, the number of test takers in cluster 5 (the largest cluster with 31 learners) was reduced by six by first identifying the six cluster-5 members whose Euclidean distances were furthest from cluster 5's center. (SPSS 19 provides these distances in the output). The average distance for all 128 learners was .47. The six individuals in cluster 5 whose distances were the greatest were those with ID numbers 127, 120, 122, 118, 106, and 109, and together their average distance was .85 (range = .64 to 1.20). These six individuals were moved to the clusters to which they were the next closest. Thus, as indicated in Figure 2, from cluster 5 one individual was moved to cluster 3, two to cluster 6, one to cluster 1, and two to cluster 4. After moving these individuals, the corresponding class sizes and their averages on the different tests were as in Table 2.

Table 2. Descriptive statistics of the classes

Cluster	Class name*	N	Average test scores		
			Self-assessment	Listening	Oral
1	Sunnyside Ups	21	116	32	3.85
2	Square Pegs	18	111	22	3.61
3	The Xs	15	77	21	1.64
4	Diamonds	26	115	40	3.95
5	Added Ingredients	25	94	30	2.89
6	Ovals	16	84	16	2.69
7	Rubies	7	64	11	1.29

Note. *Rather than assigning class names that corresponded to the English-language levels, which would have been misleading and which may have upset some learners, names unrelated to English-ability patterns were used.

The reliability and validity of the group orals

To answer the question of how reliable and valid is it to place learners into English-language listening and speaking classes using group orals, two analyses were carried out. First, the inter-rater reliability of the group orals was estimated using the scores from the two sets of raters. Second, test takers and student teachers were informally interviewed the week following the placement test to elicit their impressions of the group orals for assessing their skills.

Inter-rater reliability estimates

One way to determine if test scores are reliable is to see if the scores awarded to test takers from different raters correlate. As can be seen in Table 3, the overall inter-rater reliability on group oral scores from the two sets of raters was .72. Of interest are the correlations along the diagonal. Those correlations were expected to be high, as they represented different raters rating the same analytic traits, while correlations below the diagonal should be lower because the different traits being rated do not overlap entirely in their constructs (lower correlations indicate the measures are not tapping into the same trait or the raters are not applying the same scale to what is being tested, which should be the case for all correlated items below the diagonal.) In general, the highest correlations were along the diagonal, except for accuracy/grammar. This correlation of .49 is low, indicating unwanted variance in accuracy/grammar scores, variance that stems from the raters, not the test takers' underlying accuracy/grammar skills. In other words, the raters did not reliably measure this trait. They did best rating pronunciation, fluency, and communication skills.

Table 3. Pearson correlations between rater sets

	Measure	Rater set B					
		1	2	3	4	5	6
Rater set A	1. Pronunciation	0.69					
	2. Fluency	0.68	0.71				
	3. Accuracy/Grammar	0.50	0.58	0.49			
	4. Vocabulary/Content	0.54	0.64	0.59	0.62		
	5. Communication skills	0.48	0.60	0.60	0.60	0.67	
	6. Oral skills average	–	–	–	–	–	0.72

Note. All correlations are significant at the .01 level (2-tailed).

In the week after the group orals, eight language learners who took the group orals, two Brazilians, three Koreans, and one each from Argentina, Pakistan, and China were interviewed. They were asked the following questions: (1) How did you feel about a conversation being used to test your speaking skills? (2) What was the most difficult part of the conversation? (3) Which task did you like better, the deserted island task or the movie task, and why?

In regard to question one, six of the eight stated they liked the group orals because they mimicked real conversation and were "fun," "interesting," or "innovative." As one of the learners from Korea stated, "New experience for me. More interaction, you learn from them [the group members], get to know them." One of the students from Brazil opined the following: "I take a test in different places ... and to me is easy when you ask me about my life about "How long have you been here?" ... I know ... and sometimes it looks like I can speak very well but I know I can't [speak]. If you give me a topic, that's difficult for me, that's so hard and that's why it's so interesting ... because you have different topics, that's much better." But this impression of the group orals was not unanimous. Another learner from Korea noted that the conversations were extremely difficult. He said, "I feel more comfortable with interview. Conversation, people are from different countries with different accents. Very difficult to understand. Conversation with many people, I cannot focus." This response was similar to one from the other learner from Brazil who commented that the group oral "is great but sometimes is difficult for me understand, for example, uhm ... Chinese people, uhm, or the Asian people because they pronunciation is different than the Latin American people when they speaking English." The respondent from China commented, however, that success depends largely on the others in the group. He noted, "I prefer talking with native speakers to conversation with other English learners."

When asked which part of the conversation was most difficult, various aspects were mentioned, including difficulty in understanding the other test takers' accents, a lack of vocabulary knowledge in regard to the topics, the task of speaking itself while also

translating online, and difficulty speaking because others tended to dominate the conversation. For example, one of the test takers from Korea noted the following: "One of my
partners is a very good speaker. She talked a lot. I lost my confidence; I lost my chance to
talk." Likewise, another learner from Korea said, "I was very nervous. I've been here for
only three months. I didn't talk a lot."

When asked which of the two tasks they preferred, opinions were mixed. Four liked
the desert-island task better, three liked the movie-choice task better (with one of those
three noting that she liked both though), and one said she had no preference, that she liked
both equally well. The learner from Argentina liked the movie task better because she was
unfamiliar with the vocabulary in the desert-island task. One of the Brazilians liked the
desert-island task better because she said she had "little knowledge regarding movies."
And one of the Koreans said she liked the desert-island task best because it was just "of
greater personal interest."

Informal discussions with the student teachers and raters further clarified the suc-
cesses and problems with the group orals in this context. For the group orals, the students
had been matched with their prospective teachers. The teachers appreciated being able to
work with their future learners during the listening and speaking part of the placement
test, particularly teachers who had been assigned to teach the lower levels. During the
oral test, they got to know the learners' English level and better understand what their
class would be like. They noted, however, that the group orals could *not* be administered
to the very lowest learners because they could not speak English at all or could not read
at all. Instead of administering the group orals to these lowest-level learners, during the
time allotted for the group orals, Monica, Ashtin, and the two other raters with whom
they worked (Nuria and Chelsea) asked questions and began, essentially, teaching. They
started with "What is your name?" and worked up to very simple phrases such as "My
name is…" and "Her/his name is…" during the oral testing time. They wished they had
had the option to skip the listening test as well because for these learners, the listening test
was rather meaningless because they could not read – the multiple-choice response format
was indecipherable.

Concurring with the test takers, the raters mentioned that they had a hard time when
the learners talked too little, had long pauses between words, or when one student dominated the task discussion. Because test administrators were not supposed to interrupt
the group discussion, they hesitated to help any of the language learners out. This was in
direct contrast to Monica and Ashtin, who felt free to basically "throw the oral test out
the window" and lead a more guided discussion with their low-level learners. Other test
administrators who gave the test to lower-level learners noted that they would have liked
more leeway to intervene or direct the conversation. For example, one rater said "Some
of the students had no idea about the words on the handouts of the oral placement test.
They could not communicate to the others in English. As an instructor, I feel that if I
had a vocabulary test at that time, such as picking up pictures with words, it would have
helped me."

Discussion and conclusion

The results of this study demonstrate that group orals are as efficient and cost-effective as researchers have described (Bonk & Ockey 2003; Robison 1992). They take less time to administer than one-on-one oral proficiency interviews (Robison 1992). Additionally, the data from this study corroborate data from other studies showing that group orals reflect how most students learn to talk in the classroom (in groups) and "make sense with regard to available time" (Robison 1992:488). Verbal reports from test takers indicated that during the group orals, test takers were able to interact authentically with their peers, meaning they were able to ask questions to clarify other test takers' speech, were able to negotiate for meaning, and were involved in conversation that was, on the most part, relaxed and informal in register. Most important, as a result of this placement test method, only four out of 128 test takers asked to be moved to a different class. One wanted to move to be with his wife, another wanted to move to have a different teacher, and two wanted to move up to have more challenging classes. Thus, this placement test with group orals was a success.

Still, group orals need to be investigated for their reliability and validity and in terms of what *type* of interaction they promote. The group orals were not, in this study, audio recorded. Doing so would allow for analyses of the type of interaction that occurred. Gan and his colleagues (Gan 2008a, 2010; Gan et al. 2009) have successfully applied conversation analysis to group-oral-test discourse and have found that group orals allow for intensive conversation engagement and active participation between peers. Analysis of the group oral interaction was beyond the scope of the current study, but the interview data suggests that the learners found the group oral discourse to be active, natural, and engaging.

On another note, Gan stated that even lower-performing group-oral test takers co-construct meaning and negotiate to find the correct linguistic form – he stated even lower-level learners construct social and linguistic identity during the conversation (Gan 2010) – discourse features that may be lacking in OPI contexts (A. Brown 2003). However, this was not the case with the lowest-level, English-language learners in the present study. Gan's test takers were most likely at the intermediate level or above. In this study, some of the test takers were extremely low level or true beginners, making group orals, as designed and implemented in this study, impossible. For beginners, negotiation, turn-taking, and focus on form was impossible because fundamental and basic language skills were lacking. For such test takers, a more directed group-oral task is needed. Test administrators can provide such test takers with chances to talk, but this type of talk needs to be teacher-fronted, with, as one of the student teachers suggested, cue cards, pictures to name, direct questions to ask, and even a prepared, introductory lesson on greetings. Even though such a directed task may not be representative of most conversation varieties (Lazaraton 2002; Ross & Berwick 1992), it probably is relatively normal for beginning-level language classrooms. As stated in the literature review, placement tests should foreshadow what will be done in the language classroom. One-size-fits-all oral tasks, as we found, are not going to work equally well for all levels of speakers. Certain adjustments and accommodations need to be made for lower-level learners.

Group orals were difficult for some of the language learners precisely because the group orals were testing the types of skills to which they were not accustomed: peer-to-peer interaction, speaking with other, non-native speakers of English (with different accents), negotiating for meaning while using novel vocabulary and/or grammar forms – tasks that drive learning and L2 acquisition (Gass & Mackey 2007; Mackey 2007). The quantitative data (the high group-oral reliability estimates) and the qualitative data (reports of difficulties in communicating in the group setting) suggest that the group orals did as hoped and suggested: they tapped into communicative competency. Communication during the group orals was difficult because the learners had incomplete mastery of sociolinguistic, pragmatic, discourse, and strategic competencies.

The quantitative and qualitative data demonstrate that past concerns about the administration, reliability, and fairness of group orals (Swain 2001; van Lier 1989) are still an issue. Like all other performance assessments, group orals are plagued by construct-irrelevant variation in how raters interpret the rating rubrics. As specified by Bonk and Ockey (2003: 90), "virtually all studies that have investigated rater severity on L2 oral performance assessments (see, for example, Bachman et al. 1995; Brown 1995; Lumley & McNamara 1995; Lynch & McNamara 1998; Weigle 1998; Upshur & Turner 1999) have found significant meaningful differences among judges." Group-oral raters, like raters of any oral test, are prone to inconsistencies in assigning scores. In this light, the .72 correlation among rater sets is rather remarkable and perhaps on par with larger-scale, higher-stakes tests. The raters were novice teachers with little to no rating experience, were minimally trained (in three hours), the rating rubric was complex, and the task of listening to the test takers was multifaceted.

A way to increase rater reliability within this context may be to remove the rubric's section on accuracy/grammar. During the meaning-based group orals, test takers may not have focused on accuracy or grammar, so perhaps it shouldn't have been tested. Additionally, the raters struggled immensely to apply this part of the rubric to the test takers' speech. Reasons why are speculative, but raters mentioned they had a difficult time centering on individual test takers' grammar usage while also attending to the test takers' pronunciation, fluency, vocabulary usage, and ability to get their messages across effectively. Some raters noted that accuracy and grammar in this speaking context seemed tangential to the task at hand, thus they focused less on this category. It would be interesting to see if eliminating the heavy burden of attending to accuracy/grammar would result in an increase in reliability across the other sections. Eliminating the need for raters to think about accuracy and grammar might free up their mental resources for discerning the other categories. Another option may be using a holistic rather than analytic rating rubric, which would lessen the cognitive burden of rating.

Working accommodations into the group-oral-test format is the next step. Language testing programs that utilize group orals for a wide range of learners (in terms of proficiency) must develop a set of articulated tasks that can be administered depending on the L2-speaking level of test takers. Modifications must be made to the test-administrator instructions: if the task is not working (if test takers are not talking), test administrators should be allowed to intervene. If one learner dominates, the test administrator should step in and gently recommend someone else take a turn. Such actions will most likely not be needed with highly skilled speakers (those possessing relatively robust levels of communicative competence), but as in any testing situation, those struggling with task directions or the ability to perform at their level should be provided accommodations (Abedi 2006). Doing so may alleviate administrators' anxieties concerning group-oral-test-score interpretations and lessen the effects that personality and peer characteristics have on group-testing performance and subsequent score assignments (Davis 2009; Luk 2010; Negishi 2010; Ockey 2009; Van Moere 2006).

References

Abedi, J. (2006). Language issues in item development. In S. M. Downing & T. M. Haladyna (Eds.), *Handbook of test development* (pp. 377–398). Mahwah, NJ: Lawrence Erlbaum Associates.

ACTFL. (2004). Testing for proficiency: The ACTFL Oral Proficiency Interview. Retrieved February 3, 2004, from http://www.actfl.org

Bachman, L. F. (1990). *Fundamental considerations in language testing.* Oxford: Oxford University Press.

Bachman, L. F., Lynch, B. K., & Mason, M. (1995). Investigating variability in tasks and rater judgments in a performance test of foreign language speaking. *Language Testing, 12*(2), 238–257.

Bonk, W. J., & Ockey, G. J. (2003). A many-facet Rasch analysis of the second language group oral discussion task. *Language Testing, 20,* 89–110.

Brantmeier, C. (2006). Advanced L2 learners and reading placement: Self-assessment, CBT, and subsequent performance. *System, 34,* 15–35.

Brown, A. (2003). Interviewer variation and the co-construction of speaking proficiency. *Language Testing, 20,* 1–25.

Brown, G., Andeson, A., Shillcock, R., & Yule, G. (1985). *Teaching talk: Strategies for production and assessment.* Cambridge: Cambridge University Press.

Canale, M. (1983). From communicative competence to language pedagogy. In J. C. Richards & R. Schmidt (Eds.), *Language and communication* (pp. 2–27). London: Longman.

Canale, M. (1987). The measurement of communicative competence. *Annual Review of Applied Linguistics, 8,* 67–84.

Canale, M., & Swain, M. (1980). Theoretical bases of communicative approaches to second language teaching and testing. *Applied Linguistics, 1,* 1–47.

Chalhoub-Deville, M. (1995). A contextualized approach to describing oral language proficiency. *Language Learning, 45,* 251–281.

Chalhoub-Deville, M. (2001). Task-based assessments: Characteristics and validity evidence. In M. Bygate, P. Skehan & M. Swain (Eds.), *Researching pedagogic tasks* (pp. 210–228). Harlow: Pearson Education.

Davis, L. (2009). The influence of interlocutor proficiency in a paired oral assessment. *Language Testing, 26,* 367–396.

Day, E. M., & Shapson, S. M. (1987). Assessment of oral communicative skills in early French immersion programmes. *Journal of Multilingual and Multicultural Development, 8*(3), 237–260.

Ding, C., & He, X. (2004). K-means clustering via Principle Component Analysis. *Proceedings of the 21st International Conference on Machine Learning* (pp. 1–9). Berkeley, CA: Lawrence Berkeley National Laboratory.

Douglas, D. (1994). Quantity and quality in speaking test performance. *Language Testing, 11*, 125–144.

Douglas, D., & Selinker, L. (1992). Analyzing oral proficiency test performance in general and specific purpose contexts. *System, 20*, 317–329.

Ducasse, A. M., & Brown, A. (2009). Assessing paired orals: Raters' orientation to interaction. *Language Testing, 26*, 423–443.

Együnd, G., & Glover, P. (2001). Oral testing in pairs – a secondary school perspective. *English Language Teaching Journal, 55*, 70–76.

Everitt, B. S., Landau, S., Leese, M., & Stahl, D. (2011). *Cluster analysis* (5th edn). New York NY: Wiley.

Folland, D., & Robertson, D. (1976). Toward objectivity in group oral testing. *English Language Teaching Journal, 30*, 156–167.

Fulcher, G. (1996). Testing tasks: Issues in task design and the group oral. *Language Testing, 13*, 23–51.

Fulcher, G. (2003). *Testing second language speaking.* New York: Pearson, Longman.

Gan, Z. (2008a). Examining negotiation in peer group oral assessment: What are the implications? *Australian Review of Applied Linguistics, 31*, 1–20.

Gan, Z. (2008b). Extroversion and group oral performance: A mixed quantitative and discourse analysis approach. *Prospect, 23*, 24–42.

Gan, Z. (2010). Interaction in group oral assessment: A case study of higher- and lower-scoring students. *Language Testing, 27*, 585–602.

Gan, Z., Davison, C., & Hamp-Lyons, L. (2009). Topic negotiation in peer group oral assessment situations: A conversion analytic approach. *Applied Linguistics, 30*, 315–334.

Gass, S. M., & Mackey, A. (2007). Input, interaction, and output in second language acquisition. In B. VanPatten & J. Williams (Eds.), *Theories in second language acquisition* (pp. 175–199). Mahwah, NJ: Lawrence Erlbaum Associates.

Harlow, L. L., & Caminero, R. (1990). Oral testing of beginning language students at large universities: Is it worth the trouble? *Foreign Language Annals, 23*, 489–501.

Hymes, D. (1971). *On communicative competence.* Philadelphia, PA: University of Pennsylvania Press.

Iwashita, N. (1996). The validity of the paired interview format in oral performance assessment. *Melbourne Papers in Language Testing, 5*, 51–66.

Iwashita, N., McNamara, T., & Elder, C. (2001). Can we predict task difficulty in an oral proficiency test? Exploring the potential of an information-processing approach to task design. *Language Learning, 51*, 401–436.

Jenkins, S., & Parra, I. (2003). Multiple layers of meaning in an oral proficiency test: The complementary roles of nonverbal, paralinguistic, and verbal behaviors in assessment decisions. *The Modern Language Journal, 87*, 90–107.

Johnson, M. (2001). *The art of non-conversation. A reexamination of the validity of the Oral Proficiency Interview.* New Haven, CT: Yale University Press.

Johnson, M., & Tyler, A. E. (1998). Re-analyzing the OPI: How much does it look like natural conversation? In R. Young & A. W. He (Eds.), *Talking and testing: Discourse approaches to the assessment of oral proficiency* (pp. 27–51). Amsterdam: John Benjamins.

Kasper, G., & Ross, S. J. (2007). Multiple questions in oral proficiency interviews. *Journal of Pragmatics, 39*, 2045–2070.

Kenyon, D. M., & Malabonga, V. (2001). Comparing examinee attitudes toward computer-assisted and other oral proficiency assessments. *Language Learning and Technology, 5*(2), 60–83.

Lazaraton, A. (2002). *A qualitative approach to the validation of oral language tests.* Cambridge: Cambridge University Press.

Lazaraton, A., & Davis, L. (2008). A microanalytic perspective on discourse, proficiency, and identity in paired oral assessment. *Language Assessment Quarterly, 5*, 313–335.

Lee, H.-K., & Anderson, C. (2007). Validity and topic generality of a writing performance test. *Language Testing, 24*, 307–330.

Liski, E. (1983). A study of the statistical foundations of group conversation tests in spoken English. *Language Learning, 33*(2), 225–246.

Luk, J. (2010). Talking to score: Impression management in L2 oral assessment and the co-construction of a test discourse genre. *Language Assessment Quarterly, 7*, 25–53.

Lumley, T., & McNamara, T. F. (1995). Rater characteristics and rater bias: Implications for training. *Language Testing, 12*(1), 54–71.

Lynch, B. K. & McNamara, T. F. (1998). Using G-theory and many-facet Rasch measurement in the development of performance assessments of the ESL speaking skills of immigrants. *Language Testing, 15*(2), 158–180.

Mackey, A. (2007). Interaction as practice. In R. DeKeyser (Ed.), *Practice in second language learning: Perspectives from linguistics and psychology* (pp. 85–110). Cambridge: Cambridge University Press.

Malabonga, V., Kenyon, D. M., & Carpenter, H. (2005). Self-assessment, preparation and response time on a computerized oral proficiency test. *Language Testing, 22*, 59–92.

Malone, M. (2003). Research on the Oral Proficiency Interview: Analysis, synthesis, and future directions. *Foreign Language Annals, 36*, 491–497.

Messik, S. (1996). Validity and washback in language testing. *Language Testing, 13*, 241–256.

Mikhailova, J. (2007). Rethinking description in the Russian SOPI: Shortcomings of the simulated oral proficiency interview. *Foreign Language Annals, 40*, 584–603.

Negishi, J. (2010). Characteristics of interactional management functions in group oral by Japanese learners of English. *Journal of Pan-Pacific Association of Applied Linguistics, 14*(1), 57–79.

Norton, J. (2005). The paired format in the Cambridge Speaking Tests. *English Language Teaching Journal, 59*(4), 287–297.

Ockey, G. (2009). The effects of group members' personalities on a test taker's L2 group oral discussion test scores. *Language Testing, 26*, 161–186.

Peirce, B. N., Swain, M., & Hart, D. (1993). Self-assessment, French immersion, and locus of control. *Applied Linguistics, 14*, 25–42.

Robison, R. (1992). Developing practical speaking tests for the foreign language classroom: A small group approach. *Foreign Language Annals, 25*, 487–496.

Ross, S. J., & Berwick, R. (1992). The discourse of accommodation in oral proficiency interviews. *Studies in Second Language Acquisition, 14*, 159–176.

Saville, N., & Hargreaves, P. (1999). Assessing speaking in the revised FCE. *English Language Teaching Journal, 53*(1), 42–51.

Skehan, P. (2001). Tasks and language performance assessment. In M. Bygate, P. Skehan & M. Swain (Eds.), *Researching pedagogical tasks: Second language learning, teaching and testing* (pp. 167–185). Essex: Longman.

Swain, M. (1985). Communicative competence: Some roles of comprehensible input and comprehensible output in its development. In S. M. Gass & C. G. Madden (Eds.), *Input in second language acquisition* (pp. 235–256). Rowley, MA: Newbury House.

Swain, M. (2001). Examining dialogue: Another approach to content specification and to validating inferences drawn from test scores. *Language Testing, 18*, 275–302.

The Chauncey Group International. (2000). TOEIC can-do guide: Linking TOEIC scores to activities performed using English. Retrieved September 5, 2007 from https://www.ets.org/Media/Research/pdf/TOEIC_CAN_DO.pdf

Upshur, J. A., & Turner, C. E. (1999). Systematic effects in the rating of second-language speaking ability: test method and learner discourse. *Language Testing, 16*, 82–111.

van Lier, L. (1989). Reeling, writhing, drawling, stretching, and fainting in coils: Oral proficiency interviews as conversation. *TESOL Quarterly, 23*, 489–508.

Van Moere, A. (2006). Validity evidence in a university group oral test. *Language Testing, 23*, 411–440.

Weigle, S. C. (1998). Using FACETS to model rater training effects. *Language Testing, 15*(2), 263–287.

Appendix A

Self-assessment of English skills

Last (Family) Name: _____ First Name: _____ Identification Number: _____

Self-Assessment of English Ability - MSU English Conversation Classes

NOTE: These self-assessment items were adapted from the TOEIC Can-Do Guide, downloaded from
‹http://www.ets.org/Media/Tests/Test_of_English_for_International_Communication/TOEIC_Can_Do.pdf›.

DIRECTIONS: Please answer the questions below. You will need to record your answers to the questions in section II (questions 1 through 30) on the "General Purpose Answer Sheet" you have been given. Please write your **LAST NAME** and your **FIRST NAME** on the answer sheet where indicated. Also fill out your **BIRTH DATE** (MONTH, DATE, YEAR) and your **IDENTIFICATION NUMBER**, which is the identification number on your receipt. Record what **SEX** you are (male or female). You do <u>NOT</u> need to fill in your grade or education. Fill in the bubbles below the letters and numbers so the computer can read your information. If you have any questions, please ask a proctor for help.

SECTION I.

A. What is your native language? _____

B. What country do you come from? _____

C. How long have you been here in the United States? _____

D. What do you use English for here in the United States? (Why are you here in the USA?)

_____

SECTION II.

<u>LISTENING</u>

In ENGLISH...

	Not at all	With much difficulty	With some difficulty	With very little difficulty	Easily
1. I can understand simple questions in social situations such as "How are you?" "Where do you live?" and "How are you feeling today?"	1	2	3	4	5
2. I can understand someone who is speaking slowly and who is giving me directions on how to walk to a nearby location.	1	2	3	4	5
3. I can understand headline news broadcasts on the radio.	1	2	3	4	5
4. I can understand a recorded message that is left for me on my cell phone or answering machine.	1	2	3	4	5
5. I can understand announcements made over the loudspeaker in a store about when the store is closing or special things they have on sale.	1	2	3	4	5
6. I can understand an explanation given over the radio of why a road has been temporarily closed.	1	2	3	4	5
7. I can understand someone who is speaking slowly about his or her hobbies, interests, and plans for the weekend.	1	2	3	4	5
8. I can understand directions about what time to come to a meeting and the room in which it will be held.	1	2	3	4	5
9. I can understand an explanation of why one restaurant is better than another.	1	2	3	4	5
10. I can understand a discussion of current events taking place among a group of persons speaking English.	1	2	3	4	5

SPEAKING	Not at all	With much difficulty	With some difficulty	With very little difficulty	Easily

In ENGLISH...

	Not at all	With much difficulty	With some difficulty	With very little difficulty	Easily
11. I can tell people about myself (tell them my place of birth, who is in my family).	1	2	3	4	5
12. I can describe the plot of a movie or television program that I have seen.	1	2	3	4	5
13. I can describe a friend in detail, include how he or she looks and his or her personality.	1	2	3	4	5
14. I can order food at a restaurant.	1	2	3	4	5
15. I can talk about topics of general interest (current events, the weather).	1	2	3	4	5
16. I can describe my daily routine (when I get up, what time I eat lunch).	1	2	3	4	5
17. I can talk about my future work goals and intentions (what I plan to do next year).	1	2	3	4	5
18. I can tell someone about something humorous that recently happened to me.	1	2	3	4	5
19. I can adjust my speaking to address a variety of listeners (professional staff at work, a friend, small children).	1	2	3	4	5
20. I can tell someone directions on how to get to my house or apartment.	1	2	3	4	5

INTERACTIVE SKILLS

In ENGLISH...

	Not at all	With much difficulty	With some difficulty	With very little difficulty	Easily
21. I can telephone a restaurant to make dinner reservations for a party of three.	1	2	3	4	5
22. I can give and take messages over the phone.	1	2	3	4	5
23. I can meet with a doctor and explain the physical symptoms of my illness.	1	2	3	4	5
24. I can explain to a repair person what is wrong with an appliance I want fixed.	1	2	3	4	5
25. I can call a department store and find out if a certain item is currently in stock.	1	2	3	4	5
26. I can talk to an elementary school teacher about my child or children in general.	1	2	3	4	5
27. I can discuss my opinion on world events.	1	2	3	4	5
28. I can conduct an interview with an applicant who wants a job in my area of expertise.	1	2	3	4	5
29. I can explain school or work policies to a new person who has just started.	1	2	3	4	5
30. I can discuss with a work or school colleague how something can be improved.	1	2	3	4	5

THANK YOU!

Page 2 of 2

Appendix B

Group oral rating rubric

Group Oral Exam Score Sheet FIRST ORAL TASK (Desert Island) Test Administrator: _____

	(51) Pronunciation	(52) Fluency	(53) Accuracy/Grammar	(54) Vocabulary/Content	(55) Communicative skills/Strategies
5	Rarely mispronounces, able to speak with near native-like pronunciation	Near-native-like fluency, effortless, smooth, natural rhythm	Uses high-level discourse with near-native-like accuracy	Wide range of vocabulary with near-native-like use, vocabulary is clearly appropriate to express ideas/opinion	Confident and natural, asks others to expand on views, shows ability to negotiate meaning, shows how own and others' ideas are related
4 / 4+	Pronunciation is clear, occasionally mispronounces some words, but has mastered all sounds, accent may sound foreign but does not interfere with meaning	Speaks with confidence, but has some unnatural pauses, some errors in speech rhythm, rarely gropes for words	Shows ability to use full range of grammatical structures but makes some errors, errors do not impede the meaning of the utterances	Lexis sufficient for task although not always precisely used	Generally confident, responds appropriately to others' ideas/opinions, show ability to negotiate meaning
3 / 3+	Pronunciation is not native-like, but can be understood, mispronounces unfamiliar words, may not have mastered some sounds	Speech is hesitant, some unnatural rephrasing and groping for words	Relies mostly on simple (but generally accurate) sentences, has enough grammar to express meaning, complex sentences are used but often inaccurately	Lexis generally adequate for expressing ideas/opinion but often used inaccurately	Responds to others, shows agreement or disagreement to others opinions
2 / 2+	Frequently mispronounces, accent often impedes meaning, difficult to understand even with concentrated listening	Slow, strained speech, constant groping for words and long, unnatural pauses (except for routine phrases)	Uses simple inaccurate sentences and fragmented phrases, doesn't have enough grammar to express ideas/opinions clearly enough	Lexis not adequate for task, cannot express ideas or opinion	Does not initiate interaction, produces monologue only, shows some turn taking, may say "I agree with you," but does not relate ideas in explanation
1 / 1+	Frequently mispronounces, heavy accent, may use speech which is virtually incomprehensible	Fragments of speech that are so halting that conversation is virtually impossible	Only says a few words, cannot make a reasonable judgment of student's grammatical ability	Little lexis, inadequate for simple communication	May require prompting, shows no awareness of other speakers

Name: _____ _____ _____ _____ _____
ID#: _____

Name: _____ _____ _____ _____ _____
ID#: _____

Name: _____ _____ _____ _____ _____
ID#: _____

Chapter 14

Interaction in conversation groups
The development of L2 conversational styles

Nicole Ziegler[a], Corinne Seals[a], Steffi Ammons[a], Julie Lake[a],
Phillip Hamrick[a], and Patrick Rebuschat[b]
[a]Georgetown University and [b]Bangor University

This exploratory study examines the potential learning opportunities of interactions in the naturalistic setting of a German conversation group. Eleven intermediate L2 German learners participated in weekly conversation groups, which were recorded and then transcribed. In addition, information regarding learners' perceptions, confidence, and willingness to communicate was obtained by means of self-report surveys and interviews. A discourse analytic approach indicated that learners' styles were more passive or active depending on their ability to identify and use, consciously or unconsciously, German conversational style in the group interactions. These findings suggest that interaction in L2 conversation groups can play an important role in providing learners with opportunities to acquire native-like conversational styles and structures in an environment representative of authentic, real world conversational contexts.

Introduction

During the last few decades, numerous empirical studies and meta-analyses have demonstrated clear benefits of interaction on second language (L2) development (e.g. Keck, Iberri-Shea, Tracy-Ventura, & Wa-Mbaleka 2006; Mackey & Goo 2007; Mackey & Oliver 2002; Mackey, Oliver, & Leeman 2003). Much of the focus of these studies has been the development of lexis and grammar; however, interaction has also been shown to benefit learners by providing opportunities to produce modified output (Swain & Lapkin 2001) and receive comprehensible input (Gass & Varonis 1985), as well as negotiate for meaning and receive feedback (Pica, Lincoln-Porter, Paninos, & Linnell 1996), all of which may provide opportunities for development above the lexical and grammatical levels. Consequently, interaction may be integral to the development of discourse structures, conversational styles, and interactional features, which are all important aspects of successful L2 development.

Although L2 research tends to focus on conversation in classrooms and lab settings, these environments do not necessarily result in the kind of 'natural' oral interaction that might benefit the learning of L2 interactional conventions and styles. Although previous research acknowledges this lack of investigation of 'natural' conversation, there are few studies that have addressed this gap (see Brock, Crookes, Day, & Long 1986; McDonough & Hernández González this volume; Polio, Gass, & Chapin 2006, for exceptions). However, to our knowledge no studies have investigated the development of L2 conversational style in more naturalistic settings.

In sum, the acquisition of L2 conversational features, including conversational style and discourse structures, although important aspects of successful oral interaction, are under-investigated in second language acquisition (SLA) research overall, particularly in naturally occurring conversation. In addition, naturalistic settings, such as conversation groups, may promote the development of conversational features more than structured classrooms. However, because the majority of interaction studies have focused on lab and classroom-based environments (Mackey & Goo 2007), we argue there is a clear need for more research examining interaction in other learning environments.

In order to address these gaps, we examined interaction-driven development of L2 conversational features in intermediate level German learners outside of traditional classroom and lab-based contexts in a more naturalistic setting. We conducted our study in the context of an L2 conversation group. Given the present focus on the acquisition of conversational features, we used conventions and constructs well established within discourse analysis research to examine participants' interactions. Before proceeding to the details of the study, we first briefly review conversational interaction and its importance to SLA.

Conversational interaction and SLA

Successful L2 development is not limited to learners' development of linguistic skills, such as grammar and lexis, but also includes the development of social and interactional practices (Batstone 2010; Lantolf 2000). When engaged in face-to-face social interactions, participants draw on interactional resources, such as turn and topic management and conversational style, to successfully negotiate various communicative situations. These interactional skills, which are often acquired through observation and participation (Young 1999), may be crucial for learners to develop so that they may successfully navigate L2 interaction. When learners are able to follow the expected interactional patterns of the L2, this helps to avoid potential cross-cultural miscommunication and ensures a successful conversation between the interlocutors. Features of conversational style, such as overlap, pauses and intonation, make up the conventions through which meaning is communicated in social interactions (Tannen 2005), underscoring the importance of these features to L2 conversational development. However, despite the importance of interactional development, the acquisition of conversational features remains relatively under-researched in the field of SLA.

Acquired as part of the social process of language development (Tannen 2005), conversational style can be defined as a summation of the social norms linked to a linguistic and cultural framework (Byrnes 1986). These norms, which signal to participants the meaning of an utterance, vary across language groups and influence discourse conventions, such as the occurrence of interruptions and the ordering of turn-taking. Previous research in discourse analysis has indicated different patterns in conversational styles across linguistic and regional groups (Berry 1994; De Fina, Schiffrin, & Bamberg 1999; Sharma 2005; Tannen 2005), with results demonstrating differences in involvement, overlap, backchanneling, and collaborative sequences. In light of these differences, learners may experience a knowledge gap regarding the relevant features of L2 conversational style. Given that these features play a key role in successful interaction, they become an important part of any account of the effects of interaction on L2 development.

In the present study, we focus on U.S. native speakers of English learning German as an L2. These learners may encounter problems in learning how German conversational styles contrast with the conventions and norms of U.S. English, given that these languages differ across several dimensions, including politeness strategies, turn-taking, overlap, and discourse structure (Byrnes 1986; Kothoff 1991, 1993). However, in order to better understand how interaction may impact learners' strategies in approaching the gaps between their L1 and L2 conversational styles, we first must characterize the differences between the conversational styles associated with their L1 (U.S. English) and L2 (German). We operationalized U.S. English as North American English, from a variety of different states, and going forward will refer to it as "American English."

Use of American and German conversational style

Although there is no monolithic "American" conversational style (see Tannen 2005, and her discussion of the 'California style' versus the 'New York Jewish style'), when contrasted with other cultural and language backgrounds, commonalities among American English styles may emerge. Within Tannen's (1984) and Brown and Levinson's (1987) model of rapport strategies, Brown and Levinson (1987) isolate several key conversational American beliefs that link to solidarity, with American interlocutors striving toward a common point of view and in-group membership. Byrnes (1986), on the other hand, places emphasis on the role that language plays in conveying information as opposed to creating social bonds in German conversational styles (pp. 200–201). German conversational style is marked by overlapping, short to non-existent pauses between turn-taking, the completion of interlocutors' sentences, and a more argumentative format (Byrnes 1986; Kothoff 1991, 1993; Straehle 1998). On the other hand, American interactional style is focused more heavily on politeness strategies. The importance of politeness in the American style can be noted by clear turn-taking with relatively little overlap and a willingness to cede the floor should overlap occur (Berry 1994; Byrnes 1986).

Research comparing German and American conversational styles has shown that each group exhibits distinct communicative behavior patterns, influenced by the relationship between hearer and listener, the type of interaction, and the traits of the interlocutors (see Clyne 1995; House & Kasper 1981; Nees 2000; Schmidt 2001). For example, Straehle (1998) found differences in German and American conversational strategies, despite both being what Tannen (1984) referred to as "high-involvement" conversational styles. Straehle (1998) posited that Americans frame much of their conversation in a 'storytelling context', relying on involvement strategies while Germans frame conversation in an 'agonistic discussion', relying more on argument-building tactics. This fits into Kotthoff's (1991, 1993) German conversational 'opposition format', in which conversationalists in German are expected to undermine their interlocutors' position in order to strengthen their own. Schleef (2009), in a quantitative analysis of naturally occurring speech of American and German lecturers and their students, found differences in the academic discourse. His analysis led him to four contrastive stylistic parameters: "(1) formality; (2) student-teacher interactivity; (3) discourse structure and speech management; and (4) conversational support and conversational contrast" (Schleef 2009: 1121). These parameters support a German academic discourse style with a higher degree of formality, less speech management devices to maintain student comprehension, and more use of linguistic devices (e.g., but, well) that express contrasting opinions in a turn-initial position.

Overall, patterns of conversational style suggest some differences between American speakers of English and native German speakers. Before detailing learners' reactions to these differences, we first review some of the necessary constructs of discourse analysis relevant to the present study.

Features of conversational interaction

One feature of conversational style relevant to the investigation of a naturalistic interactional L2 setting is control of the conversational floor. Edelsky explains conversational floor control as a conversational setting that can be either a "one-at-a-time type of floor" or "a collaborative venture where two or more people either t[ake] part in an apparent free-for-all or jointly buil[d] one idea," (1981: 384). Within the context of this study, when the L2 conversation group meets and holds a group discussion, they are all building a "collaborative floor." This is distinct from a classroom setting where a "one-at-a-time" structure typically occurs, with the instructor controlling the overall allowance of turn-taking by "calling" on participants and then "yielding the floor" to them (Duncan 1972). Thus, there are clues in how students in a conversation group are participating in their own L2 acquisition by the frequency and character of their turns as they collaboratively build the floor. However, learning to share the floor in the L2 style may not be a simple task. There is a difference between *sharing* the floor through collaborative overlap and *taking* the floor through interruption (Schegloff 2000; Tannen 1990), and it is plausible that learners may have difficulty distinguishing between the two. Interruption involves a second speaker beginning her turn while the first speaker is still taking her turn, with the effect of the second speaker ultimately taking the floor from the first. Collaborative overlap, as defined by Schegloff (2000), occurs when "one participant initiates an utterance and provides for another to complete it," (p. 6). Thus, collaborative overlap is a sharing of the floor between participants who often have the same linguistic style (Tannen 1990). However, communication issues can arise when participants do not or cannot negotiate this practice of sharing the floor, and may instead interpret collaborative overlap as interruption. This miscommunication may lead to social misunderstanding, or may even impact the effectiveness of subsequent interactions and opportunities for negotiation of meaning. Moreover, learning the conversational features that permit successful and acceptable control of the floor may lead to more opportunities for production and modified output, making floor control an area of L2 development worthy of investigation. Although previous sociolinguistic research has examined control of the floor using number and length of turns (Schegloff 2000; Tannen 1990), these conversational structures have been underexplored in interaction research in SLA settings.

Another conversational feature worthy of study in an L2 context is topic change. Traditional discourse analysis (e.g. Murray 1985; Sacks, Schegloff, & Jefferson 1974) has suggested that the initiation of topic changes can be considered as a specific type of turn used to gain control of the floor through negotiation rather than sharing. Speakers who take the most turns or who are successfully able to initiate the majority of topic changes in a conversation, may also negotiate more control of the floor. Once again, such successful management of the floor may potentially lead to increased production and modified output opportunities.

Overall, fostering learners' abilities to notice, and potentially adopt, features of L2 conversational style is an important interaction-driven aspect of L2 learning not often addressed within traditional lab-based and classroom contexts. Naturalistic settings, such as the conversation groups from which our data are extracted, may offer learners more authentic conversational opportunities than the classroom. Thus, the social and collaborative nature of the conversation groups offers learners opportunities to acquire features of L2 conversational structure, as well as grammatical structures and lexical items. Seeking to address these gaps in the literature, this exploratory study uses a discourse analysis approach to explore interaction-driven development in the unique L2 context of a conversation group.

Methods

Context of the study

Regularly used as supplementary practice to formal instruction within educational contexts, L2 conversation groups provide learners opportunities to practice oral language skills in a naturalistic and authentic language setting. Conversation groups may take on various forms depending on the linguistic, social, or educational context, varying widely in structure and formality, with some groups relying on prepared topics, tasks, or games to ensure continuous conversation and inclusion of all proficiency levels, while others may rely solely on the participants to conceive of topics for spontaneous conversation. Conversation groups may be led by native or non-native speakers of the target language and may include participants of similar or varying levels of proficiency.

However, regardless of the leadership structure or levels of formality, conversation groups provide students of all proficiency levels the opportunity to practice oral interaction in a less formal setting than the classroom. Because conversation groups are designed to reduce anxiety and provide a comfortable atmosphere, they provide an environment in which learners can practice their L2 skills and test their hypotheses about the language. Additionally, conversation groups offer components found in well-structured tasks, e.g., a setting in which learners can freely make mistakes and participate in authentic oral interaction. In addition, they give speakers a unique setting in which to observe and acquire L2 conversational features, including conventions of topic initiation and turn taking, through the use of naturally occurring language. Although there may be a great deal of individual variation across cultural and social contexts, conversation groups provide an informal atmosphere outside of the classroom for learners to practice and improve their L2 abilities.

In terms of SLA, conversation groups also present researchers with unique opportunities not often found within classroom contexts. For example, social context is an important factor in interactions, and native speakers may be more likely to be perceived by participants as a true conversational partner rather than an instructor within a conversation group. This perception of the more experienced speaker as a partner may provide the researcher with differential interactional outcomes than what might occur in a more formal, structured classroom or lab environment.

Participants

The eleven German as a second language learners who participated in the research were recruited from intermediate level undergraduate German courses at Georgetown University. Biographical details appear in Table 1 below, and pseudonyms have been given for all participants. All participants were native speakers of English. The participants' length of previous German instruction ranged from one semester to seven years, with an average of 2.46 years ($SD = 2.42$) of formal instruction. Only one student, who also happened to have had the most formal instruction, was a declared German major with previous experience participating in a conversation group. All other participants were enrolled in German courses as electives or to meet foreign language requirements, and had no previous experience in conversation groups. Proficiency levels were determined by the German Department's placement test and were also self-reported on a questionnaire.

Table 1. Biographical data of participants

German pseudonym	Gender	Age	Years studying
Nathaniel	M	19	.5
David	M	20	5
Bryan	M	19	7
Jacob	M	18	1
Meg	F	18	3
Katherine	F	21	6
Molly	F	20	1
Amanda	F	20	1.5
Deanna	F	19	1
Mark	M	19	.5
Anne	F	18	1

Design

In order to keep the group size small and to encourage a friendly and intimate atmosphere, participants were assigned to one of two conversation groups depending on their schedule and availability. Each conversation group met for one hour each week for six consecutive weeks. Each of the 11 participants completed a biographical data and language survey prior to the first conversation group meeting, as well as a language survey, exit survey, and exit interview following the last meeting. Language surveys were designed to elicit participants' self-assessment of their speaking, listening, grammar, and vocabulary skills, while the exit survey and interview were designed to obtain richer data regarding learners' experiences and perceptions regarding the conversation group.

Data collection procedure

The data for the current research came from audio and video recordings of two German as an L2 conversation groups, as well as surveys and interviews prior to and following completion of the study. All conversation group meetings were held in a conference room located on the participants' university campus. Meetings were both audio taped using handheld digital recorders and video taped using a Flip video camera stationed on a tripod. They were moderated by the third author, who is a native speaker of German and an experienced German as a foreign language instructor. None of the participants were currently in a class taught by the moderator, thus eliminating the possibility of confusion surrounding the moderator's role in the different contexts.

Because the overall goal of this study was to examine what happens in learner interactions in a naturalistic setting, the moderator aimed to create an environment that maintained learner engagement regardless of their level of language production. Following Gamble and Gamble (2004), who state that in conversation "speakers need to speak so that listeners can listen, and listeners need to keep in mind that they are not just waiting to speak but need to be actively involved in listening" (p. 123), the moderator encouraged participants to actively listen as well as speak. In addition, this allowed the moderator to assume a role more akin to a knowledgeable peer rather than an instructor. This allowed her to scaffold participants' learning and coordinate their turns as needed, maximizing the interaction between the participants rather than between the moderator and individual learners.

In order to retain a supporting rather than instructional role, thus limiting the provision of corrective feedback and maintaining the naturalistic features of interpersonal conversation, the moderator focused on responding to the content of participants' utterances through verbal and non-verbal messages, such as signaling interest and encouragement or opening the floor with general questions. However, in an effort to prevent learner frustration and to provide guidance when necessary, the moderator provided linguistic scaffolding in the form of lexical or grammatical suggestions, either when explicitly asked by a participant or when it was deemed necessary to aid the continuing flow of natural conversation. The moderator also used pre-selected discussion topics when it was necessary to initiate a topic to maintain continuous conversation within the group. Topics for discussion were self-selected by the participants through responses on the pre-study language survey, including general themes such as undergraduate life, German and American film and music, and life in Germany.

Although all conversation group meetings were recorded, only the initial, medial and final sessions were transcribed and analyzed for the current research (please see Appendix for transcription conventions). Table 2 provides additional details regarding the analyzed data and the data collection timeline.

Table 2. Data collection timeline used for the current study

Timeline	Data
Pre-study	Background survey
	Language survey
Week 1	Initial conversation group meeting
	Audio recording and transcription
	Video recording of initial meeting
Week 3	Medial conversation group meeting
	Audio recording and transcription
	Video recording of medial meeting
Week 6	Final conversation group meeting
	Audio recording and transcription
	Video recording of final meeting
Post-study	Exit surveys and interviews
(most interviews	Language survey
conducted within	Data validation interviews
2 weeks of the	
end of the study)	

Analysis

This study was exploratory in nature and sought to investigate how the development of L2 learners benefited from interaction in a naturalistic setting. Using a data-driven approach to identify key themes with minimal *a priori* assumptions, we began by watching the videos and listening to the audio recordings of each conversation group meeting. In order to gain a holistic perspective of the significant themes emerging within the data, sessions were examined on an individual level as well as across the six weeks of the study. Out of six sessions, the first, third, and sixth sessions were selected based on their representation of participants' baseline, middle and final conversational behaviors. After reviewing these sessions, we noticed that the amount of overlap occurring between the moderator and the learners, as well as between the learners themselves, varied across the sessions. In addition, the conversational format of the interaction, for example, whether it was more representative of a classroom question and answer with the moderator controlling the floor, or if it was more of a natural conversational style, also emerged as a dominant theme. These initial analyses seemed to indicate that the moderator was holding the floor most often during the first meeting. However, by the sixth and final meeting, we noticed that a number of learners in each conversation group had begun to collaboratively overlap through sharing control of the floor with the moderator and appeared to be imitating her conversational style. These data-driven observations were then triangulated with participants' independent reactions, including their observations and perceptions of group dynamics and conversational styles, in a second set of interviews. During these interviews, participants listened to playback of the sessions used for analysis, and provided their perspective of the interactions. In addition, transcripts of sections selected for analysis were checked and confirmed by the participants.

To further investigate the data, the researcher/moderator coded 100% of the transcriptions of the initial, medial, and final conversation group meetings selected for analysis. Transcripts were coded for the number of turns for each individual learner and occurrence of topic initiation, including if a previous topic was re-introduced. Transcripts were then coded to identify learners' control of the floor and participation in the group meeting. Floor control was operationalized as the number of topic introductions by each learner while participation was operationalized as the number of turns. A co-researcher then reviewed the coding and either agreed or disagreed with what was marked as a new topic or a return to a topic. Disagreements were discussed, and the researchers reached 100% agreement before continuing with further analyses.

Results and discussion

Overall, the analyses suggest that over the six weeks of the study, the participants either became more active interactors, by which we mean that they increased their participation and control of the floor from the first to the final meeting, or more passive interactors, indicating that they reduced their participation and adopted the role of listeners more than speakers over the course of the study. We argue that one reason learners became more passive interactors was because they were less able to identify and adapt to the native German conversational style, either consciously or unconsciously, defined by the pace and flow of the discourse, while the more active interactors were more able to recognize and utilize German discourse structure.

We support this argument by first providing native speaker and learner examples of typical German conversational style found in this data and in previous research. We then illustrate how learners' success or failure to adopt German conversational style led to the learners' more active or passive roles. Although some learners may have been more successful than others at using German discourse structure, regardless of their level of interaction, we suggest that all learners appeared to benefit in some way from participation, particularly regarding their levels of confidence and willingness to communicate (WTC), as evidenced from their interview and survey data.

Conversational style and control of the floor

The analysis of participation and control of the floor reveals striking changes in some of the learners' conversational styles across the six weeks of the study. For example, the interaction in the first meeting in Group B follows what might be considered an American conversational style, with the control of the floor relatively evenly shared between the learners. One speaker speaks at a time, with minimal instances of overlap. As this was the first group meeting and much of the conversation consisted of sharing information and discussing introductory topics designed to help students get to know one another, this was not an unexpected finding. However, discussions of general topics produced similar interactions, with learners sharing the control of the floor. In the Excerpt (1) below, taken from Group B's first group meeting, this shared control of the floor is illustrated through the learners' lack of interruptions or overlap. Rather, speakers only seem to respond to a previous utterance when it is clear the interlocutor's turn is complete. Excerpt (1), which follows American discourse style, is taken from a conversation involving Bryan, Meg, and Jacob, three of the learners in Group B, and S., the moderator.

(1)   1   B: Ähm es ist bei ähm Tenleytown.
      2   M: Welche Instrument.
      3   B: Ich spiele Gitarre,
      4   M: Hm.
      5   B: Bluesguitarre. (laughs)
      6   S: Und ihr macht Bluesmusik.
      7   B: Ja.=
      8   S: =Oh cool.
      9   B: Ich habe ein Radioshow am Georgetown Radio… Donnerstag elf
    10   bis midnight. (laughs)

11	M:	Kennst du das wir haben or wir recording studios?
12	S:	Hä?
13	M:	Recording studios. Wie sagt man recording studios?
14	S:	Aufnahmestudios.
15	M:	Aufnamestudios hier in Georgetown du kannst äh für kostenlos…
16		äh… rent? Wie sagt man rent or like check out?
17	J:	Meit.
18	S:	Mieten.
19	M:	Mieten, ja in Lau also.
20	B:	Für keine Geld?
21	M:	Kein Geld. Du musst zu Gelardin gehen. (laughs)

1	B:	*Um it is near um Tenleytown.*
2	M:	*What instrument.*
3	B:	*I play the guitar.*
4	M:	*Hm.*
5	B:	*Blues guitar. (laughs)*
6	S:	*And you are playing blues music.*
7	B:	*Yes.=*
8	S:	*=Oh cool.*
9	B:	*I have a radio show at the Georgetown radio… Thursday eleven*
10		*till midnight. (laughs)*
11	M:	*Do you know that we have or we recording studios?*
12	S:	*Um?*
13	M:	*Recording studios. How do you say recording studios?*
14	S:	*Recording studios.*
15	M:	*Recording studio here at Georgetown you can um for free…*
16		*um… rent? How do you say rent or like check out?*
17	J:	*Rent. ((mispronounced))*
18	S:	*Rent. ((infinitive))*
19	M:	*Rent, yes, in Lau, so.*
20	B:	*For no money?*
21	M:	*No money. You have to go to Gelardin. (laughs)*

In line 13, Meg, identified by 'M' in the excerpt above, is making a bid for help with the use of the lexical item with rising intonation *recording studios?*, which indicates to the other learners and the moderator that she is seeking assistance. After the needed item is provided, Meg continues to speak in lines 15–16, again seeking help with a lexical item. Jacob provides the needed verb in line 17, although he mispronounces it. He is corrected by the moderator, at which point Meg seeks confirmation of the word and proceeds with her previous thought. Yet, throughout this process, the conversational participants take turns one at a time without overlap, thus following a more American conversational style.

By the third week, the moderator's control of the floor had increased from 16.7% to 42.4%, indicating that participants had progressed from shared control in session 1 to reduced floor control in session 3. Nathaniel, Jacob and David dramatically decrease their control of the floor, reducing control from approximately 16% to 3% in some cases, while only two learners, Bryan and Meg, maintain control rates similar to session 1. The Excerpt (2) below demonstrates that although learners are controlling the floor less than in the first session, they maintain a polite discourse style more similar to an American than a German style, with minimal overlap and clear turn-taking. Note that in this excerpt Meg is using the same conversational style as S., as seen in the latching done by the two of them (denoted by "="). David latches in line 5 and overlaps with Meg in line 12. This latching demonstrates a move from an American to a more German conversational style (in comparison to previous excerpt).

(2) 1 S: Ich bin am Montag nach Leesburg gefahren.
     2   Ich wollte in ein- in ein deutsches Restaurant gehen. (laughs)
     3   Und da gibt es ein Döner- kennt ihr Döner Kebab?
     4 M: Oh ja… Dön-
     5 D: =Ja, ja, ja.=
     6 M: =Ja. Wie Türkisch-
     7 S: =Ja.=
     8 M: =essen.=
     9 S: =Genau. Das gibt es in Leesburg. Und ich bin eine Stunde
    10   nach Leesburg gefahren und dann war es geschlossen.
    11 M: [Oh!]
    12 D: [Oh!] That sucks.
    13 S: Aber wenn ihr mal,
    14   Döner Kebab essen wollt oder,
    15   äh Currywurst-
    16 M: =Um: ja.=
    17 S: =oder deutsches Bier. Das gibt es in einem Restaurant in Leesburg.

     1 S: *I went to Leesburg Monday.*
     2   *I wanted to go to a- to a German restaurant. (laughs)*
     3   *And there is Döner there- do you guys know Döner Kebab?*
     4 M: *Oh yeah… Dön-*
     5 D: *=Yeah, yeah, yeah.=*
     6 M: *=Yeah. Like Turkish-*
     7 S: *=Yeah.=*
     8 M: *=food.=*
     9 S: *=Exactly. It's in Leesburg. And I went an hour*
    10   *to Leesburg and then it was closed.*
    11 M: *[Oh!]*

12   D: *[Oh.!] That sucks.*
13   S: *But if you guys want to eat,*
14   *Döner Kebab or,*
15   *uh Currywurst-*
16   M: *=Um: yeah.=*
17   S: *=or German beer. There's a restaurant in Leesburg with it.*

We hypothesize that the reduction in learner participation may have been a reaction to the unfamiliar German conversational style, with learners not noticing the new style or failing to adjust to a more native speaker structure. However, it should also be acknowledged that speakers may also not have felt the need to adjust to the more aggressive German speaker style due to the relaxed environment of the conversation group. Bryan and Meg, the two most experienced German learners in this group, seem to encounter the least amount of difficulty here, evidenced by their relatively stable amount (less than six percent change) of floor control from session 1 to session 3. This is increasingly evidenced by the fact that by the final meeting in the sixth week, these same participants are relatively equal with the moderator in terms of control of the floor. Table 3 illustrates Group B's control of the floor across session 1, 3, and 6.

Table 3. Group B (topics/control of floor)

Participant	Week 1	Week 3	Week 6
Moderator	16.7%	42.4%	27.3%
Nathaniel	16.7%	3.0%	3.1%
David	16.7%	9.1%	12.5%
Bryan	20.8%	18.2%	30.3%
Jacob	12.5%	3.0%	3.1%
Meg	18.3%	24.2%	21.9%

In the sixth session, Nathaniel and Jacob have not increased their control of the floor more than 1/10 of a percent, suggesting that they have not adjusted to the German conversational style. Although David increases his participation by approximately 3% from session 3 to session 6, the floor control of these three learners in the last session is markedly different than the first session, with all three learners controlling the floor less than the other participants. As demonstrated in the following Excerpt (3), Bryan and Meg seem to have picked up on the native German conversational style modeled by the moderator and have adapted their interactions accordingly, sharing the floor nearly equally with the native speaker and successfully imitating the features of her conversational style.

(3)   1   B: Kennen Sie failblog=
      2   M: =Mhm.
      3   D: Was?
      4   M: [Failblog].

```
 5   B:   [Failblog] dot com… es ist- es gibt viele videos und Bil-
 6        Bilder das zeigt… ah… fails… [₂ von Leute].
 7   D:                                 [₂ Oh ja.]
 8   M:                                 [₂ Oh wie] Engrish dot com…
 9        [₃ fails].
10   B:   [₃ Es] ist viel besser aber nicht When Parents Text.=
11   M:   =Hm, ja!=
12   B:   =Das ist besser.=
13   M:   =Oder den XXX.
14   S:   Was ist das?
15   B:   When Parents Text like es ist es gibt texts ähm zwischen eltern und
16        ähm [kin]dern, und eltern kennt.
17   M:        [Kin-]
18   B:   Kennts- [₂ kennen] sie nicht über das technology… so das ist
19        lustig.=
20   M:              [₂ (laughs)]
21   S:   =Wie haben woher haben sie ähm die SMS…
22        SMS heißt [₃ text] message woher haben sie das?
23   M:              [₃ Ja.]
24   B:              [₃ Hm.]
25        Woher?=
26   M:   =Oh ähm internet, es gibt es die sie- sie [kann das-]
27   S:                                              [Aber ist] das nicht privat
28        oder-
29   M:   =Ähm, man kann das like senden [₂ und checken] XXX.
30   B:                                  [₂ You post it].
31   S:                                  [₂ Oh].
32   B:   [₃ Wenn seine eltern] lustig sind du [₄ gehst] an web.
33   M:   [₃ XXX]                               [₄ Ja].
 1   B:   Do you know failblog=
 2   M:   =Mhm.
 3   D:   What?
 4   M:   [Failblog].
 5   B:   [Failblog] dot com… there is- there are many videos and pic-
 6        pictures which show… uh… fails [₂ from people].
 7   D:                                  [₂ Oh yes].
 8   M:                                  [₂ Oh like] Engrish dot com…
 9        [₃ fails].
10   B:   [₃ It] is much better but not When Parents Text.=
11   M:   =Hm, yes!=
12   B:   =That is better.=
```

13 M: =Or the XXX.
14 S: What is that?
15 B: When Parents Text like it is there is texts um between parents and
16   um [chil]dren, and parents knows.
17 M: [Chil-]
18 B: Knows- [₂ know] they not about technology... that is so
19   funny.=
20 M: [₂ (laughs)]
21 S: =How have where do they have them from um the SMS...
22   SMS means [₃ text] message where do they have it from?
23 M: [₃ Yes].
24 B: [₃ Hm].
25   Where from?=
26 M: =Oh um internet, there is the they- they [can that-]
27 S: [But that] is not private
28   or-
29 M: =Um, one can um one can like send [₂ and check] XXX.
30 B: [₂ You post it].
31 S: [₂ Oh].
32 B: [₃ When his parents] are funny you [₄ go] to the web.
33 M: [₃ XXX]   [₄ Yes].

In line 11, Meg is latching on to Bryan's utterance when she utters *hm ja!*, which is indicative of German discourse style. Bryan and Meg continue to follow this style as they collaborate in the construction of the dialogue, building on each other's utterances and sharing the control of the floor. In lines 16–17, for example, Meg collaboratively overlaps with Bryan when she begins to say *children*. Bryan continues, and Meg, instead of finishing her utterance, agrees with Bryan's statement and pauses as the moderator becomes involved in the topic discussion. Line 25 demonstrates a comprehension check from Bryan when he utters *woher*, as he attempts to clarify his understanding of the moderator's question. Meg provides the response in line 26, quickly latching on to Bryan's response and providing the information herself. The native speaker moderator then interrupts Meg's utterance in lines 27–28 by saying *aber ist das nicht privat oder*. These learners, having figured out the native speaker style modeled by the moderator, have become the more active interactors, sharing the floor with the native speaker and dominating the conversation more than the remaining participants. The learners who became more passive participants, on the other hand, spend a sizeable portion of the interactions providing American style backchanneling (e.g. *ja* [yeah]), which the more active learners talk over.

Turning to Group A, learners demonstrate a similar pattern regarding the adoption of German conversational style, yet the interactions are slightly different due to the presence and absence of Anne, suggesting that the social relationships between learners played a particularly influential role in determining learners' levels of floor control.

For example, when Anne is present in the first session, she immediately shares the floor with the moderator (39.5%), although her floor control remains at a slightly lower level (26.3%). The remaining learners, with the exception of Deanna, share control of the floor less than 8% of the time. This is in stark contrast to the first session in Group B, in which all of the learners shared the floor somewhat equally with the moderator, controlling the floor between 8%–16.7%. When Anne is absent in the third session, the other learners share floor control more equally, with most participants (especially Katherine, Molly, and Amanda) raising their control of the floor noticeably from session 1 to session 3. Table 4 illustrates floor control for Group A.

Table 4. Group A (topics/control of floor)

Participant	Week 1	Week 3	Week 6
Moderator	39.5%	33.3%	30.1%
Katherine	7.9%	20.0%	12.8%
Molly	2.6%	13.3%	5.1%
Amanda	5.3%	16.7%	15.4%
Deanna	15.8%	10.0%	12.8%
Mark	2.6%	6.7%	5.1%
Anne	26.3%	Not present	17.9%

However, when Anne returns in the final session, she again takes back a large amount of floor control in proportion to the other learners. Despite Anne's dominance and success in taking control of the floor, Amanda and Deanna maintain a high degree of participation as well. Katherine's participation also remains relatively high, in contrast to the decrease in floor control exhibited by Molly and Mark. The primary contributors to these discussions are the moderator, Amanda and Deanna, with Mark and Molly as more passive interactors, providing mainly backchanneling. The decreased participation of Mark and Molly seems to indicate that they have not yet successfully negotiated the interactional structure of German discourse, while Katherine, Amanda, and Deanna have begun to adopt features of a more German conversational style. Nathaniel and Jacob, in Group B, have likewise not adapted to the native German conversational style, and are frequently unsuccessful at taking the floor and regularly interrupted by the other learners. Similar to the passive interactors in Group A, their continued use of a more American conversational style, which does not use overlap and interruptions to the same degree as the German style, results in reduced floor control, subsequently leading to decreased interactional opportunities. In failing to adopt the German conversational style, Nathaniel, Jacob, Molly, and Mark have become more passive interactors, participating through listening rather than through speaking.

Although they continue to receive the same input as the more active participants, their opportunities for output have decreased along with their control of the floor. However, as previous research has suggested (Ellis, Tanaka, & Yamazaki 1994; Mackey 1999; Pica

1992), learners need not be active interactors to still benefit developmentally. For example, Mackey found that learners who observed interactions but did not participate, still demonstrated slight increases in developmental stages, suggesting that passive interaction may also be somewhat beneficial to L2 development. Similar to the observer group in Mackey's study, the more passive interactors in the current research were exposed to negotiations for meaning, modified output opportunities, and corrective feedback that may have occurred between the moderator and the active interactors. Swain's Output Hypothesis (Swain 1985, 1995) suggests that output is a critical component of L2 development, and because of the exposure to modified output opportunities produced by the more active participants, passive interactors may also be able to benefit from these interactional opportunities. For example, in the following Excerpt (4), we see that the moderator has asked one of the learners about her weekend. When the moderator (indicated by S.) asks Deanna about the film she watched, she doesn't understand, and the moderator repeats the question. However, rather than Deanna providing the answer, Mark, a more passive interactor, provides the target word. Although Mark's involvement overall is more passive than active, this example demonstrates that despite not having produced the original utterance, Mark is still presented with opportunities for interactional benefit. That is, although Mark was not actively participating in the interaction, he was still attending to the input and was able to produce output in response to the moderator's repetition, suggesting that passive interactors are still able to benefit from the positive effects commonly associated with interaction.

(4) 1 S: Und hast den Film gesehen mit deinem Freund?
2 D: Ja. (laughs)
3 S: Hat sich's gelohnt?
4 D: Was?
5 S: Hat sich der Film gelohnt? Lohnen. Kennt ihr das?
6 Das lohnt sich?
7 M: Is it worth it?
8 S: Ja.
9 D: Oh. Yeah.

1 S: *And you saw the film with your boyfriend?*
2 D: *Yeah. (laughs)*
3 S: *Was it worth it?*
4 D: *What?*
5 S: *Was the film worth it? Worth it. Do you guys know that?*
6 *To be worth it?*
7 M: *Is it worth it?*
8 S: *Yeah.*
9 D: *Oh. Yeah.*

Although passive interactors' abilities to adapt to the dominant conversational style may impact their interaction, low floor control does not necessarily indicate low participation. For example, when considering the number of turns for Group B, Jacob, a more passive interactor according to his low proportion of floor control, produces a high number of turns. Although the data indicate that Jacob does not introduce as many topics as his peers, he continues to participate in the conversations. However, his turn taking and topic control follow an American style, thus reducing his possibilities for interaction despite his continued turn taking. Active interactors, on the other hand, seem to not only maintain a high proportion of control of the floor, but also a greater number of turns overall when compared to the passive interactors. For example, the more active interactors in Group B, Bryan and Meg, initiate more turns in both session 3 and session 6, while Anne, Deanna, and Katherine in Group A produce the most turns of the learners in their middle and final sessions. Tables 5 and 6 indicate the turns per learner in each group.

Table 5. Group A (turns/participation)

Participant	Week 1	Week 3	Week 6
Moderator	27.9%	26.3%	25.3%
Katherine	15.1%	12.4%	20.1%
Molly	4.7%	12.4%	5.2%
Amanda	11.8%	12.7%	6.5%
Deanna	14.8%	25.4%	18.8%
Mark	7.4%	10.9%	6.5%
Anne	18.4%	Not present	17.6%

Table 6. Group B (turns/participation)

Participant	Week 1	Week 3	Week 6
Moderator	21.3%	24.9%	24.8%
Nathaniel	15.2%	6.2%	3.6%
David	13.4%	15.6%	9.2%
Bryan	13.4%	17.0%	27.1%
Jacob	19.1%	9.7%	13.2%
Meg	7.6%	26.6%	22.1%

Overall, the data suggest that within naturalistic settings, the passive interactors are those learners who did not change their conversational style to match that of the more advanced speakers, as evidenced in their control of the floor, resulting in reduced interactional opportunities. Although the more active interactors, defined as those learners who were successful in adapting to the native German speaker style, may have had more output opportunities due to their higher floor control and participation, all learners were exposed to the same amounts of input. Our findings indicate that regardless of whether learners are passively or actively involved in the interaction, they are still provided with input, feed-back, and output opportunities. This suggests that learner participation in conversation groups may still result in positive effects commonly associated with interaction, such as increased opportunities for modified output and meaning negotiation, regardless of their level of interaction. For example, learners who did not initiate topics were still able to participate in the ensuing discussion, thereby producing speech and increasing their opportunities for modified output. Learners that had low levels of participation were still able to attend to input through active listening and observation of other learners in the group. This provided additional opportunities for learners to notice mismatches between their language and that of their peers when compared to the language of more advanced learners or a native speaker.

Confidence and willingness to communicate

Learners' exit surveys and interviews indicated additional benefits, namely that they felt more confident and willing to communicate due to participation in the conversation group. For example, in his exit interview, Jacob, who was one of the more passive interactors, said, "I feel like I'm confident enough that I could stumble through German in front of a native speaker and not be embarrassed." Although the data demonstrate that Jacob's control of the floor and turn taking were some of the lowest in his group, 4% and 13.2% respectively, his interview data indicate that he felt he benefited from participation and was now confident enough to communicate with native speakers in the target language environment. Even though his participation in the interactions was minimal compared to other learners, he was able to benefit from the interaction in a positive way.

In addition, learners reported feeling more confident in class. For example, on his exit survey, David remarked that "as a result of the German conversation group, I am more willing to communicate to another German speaker inside or outside of class." This quote demonstrates that the conversation group contributed to his willingness to communicate in both naturalistic settings and classroom contexts. The ability of conversation groups to improve WTC and confidence for in-class communication is further evidenced by Amanda, who stated on her exit survey that she had "more confidence speaking in class." These findings suggest that interaction within conversation groups may have wide ranging positive effects for learners in both academic and social settings.

Participation in the informal, and more social, atmosphere of the conversation group seems to have provided learners with an environment free from judgment in which they felt they could freely test their hypotheses and make mistakes. This notion is supported by learner interview data in which learners discussed that they felt more comfortable making mistakes with each other than they did in class. For example, Anne remarks that "it was more relaxed…if people feel less pressured that everything has to be perfect, then that means they'll be more willing to speak out, and that means they get to practice more." This statement demonstrates that settings such as conversation groups, where the informal nature of the context is emphasized, may provide anxious or introverted learners with interaction and speaking opportunities they may not have had in class. Furthermore, in his interview, David discusses how in his German class, he felt he needed to prepare all his utterances on paper, checking for grammar and practicing the pronunciation silently to himself, before speaking or interacting with other students. He was afraid he would be corrected harshly by his instructors and did not want to embarrass himself in front of his peers. In the conversation group, however, the more relaxed environment contributed to his ability to produce more spontaneous speech.

Learners also found the conversation group to be an environment encouraging of collaborative learning. For example, because the moderator's role was one more akin to participant than instructor, learners were largely responsible for providing each other with corrective and interactional feedback, or lexical and grammatical assistance. In an exit interview, when asked what role correction played with the group, Jacob responded, "It wasn't so much correction, but looking for a word and someone would supply it. Or if it was a little bit off, it wasn't correction but filling in gaps. And that worked really well, actually." The learner is describing how participants assisted one another with form and meaning during their interactions by "filling gaps" and supplying words, thus providing one another with feedback and modified output opportunities. Referring to instances where a speaker may not know a lexical item, Bryan states, "Everyone would start guessing together. We'd all shoot out our guesses and if not one could figure it out, we'd be like "(Moderator)"?" This remark demonstrates how the learners interacted as a group to address the gaps in their language abilities, demonstrating how interaction was shared among the participants.

Because the moderator only provided feedback when requested, the learners pushed each other to find the language to further the conversation. By having to assist one another in solving form and meaning difficulties, learners received needed opportunities to test their hypotheses and demonstrate their knowledge of the target language, subsequently building their confidence in their abilities to make online linguistic decisions in real time. This confidence may have led to learners' increased WTC in classroom and real world contexts, suggesting that overall, conversation groups positively contributed to learners' development through the improvement of their communicative abilities.

To summarize, this study examines the interaction-driven development of L2 conversational style in an environment representative of authentic, real-world conversational contexts. Following the model of the native speaking moderator, learners developed into either more passive or more active interactors based on their ability to identify and use, consciously or unconsciously, German conversational style in the group interactions. Based on our analysis, learners who did not identify and adapt to the native German conversational style, such as the pace and flow of the discourse, had less control of the floor and fewer topic initiations than learners that did adapt to German conversational style, and thus assumed a more passive interactor role. The more active interactors may have had more interactional opportunities due to their increased floor control and overall participation; however, passive learners were still able to attend to the input and modified output of their peers, providing them with opportunities to benefit from the positive effects associated with interaction. Finally, although adoption of German conversation styles was not uniform, nearly all learners reported positive outcomes due to participation in the conversation group, with many learners reporting improved willingness to communicate and greater confidence in their exit interviews and surveys.

Conclusion

This exploratory study provides an initial look at the developmental benefits of interaction in the naturalistic, informal context of L2 conversation groups. We argue that the results from these data demonstrate that L2 conversation groups are valuable in that they provide participants with interaction-driven learning opportunities. In addition, conversation groups give learners the opportunity to learn native-like conversational structure in an environment more representative of real world conversational contexts than a traditional classroom or lab-based interaction might be. Conversation groups with native speaker participants may result in improved knowledge of L2 conversation structures by providing opportunities for learners to become more fluent in language specific turn-taking structure, including knowledge of specific floor-taking and floor-holding strategies. By developing these abilities, learners may gain more opportunities for interaction as they improve their ability to more evenly distribute control of the floor. However, regardless of their ability to identify and use conversational styles, learners still stand to benefit from exposure to modified input and output opportunities occurring within the conversation group, suggesting that conversation groups may provide both active and passive learners with interactional benefits. Furthermore, participation in these conversation groups seemed to have a clear positive impact on learners' confidence and willingness to communicate in real-world authentic contexts. These results suggest that conversation groups may drive L2 development by providing opportunities for learners to acquire conversational features important to L2 communication, as well as additional opportunities for learners to experience the positive developmental benefits commonly associated with interaction. The current data suggest that conversation groups, when used as a supplement to foreign language instruction, afford learners valuable speaking and listening practice in a naturalistic setting, providing them with an environment where they might feel more comfortable trying out new words and hypotheses, thus potentially leading to increased output or interaction.

Conversation groups not only provide learners with unique opportunities to develop L2 conversational competence. They also present valuable second language research opportunities. The naturalistic context of conversation groups not only provides SLA researchers with the chance to examine naturally occurring oral interactions, but also with additional research opportunities not often found within classroom or lab-based environments. For example, complex social aspects of language learning, such as the effects of peer relationships on L2 development, may be more accessible in the informal setting of the conversation group than in structured classrooms. Although this study takes an initial step in examining the L2 learning outcomes associated with conversation groups, more research is needed to explore such hypotheses in this unique and under-investigated context.

Limitations and future research

Although this exploratory research provided general and particular descriptions of the discourse-level L2 development associated with interaction in conversation groups, giving a fresh perspective on the benefits of multiple levels of interaction in a naturalistic, informal setting, it is important to acknowledge the limitations of this study. Perhaps the most prominent limitation is that the conclusions drawn from this descriptive research are based on two groups of learners in a specific social context at a single educational institution and therefore should not be generalized to other social and educational contexts without a more diverse pool of data. A further limitation is the short duration of the study. Participants met only once per week for six consecutive weeks, a short amount of time considering language learning is a complex and difficult process. Future research should consider examining the effects of conversation groups over a longer period of time more representative of educational contexts, such as a semester or academic year. In addition, future research in other foreign language learning environments with learners of different proficiency levels will provide more information regarding the benefits of interaction in conversation groups. It also would be of value to compare conversation groups with different levels of structure, examining relatively informal groups, like the one in this study, with more formal groups with added structure.

Overall, this study takes an important first step in examining the effects of interaction on second language development outside of the traditional lab and classroom-based contexts, finding that conversation groups provide learners with opportunities to learn L2 conversational structure in an informal environment, as well as improve their confidence and willingness to communicate in the target language. This research highlights the fact that learners acquire language in a variety of contexts, and in order to further our understanding of the benefits of interaction on multiple levels, additional research in naturalistic settings is needed.

References

Batstone, R. (Ed.). (2010). *Sociocognitive perspectives on language use and language learning*. Oxford: Oxford University Press.
Berry, A. (1994). Spanish and American turn-taking styles: A comparative study. *Pragmatics and Language Learning Monograph Series, 5*, 180–190.
Brock, C., Crookes, G., Day, R. R., & Long, M. H. (1986). Differential effects of Corrective feedback on second language performance. In R. R. Day (Ed.), *"Talking to learn": Conversation in second language acquisition* (pp. 229–36). Rowley, MA: Newbury House.
Brown, P., & Levinson, S. (1987). *Politeness: Some universals in language usage*. Cambridge: Cambridge University Press.
Byrnes, H. (1986). Interactional style in German and American conversations. *Text, 6*, 189–206.
Clyne, M. (1995). *The German language in a changing Europe*. Cambridge: Cambridge University Press.

De Fina, A., Schiffrin, D., & Bamberg, M. (1999). *Reinventing identities: The gendered self in discourse.* Oxford: Oxford University Press.

Duncan, S. (1972). Some signals and rules for taking speaking turns in conversation. *Journal of Personality and Social Psychology, 23*, 283–293.

Edelsky, C. (1981). Who's got the floor? *Language in Society, 10*, 383–421.

Ellis, R., Tanaka, Y., & Yamazaki, A. (1994). Classroom interaction, comprehension, and the acquisition of L2 word meanings. *Language Learning, 44*, 449–491.

Gamble, T. K., & Gamble, M. W. (2004). *Contacts: Interpersonal communication in theory, practice, and context.* Upper Sadle River, NJ: Prentice Hall.

Gass, S. M., & Varonis, E. M. (1985). Task variation and non-native/non-native negotiation of meaning. In S. M. Gass & C. G. Madden (Eds.), *Input in second language acquisition* (pp. 149–161). Rowley, MA: Newbury House.

House, J., & Kasper, G. (1981). Politeness markers in English and German. In F. Coulmas (Ed.), *Conversational routine: Explorations in standardized communication situations and prepatterned speech* (pp. 157–185). The Hague: Mouton.

Keck, C. M., Iberri-Shea, G., Tracy-Ventura, N., & Wa-Mbaleka, S. (2006). Investigating the empirical link between task-based interaction and acquisition: A meta-analysis. In J. M. Norris & L. Ortega (Eds.), *Synthesizing research on language learning and teaching* (pp. 91–131). Amsterdam: John Benjamins.

Kotthoff, H. (1991). Lernersprachliche und interkulturelle Ursachen für kommunikative Irritationen. *Linguistiche Berichte, 135*, 375–397.

Kotthoff, H. (1993). Disagreement and concession in disputes: On the context sensitivity of preference structures. *Language and Society, 22*, 193–216.

Lantolf, J. P. (Ed.). (2000). *Sociocultural theory and second language learning.* Oxford: Oxford University Press.

Mackey, A. (1999). Input, interaction and second language development: An empirical study of question formation in ESL. *Studies in Second Language Acquisition, 21*, 557–587.

Mackey, A., & Goo, J. (2007). Interaction research in SLA: A meta-analysis and research synthesis. In A. Mackey (Ed.), *Conversational interaction in second language acquisition: A collection of empirical studies* (pp. 407–452). Oxford: Oxford University Press.

Mackey, A., & Oliver, R. (2002). Interactional feedback and children's L2 development. *System, 30*, 459–477.

Mackey, A., Oliver, R., & Leeman, J. (2003). Interactional input and the incorporation of feedback: An exploration of NS-NNS and NNS-NNS adult and child dyads. *Language Learning, 53*, 35–66.

Murray, S. O. (1985). Toward a model of members' methods for recognizing interruptions. *Language in Society, 14*, 31–40.

Nees, G. (2000). *Germany: Unraveling an enigma.* Yarmouth, ME: Intercultural Press.

Pica, T. (1992). The textual outcomes of native speaker–nonnative speaker negotiation: What do they reveal about second language learning? In C. Kramsch & S. McConnell-Ginet (Eds.), *Text and context: Cross-disciplinary perspectives on language study* (pp. 198–237). Lexington, MA: D. C. Heath & Co.

Pica, T., Lincoln-Porter, F., Paninos, F., & Linnell, J. (1996). Language learners' interaction: How does it address input, output and feedback needs of L2 learners? *TESOL Quarterly, 30*, 59–84.

Polio, C., Gass, S., & Chapin, L. (2006). Using stimulated recall to investigate native speaker perception in native-nonnative speaker interaction. *Studies in Second Language Acquisition, 28*, 237–267.

Sacks, H., Schegloff, E. A., & Jefferson, G. (1974). A simplest systematics for the organization of turn-taking for conversation. *Language, 50*, 696–735.

Schegloff, E. A. (2000). Overlapping talk and the organization of turn-taking for conversation. *Language in Society, 29*, 1–63.

Schleef, E. (2009). Cross-cultural investigation of German and American academic style. *Journal of Pragmatics, 41,* 1104–1124.

Schmidt, P. L. (2001). *Understanding American and German business cultures.* Montreal: Meridian World Press.

Sharma, D. (2005). Dialect stabilization and speaker awareness in non-native varieties of English. *Journal of Sociolinguistics, 9,* 194–224.

Straehle, C. (1998). German and American conversational styles: A focus on narrative and agonistic discussion as a source of stereotypes. Unpublished PhD dissertation. Georgetown University.

Swain, M. (1985). Communicative competence: Some rules of comprehensible input and comprehensible output in its development. In S. Gass & C. Madden (Eds.), *Input in second language acquisition* (pp. 235–253). Rowley, MA: Newbury House.

Swain, M. (1995). Three functions of output in second language learning. In G. Cook & B. Seidlhofer (Eds.), *Principle and practice in applied linguistics: Studies in honour of H. G. Widdowson* (pp. 125–144). Oxford: Oxford University Press.

Swain, M., & Lapkin, S. (2001). Focus on form through collaborative dialogue: Exploring task effects. In M. Bygate, P. Skehan, & M. Swain (Eds.), *Researching pedagogic tasks: Second language learning, teaching and testing* (pp. 99–118). Harlow: Pearson Education.

Tannen, D. (1984). The pragmatics of cross-cultural communication. *Applied Linguistics, 5,* 189–195.

Tannen, D. (1990). *You just don't understand: Men and women in conversation.* New York, NY: Ballantine.

Tannen, D. (2005). *Conversational style: Analyzing talk among friends* (2nd edn). New York, NY: Oxford University Press.

Young, R. (1999). Sociolinguistic approaches to SLA. *Annual Review of Applied Linguistics, 19,* 105–132.

Appendix

Transcription conventions

…	Indicates a time gap of over half a second (roughly).
.	Periods indicate the end of an intonational unit with falling intonation.
,	Commas indicate the end of an intonational unit with a continuing intonation.
=	Indicates 'latching' between utterances.
[ ]	Square brackets between adjacent lines of concurrent speech indicate the onset and end of a spate of overlapping talk.
( )	A description enclosed in brackets indicates a non-verbal activity.
(( ))	Indicates commentary from transcriber
-	A dash indicates the sharp cut-off of the prior sound or word, as well as a false start.
:	Colons indicate that the speaker has stretched the preceding sound or letter.
?	A question mark indicates a rising inflection. It does not necessarily indicate a question.
XXX	Unintelligible speech.
Under	Underlined fragments indicate speaker emphasis.
CAPS	Words in capitals mark a section of speech noticeably louder than that surrounding it.

Chapter 15

Language production opportunities during whole-group interaction in conversation group settings

Kim McDonough and Teresa Hernández González
Concordia University

This study analyzes the whole-group interaction between preservice teachers (*N* = 15) and ESL speakers during conversation groups that were organized as part of the requirements of a TESL methods course. Analysis of the teacher-led interactions focused on the occurrence of language production opportunities provided to the ESL speakers as reflected through the amount of talk and questioning styles that occurred in four interactional contexts: communication, content, management and language. The findings indicate that the participants generated less talk than the teachers, management and content segments occurred most often, and referential questions were most frequent during content segments. Implications are discussed in terms of strategies for helping conversation group facilitators create language production opportunities.

Introduction

Reflecting its theoretical and methodological diversity, interaction research to date has demonstrated that a variety of language production opportunities, such as responses to interactional feedback, structural priming, and collaborative dialogue, positively impact L2 learning (eg., Lyster 2004; Mackey 1999; McDonough & Chaikitmongol 2010; Swain & Lapkin 2002). In this chapter, we focus on language production opportunities with the aim of identifying effective strategies used by preservice teachers to elicit talk during conversation groups organized as part of a TESL BEd program. Our long term goal is to positively impact the conversation group experience for the participating ESL speakers, thereby ensuring that both parties benefit from the partnership. Because prior studies have not analyzed teacher talk during practical training experiences, we instead review studies that have analyzed features of teacher talk in L2 classrooms or compared the interaction of experienced and novice teachers. The classroom discourse studies identify key characteristics of classroom talk that distinguish it from informal conversation, which will help situate the conversation groups within a continuum ranging from classroom discourse to informal conversation. The comparative studies of ESL teachers with varying levels of experience highlight the issues that may impact preservice teachers' interactions with ESL participants during the conversation groups (see Ziegler et al., this volume, for a description of interaction in a German conversation group).

Comparative studies of classroom discourse and informal conversation were carried out in the early interaction research to describe the linguistic and discourse features of conversation. Influenced by the literature on foreigner talk and claims about the importance of comprehensible input, these studies largely focused on how native speakers modify the linguistic or discourse features of conversation in order to facilitate communication with less proficient speakers. Situated in this framework, several studies (Long & Sato 1983; Pica & Long 1986) compared informal conversations between English L1 and L2 speakers with the whole-group classroom discourse (e.g., teacher-fronted interaction or teacher-led discourse) of ESL teachers with varying degrees of experience. In terms of discourse features, the classroom interaction contained more comprehension questions (i.e., the teacher asking whether the learners had understood what she said), while the informal conversations contained more confirmation and clarification questions (i.e., the native speakers clarified or confirmed whether they had understood the learner correctly). While the teacher talk consisted of a large number of display questions (questions that elicit known information), the informal conversations contained few display questions and were characterized by referential questions (questions that elicit unknown information). The findings suggested that unlike informal conversations, whole-class interaction was oriented toward comprehension, which manifested in the teachers' greater use of display questions and comprehension checks.

Whereas the early comparative studies detected few differences in the question types or quantity of talk produced by experienced and novice teachers (Pica & Long 1986), subsequent comparative research has identified some differences in experienced and novice teachers' whole-group interactions with L2 learners. In a classroom study, Mackey, Polio, and McDonough (2004) compared the classroom discourse of experienced and novice teachers who implemented lesson plans created by the researchers. Experienced teachers used significantly more explicit feedback, recasts, and preemptive techniques than the novice teachers, but there were no significant differences in the occurrence of negotiation (clarification and confirmation questions). A small scale follow up investigation revealed that novice teachers expressed concerns with whether the ESL learners had understood them and were less focused on the grammaticality of the learners' utterances. The tendency for novice teachers to focus on meaning, rather than language form, was also reported by Polio, Gass, and Chapin (2006), who investigated the impact of experience on L2 teachers' interactions with ESL learners during informal conversation. Learners who interacted with experienced teachers tended to produce more words than the learners who interacted with novice teachers, but there were no differences in the percentage of learner errors that were ignored, negotiated, or recast.

One interesting qualitative finding reported by Polio et al. (2006) may help explain the tendency for ESL learners to produce more language when they interacted with the experienced teachers. The task instructions given to the teachers emphasized that they should try to 'get the learner to talk' (p. 247). Based on the stimulated recall comments, the researchers suggested that the experienced teachers oriented to the goal of eliciting language production from the ESL learners, while the novice teachers were more oriented toward their own feelings about the interaction, such as their comprehension of the ESL learners' utterances. Unfortunately, the researchers did not report the number of words or turns produced by the teachers, so it is difficult to determine whether their differing orientations toward the task also impacted the quantity of teacher talk produced by the two groups. And although the teachers produced similar quantities of negotiation, they may have been negotiating for different reasons, with experienced teachers using negotiation sequences to elicit learner talk while novice teachers were negotiating to facilitate their own comprehension.

Research in other educational contexts, such as face-to-face writing conferences, similarly investigated the quantity of talk produced during tutor-learner interaction and revealed a tendency for the teacher or tutor to dominate conversation (Ewert 2009; Patthey-Chavez & Ferris 1997; Williams 2004). Prior studies have also shown that classroom discourse is characterized by the frequent use of display questions to elicit and evaluate learner knowledge (Abd-Kadir & Hardman 2007; Banbrook & Skehan 1989; Brock 1986; Golkar 2003; Gourlay 2005; Lee 2007; Muscumeci 1996; Nassaji & Wells 2000; Nunan 1990; Tan 2007; Waring 2009; Wu 1993), which impacts the quantity of learner talk generated in L2 classrooms. Fewer studies, however, have considered the quality of learner talk, specifically whether it reflects genuine communication. Genuine communication has been characterized as interaction in which interlocutors can decide how, what, and when to contribute, make efforts to ensure meaning has been communicated successfully (such as through efforts to clarify and confirm), have opportunities to nominate and change topics, and the distribution of unknown information is bidirectional (Nunan 1987). Although this type of communication is possible in a range of interactional settings, L2 classroom discourse may have an uneven distribution of speaking opportunities that makes genuine communication difficult (Dalton-Puffer 2005; Golkar 2003). Previous research with young English L2 learners (Oliver & Mackey 2003; Huang 2011) has shown that learner participation in classroom discourse is influenced by interactional context and whether that context is oriented toward content or language.

To summarize, prior studies have indicated that whole-group, teacher-led interaction in educational settings may be characterized by lower quantities of learner talk compared to informal conversation (Pica & Long 1986; Sato & Long 1983), and that preservice teachers may orient toward their own understanding rather than to the characteristics of learner talk (Mackey et al. 2004; Polio et al. 2006). Furthermore, learner talk in educational settings may not be characteristic of genuine communication, particularly when the topic is language form (Huang 2011) or there is an uneven distribution of speaking opportunities (Dalton-Puffer 2005; Golkar 2003).

These studies raise interesting questions about whether preservice teachers interacting with ESL speakers during conversation groups would demonstrate similar tendencies. One possibility is that the conversation group setting might lead preservice teachers to show less orientation to linguistic form or learners' accuracy because the goal of the conversation group is to provide the ESL speakers with opportunities to engage in meaningful, genuine communication. In this scenario, the conversation groups might be characterized by lower quantities of teacher talk and more referential questions, which are more associated with informal conversations. An alternate possibility, however, is that regardless of the setting (i.e., conversation group versus classroom versus informal conversation), preservice teachers may assume traditional teacher roles, such as knowledge holder or discourse manager (Nassaji 2000), which may lead them to dominate the interaction and ask questions that check understanding, similar to teacher talk, and fewer instances of interaction that reflects genuine communication. The current study aims to clarify these possibilities by identifying the language production opportunities that occur during whole-group interaction when preservice teachers facilitate conversation groups for ESL speakers.

Method

Participants

Preservice teachers
The 15 preservice teachers (six men and nine women) were enrolled in a TESL methods course during their first year in a BEd TESL program. They ranged in age from 19 to 47 years, with a mean age of 25.4 years ($SD = 8.2$). In terms of their self-reported language backgrounds, 10 teachers were French-English bilinguals, two were English monolinguals, and the remaining three teachers were a Greek-English bilingual, a Romanian-English bilingual, and an English-French-Italian trilingual. All but two of the teachers reported having studied a second language previously, which included French, English, German, Spanish, Italian, Chinese, Arabic, and Polish. Five teachers reported prior L2 teaching experience (English or French) through summer camps, individual tutoring, or volunteer activities, while two teachers reported that they had taught an L2 course for one to two semesters. The remaining eight teachers reported no experience teaching or tutoring L2 learners. None of them indicated any experience teaching ESL at the tertiary level or for adults.

These preservice teachers were representative of first year students in the BEd program, which includes students studying their first university degree as well as mature students seeking a career change. The BEd curriculum provides courses in TESL methods, language analysis (phonology and grammar), and language acquisition along with four practical training opportunities. The first practical training opportunity is leading conversation groups, the focus of the current study, which is integrated into the first TESL methods course in the curriculum. The methods course covers general topics in ESL pedagogy, such as lesson planning, giving feedback, targeting language skills, giving instructions, and monitoring student learning, with subsequent methods courses focusing more narrowly on specific educational contexts (primary or secondary schools). The TESL methods course was taught by a team of two instructors who collaborated throughout the semester. One instructor was responsible for delivering course content through lectures and assessing the preservice teacher's understanding of that content. The other instructor, who was the second researcher, helped the preservice teachers prepare for the conversation groups and facilitated peer and self-evaluation of the conversation group sessions.

ESL participants

The ESL participants who attended the conversation groups were taking ESL courses at the participating community center or were enrolled in undergraduate or graduate degree programs at the same university as the preservice teachers. The community center ESL participants were taking a six-week ESL class taught by the community center staff. Depending on their level, they attended class either four times per week (beginning and intermediate levels) or twice per week (high-intermediate). The university ESL participants were enrolled in undergraduate and graduate degree programs. Some of them were taking an academic English course (two, 2.75 hour classes per week), but others had fulfilled all language requirements and were only taking courses in their degree programs. Across the two settings, the ESL participants included permanent residents of Canada who emigrated from various countries (including Argentina, France, Iran, Korea, Mexico, Spain, and Syria), international students in Canada on student visas (from countries such as China, Korea, Japan, and Saudi Arabia), and native Quebecers. The conversation groups were an optional speaking practice activity, and the participants paid a small administrative fee to attend the conversation group that was most convenient for their class schedules.

Procedure

The conversation group sessions were organized and video-recorded according to the procedures created and implemented by the TESL methods course instructors. The instructors created teams of two preservice teachers who were assigned to lead conversation groups at either the community center or the university. Each team was responsible for four, 45-minute conversation group sessions over a one-month period, with each session held on the same day and time slot each week. The team members alternated between leading the conversation group and videotaping the session. For example, one preservice teacher led the conversation group in weeks one and three, and videotaped her partner in weeks two and four. The preservice teachers were required to video-record the conversation group sessions as part of the assessment of the TESL methods course. They were then required to select segments from the video-recordings to present to the class as self-evaluation and reflection activities. The partnership between the TESL program and the participating ESL programs required that (a) the video-camera remain focused on the preservice teachers at all times, (b) only the ESL participants in the immediate proximity of the preservice teachers would be video-recorded, and (c) no additional audio-recording or data collection from the ESL participants was permitted.

At the end of the semester after the TESL methods course grades had been submitted, the video-recordings from the participating preservice teachers were transcribed by paid research assistants. Fifteen transcripts were selected for inclusion in the analysis with each teacher contributing one session to the dataset. The selection of a session was first determined by technical issues (i.e., incomplete or missing video-recordings and sound quality), and then balanced across the first and second sessions based on the teachers' prior experience (none versus some prior teaching or tutoring experiences) and the school site (community center or university). Nine transcripts were from a teacher's first conversation group session and six transcripts were from a teacher's second session.

Data coding

The focus of the study was to examine the nature of whole-group, teacher-led interaction in conversation group settings, which was analyzed in terms of interactional contexts and the types of questions produced by the preservice teachers. To identify interactional contexts, we first reviewed the transcripts to form preliminary impressions about the categories of talk that were apparent in the data. Next, we compared our preliminary impressions and consulted previous studies that had identified distinct interactional contexts in L2 classroom discourse (e.g., Huang 2011; Lyster & Ranta 1997; Oliver & Mackey 2003). This process resulted in a final list of four interactional contexts (communication, content, explicit language, and management) and their definitions. We each independently coded one transcript and compared our results. Based on this discussion, we revised the initial definitions, identified examples of each context, and resolved queries about context length and boundaries. For example, explicit language often occurred within content when the teacher asked learners whether they knew the meaning of a vocabulary word. The interaction prior to the explicit language was coded as content while the language-focused exchange was coded as explicit language. Once the vocabulary item was defined, the teacher returned to the content focus of the activity, and this interaction was coded as content. Following this discussion, we independently coded the remaining transcripts and classified all of the teacher-fronted interaction according to the four interactional contexts (for examples, see Table 1).

Communication

Communication contexts were interaction in which the teacher engaged the ESL speakers in an exchange of information that did not directly support the topic or activities that were the main focus of the conversation group session. Communication involved the exchange of information about topics that arose during the session, such as shared interests, personal information, topics initiated by the learners, or invitations for the ESL speakers to provide feedback to the teachers. They occurred when the teacher created opportunities

Table 1. Examples of interactional contexts

Context	Background to the example	Example
Communication	Chatting at the end of class	P: I will try to do bartending T: Oh! I started working in a bar this weekend P: Really? T: Yeah
Content	Discussing ethical dilemmas	T: you said about finding $50,000 you would keep it? P: yeah keep it T: why? P: because I would want to save my daughter T: no matter what? P: yeah
Explicit language	Talking about past tense	T: so for example if the word is awake, what's that in the past? P: uh what? T: awake in the past P: awoke
Management	Giving instructions for pair work	T: Uh, actually there's a couple more, you guys can read them, I wrote them down. *(hands out papers)* So with your partner you can pick a few to look at and discuss. And we'll come back as a group after and you know go through them. P: We have to discuss about the same dilemma? T: Uh, yeah just pick a few that you like. And you guys can discuss.

Note: T = Preservice teacher; P = ESL participant.

for follow-up questions, when the ESL participants nominated topics, or when the teacher shared personal information or gave an opinion to illustrate a concept. Because communication involved a bidirectional distribution of unknown information (i.e., the teachers did not already know the answers to their questions) and both the ESL participants and teachers had opportunities to nominate and change topics, these contexts were considered most representative of genuine communication (Nunan 1987).

Content

Content contexts involved interaction in which the teacher provided or elicited information about the topic, theme, or situations that were the focus of the conversation group session. In content contexts, the ESL participants typically answered questions posed by the teacher, and asked for clarification of the meaning of lexical items introduced by the teacher. Content often involved interaction in which the teacher asked comprehension questions and the ESL participants shared knowledge about the topic or theme.

Explicit language

Explicit language contexts were interaction in which the teacher explicitly provided or elicited knowledge about language form, which could include vocabulary, grammar, or pronunciation. Explicit language occurred when the teacher had selected a language form as the topic of the conversation group and when a particular language form arose within content or communication contexts. ESL participant contributions to explicit language segments typically involved responding to display and comprehension questions, providing forms requested by the instructor, or requesting information about language forms.

Management

Management contexts consisted of interaction in which a teacher talked about the organization of activities, such as starting and ending the conversation groups, giving and clarifying instructions, allocating turns, and integrating late-arriving students. ESL participant contributions in management contexts typically consisted of providing requested information, requesting clarification about instructions or procedures, or acknowledging that they had understood instructions.

To gain additional insight into the language production opportunities received by the ESL participants during the conversation groups, we also analyzed the types of questions asked by the preservice teachers. Based on the previous interaction studies that described teachers' questioning styles (e.g., Brock 1986; Long & Sato 1983; Pica & Long 1986), four types of questions were coded: referential, comprehension, display, and clarification questions. We met to review the definitions and independently code one transcript. After discussing that transcript, we clarified and revised the initial definitions, and then independently coded the remaining transcripts and classified all of the teacher questions into to the four categories that follow.

Referential questions

Referential questions were operationalized as questions that elicited information that was not already known to the preservice teachers. Referential questions also occurred in a variety of forms, including yes/no questions (*have you ever tasted it? do they have a lot of dried mangoes in Asia?*), wh-questions (*what do you like about it? how do you eat a coconut? what does your name mean?*) and declarative sentences with rising intonation (*they grow everywhere? they break the coconut? you live with your family here?*).

Comprehension questions

These were operationalized as a subcategory of referential questions that served to establish whether the ESL participants had understood something previously mentioned by the teacher, such as a word, concept, or instructions. Comprehension questions occurred in a variety of linguistic forms, including yes/no questions (*do you understand? do you know what an adjective is? does everybody know what small means? do you know what formal means?*) and declarative utterances with rising intonation (*you understand bad? everybody knows what happy is? got it? you know what I mean?*).

Display questions
Display questions were operationalized as questions that elicited information already known to the preservice teachers, which typically occurred in the form of *wh*-questions (*what is an adjective? what do you call your sister's children?*) but also occurred as declarative utterances with rising intonation (*we is plural?*).

Clarification questions
Clarification questions were questions that served to verify information previously supplied by an ESL participant. Clarification questions occurred in the form of single word utterances (*pardon? sorry? when?*), declarative utterances with rising intonation (*you have two? you cook?*), and yes/no questions (*could you say it again?*).

   After independently coding all of the transcripts, we met to compare our analysis of interactional contexts and questions. Agreements and disagreements were summed across the dataset for each analysis. Simple percentage agreement was 98% for questions and 97% for segments. Disagreements were resolved through discussion and the final decision was included in the dataset. If one researcher missed a question or segment that had been coded by the other researcher, then it was considered a coding omission (rather than a disagreement) and was subsequently included in the dataset (5% of the interactional contexts and 2% of the questions were missed by one researcher).

Results

Overview of the dataset

As noted earlier, the dataset consisted of 15 conversation group sessions that were video-recorded and transcribed. The number of ESL participants present during the conversation group sessions ranged from 2 to 16, with a median of 8 participants ($IQR = 7$). The total length of the video-recordings ranged from 28 to 58 minutes, with a median length of 50 minutes ($IQR = 11$). Five of the conversation group sessions consisted of whole class, teacher-led interaction exclusively, while 10 sessions included both teacher-led and small group activities. For the sessions with both types of interaction, approximately two-thirds of each session consisted of teacher-led interaction. The teacher-led interaction contained a relatively equal number of turns taken by the teacher (51%) and the ESL participants (49%), with the total turns per conversation group session ranging from 171 to 995 ($mdn = 444$, $IQR = 237$). However, whereas nearly one-third (32%) of the ESL participants' turns consisted of a single word, such as *yeah* or *uh-huh*, only 16% of the teacher turns contained only one word.

Because the teachers took longer turns that contained multiple interactional contexts (communication, content, language, and management), contexts were taken as the unit of analysis rather than turns. The total number of contexts generated by each teacher ranged from 15 to 100, with a median of 61 segments (*IQR*=48) per conversation group session. The variation across teachers was influenced in part by the total length of their recording as well as whether they had allocated time to small group activities. Individual style likely influenced the variation as well, with some teachers alternating between contexts frequently, such as repeated cycles of short content and management contexts, while other teachers spent more time in a particular context type.

Language production opportunities

The research question asked what types of language production opportunities ESL speakers received during whole group, teacher-led interaction in conversation group settings. In terms of the quantity of talk, the preservice teachers produced 78% of the total words (49,482/63,533) while the ESL participants produced only 22% of the total words that occurred during the conversation group sessions (see Table 2). The pattern for the ESL participants to produce less language than the teachers was consistent across all four interactional contexts. The predominance of teacher talk was most evident during management with the teachers producing a median of 23.5 words per context while the learners rarely spoke, and during communication (24.5 words for teachers but only 5 words for the learners). The quantity of talk by the ESL participants was greatest in content contexts (*mdn* = 18 words).

Table 2. Words by context and participant

Context	Teachers			ESL participants		
	Sum	*mdn*	IQR	Sum	*mdn*	IQR
Communication (*n*=92)	4,106	24.5	47	1,583	5	17
Content (*n*=259)	10,273	24	41	8,709	18	30
Explicit language (*n*=192)	16,035	37	96	2,938	9	15
Management (*n*=314)	19,068	23.5	52	821	0	2
Total (*N*=857)	49,482	26	53	14,051	4	18

In terms of the types of questions that the teachers asked, referential questions were most frequently used (41% of all questions), followed by clarification requests (21%). Comprehension checks and display questions each represented 19% of the total questions asked by the teachers. In terms of the distribution of question types by context (see Table 3), comprehension and display questions occurred most often during explicit language, while clarification requests occurred frequently during content contexts. Referential questions occurred during content and communication, but were also frequent during management. Interestingly, content contexts contained the greatest amount of talk produced by ESL participants, and also had the highest number of referential questions.

Table 3. Questions by context

	Referential	Display	Comprehension	Clarification
Communication	103	0	5	37
Content	173	66	8	108
Explicit language	17	155	119	45
Management	92	22	42	10
Total	385 (41%)	177 (19%)	174 (19%)	200 (21%)

To provide greater insight into the quantitative findings, examples that illustrate the types of interaction that occurred in the four contexts follow.

Communication

Communication contexts were infrequent (11% of all segments) in the conversation group sessions, but contained over one-quarter (27%) of the referential questions. They typically occurred at three times in the conversation group sessions: (a) at the beginning when the teacher and ESL participants were introducing themselves, (b) during content or explicit language contexts when an ESL participant's prior utterance led to follow-up questions or comments, and (c) at the end when a teacher requested feedback about the activities. Example (1) illustrates communication embedded within a content context. The ESL participants had been asked to create sentences about daily life activities that are typically done in the morning, afternoon, and evening. The teacher was eliciting sentences and writing them on the board. After repeating a sentence and writing it on the board, the teacher initiates communication by asking the ESL participant if the information is actually true.

(1) T: in the morning at seven forty-five, Michael makes exercise (*writing on board*). Okay. Can you – do you – is that true? Michael? Do you – do you make exercise in the morning? Is this true?

S7: huh?

T: Is – is this the reality? In your real life, do you use a bike and or exercise?

S7: Bicycle?

T: The bicycle, mhm. Do you have a bicycle? In your life? In the reality?

S7: no

T: You don't (*laughs*) have a bicycle okay.

SS: (*laugh*)

After establishing that the ESL participant does not in fact own a bicycle, the teacher returns to the content focus of the activity by eliciting a sentence from another learner. Communication was also initiated by the ESL participants. For example, in one conversation group session, the content focus was introductions and the ESL participants were sharing their names and jobs. One ESL participant stated that he worked for an extermination company, which led to communication in the form of numerous follow-up questions initiated by the other ESL participants.

Communication that occurred at the end of a conversation group session typically involved the teacher inviting feedback and suggestions about activities for subsequent sessions. The teacher in (2) had organized the conversation group session into teacher-fronted interaction in which the ESL participants took turns thinking of a famous person while the other students asked questions until the person's identity could be guessed. At the end of the session, the teacher requested feedback.

(2)   T: So could you tell me if uh it was ok for you to do some vocabulary or you just want to practice some more conversation. How would you like to do that?

     S2:   Both of them

     T: So this is a good combination?

     SS: yes

     T: And the game is working for you? Or would you like something more like we discuss more?

     S1:   we discuss more. We want to lead more conversation because in one hour we speaking five seconds ten seconds, so yeah we need more

     T: *(nods)*

     S13:   The problem is there is many persons here

     S1:   yeah so maybe I – we need to make a group and then you ... change the mistakes /---/ and then we have to /---/

     T: So role play

     S1:   yeah role play and uh more activities

     T: So do you think that it would be ok to do role play? Do you think that would bring about more conversation?

     SS: yes

Although communication segments were infrequent in the conversation group sessions, they typically involved instances of genuine communication in which the ESL participants nominated or pursued topics that they were interested in, expressed their opinions about the conversation group sessions, and asked and answered referential questions.

Content

Content-focused interaction occurred frequently in the dataset (30%), elicited the greatest amount of talk by the ESL speakers (62% of all their words), and contained the most referential and clarification questions. The prevalence of content is likely due to the preservice teachers' organization of the conversation group session around a particular topic or theme. The content foci of the conversation group sessions included making introductions and talking about family or daily activities (4 sessions), describing people or music (4 sessions), describing holidays and festivals (2 sessions), discussing controversial topics or scenarios (2 sessions), and shopping (1 session). However, two teachers organized the conversation group session around a specific language form (past tense and affixes) that was not embedded in a more global content focus. Unlike communication, however, content contexts did not provide many opportunities for ESL speakers to talk about their own lives or experiences, even when the content focus of the session allowed for the exchange of personal information. For example, all four conversation group sessions that involved describing people or movies consisted of talk about famous people in the form of guessing games or talk about songs that the teacher had preselected. The conversation group sessions about festivals and holidays also focused on the history and traditions associated with popular holidays in various countries, and elicited less talk about their own activities or beliefs. This tendency was also evident in the conversation sessions about describing families. For example, one conversation session included several activities in which the ESL participants pretended to belong to fictional families (such as the Simpsons) and then described their family members (i.e., Homer, Marge, Bart, and Lisa). Similarly, another conversation group session included an activity in which the ESL participants discussed daily activities and chores, but the focus remained on things people in general are likely to do in a day, rather than their actual routines.

The two conversation group sessions that focused on controversial topics or scenarios elicited more talk from the ESL participants, with those two sessions accounting for 26% of their words across all content contexts. Whereas content contexts that involved guessing games tended to elicit short turns consisting of phrases, these two sessions contained longer learner turns in response to referential questions and opportunities to elaborate in response to clarification requests. In the conversation group session that focused on the advantages and disadvantages of the internet, the teacher in the example below (3) asked a group to explain the benefits of internet use.

(3) T: Okay and what's your third idea?   (Referential)
    S9: is uh best solution for everything
    T: Everything (*laughs*) what do you mean by everything?   (Clarification)
    S9: ok if you are looking for something to buy to sell uh you're looking for an address like Google Map
    T: in what – uh do you think – is that what you meant by uh great for everything?
                                                                  (Clarification)
    S5: business
    T: ah okay so business, communication and good for
    S5: education
    S2: and if you need to develop some idea you can choose sources
    T: okay so a research uh engine
    S2: yeah
    T: okay great
    S5: We need – we needed to talk with people uh to know uh places or addresses or ... or dates of ... exams or ... we can discover that we can uh
    S9: find it
    S5: look in it or find it. It's in the internet

This contrasts with the type of talk elicited through guessing games. In (4), the teacher had organized the conversation group session as a whole-class game of 20 questions. One ESL participant (S13) was thinking of a famous person and the other students asked questions. Many of the turns were a single word (*yes, no, no*) or phrases (*a tennis player? Spanish guy?*) as complete sentences and elaborated utterances were not necessary for task accomplishment.

(4) S14: are you woman?
     S13: no
     S14: single?
     S13: no
     S10: is a man?
     S13: yes
     S14: are you uh American?
     S13: no
     S10: European?
     S13: Yes he's from Europe
     S10: ah European
     S14: a tennis player?
     S13: yes
     S14: Spanish guy?
     S10: Nadal?
     S13: yeah

In sum, most of the teachers organized the conversation group sessions around a particular topic or theme, but many of the activities did not provide opportunities for the ESL participants to talk about their own lives or experiences. The sessions that focused on the exchange of opinions about controversial topics elicited talk in the form of longer turns and elaborated responses, but the sessions based on guessing games or hypothetical activities generally elicited shorter turns.

Explicit language

Explicit language accounted for 22% of the total contexts and contained the greatest number of display and comprehension questions. As described previously, most teachers organized the conversation sessions around a central theme or topic, although two teachers organized an entire session around a language form (past tense and affixes). Explicit language typically occurred when the teachers provided or elicited information about language form before the ESL participants were given an activity. For example, one teacher structured the conversation group session as an extended role play activity in which the ESL participants took on roles as shopkeepers or customers and moved around the classroom to make purchases at various stores. The teacher elicited and reviewed expressions that would be useful for shopping (*where can I find X? can I help you? Do you need anything else?*). These explicit language contexts often contained display questions that elicited relevant forms, such as *what would you say if you don't have the item? what would you say to buy an item? what other words can you use besides 'buy'?*

The conversation group sessions that involved describing people often contained explicit language contexts in which the teacher reviewed different types of adjectives and their meanings before the learners began the activities. The segment in (5) illustrates a typical combination of comprehension and display questions found during explicit language. Before beginning a guessing game activity about famous people, the teacher distributed a list of adjectives.

(5) T: Anybody know what an adjective is?   (Comprehension)
     S1: Yeah
     T: Can you tell me?   (Display)
     S1: Adjectives is uh like describe
     T: yes describes a noun (writes on board). And an example would be what?
                                                           (Display)
     S1: slow

Explicit language also occurred during content or communication contexts when teachers provided a lexical item and then checked whether everyone was familiar with the term. In (6) the ESL participants were describing a holiday that is celebrated in their country of origin. The participant was describing the Mexican Revolution and was searching for the lexical item '*speeches*.' After providing the word, the teacher then stops to ask whether they know what it means.

(6) T: There are speeches … people that talk about the revolution? Is that it?
         Speeches? Do you know what a speech is?   (Comprehension)
     S1: Speeches?
     S3: Can you write it?
     T: Yeah I'll write it. Do you know what that is a speech? Speech? No.
                                                           (Comprehension)

After that exchange, the teacher then explained the meaning of speech by defining it and giving examples of North American politicians. He then asked several more comprehension questions, and once the explicit language concludes, the ESL participants continued describing their holidays. In sum, whereas explicit language typically occurred when the teachers used comprehension and display questions to assess understanding, in a few cases the teachers organized the entire conversation group session around a specific grammatical form.

Management

Management occurred most frequently in the data set, accounting for 37% of the total contexts, and contained both referential and comprehension questions. They occurred when the teachers began and ended the conversation group sessions, and when they provided instructions and modeled how to do an activity, as illustrated in (7):

(7) T: okay… so first we're going to start by playing a game. Okay so let's say I were to write the word 'pencil' on the board. Now you use adjectives to explain this word to me. So I can't see the word, so I don't know, let's pretend that I don't know this word. So we're going to use adjectives to describe this word

S1: small

T: okay yeah just think for a little bit and think of different adjectives you can use to describe that word

The management contexts that contained instructions often concluded with one or more comprehension questions (*Do you all understand? Does that make sense? Do you understand what we're going to do?*).

Management also occurred during content contexts when the teachers allocated turns. Often these management segments contained referential questions, shown in (8), which functioned to identify who would speak next.

(8) Okay everybody's going to have to go a few times. Who wants to pick?
Who are you interested in asking?
Okay so who's two more volunteers?
Are you ready to join in?

Management also occurred when the teacher asked referential questions related to the use of the materials (*do you guys mind if I erase this?*) and reminded the ESL participants about the goal or procedure for carrying out an activity (*ask questions to find out who she is*). Although management was frequent in the dataset, these contexts primarily elicited one-word confirmations that the ESL participants had understood.

Discussion and conclusions

The present study aimed to the identify language production opportunities that ESL participants received during whole-group, teacher led interaction in a conversation group setting. The findings indicated that the preservice teachers dominated the conversation groups in terms of total words, which parallels the findings of studies that explored the amount of teacher talk that occurs during writing conferences (Ewert 2009; Williams 2004) and in L2 classrooms (Abd-Kadir & Hardman 2007; Salhberg & Boci 2010). Teacher talk was most frequent in management and explicit language contexts, during which they asked numerous display and comprehension questions. The ESL participants, who produced less than 25% of the total words, had opportunities to produce the greatest quantity of talk during content, which contained the most referential and clarification questions.

When compared to the early interaction studies that contrasted teacher talk and informal conversation (Long & Sato 1983; Pica & Long 1986), these conversation groups had characteristics associated with both types of interaction. Similar to classroom discourse, the preservice teachers asked display and comprehension questions, but typically used these question types during explicit language and management contexts, which are most similar to classroom discourse. However, similar to the informal conversation reported in these early studies, the preservice teachers asked referential and clarification questions during content and communication contexts. Prior studies also reported a tendency for novice ESL teachers to elicit less talk than experienced teachers (Polio et al. 2006), which was confirmed by the low quantity of talk elicited by the preservice teachers in the current study.

An important question raised by the findings concerns the factors that contribute to the preservice teachers' tendency to dominate conversation group interaction. Despite the fact that the conversation groups were organized specifically to provide oral communication opportunities for the ESL participants, the preservice teachers may have perceived their role as teachers rather than as facilitators. Consequently, they may have been influenced by interactional patterns associated with the teacher roles of knowledge holder and discourse manager (Nassaji 2000). In terms of the role of knowledge holder, the preservice teachers may have regarded themselves as the primary source of content knowledge. The role of knowledge holder was apparent in the conversation group sessions when the teachers asserted their own opinions over those of the ESL participants, and failed to elicit information in contexts where the ESL participants may have greater knowledge. For example, in (9), the teacher was eliciting opinions about Oprah Winfrey by asking the ESL participants to provide adjectives that describe her. When one speaker suggested that Oprah is not attractive, the teacher responded by saying *okay it's your opinion*. When another speaker then suggested that Oprah is *elegant* the teacher confirmed the opinion as fact (*yes she is*) and then explained that Oprah is generous.

(9) S1: Beautiful.
　　 S2: And powerful?
　　 S3: She's ugly.
　　 T: She's ugly? That's ok it's your opinion. (writes) It's still an adjective so... put it up here.
　　 S?: Elegant
　　 T: Yes she is. And you know what? There's one thing that Oprah is and she does, every time she has her shows... she gives a lot of gifts... to people. So she's very generous.

Through this exchange, the preservice teacher's role as knowledge holder becomes apparent when she positions some contributions as being personal opinions, but validates other responses. Assuming the role of knowledge holder may result in interaction where the teacher accepts and dismisses contributions without creating opportunities for the ESL participants to expand or develop their opinions, which could facilitate more talk involving a bidirectional flow of information (Ellis 1998).

In addition to the role of knowledge holder, the preservice teachers also adopted a role as discourse manager, which is reflected in the prevalence of management contexts (37% of the total contexts). Their role as a discourse manager is illustrated in (10) when one ESL participant asks another speaker about her religion. The teacher intervened in the exchange by evaluating the question (*that's a good question*) and then directing the question to the intended recipient.

> (10) T: I'm going to find this for you. I'm sorry, uh…
> S1: (*to S3*) Wha – what is, uh… your religion?
> T: That's a – that's a good question…. (*to S3*) what is your religion?

Similarly, in (11) the teacher signaled that the ESL participants should begin the activity, which was to roll some dice and then ask the question indicated by the dice. The first speaker (S1) asks a peer (S4) about his occupation. The teacher then appropriated the question, acknowledged the response, and asked a follow up question. After receiving an answer to the follow-up question, the teacher then instructed a new speaker (S2) to take a turn. Although this activity appears to have been designed to create opportunities for an exchange of personal information, the teacher managed the questions, which resulted in fewer opportunities for talk by the ESL participants.

> (11) T: Is that fine? Ok, here we go.
> S1: (*rolls dice*) What is your… occupation? (*asks S4*)
> T: Yeah, what is your occupation? (*asks S4*)
> S4: Actually, uh… I am a student.
> T: You are a student. What do you study?
> S4: English. And uh in course, uh in… lesson of uh… medicine.
> T: Medicine? Alright, perfect. Ok. Your turn.
> S2: (*rolls dice*)

The teachers' role of discourse manager was also apparent in their use of referential questions during management segments. Many of these referential questions were used as polite requests for the ESL participants to provide information and to allocate turns. In (12), the teacher's referential question was a request for a speaker to take the next turn in the activity. She seemed to recognize the dual function of the question by first acknowledging her ability to participate and then fulfilling the request.

(12)   T: Ok let's get a fresh perspective… Uh, [S6]? Could you help us with a personality?
         S6:   Yes (*other students begin asking questions*)

Interestingly, these requests were occasionally declined, which suggests that management-oriented referential questions provide choices to continue or discontinue the interaction. The declined request in (13) triggered laughter and an evaluative comment from the teacher.

(13)   T: To play soccer, alright. Do you want to ask him another question?
         S2:   No (*laughs*)
         T: No you don't? (*laughs*)
         SS: (*laugh*)
         T: You should!

The occurrence of laughter as a face-saving strategy which minimizes confrontation suggests that these referential questions were a means of allocating turns rather than a tool for eliciting genuine communication.

Based on the analysis of the interaction between the teachers and ESL participants, we have identified several areas for further reflection and development that may help preservice teachers elicit talk that involves genuine communication. First, in terms of questioning styles, it may be useful to expose preservice teachers to examples of how the same type of question can serve different communicative functions in specific interactional contexts. For example, the use of referential questions for management may not be the most efficient or transparent way to allocate turns or elicit responses (Scrivener 2011). The complex function of these questions can be challenging for lower proficiency learners or learners who are less familiar with the norms and politeness strategies associated with North American classroom discourse. However, the use of referential questions in communication or content segments may be an effective strategy for eliciting learner talk.

Unlike the practical training conversation partner program reported in Williams (2009), where a lack of clear goals led to confusion about the purpose of the teacher-learner interactions, the conversation groups in the current study may have had an instructional orientation that resulted in interaction that resembled classroom discourse rather than informal conversation. One possible solution may be to structure the conversation groups as discussion sessions, similar to the types of content-based discussion that ESL students encounter in academic courses. Being able to conduct interactive classroom discussion has been recognized as an important skill for teachers of a variety of subjects, including math, science, and English (Applebee, Langer, Nystrand, & Gamoran 2003; Rosaen, Lundeberg, Terpstrac, Niu, & Jing 2010), but preservice teachers may not receive the information and practice opportunities necessary to facilitate interactive discussions and assess their effectiveness. Raising preservice teachers' awareness of more diverse teacher roles, such as facilitator, organizer, prompter, or observer, may help them create opportunities for interaction that does not require the teacher to manage the discourse or serve as the primary knowledge holder (Téllez & Waxman 2006).

Although the present study provides a modest contribution to understanding interaction in other educational contexts, specifically the interaction that occurs between preservice teachers and ESL speakers during practical training experiences, it has several limitations that should be acknowledged. Due to the partnership agreement between the TESL program and the ESL programs, it was not possible to supplement the video-recordings of the preservice teachers with audio-recordings of the ESL participants' small group activities. Audio-recording the small group activities would allow for comparisons between learner-learner interaction and whole-class, teacher-fronted discourse, which could further illuminate the language production opportunities that occur in conversation group settings. It would also provide greater insight into the teachers' use of questions and strategies for eliciting talk in a wider variety of classroom activities.

Future research should also include the perceptions of the ESL participants who participate in practical training experiences so that teacher educators can ensure that they are benefiting from the partnership. As in the current study, practical training experiences often rely on volunteer L2 participants so it is important to consider their benefits of participation. Some insight into their perceptions about the conversation groups was provided when the preservice teachers requested suggestions at the end of the sessions, but future studies might solicit feedback more systematically. By incorporating systematic evaluation into the conversation groups, each teacher would be able to obtain suggestions that could be incorporated into a subsequent session. Adopting a longer-term perspective would also be useful, as the current practical training program allows each preservice teacher to facilitate only two conversation group sessions separated by one week. Consequently, it was not possible to explore their professional development over time. A case study approach in which one or two teachers are tracked throughout all four practical training experiences would provide greater insight into how their interactional routines develop over time.

In conclusion, the findings of the current study suggest that conversation groups show promise as a vehicle for providing preservice teachers with practical training experiences. By targeting adult ESL participants who were motivated to participate, the preservice teachers did not encounter the discipline problems or lack of attention that can arise in other educational contexts. Unfortunately, these preservice teachers did not elicit large quantities of talk from the ESL participants, which suggests that future efforts to improve their training are needed. We hope that future interaction research situated in educational settings can help inform the design, implementation, and evaluation of practical training programs that help preservice teachers create interaction that elicits genuine communication and encourages more equal participation in the discourse so that L2 speakers receive the language production opportunities that have been shown to be developmentally-helpful.

References

Abd-Kadir, J., & Hardman, F. (2007). The discourse of whole class teaching: A comparative study of Kenyan and Nigerian primary English lessons. *Language and Education, 21*, 1–15.

Applebee, A., Langer, J., Nystrand, M., & Gamoran, A. (2003). Discussion-based approaches to developing understanding: Classroom instruction and student performance in middle and high school English. *American Educational Research Journal, 40*, 685–730.

Banbrook, L., & Skehan, P. (1989). Classrooms and display questions. In C. Brumfit & S. Mitchell (Eds.), *Research in the language classroom* (pp. 141–152). London: MEP/British Council.

Brock, C. (1986). The effects of referential question on ESL classroom discourse. *TESOL Quarterly, 20*, 47–59.

Dalton-Puffer, C. (2005). Negotiating interpersonal meaning in naturalistic classroom discourse: Directives in content-and-language-integrated classrooms. *Journal of Pragmatics, 37*, 1275–1293.

Ellis, R. (1998). Discourse control and the acquisition-rich classroom. In W. Renandya & G. Jacobs (Eds.), *Learners and language learning* (pp. 145–171). Singapore: RELC.

Ewert, D. (2009). L2 writing conferences: Investigating teacher talk. *Journal of Second Language Writing, 18*, 251–269.

Golkar, M. (2003). Classroom observation: Interaction time and question and answer patterns. *Indian Journal of Applied Linguistics, 29(2)*, 79–89.

Gourlay, L. (2005). OK, who's got number one? Permeable triadic dialogue, covert participation and the co-construction of checking episodes. *Language Teaching Research, 9*, 403–422.

Huang, K. (2011). Motivating lessons: A classroom-oriented investigation of the effects of content-based instruction on EFL young learners' motivated behaviors and classroom verbal interaction. *System, 39*, 186–201.

Lee, Y. (2007). Third turn position in teacher talk: Contingency and the work of teaching. *Journal of Pragmatics, 39*, 1204–1230.

Long, M., & Sato, C. (1983). Classroom foreigner talk discourse: Forms and functions of teachers' questions. In H. Seliger & M. Long (Eds.), *Classroom oriented research in second language acquisition* (pp. 268–286). Rowley, MA: Newbury.

Lyster, R. (2004). Differential effects of prompts and recasts in form-focused instruction. *Studies in Second Language Acquisition, 26*, 399–432.

Lyster, R., & Ranta, L. (1997). Corrective feedback and learner uptake: Negotiation of form in communicative classrooms. *Studies in Second Language Acquisition, 19*, 37–66.

Mackey, A. (1999). Input, interaction and second language development: An empirical study of question formation in ESL. *Studies in Second Language Acquisition, 21*, 557–587.

Mackey, A., Polio, C., & McDonough, K. (2004). The relationship between experience, education and teachers' use of incidental focus on form techniques. *Language Teaching Research, 8*, 301–327.

McDonough, K., & Chaikitmongkol, W. (2010). Collaborative syntactic priming activities and EFL learners' production of *wh*-questions. *Canadian Modern Language Review, 66*, 817–841.

Musumeci, D. (1996). Teacher-learner negotiation in content-based instruction: Communication at cross-purposes? *Applied Linguistics, 17*, 286–325.

Nassaji, H. (2000). Towards integrating form-focused instruction and communicative interaction in the second language classroom: Some pedagogical possibilities. *Modern Language Journal, 84*, 241–250.

Nassaji, H., & Wells, G. (2000). What's the use of 'triadic dialogue'? An investigation of teacher–student interaction. *Applied Linguistics, 21*, 376–406.

Nunan, D. (1987). Communicative language teaching: Making it work. *ELT Journal, 41*, 136–145.

Nunan, D. (1990). The questions teachers ask. *JALT Journal, 12(2)*, 187–202.

Oliver, R., & Mackey, A. (2003). Interactional contexts and feedback in child ESL classrooms. *Modern Language Journal, 87,* 519–533.

Patthey-Chavez, G. G., & Ferris, D. (1997). Writing conferences and the weaving of multi-voiced texts in college composition. *Research in the Teaching of English, 31,* 51–90.

Pica, T., & Long, M. (1986). The linguistic and conversational performance of experienced and inexperienced teachers. In R. Day (Ed.), *Talking to learn: Conversation in second language acquisition* (pp. 85–98). Rowley, MA: Newbury.

Polio, C., Gass, S., & Chapin, L. (2006). Using stimulated recall to investigate native speaker perceptions in native-nonnative speaker interaction. *Studies in Second Language Acquisition, 28,* 237–267.

Rosaen, C., Lundeberg, M., Terpstra, M., Cooper, M., Niu, R., & Fu, J. (2010). Constructing videocases to help novices learn to facilitate discussion in science and English: How does subject matter matter? *Teachers and Teaching: Theory and Practice, 16,* 507–524.

Salhberg, P., & Boci, E. (2010). Are teachers teaching for a knowledge society? *Teachers and Teaching: Theory and Practice, 16,* 31–48.

Scrivener, J. (2011). *Learning teaching: The essential guide to English language teaching.* Oxford: Macmillan Education.

Swain, M., & Lapkin, S. (2002). Talking it through: Two French immersion learners'response to reformulation. *International Journal of Educational Research, 37,* 285–304.

Tan, Z. (2007). Questioning in Chinese university EL classes: What lies beyond it? *RELC, 38,* 87–103.

Téllez, K., & Waxman, H. C. (2006). A meta-synthesis of qualitative research of effective teaching practices of English language learners. In J. M. Norris & L. Ortega (Eds.), *Synthesizing research on language learning teaching* (pp. 245–277). Amsterdam: John Benjamins.

Waring, H. (2009). Using explicit positive assessment in the language classroom: IRF, feedback, and learning opportunities. *Modern Language Journal, 92,* 577–594.

Williams, J. (2004). Tutoring and revision: Second language writers in the writing center. *Journal of Second Language Writing, 13,* 173–201.

Williams, J. (2009). Beyond the practicum experience. *ELT Journal, 63,* 68–77.

Wu, K. (1993). Classroom interaction and teacher questions revisited. *RELC Journal, 24*(2), 49–68.

Author note

This research was supported by a team infrastructure grant from *Fonds québécois de la recherche sur la société et la culture* (FQRSC).

Appendix

Common European Framework of Reference (CEFR) for Languages

Common Reference Levels: Global scale

Proficient user	C2	Can understand with ease virtually everything heard or read. Can summarise information from different spoken and written sources, reconstructing arguments and accounts in a coherent presentation. Can express him/herself spontaneously, very fluently and precisely, differentiating finer shades of meaning even in more complex situations.
	C1	Can understand a wide range of demanding, longer texts, and recognise implicit meaning. Can express him/herself fluently and spontaneously without much obvious searching for expressions. Can use language flexibly and effectively for social, academic and professional purposes. Can produce clear, well-structured, detailed text on complex subjects, showing controlled use of organisational patterns, connectors and cohesive devices.
Independent user	B2	Can understand the main ideas of complex text on both concrete and abstract topics, including technical discussions in his/her field of specialisation. Can interact with a degree of fluency and spontaneity that makes regular interaction with native speakers quite possible without strain for either party. Can produce clear, detailed text on a wide range of subjects and explain a viewpoint on a topical issue giving the advantages and disadvantages of various options.
	B1	Can understand the main points of clear standard input on familiar matters regularly encountered in work, school, leisure, etc. Can deal with most situations likely to arise whilst travelling in an area where the language is spoken. Can produce simple connected text on topics which are familiar or of personal interest. Can describe experiences and events, dreams, hopes and ambitions and briefly give reasons and explanations for opinions and plans.
Basic user	A2	Can understand sentences and frequently used expressions related to areas of most immediate relevance (e.g. very basic personal and family information, shopping, local geography, employment). Can communicate in simple and routine tasks requiring a simple and direct exchange of information on familiar and routine matters. Can describe in simple terms aspects of his/her background, immediate environment and matters in areas of immediate need.
	A1	Can understand and use familiar everyday expressions and very basic phrases aimed at the satisfaction of needs of a concrete type. Can introduce him/herself and others and can ask and answer questions about personal details such as where he/she lives, people he/she knows and things he/she has. Can interact in a simple way provided the other person talks slowly and clearly and is prepared to help.

http://www.coe.int/t/dg4/linguistic/CADRE_EN.asp

Index